Emotional Disorders:

A Neuropsychological, Psychopharmacological, and Educational Perspective

EDITED BY
Steven G. Feifer, D.Ed.
and Gurmal Rattan, Ph.D.

Emotional Disorders: A Neuropsychological, Psychopharmacological, and Educational Perspective
Edited by Steven G. Feifer, D.Ed. and Gurmal Rattan, Ph.D.

Published by School Neuropsych Press, LLC
PO Box 413
Middletown, MD 21769
snpress@comcast.net
www.schoolneuropsychpress.com

Cover design: Enforme Interactive, Frederick, MD

ISBN # 0-9703337-5-7

Printed in the United States of America by Signature Book Printing, www.sbpbooks.com

Acknowledgements

The opportunity to write a scholarly book on emotional disorders represented a journey back into my formative years as a psychologist, and allowed me to reconnect with the philosophical tenets of behavior which so richly attracted me to this field. To explore the evolution of temperament into personality, of empathy into morality, of aggression into psychopathology from a brain-behavioral perspective was not a reductionist exercise, but rather an enriching one. There is no mystery as perplexing as the human mind, and nothing more misunderstood than the resolve of the human spirit. This manuscript was constructed to recognize the technological advances in capturing the dynamic properties of the brain. In addition, this manuscript was also written to capture the social advances in recognizing that ethics and morality may indeed have neurological underpinnings. Perhaps a complete understanding of human behavior will always be elusive due to our own philosophical orientations that shape how we view the world around us. For instance, most school personnel and educators alike tend to follow a strict teleological position where countless hours are spent determining causal agents or antecedents in hopes of altering a particular behavioral response. On the other hand, many psychologists tend to adopt a more empirical position, and examine a student's background experiences, interpersonal relationships, and family dynamics as the shaping agents which dictate a behavioral response. This book represents a cognitive neuroscientific perspective, which adopts a 21st century brand of epistemology that views behavior as a manifestation of biological impulses stemming from a brain interacting with its environment. Hence, psychopathology and emotional disorders are explained not only by their surface features, but also from their underlying structure and form. Certainly, there is no one book that can possibly represent the complexities of human behavior nor serve as a compendium of knowledge about our species. The aim of this book is merely to shed light on a few fundamental neurological principles that shape the mind, and provide educators with a closer inspection of the biological phenomena which molds cognition and behavior.

To embark on such an ambitious endeavor, I naturally turned to some of the brightest minds in the field, friends and colleagues who inspired me personally and influenced me professionally. I am deeply indebted to my advisor and now my esteemed colleague and friend, Dr. Gurmal Rattan. Thank you for agreeing to serve as my co-editor and intellectual confidant throughout the project. It was an honor to finally work with my friend, Dr. George McCloskey, whose unique perspectives on executive functioning remain unparalleled in the field. The contributions of Dr. James B. Hale, whose intellectual prowess in school neuropsychology is nothing short of brilliant, and Dr. Lisa Hain were both scholarly and insightful. It was a privilege to work with a pioneer in the field of mind, brain, and education, Dr. Mary Helen Immordino Yang. Of course, my dear friend Ronald Sudano was included as well, whose constant support and friendship remains matched only by his professional contributions to the field of school psychology. Many thanks to Dr. Jeb Yalof, whose expertise in nonverbal learning disabilities was such a crucial component for this project. Also, it was a thrill to have Dr. Amy Gabel assist with the assessment portions of this manuscript, and an honor to have a leading expert in resiliency, Dr. Beth Doll, contribute as well. Furthermore, the contributions of an aspiring scholar, John Garruto were most appreciated, and it was a pleasure to lean on the expertise of my teaching colleague, Dr. Ann Leonard-Zabel. Lastly, it was wonderful to have the perspective from a teacher trainer and expert in classroom management, Mary Fowler.

ACKNOWLEDGEMENTS

As always, I could not imagine embracing any book project without the creative talents of Mark Burrier at Enforme Interactive. Finally, there are my students and fellow psychologists whom I am so fortunate to have encountered in my many travels abroad. Your sense of loyalty and unwavering support for all of my endeavors is so very much appreciated. As always, my emotional pillars and source of inspiration will always be my loving wife, Darci, and our three children, Brendan, Madison, and Brianna. Each day, I am emphatically reminded that my own emotional world would ring hollow without the greatest gift of all: your unconditional love.

Steven G. Feifer, D.Ed.

Dedication

To the emotional pillars of my life, my wife Darci, and children Brendan, Madison, and Brianna.
—SGF

I would like to dedicate this book to my wonderful and loving wife, Tina M. Rattan, who has always supported me in all of my endeavors. And to my children, Ashley T. Rattan and Michael R. Rattan whose accomplishments have made me very proud. And lastly, to the ECK which provides a graceful and abundant life to all.
—GR

Preface

The interest in neuropsychology is clearly evidenced by the burgeoning number of articles exploring brain-behavior relationships for disorders associated with emotional, learning, behavioral, and the like. With the advent of more sophisticated neuroimaging techniques such as the functional magnetic resonance imaging (fMRI), it becomes evident that clear and meaningful patterns exist between behavior and their corresponding nerve impulses. These patterns, however, do not follow a simple stimulus-response paradigm. For instance, a simple task such as reading evokes a sophisticated array of interconnected neural responses involving multiple brain regions throughout the cortex. This includes the prefrontal cortex and executive functions where cognitive decisions are made regarding the information received. In a likewise fashion, emotional responses have a primary limbic system activation with subsequent prefrontal cortex involvement to assess behavioral regulation and response inhibition. This oversimplification doesn't include the further action by the prefrontal region in making cognitive decisions based on whether this emotional experience is viewed as positive or negative. Clearly, the observed outward behavior, whether calm or frenzied, is orchestrated by electrical and chemical signals sent selectively, or in some cases, in disarray, to the over 100 billion neurons in the human brain. To understand how this works, then is no easy task.

The above notwithstanding, the goal of the current text is to present an understanding of emotional disorders from a neuropsychological, psychopharmacological, and educational perspective. The intent is to provide the reader with useful information not only to understand the complexity of emotional behavior, but also to find meaningful information that may prove instrumental in their practice or repertoire of knowledge. This text is written with the psychologist, educator, and allied mental health provider in mind. Although some of the information is clearly technical, efforts have been made to explain jargon related terminology and simplify the content by using vignettes, tables, figures, and other illustrations to magnify salient information. The first section deals with the neuropsychological component of emotional disorders and provides both a theoretical and practical description with discussions ranging from dysfunctional executive functions to right hemisphere disorders. The second section of the book is devoted to the psychopharmacological aspects of emotional disorders. All too often, psychotropic medication is used as a primary or adjunctive treatment for emotional disorders, but understanding how these drugs work is often left to the medical professional. Yet, as providers of mental health or educational attainment, it is incumbent that we understand the principles of psychopharmacology and the underlying mechanisms associated with drug action. As a consequence, it allows us to converse with both the end user and the medical community with more confidence. The final section deals with the educational aspects of this disorder with topics ranging from the effects of psychopathology on learning, school achievement, measurement issues, the concept of mindfulness, and positive behavioral support programs. It is our fond hope that the information in this volume is presented in an academic yet easy to understand manner—but as always, the consumer is the final arbiter.

Gurmal Rattan, Ph.D.

About the Editors

Steven G. Feifer, D. Ed., NCSP, ABSNP is a nationally renowned speaker and author in the field of school neuropsychology and has conducted nearly 200 professional seminars for educators and psychologists. He is dually trained as both a Nationally Certified School Psychologist from James Madison University, and is also a diplomate in school neuropsychology. His doctorate work was conducted at Indiana University of Pennsylvania, with research stints at the National Institute of Health (NIH). He currently works as a school psychologist in Frederick, MD, and is a course instructor in the ABSNP school neuropsychology training program. Dr. Feifer was voted the Maryland School Psychologist of the Year in 2008, and also awarded the National School Psychologist of the Year in 2009 by the National Association of School Psychologists.

Website: ***www.schoolneuropsychpress.com***
Email: feifer@comcast.net

Gurmal Rattan, Ph.D. NCSP is a nationally certified school psychologist and a licensed psychologist in Pennsylvania. Dr. Rattan obtained his undergraduate and master's degrees from the University of British Columbia and his doctorate from Ball State University. Dr. Rattan is currently a professor at Indiana University of Pennsylvania where he teaches graduate courses in neuropsychology and psychopharmacology to students in the doctoral School Psychology program. Dr. Rattan's research interest and publications have been in the areas of neuropsychology, learning disabilities, psychopharmacology, and information processing.

Website: ***www.coe.iup.edu/rattan***
Email: gurmalra@iup.edu

Chapter Contributors

Eleazar Cruz Eusebio, M.A, Ed.S., NCSP is a nationally certified school psychologist currently practicing in Delaware. He holds a master's degree in psychology and an education specialist degree in school psychology from The Citadel Graduate College. He is an instructor and a doctoral student in psychology at the Philadelphia College of Osteopathic Medicine focusing on cross-cultural and neuropsychological issues of children and adolescents.

Beth Doll, Ph.D. is Professor and Director of the School Psychology Program at the University of Nebraska Lincoln. She has worked as a school psychologist in four states across school districts, child guidance clinics, and universities. The central premise of her work is that school environments can prompt children to be developmentally competent or predispose them to be maladjusted.

Mary Fowler, B.A. is an independent education consultant and the author of four books and numerous book chapters on ADHD and related behavioral/emotional disorders. She trains teachers worldwide on classroom management and teaching strategies for students with emotional and behavioral issues

Amy Dilworth Gabel, Ph.D. is the Training and Client Consultation Director with Pearson Clinical Assessment, and formerly Clinical Sales Director with The Psychological Corporation. She earned her Ph.D. and MS in school psychology from The Pennsylvania State University. Her undergraduate training is in psychology and elementary education from Gettysburg College. As a licensed school psychologist in Virginia, her specialty is the comprehensive evaluation of preschool and school-aged students. Dr. Gabel has provided training workshops both nationally and internationally on a wide range of topics, including linking assessment to effective teaching, AD/HD, reading disorders/literacy, executive function disorders, and a variety of assessment and intervention methodologies.

John M. Garruto, M.S., NCSP is currently a doctoral candidate at Indiana University of Pennsylvania. He has been a practicing school psychologist for eleven years (ten of which were in the Oswego City School District) and currently teaches two courses at SUNY Oswego in cognitive assessment and ethics. His professional interests include cognitive and neuropsychological assessment, professional and ethical issues in school psychology, and the use of cognitive-behavioral techniques for the treatment of anxiety disorders.

Lisa A. Hain, Psy.D., NCSP, LPC is a Pennsylvania and nationally certified school psychologist in private practice as well as an adjunct faculty member in Psychology at the Pennsylvania State University. She has extensive experience in assessment of learning and emotional disorders in children, adolescents, and young adults and provides direct therapeutic intervention services. In addition, Dr. Hain also maintains licensure as a professional counselor in Pennsylvania.

James B. Hale, Ph.D., M.Ed., ABSNP is a licensed psychologist, certified school psychologist, and certified special education teacher. He is an Associate Professor and Associate Director of Clinical Training in the Department of Psychology at the Philadelphia College of Osteopathic Medicine. Dr. Hale has pursued multiple lines of research, including studies that differentiate reading and math disability subtypes, challenge assumptions about the validity of global IQ interpretation, examine language and psychosocial functions associated with right hemisphere learning disabilities, and explore neuropsychological aspects of ADHD and medication response. Dr. Hale is an active researcher, practitioner, presenter, and author, including his co-authorship of the critically-acclaimed, bestselling book, School Neuropsychology: A Practitioner's Handbook.

Julie Henzel, M.A., NCSP is a doctoral student and instructor in the School Psychology Program at Philadelphia College of Osteopathic Medicine and a nationally certified school psychologist practicing in Pennsylvania. She earned her master's degree from The Ohio State University and also holds certificates in cognitive behavioral therapy. Julie's professional interests include the neuropsychology of mental illness and the integration of cognitive behavioral therapy with neuropsychology.

Joseph C. Hewitt, D.O. is a board certified child, adolescent, and adult psychiatrist currently in private practice in Lawnside, New Jersey. Dr. Hewitt is a consulting psychiatrist at Swarthmore College in Swarthmore, Pennsylvania and provides school consultative services for children with special education needs. He attended medical school at UMDNJ –School of Osteopathic Medicine, and his child and adolescent psychiatry residency was completed at Thomas Jefferson University Hospital in Philadelphia, PA.

Mary Helen Immordino-Yang, Ed.D. is a cognitive neuroscientist and educational psychologist who studies the brain bases of social emotion and culture and their implications for development and schools. She is an Assistant Professor of Education at the Rossier School of Education and an Assistant Professor of Psychology at the Brain and Creativity Institute, at the University of Southern California. As a former junior high school teacher, she earned her doctorate at the Harvard University Graduate School of Education. She is also the Associate Editor for North America for the journal *Mind, Brain and Education*.

Jessica G. Kendorski, Ph.D., NCSP is an Assistant Professor at the Philadelphia College of Osteopathic Medicine (PCOM). She obtained her Ph.D. in School Psychology from Temple University where she also served as an adjunct faculty member. She has extensive experience in supporting the emotional, social, and behavioral needs of children with developmental disabilities. In addition, Dr. Kendorski actively works with school districts to improve systems through the reform of school and district-wide academic and behavioral policies and practices. She maintains certifications as a School Psychologist both nationally, and in the states of PA and NJ.

Ann Leonard-Zabel. Ed.D., ABSNP, NCSP is an Associate Professor of Psychology at Curry College in Milton, Massachusetts. She is a clinical cohort instructor for the School Neuropsychology Post-Graduate Certificate Program under the direction of Texas Woman's University, Kids, Inc., and the American Board of School Neuropsychology in the state of Connecticut. Dr. Leonard-Zabel is a member of the Board of Directors of the Massachusetts School Psychologist Association and is an Executive Board Member of the American Board of School Neuropsychologists. She holds several diplomat and fellow certificates and certifications in the field of Neuropsychology, Homeland Security, Forensic Counseling, Clinical Counseling, Cognitive-Behavioral Therapy, and Disability Analysis.

George McCloskey, Ph.D. is a Professor and Director of School Psychology Research in the Psychology Department of the Philadelphia College of Osteopathic Medicine. He frequently presents at national, regional and state meetings on cognitive and neuropsychological assessment topics. Dr. McCloskey is the lead author the text *Assessment and Intervention for Executive Function Difficulties* and the text *Essentials of Executive Function Assessment* (in press). Dr. McCloskey has been involved in test development and publishing activities for more than 25 years. He directed the development of the WISC-IV Integrated and was a Senior Research Director and the Clinical Advisor to the Wechsler Test Development Group for The Psychological Corporation (Harcourt Assessment) and Associate Director of Test Development for AGS.

Ronald A. Sudano, Ed.S., NCSP/Licensed Psychologist, is employed as an educational consultant with the Pennsylvania Training and Technical Assistance Network (PaTTAN) in Pittsburgh, PA. Mr. Sudano has worked in the educational field for 31 years, serving as a school psychologist, emotional support program manager, trainer for crisis prevention and CASSP Core Team member. He is currently enrolled in the school psychology doctoral program at Indiana University of Pennsylvania with a concentration in the neuropsychological assessment and intervention of learning and behavior disorders.

Jed Yalof, Psy.D., ABPP, ABSNP, is Professor and Chair of the Department of Graduate Psychology at Immaculata University, and Coordinator of the Psy.D. Program in Clinical Psychology. He holds a doctorate in clinical psychology, and is also a school and neuropsychologist. He has published in the areas of learning disability diagnosis, nonverbal learning disability, and other areas, including college counseling, psychoanalytic interviewing, and ethics and assessment.

Table of Contents

CHAPTER 1

SOCIAL NEUROSCIENCE AND ITS APPLICATION TO EDUCATION

Mary Helen Immordino-Yang, Ph.D.

"I've had three friends die of gang violence, and they weren't even from a gang... I cried for two of them, and then the third one, I was just like, in shock. I was like... I can't believe that just happened again."
(as heard on KPCC Southern California Public Radio, story by F. Stoltze, 5-22-08)

Fifteen-year-old Alan's story is one of fear and sadness, of turning from compassion and embodied, tearful awareness to numbness and *"shock."* It is a story of empathy come and gone, of emotion felt and lost, of consciousness altered by engagement changed to disbelief. Alan speaks of his life in Los Angeles, but he could be telling the story of many young people caught in zones of urban violence worldwide.

As many young people do, in talking about their experiences, Alan gives away what social and affective neuroscience is just beginning to understand, namely, that the body and mind are linked and that our very consciousness, the biological mechanisms that make possible our subjective sense of self, form the sounding board for our understanding of other people. Alan cries for the deaths of his first two friends, innocent bystanders caught in gang violence. He feels the sadness of their loss as an emotion that changes his body through crying as well as other physiological changes, which typically include a decrease in overall activity level, lowered heart rate, a sad facial expression, and restricted bodily posture. His friends' deaths and the ensuing emotions he feels also alter his mind in uncharacteristic ways, most likely causing him to dwell on and re-experience the event, shattering his focus and concentration, and perhaps even causing trouble in his relationships with loved ones due to the fear that he will lose them.

Beyond the emotions that Alan reports for his first two friends' deaths, Alan's experience exemplifies another recent neuroscientific discovery about the relationship between the mind and body. When his third friend dies, Alan's reaction moves past his former extreme sadness to induce a state that he cogently describes as "shock." From a neuroscientific perspective, Alan is describing the altered state of consciousness he experienced at such an overwhelming event, and alluding to a disjunction between his previous experiences and this new occurrence by stating that he could not *"believe"* what had just happened. Unable to reconcile the events he knows are true with his knowledge about what ought to be true based on his past experiences, his emotion and sense of self are temporarily dampened. Alan is unable to cry for his third friend's death, because he simply cannot connect his current knowledge to his past experiences in order to properly engage his body and mind to foster an appropriate emotional reaction. Instead, the resulting state is "shock," or the emotional numbness and disembodiment that many people feel during traumatic events that would otherwise trigger overwhelming emotion.

To sum up the discussion of Alan, what have we learned? The answer forms a conceptual outline for the rest of this chapter, and leads us into a discussion of the neuroscience of emotion, social interaction, and their implications for learning and education. First, Alan's tearful reaction to his first two friends' deaths highlights the relationship between the cognitive and emotional aspects of Alan's experience. Alan's emotions and thoughts are intertwined, not separate. What he feels influences and is influenced by what he thinks, and in fact his thoughts and emotions are two aspects of the same process (Fischer & Bidell, 2006), a concept that we have previously termed *"emotional thought"* (Immordino-Yang & Damasio, 2007).

Second, emotions involve an interdependency of the body and brain, and both the body and brain are involved in the induction of an appropriate response to Alan's tragic news. Alan learns of his friends' deaths, a circumstance that automatically triggers the emotional reaction of sadness; and this reaction modulates basic physiological life-regulatory processing in the body. Alan manifests bodily changes through crying, and if we measured, we would expect to see changes in heart rate, blood pressure, and breathing pattern as well. In turn, these physiological changes are sensed by the brain, and used to shape the contents of Alan's mind. In this way, Alan's "cognitive" knowledge triggers an "emotional" response that involves bodily changes as well as the accommodation of Alan's thoughts to the feeling of these changes. In this body ↔ brain/mind cycle, emotions and cognition are intertwined, and together influence and are influenced by changes in the state of the body.

Third, Alan's reaction to his third friend's death demonstrates how the relationships between the body, brain, and mind are connected to neuropsychological mechanisms of consciousness. When Alan is unable to assimilate the knowledge of his third friend's death, he cannot mount an appropriate emotional response in his body and mind. The result is a change or void in his consciousness level, experienced as "shock," "disbelief," and, although Alan does not directly say this, a perceived detachment or disembodiment, as evidenced by a lack of crying or emotional reaction.

Fourth, and perhaps least obvious but most important, all of the reactions that Alan describes involve his own body and mind, and yet they are induced by events that happened to other people. Here, Alan reveals that, from a neuroscientific perspective, the mechanisms involved in the feeling and control of the body form a platform for the *social mind*. In essence, we understand and mount reactions to others' situations by feeling the response of our own viscera or "gut" as our mind perceives and deliberates on the situation at hand. Related to the third point above, the feeling of our own "self" appears to involve the organized recruitment of brain networks for feeling and regulating the body, connected to memories for experiences within the social and physical worlds. In summary, affective neuroscience is discovering and describing the interrelatedness of the body and mind in processes of emotion, thinking and consciousness. Further, the neuroscientific evidence is increasingly demonstrating that we understand, evaluate, and react to the situations of other people by vicariously imagining them on the substrate of our own self.

What Is Emotion?

As an entry point to the discussion of educationally-relevant advances in affective and social neuroscience, it is useful to lay out a neuroscientific definition of emotion. Although lay views of emotion abound, here we understand emotion as a set of cognitive and physiological processes that constitute a person's automatic evaluative reaction to a perceived, remembered, or imagined circumstance. As such, emotions involve both the body and mind, and utilize brain systems for body regulation (e.g., for blood pressure, heart rate, respiration, or digestion) and sensation (e.g., for physical pain or pleasure, or for stomach ache) (Damasio et al., 2000). Emotions also influence brain systems for cognition, changing thought in characteristic ways—from the desire to seek revenge in anger, to the search for escape in fear, to the receptive openness to others in happiness, to

> **KEY LEARNING POINTS:**
> **Emotion and Cognition**
>
> This chapter is about the cognitive neuroscience of emotion and social interaction, and the implications of a cognitive neuroscientific perspective on these topics for education. By capturing a brief vignette about a teenage boy whose innocent friends are gunned down in a slew of urban violence, this section introduces several recent developments in the neuroscientific study of emotion. Most importantly:
>
> - Emotion and cognition are intertwined, and actively involve both the body and mind.
> - Social processing and learning happen by internalizing subjective interpretations of other people's beliefs, goals, feelings, and actions, and vicariously experiencing these as if they were our own.

the ruminating on lost people or objects in sadness. In each case, the emotion is played out on the face and body, a process that is felt via neural systems for sensing and regulating the body. And in each case, these feelings of the body interact with other thoughts to change the mind in characteristic ways, and to help people learn from their experiences.

It is important to understand that in this view, emotion and thinking are never truly separated, and learning always involves both emotional evaluation and cognitive processing (see Figure 1-1, from Immordino-Yang & Damasio, 2007). Even solving the driest academic problem involves emotional as well as cognitive processing. For example, what neurocognitive processes are required for Amy, a typical 10th grade student void of any particular learning condition, to solve a typical mathematical equation? It is readily apparent that the initial steps to engage in successful problem solving are more emotional in nature. For instance, to apply problem-solving skills usefully in math, Amy must first motivate and engage herself sufficiently, recognize the degree of complexity required to tackle the equation and make a value judgment as to whether or not her efforts are worthwhile, identify the type of problem that is before her, and retrieve the necessary neurocognitive and academic information and strategies that will steer her toward a correct solution. Emotion plays a critical role in all of these stages of problem solving, helping Amy to consciously or non-consciously evaluate which sets of knowledge, skills, and abilities are likely relevant, and which will lead to the correct solution based on previous learning experiences. As she begins the cognitive journey of thinking through the solution, Amy is emotionally evaluating whether each cognitive step is likely to bring her closer to a correct solution, or whether it seems to be pointing her down an incorrect path.

From a neuropsychological perspective, the brain systems for emotion form the "rudder" that steers a student's thinking toward the development and recruitment of an effective skill or solution (Immordino-Yang & Damasio, 2007). in this case for the solving of math problems. Through regulating and inciting attention (Posner & Rothbart, 2005), motivation, and evaluation of possible outcomes, emotion serves to modulate Amy's recruitment of brain networks that support the mathematical skills she is developing. These same mechanisms would be at play in the solving of most other academic endeavors, thereby blurring the oft artificial distinction between cognition and emotion.

FIGURE 1-1

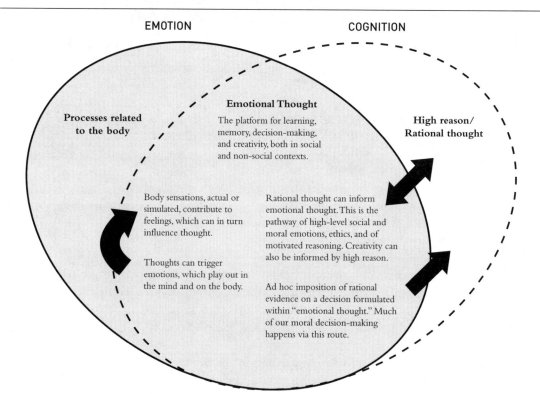

Figure 1-1. The thought processes that educators care about, among them learning and memory, involve both emotional and cognitive aspects, and the body as well as the mind. In the diagram, the solid ellipse represents emotion; the dashed ellipse represents cognition. The extensive overlap between the two ellipses represents the domain of "emotional thought." Emotional thought can be conscious or non-conscious, and is the means by which bodily sensations influence the mind during learning. High reason is a small section of the diagram, and refers to the most abstract and logical of thought processes, which are nevertheless informed by emotional thought. Reprinted with permission from Immordino-Yang and Damasio (2007).

From "Self" to "Other" and Back Again

Many emotions are social, and anyone involved in educating children, from teachers and parents to coaches, counselors and beyond, realizes all too well that social learning is a major force in children's development. Typical children watch and engage with other people, imitate other people's actions (including mental actions and beliefs), and look to trusted adults and peers for emotional and other feedback on their behavior. They imagine how other people feel and think, and those thoughts in turn influence how they feel and think.

Educators have long known that thinking and learning, as simultaneously cognitive and emotional processes, are not carried out in a vacuum, but in social and cultural contexts (Fischer & Bidell, 2006). A major part of a child's decision-making process involves previous social experiences, moral and ethical boundaries, and cultural history. For example, Alan and Amy clearly utilize past experiences to guide their current behavior, thoughts, feelings, and ultimately their learning. In Alan's case, experiencing the emotional connection involved in friendship leads him to an appreciation of the emotional implications of losing them. Furthermore, knowing and empathizing with the feelings of being physically and emotionally hurt helps him to understand what his friends must have experienced during their deadly encounter. With respect to the emotional interplay of solving a mundane mathematical problem, Amy's reasons may include the desire to

> **KEY LEARNING POINTS:**
> **Defining Emotion**
>
> Emotions are packages of behaviors and cognitive strategies that are automatically triggered in certain contexts, either real, imagined, or remembered (Damasio, 1994/2005). Often the term "emotional thought" is used to describe the mental platform that supports important educational processes like learning, memory, and problem solving, because in real-life learning, emotional and cognitive aspects of mental processing are never truly separate (Immordion-Yang & Damasio, 2007). In emotional thought, emotion-related changes in the mind and body form feedback loops that steer thought and behavior. In essence, emotion can be seen as the rudder for learning, as it guides thought and behavior in order to foster the development of effective skills for acting in the social and physical worlds.

please her parents, the intrinsic reward of finding the solution, the avoidance of punishment or the teacher's disapproval, or the desire to attend a good college. From a neuroscientific perspective, we do not usually think of math problems as emotional; nevertheless, each of these reasons involves an implicit or explicit social or emotional value judgment. As Amy imagines how it would feel to solve the mathematical problem, she engages feedback loops between neural systems supporting memories, sensations, and cultural values, including how she may have benefited from previous learning situations. This emotional chain of processing eventually comes together to help steer Amy's current thinking and behavior, while at the same time giving her a context in which to interpret and learn from her new experiences. Despite the differences in Alan's and Amy's experiences, both adolescents' behavior is guided at every step by their ability to make social and emotional evaluations and predictions, and by their ability to use their own selves as a platform for decision-making.

The Neuroscience of Self and Other: "Mirror Neurons"

Social neuroscience is revealing some of the basic biological mechanisms by which such social and

KEY LEARNING POINTS:
Emotional Predictions

Many emotions are social in nature, and fueled by feelings toward others. Such emotions play an important role in helping to guide students' and teachers' behavior and thinking, because they enable educators to formulate predictions about how students may react to decisions and actions. These predictive processes form a basic mechanism for social learning, as they enable educators to learn from the behavior of their students, while also guiding their own behavior in directions that will lead to positive outcomes. These processes also underscore the subjective nature of social processing, as predictions and evaluation are made in relation to a persons own culture mores, memories, biases, and preferences (Immordino-Yang, 2007).

emotional processing takes place (Frith & Frith, 2007; Mitchell, 2008), although applications to classroom practice are only just beginning (Immordino-Yang, 2009). According to current evidence, social processing and learning generally involve internalizing one's own subjective interpretations of other people's feelings and actions (Uddin, Iacoboni, Lange, & Keenan, 2007). We perceive and understand other people's feelings and actions in relation to our own beliefs and goals, and vicariously experience these feelings and actions as if they were our own (Immordino-Yang, 2008). This processing allows us to empathically experience the emotional and cognitive effects of another person's circumstances, be they about urban violence or about math problems, and to use these empathic experiences to guide our own behavior and learning.

Notably, empathically experiencing another person's feelings and actions involves neural systems relating actions with their resulting perceptions. Bringing this discussion to the level of neuroscience explanations, recent research findings regarding empathetic behavior in the brain has led researchers toward further exploring the "mirror neuron" systems (Oberman & Ramachandran, 2007; Rizzolatti, Fogassi, & Gallese, 2001; Umiltà et al., 2001). The "mirror systems" are essentially networks in the brain where systems for perception, and systems for action, converge and feed into one another (Damasio & Meyer, 2008). What are the implications of this relatively obscure brain system for school based educators? Simply put, in order for these convergence areas to be activated in an observer watching another person, the observer must have some context in which to understand the purpose or goal of the action being observed. Furthermore, in order for an action to be perceived as goal-directed or purposeful, the observer must have some sense of the change in circumstances that the action will produce, i.e. "the goal." In turn, the change in circumstances the action produces will be perceived, and then fed back into motor systems to inform the planning of future actions. (For a more complete treatment of the role of mirror systems in the production of meaningful skills, see Immordino-Yang, 2008.)

To understand how this process is invoked in empathically assessing other people's actions, think, for example, of the last time you were in a quiet meeting, when suddenly someone began frantically groping for a ringing cell phone. Everyone in the room instantly knew why this person was searching their pockets in order to avoid further embarrassment. Furthermore, everyone in the room likely felt some of the accompanying emotions this hapless person felt while searching. Why? Because everyone in that room shared a common cultural understanding of the appropriate use of technology in a meeting, and of the embarrassment that results from a breach of conduct. Lastly, what did several people in the room do after watching this unpleasant predicament? Of course, they turned off or muted their own cell phones!

To understand what this means for education, think about a typical classroom, with students engaged in problem-solving activities while the teacher demonstrates and explains a myriad of concepts. Beyond the obvious linguistic and visual necessities, what is required for a student to understand and learn from a teacher? And, conversely, what can the teacher do to facilitate a student's comprehension of the information presented? Clearly, for students to accurately perceive, understand, and conceptually grasp the information offered the student and teacher must implicitly understand each other's goals. In essence, to perceive another person's actions as meaningful, a process which involves empathic activation of motor planning systems (via sectors of these systems known as "mirror neuron" areas) and many other neural systems for various aspects of emotional thought, requires that the perceiver have some background in addition to some prior experience with the topic at hand. Despite the teacher's best efforts, if the students are not in tune with the purposes of the lesson and subsequently not able to empathically internalize the aim of the teacher's actions and words, they may overlook the features of the lesson that the teacher intended to convey. To them, the teacher's words and gestures may seem irrelevant, meaningless, or pointless. Additionally, the students may impute the wrong goal to the teacher's actions and misinterpret the social exchanges of the learning situation. Consequently, an erroneous conclusion is reached as students may feel the teacher is only interested in boring them, or in making them feel unintelligent, or in making them learn something that is entirely different from what the teacher intended.

SUMMARY

Just as affective neuroscientific evidence links our bodies and minds in processes of emotion, social neuroscientific evidence links our own selves to the understanding of other people. From a neuroscientific standpoint, understanding other people's actions, and hence learning from others, is a process that involves an observer imagining another person's actions as if they were his own. This process is inherently subjective and biased, as the observer imputes goals to the other person's actions based on their own experience within similar contexts. In educational settings, this suggests that if students do not understand the teacher's goals, they may not perceive the teacher's lesson as intended, and the content may be lost. In other words, the social exchanges of learning are paramount before the sharing of knowledge can take place. Therefore, teachers should strive to learn about the culture, mindset, mores, and values of their students to forge a strong social connection that can then lay the foundation for a successful learning experience. Further, teachers should work to make their goals as explicit as possible for students, rather than hidden underneath the veil of the subject matter.

To conclude, social emotions and their associated thoughts and actions are biologically built but culturally shaped; they reflect our neuropsychological propensity to internalize the actions of others, but are interpreted in light of our own social, emotional and cognitive experiences. These social, emotional, and cognitive experiences, in turn, can be interrelated under the heading of "emotional thought," which can originate in the mind but involves interplay between the body and brain. Social and affective neuroscience, while it cannot directly show teachers how to interact with students, can inform educators' knowledge of why and how students learn, especially in social contexts. Incorporating this new information into traditional models of teaching and learning may lead to innovative, effective methods for engaging students in meaningful learning experiences.

REFERENCES

Damasio, A. R. (1994/2005). *Descartes' error: Emotion, reason and the human brain.* London: Penguin Books.

Damasio, A. R., Grabowski, T. J., Bechara, A., Damasio, H., Ponto, L. L. B., Parvizi, J., et al. (2000). Subcortical and cortical brain activity during the feeling of self-generated emotions. *Nature Neuroscience, 3*(10), 1049-1056.

Damasio, A. R., & Meyer, K. (2008). Behind the looking-glass. *Nature, 454*(7201), 167-168.

Fischer, K. W., & Bidell, T. (2006). Dynamic development of action and thought. In W. Damon & R. Lerner (Eds.), *Handbook of Child Psychology, Vol. 1: Theoretical Models of Human Development* (6th ed., pp. 313-399). Hoboken, NJ: John Wiley & Sons.

Frith, C. D., & Frith, U. (2007). Social cognition in humans. *Current Biology, 17*(16), R724-R732.

Immordino-Yang, M. H. (2007). A tale of two cases: Lessons for education from the study of two boys living with half their brains. *Mind, Brain and Education, 1*(2), 66-83.

Immordino-Yang, M. H. (2008). The smoke around mirror neurons: Goals as sociocultural and emotional organizers of perception and action in learning. *Mind, Brain, and Education, 2*(2), 67-73.

Immordino-Yang, M. H. (2009). Our bodies, our minds--Our cultures, our "selves": Implications of affective and social neuroscience for educational theory. *Educational Philosophy and Theory.*

Immordino-Yang, M. H., & Damasio, A. R. (2007). We feel, therefore we learn: The relevance of affective and social neuroscience to education. *Mind, Brain and Education, 1*(1), 3-10.

Mitchell, J. P. (2008). Contributions of functional neuroimaging to the study of social cognition. *Current Directions in Psychological Science, 17*(2), 142-146.

Oberman, L. M., & Ramachandran, V. S. (2007). The simulating social mind: The role of the mirror neuron system and simulation in the social and communicative deficits of autism spectrum disorders. *Psychological Bulletin, 133*(2), 310-327.

Posner, M. I., & Rothbart, M. K. (2005). Influencing brain networks: Implications for education. *Trends in Cognitive Sciences, 9*(3), 99-103.

Rizzolatti, G., Fogassi, L., & Gallese, V. (2001). Neurophysiological mechanisms underlying the understanding and imitation of action. *Nature Reviews Neuroscience, 2*(9), 661-670.

Uddin, L. Q., Iacoboni, M., Lange, C., & Keenan, J. P. (2007). The self and social cognition: The role of cortical midline structures and mirror neurons. *Trends in Cognitive Sciences, 11*(4), 153-157.

Umiltà, M. A., Kohler, E., Gallese, V., Fogassi, L., Fadiga, L., Keysers, C., et al. (2001). I Know What You Are Doing: A Neurophysiological Study. *Neuron, 31*(1), 155-165.

CHAPTER 2

SOCIAL BRAIN CIRCUITRY AND BEHAVIOR: THE NEURAL BUILDING BLOCKS OF EMOTION

Steven G. Feifer, D.Ed.

"Empathy is at the heart of my moral code. It is how I understand the golden rule, not simply as a call to sympathy or charity, but as something more demanding, a call to stand in somebody else's shoes and see through their eyes."

—Barack Obama, 2006

The very fabric of American school culture has been undermined in recent years by an unprecedented and dramatic wave of violence whose very magnitude has fostered a shift in educational resources and public policy toward early identification of and treatment for students with social and emotional disorders. The intense public scrutiny on safety in our schools cascaded to epic proportions between 1997 and 1998, when children as young as 11 years of age shot classmates and teachers in mass shootings in Pearl, Mississippi; West Paducah, Kentucky; Jonesboro, Arkansas; Edinburg, Pennsylvania, and Springfield, Oregon leaving 13 dead and 45 wounded (Filley et al., 2001). However, the most disturbing incident of mass terror which riveted the nation occurred in Littleton, Colorado, where two high school seniors killed 12 classmates and a teacher at Columbine High School before turning their guns on themselves. In each of these instances, there were teachers, counselors, administrators, and psychologists familiar with the perpetrators, though a common decry echoed by all was shock, horror, and disbelief. Unfortunately, the recent trend of school shootings and senseless violence has persisted since the 1999 Columbine tragedy, as depicted in Table 2-1. Consequently, a new breed of educational curriculum that invokes a healthy school climate by promoting character education programs, peer mediation techniques, bullying prevention methods, and conflict resolution scenarios has now permeated the boundaries of public education.

According to the National Center for Educational Statistics (2007), the sobering truth remains that 78 percent of all schools have experienced one or more violent incidents of crime. Both primary schools and high schools have lower rates of violent crime per 1,000 students than middle schools. Perhaps most disconcerting was the fact that the percentage of schools experiencing crimes in 2005–06 that was not measurably different from the percentage of schools experiencing crimes in 1999–2000, despite the new wave of curricular changes aimed at enhancing character education. Certainly, school violence can heighten levels of arousal, detract from a positive school climate, and ultimately affect students' ability to learn.

TABLE 2-1
A Time Line of School Shootings Since Columbine (April, 1999)

Adapted from: http://www.infoplease.com/ipa/A0777958.html

May 20, 1999, Conyers, GA
Six students injured at Heritage High School by Thomas Solomon, 15, who was reportedly depressed after breaking up with his girlfriend.

Nov. 19, 1999, Deming, NM
Victor Cordova Jr., 12, shot and killed Araceli Tena, 13, in the lobby of Deming Middle School.

Dec. 6, 1999, Fort Gibson, OK
Four students wounded as Seth Trickey, 13, opened fire with a 9mm semiautomatic handgun at Fort Gibson Middle School.

Feb. 29, 2000, Mount Morris Township, MI
Six-year-old Kayla Rolland shot dead at Buell Elementary School near Flint, Mich. The assailant was identified as a six-year-old boy with a .32-caliber handgun.

March 10, 2000, Savannah, GA
Two students killed by Darrell Ingram, 19, while leaving a dance sponsored by Beach High School.

May 26, 2000, Lake Worth, FL
One teacher, Barry Grunow, shot and killed at Lake Worth Middle School by Nate Brazill, 13, with .25-caliber semiautomatic pistol on the last day of classes.

Sept. 26, 2000, New Orleans, LA
Two students wounded with the same gun during a fight at Woodson Middle School.

Jan. 17, 2001, Baltimore, MD
One student shot and killed in front of Lake Clifton Eastern High School.

March 5, 2001, Santee, CA
Two killed and 13 wounded by Charles Andrew Williams, 15, firing from a bathroom at Santana High School.

March 7, 2001, Williamsport, PA
Elizabeth Catherine Bush, 14, wounded student Kimberly Marchese in the cafeteria of Bishop Neumann High School; she was depressed and frequently teased.

March 22, 2001, Granite Hills, CA
One teacher and three students wounded by Jason Hoffman, 18, at Granite Hills High School. A policeman shot and wounded Hoffman.

March 30, 2001, Gary, IN
One student killed by Donald R. Burt, Jr., a 17-year-old student who had been expelled from Lew Wallace High School.

Nov. 12, 2001, Caro, MI
Chris Buschbacher, 17, took two hostages at the Caro Learning Center before killing himself.

Jan. 15, 2002, New York, NY
A teenager wounded two students at Martin Luther King Jr. High School.

October 28, 2002, Tucson, AZ
Robert S. Flores Jr., 41, a student at the nursing school at the University of Arizona, shot and killed three female professors and then himself.

April 14, 2003, New Orleans, LA
One 15-year-old killed, and three students wounded at John McDonogh High School by gunfire from four teenagers (none were students at the school). The motive was gang-related.

April 24, 2003, Red Lion, PA
James Sheets, 14, killed principal Eugene Segro of Red Lion Area Junior High School before killing himself.

Sept. 24, 2003, Cold Spring, MI
Two students are killed at Rocori High School by John Jason McLaughlin, 15.

March 21, 2005, Red Lake, MI
Jeff Weise, 16, killed grandfather and companion, and then arrived at school where he killed a teacher, a security guard, 5 students, and finally himself, leaving a total of 10 dead.

Nov. 8, 2005, Jacksboro, TN
One 15-year-old shot and killed an assistant principal at Campbell County High School and seriously wounded two other administrators.

Aug. 24, 2006, Essex, VT
Christopher Williams, 27, looking for his ex-girlfriend at Essex Elementary School, shot two teachers, killing one and wounding another. Before going to the school, he had killed the ex-girlfriend's mother.

Sept. 26, 2006, Bailey, CO
Adult male held six students hostage at Platte Canyon High School and then shot and killed Emily Keyes, 16, and himself.

Sept. 29, 2006, Cazenovia, WI
A 15-year-old student shot and killed Weston School principal John Klang.

Oct. 3, 2006, Nickel Mines, PA
32-year-old Carl Charles Roberts IV entered the one-room West Nickel Mines Amish School and shot 10 schoolgirls, ranging in age from 6 to 13 years old, and then himself. Five of the girls and Roberts died.

Jan. 3, 2007, Tacoma, WA
Douglas Chanthabouly, 18, shot fellow student Samnang Kok, 17, in the hallway of Henry Foss High School.

April 16, 2007, Blacksburg, VA
A 23-year-old Virginia Tech student, Cho Seung-Hui, killed two in a dorm, then killed 30 more 2 hours later in a classroom building. His suicide brought the death toll to 33, making the shooting rampage the most deadly in U.S. history. Fifteen others were wounded.

Sept. 21, 2007, Dover, DE
A Delaware State University Freshman, Loyer D. Brandon, shot and wounded two other Freshman students on the University campus. Brandon is being charged with attempted murder, assault, reckless engagement, as well as a gun charge.

Oct. 10, 2007, Cleveland, OH
A 14-year-old student at a Cleveland high school, Asa H. Coon, shot and injured two students and two teachers before he shot and killed himself. The victims' injuries were not life-threatening.

Nov. 7, 2007, Tuusula, Finland
An 18-year-old student in southern Finland shot and killed five boys, two girls, and the female principal at Jokela High School. At least 10 others were injured. The gunman shot himself and died from his wounds in the hospital.

Feb. 8, 2008, Baton Rouge, LA
A nursing student shot and killed two women and then herself in a classroom at Louisiana Technical College in Baton Rouge.

Feb. 11, 2008, Memphis, TN
A 17-year-old student at Mitchell High School shot and wounded a classmate in gym class.

Feb. 12, 2008, Oxnard, CA
A 14-year-old boy shot a student at E.O. Green Junior High School causing the 15-year-old victim to be brain dead.

Feb. 14, 2008, DeKalb, IL
Gunman kills seven students and then himself, and wounds 15 more when he opens fire on a classroom at Northern Illinois University. The gunman, Stephen P. Kazmierczak, was identified as a former graduate student at the university in 2007

A compelling argument can be made that a strong relationship exists between committing violent acts and the existence of social-emotional disorders in children. For instance, Swanson, Holser, and Ganju (1990) noted that violence increased five times among persons diagnosed with schizophrenia, major depression, and bipolar disorder; and 12 to 16 times among those with alcohol or substance abuse disorders. Likewise Eronen, Tiihonen, and Hakola (1996) found that homicides substantially increased for both men and women who suffered from schizophrenia, anti-social personality disorder, and alcoholism compared with the general population in Finland. Similarly, Worling (2001) examined male sexual offenders and noted those who presented as having an anti-social personality disorder or as being more socially isolated in their manner were charged with more violent types of sexual offenses. Lastly, Valliant et al. (1999) found a relationship between elevated scores on the Psychopathic Deviate, Paranoid and Schizophrenic scales of the *Minnesota Multiphasic Personality Inventory* (MMPI) and violent offenses among incarcerated males. Nevertheless, most of these studies used rather skewed population samples; namely, juvenile offenders currently incarcerated, and did not control for critical variables such as intelligence, educational level, previous violent offenses, family background, or history of being victimized or abused (Filley et al., 2001).

Conventional wisdom in our society maintains that children with disruptive behavior problems lack either a moral foundation, have little incentive to conform with societal demands, or simply are the byproduct of an unstable home environment. Therefore, if a child struggles to conform with behavioral rules and expectations, the prudent educator, crafty parent, or cunning therapist must somehow find a way to develop suitable behavior incentive plans to motivate these students toward behaving in a more appropriate manner. As Cicerone (2002) noted, the goal of most behavior plans is to induce task specific performance, as opposed to the internalization of self-regulatory processes. Thus, some children may demonstrate more desired behaviors in the artificial contextual environment of the classroom when explicitly rewarded, but these children rarely internalize their behavior to guide and regulate emotional functioning in other social situations and contexts. Why? Simply put, behavior modification does not work in a vacuum, as each individual child has a unique brain that must ultimately guide the development of social integration through trust, empathy, and attachment, while simultaneously learning to temper emotional aggression. According to Barkley (2001), effective school performance in part requires successful social and emotional management through a milieu of interpersonal encounters and challenges, where frustration and anger must be tempered for the pursuit of goal attainment. Therefore, simplistic solutions for complex emotional problems may provide an artificial sense of comfort, but truly effective interventions must be comprehensive in scope to address both internalizing *and* externalizing factors to produce lasting change. Today, the subsequent failure to integrate children with emotional disorders back into the classroom, let alone society, remains rather striking. For instance, children with emotional disorders remain the single most challenging group to educate successfully, are twice as likely to drop out of school, and tend to earn lower grades than children with other disabilities (Reddy, 2001). Furthermore, children with emotional disturbances comprise approximately one-third of all students with disabilities who receive homebound instructional services (Leone & McLaughlin, 1995).

According to Moeller (2001), available research indicates that some of the variability in children's aggressive behaviors is actually due to genetic factors, and not entirely to deficits of character, poor behavioral motivation, or family dynamics. Therefore, the question must be asked: how some 80,000 to 100,000 genes located within 3 million base pairs of DNA on 23 chromosomes express themselves through mental processes and ultimately observable behavior? The answer remains as elusive as ever, though the fledgling discipline of affective neuroscience has provided a beacon of light for future scientists to explore. As William James (1890) so poignantly stated, "Psychology is the science of mental life."

The Neurobiological Architecture of Human Emotion
The idea of connecting mental processes to brain activity is certainly not new. Perhaps the most celebrated case highlighting the association between brain activity and emotional processing dates

back to 1848 in a small Vermont town. It was here that the miraculous story of a railroad worker named Phineas Gage emerged. Gage, a railroad construction foreman, actually survived a 13 pound spike that completely penetrated the orbitofrontal cortex of his right hemisphere. As a result, he developed profound personality and emotional changes, but was spared any cognitive decline. Today, there is compelling evidence from cognitive neuroscience that a distributed network of interdependent brain regions dictate a variety of affective processes that gradually become integrated during the course of social development (Cicchetti & Posner, 2005; Yeates et al., 2007). These neurobehavioral systems are involved with emotional processing and work in unison to modulate social behavior (Dahl, 2001). For instance, the left hemisphere of our brains is involved with positive emotions such as love and happiness, while the right hemisphere modulates negative emotions such as fear, hatred, and anger. Consequently, damage to the left frontal cortices are associated with negative emotions such as depression, fearfulness, and social withdrawal, while damage to the right frontal cortices are often associated with excessive emotionality, jocularity, and disinhibition of behavior (Powell & Voeller, 2004). However, the complexity of social emotional functioning goes far beyond simple right versus left hemispheric dichotomies in the brain. As stipulated by Posner, Russell, and Peterson (2005), emotions are actually complex cognitive machinations that are interpreted from core physiological experiences. For instance, most animal research also emphasizes the role of subcortical and other limbic system brain structures in the processing of emotions, whereas human research demonstrates the importance of neocortical structures (Posner, Russell, & Peterson, 2005). Perhaps over time, organizational changes in neural networks in the brain may occur so that multiple brain regions contribute to emotional processing. For any parent who survived the *"terrible-two"* stages of behavior, it becomes readily apparent that children gradually learn to temper their immediate emotional outbursts through the development of other cognitive self-regulation skills.

Quite early in development, the general architecture of emotional functioning takes shape as specific brain regions branch out through the development of white matter pathways. These pathways cross vast terrains deep within the brain, forging a complex web of functional connectivity and communication vital to adaptive social behavior. The development of white matter pathways, or myelination, involves a fatty substance that covers and protects nerve cells by wrapping itself around axonal connections. This sheath around the axon acts like a conduit in an electrical system, ensuring that messages sent by axons are not lost en route while speeding up neural connectivity exponentially (Fields, 2008). The myelination and ultimate maturation of the brain occurs gradually during the first 25 years of life, and proceeds from the back of the brain toward the frontal regions (Fields). The frontal lobes are the final frontier of brain development, and remain the seat for higher level planning, reasoning, and executive functioning skills. Schwann cells, supporting glial cells that provide myelin insulation, dictate both the timing and degree of completion of white matter pathways. This is viewed as a critical prerequisite for the ultimate emergence of the social brain network (Yeates et al., 2007). For instance, Johnson et al. (2005) found white matter aberrations in autistic children actually correlated with the failure to develop early social skills such as eye gaze cuing and joint attention. According to Fields, abnormal myelin formation alters the timing of neural connectivity, which may subsequently contribute to many mental illnesses such as schizophrenia, bipolar disorder, and autism.

The overall integrity of the emotional brain may very well have its genesis in early emotional experiences. Children who are abused or neglected or deprived of the emotional warmth and a give-

KEY LEARNING POINTS:
Stress and the Brain

The stress system most likely evolved to help human beings recognize danger and adapt to a constantly changing environment. The *hypothalamic-pituitary-adrenal (HPA)* axis coordinates secretion of corticotropin-releasing hormone *(CRH)* from the hypothalamus, adrenocorticotropin *(ACTH)* from the pituitary, and *cortisol* from the adrenal glands in response to stress. This chemical cascade stimulates the fight or flight system causing an increase in cardiovascular activity, enhanced selective memory, increased alertness, and suppression of nonessential bodily functions. Lower levels of cortisol have been linked to antisocial behavior and aggression (Susman, 2006). Higher cortisol levels, such as those produced from chronic stress, are associated with severe fatigue, weak muscles, high blood pressure, anxiety, and hormonal disorders such as *Cushing's Syndrome*.

and-take exchange from a passionate caregiver may not develop an appropriate emotional foundation for higher level social skills via white matter connectivity (Yeates et al.,2007). According to Gunnar and Quevado (2008), early stressful experiences can alter brain chemistry through the atypical release of cortisol. Cortisol is an important stress hormone whose release activates the body's *"fight or flight"* system. During prolonged periods of chronic stress, elevated cortisol levels can actually destroy brain cells and alter crucial cortico-limbic circuits, which are vital in processing social-emotional experiences (Gunnar & Quevado, 2008). According to Susman (2006), bi-directional changes in cortisol reactivity, whether extremely high or extremely low, are related to antisocial behavior. In other words, each child has a set point for optimum functioning during periods of stress. If the set point is unusually low, this creates a dampening of the stress system, thereby rendering it inactive and possibly leading to more sociopathic behaviors. Conversely, too much cortisol, which often stems from periods of chronic stress, results in a very high set point, which can lead to hormonal disorders and more negative social reciprocity unless the causative stress can be reduced (Susman, 2006).

In summary, brains may actually undergo a sort of regional specialization, with higher level brain functions eventually overtaking the responsibility of basic emotional processes generated at a more subcortical level in the brain (Yeates et al., 2007). Therefore, students who have difficulty in the physiological regulation of emotion and stress, may eventually have difficulty in the development of higher-order self regulation skills (executive functioning skills) in order to manage their stress (Blair, 2002). There is no doubt that emotional behavior involves a complex array of cortical and subcortical brain regions, each connected via white matter pathways, with an end result to ultimately define our emotional adaptability. Table 2-2 provides a general overview of the neural machinery involved with the regulation of social behavior, and is followed by a short vignette.

TABLE 2-2
Brain Structures and Social Emotional Processes

Adapted from Yeates et al. (2007) and Whittle et al. (2006)

BRAIN STRUCTURE	SOCIAL EMOTIONAL PROCESS
• Somatosensory cortex	• Representation of emotional stimuli
• Fusiform gyrus (right hemisphere)	• Face perception
• Superior temporal gyrus	• Representation of perceived action • Perception of gaze and motion
• Amygdala	• Ascribing emotional valence to stimuli • Threat appraisal • Fear conditioning
• Hippocampus	• Emotional learning and memory • Anxiety
• Nucleus Accumbens	• Positive emotions and anticipation of reward
• Corpus striatum	• Detects the presence of rewards and represents reward related goals
• Anterior Cingulate Cortex	• Motivation and reward-based decision making • Distributed attention system involved with "theory of mind" • Response inhibition and constraint
• Orbitofrontal cortex (right hemisphere)	• Self regulation of behavior • Monitor reward valued of stimulus • Response-reversal learning • Emotional executive functions
• Ventromedial prefrontal cortex	• Response inhibition • Emotional regulation and executive functioning. • Theory of mind
• Dorsolateral Prefrontal Cortex	• Cognitive executive functions • Working memory
• Left Prefrontal Cortex	• Modulates positive emotions such as love, happiness, and euphoria.
• Right Prefrontal Cortex	• Modulates negative emotions such as fear, hatred, and anger.

*Vignette #1: Brianna is celebrating her sixth birthday party and after becoming intoxicated with cake, two scoops of ice cream, and good cheer by all, the time has come for her friends to gather in a circle and open presents and gifts. Brianna is brimming with excitement as her **nucleus accumbens** is anticipating gifts of magnanimous proportions. Her **fusiform gyrus** immediately recognizes her best friend Megan from her kindergarten class, while her **somatosensory cortex** enhances this recognition with feelings of positive regard. She opens Megan's gift first and immediately recognizes a Cinderella ballroom dress, glass slipper, crown, and jewelry all neatly* *packaged in a gift box. Brianna's **amygdala** responds intensely with excitement, while her **hippocampus** remembers this was the one present she wanted most. Immediately, her **orbitofrontal cortex** recognizes the value of such a wonderful gift, which cues her **dorsolateral prefrontal cortex** on the importance of expressing good manners in social situations. However, Brianna's **ventromedial prefrontal cortex** cannot restrain her emotional response to a simple thank you, thereby compelling her to physically act out her feelings in some capacity. Brianna immediately throws her arms around Megan to give her a bear hug of such veracity, that Megan is literally swept off her feet. As Brianna proceeds to open the next gift, she remembers Megan's birthday is the following week and begins to think about a gift that would match the euphoria she is now experiencing in her **left prefrontal cortex**. Brianna's **anterior cingulate cortex** allows her to step outside of herself and imagine how Megan would feel if she were to receive a Disney Leapster the following week.*

Empathy: The Underpinnings to Social Competence

As noted in Table 2-2, there are numerous biological factors that can lead to profound deficits in the development of social competence and emotional self-regulation. However, the ability of each child to develop an effective social arsenal goes far beyond the sheer learning of individual tasks and functions. For instance, simply teaching a child isolated social skills such as appropriate manners at the dinner table, reinforcing the need for eye contact when someone is speaking, taking turns, resolving conflicts with words, learning to smile at another's good fortune, and comprehending the virtues of teamwork may very well ring hollow unless children initially learn to cultivate an exceedingly complex emotional skill such as *empathy*.

Empathy entails the natural ability to understand the emotions and feelings of others and to experience a sense of similarity between the feelings one experiences and those expressed by another (Decety & Jackson, 2004). In many ways, empathy promotes the development of ethical behavior by distinguishing between the social-emotional needs of *"self"* versus *"other."* This process begins very early in school, as classroom rules and behavioral expectations are explicitly stated and reinforced in order to shape a more positive learning climate. Therefore, virtues such as sharing, using polite manners, and turn-taking in kindergarten sometimes take precedence over academic skill development. In fact, an overwhelming majority of kindergarten teachers deemed social competence and the ability to self-regulate behavior during school activities as being more critical to academic success than development of cognitive and reading readiness skills (Blair, 2002). According to Yeates et al. (2007), the essence of *social competence* is the ability to achieve personal goals in social interactions while simultaneously maintaining positive relationships with others. A further examination of social competence is provided in Table 2-3:

TABLE 2-3
Three Aspects of Social Competence

(Yeates et al., 2007)

1. *Social skills*—a child's individual abilities or characteristics needed to behave competently in social settings.
2. *Social performance*—refers to the child' actual behavior in social interactions and to determine whether a child's responses are effective in both achieving their own goals and in maintaining positive relationships.
3. *Social adjustment*—reflects the extent in which children attain socially desirable goals and encompasses the quality of a child's interpersonal relationships.

The conceptual notion of empathy being a byproduct of brain functioning may seem rather jarring to some, especially those who perceive empathy as a direct extension of morality extrapolated from one's religious beliefs and cultural upbringing. However, cognitive neuroscience is beginning to put together compelling evidence that empathy may very well be related to a series of specific neural constellations in the brain, beginning at the cellular level. Is it truly possible that such a noble and compassionate human endeavor can actually be hardwired into the brain's circuitry? Perhaps. The evolution of an empathetic brain may have stemmed from the sheer survival need to rapidly evaluate the motivation and intent of potential predators (Decety & Jackson, 2004). Certainly, understanding emotional signals has an adaptive advantage in the formation of trust, bonding, and enduring social relationships. According to Decety and Jackson (2004), empathy involves both the recognition and understanding of another person's emotional state, coupled with the ability to affectively experience the emotional valence of that state. In essence, there are three major functional components of empathy whose synergy creates the uniquely human quality of caring and compassion. These are listed in Table 2-4:

TABLE 2-4
Three Components of Empathy

(Decety & Jackson, 2004)

1. *Affective Sharing*—the ability to share and fully experience the emotional experiences of another through shared sensory perceptions.
2. *Self-Other Awareness*—a clear and distinct representation between the thoughts, actions, and feelings of another with the thoughts, actions, and feelings of oneself.
3. *Mental Flexibility*—the ability to adopt the subjective perspective of another, or what is sometimes referred to as *"theory of mind,"* by the development of an internal frame of reference.

1. Affective Sharing: There is emerging evidence that numerous brain regions may be responsible for the development of compassionate feelings toward others (Ramacandran & Oberman, 2006). The seeds of an empathetic brain are planted very early in life, through intrinsic biological mechanisms that are uniquely tailored to detect the basic emotional impulses of others. In order to establish a sense of *affective sharing*, as defined by the ability to fully share in the emotional experiences of others, researchers have begun to investigate the role of mirror neurons. Theses neurons are present in both most mammalian and human brains, and are primarily housed in the prefrontal cortex (Decety & Jackson, 2004). Mirror neurons are stimulated both during self-directed goal attainment and when observing others engaged in the same action (Ramachandran & Oberman, 2006). Mirror neurons were so named because they are thought to *"mirror"* movement by incorporating the actions or movement of others as their own. Such a unique discovery prompted the preeminent neuroscientist V.S. Ramachandran to claim that mirror neurons may be the single most important discovery in neuroscience in the last decade. Furthermore, mirror neurons may ultimately do for psychology what DNA did for biology; namely, to provide a unifying framework that may ultimately explain a plethora of social-emotional abilities. Mirror neurons have been linked to empathy because certain brain regions in the prefrontal cortex *(e.g., anterior insular cortex, anterior cingulate cortex,* and *inferior frontal cortex)* tend to become active when a child both experiences an emotion and when they see another person experience the same emotion (Wicker et al., 2003; Jabbi, Swart & Keysers, 2007). Therefore, observing an emotion in others may actually trigger the neural representation of that emotion in ourselves. Why do we cry at the movies, become nervous when the game is on the line in the fourth quarter, or shudder with fear at the latest terrorist news from Iraq? In each of these scenarios, we are vicariously experiencing an emotion by watching others. Keysers and Gazzola (2006) reported that persons demonstrating high levels of empathic behavior tend to have stronger activations in the mirror system for emotions. Conversely, persons with more dysfunctional mirror neuron systems, such as autistic children, have a litany of social-emotional limitations such as poor self-awareness, a lack of instrospection, the inability to imitate when young, and poor affective matching (Ramachandran & Oberman, 2006). In summary, mirror neurons may play a crucial role in affective sharing by mapping the bodily feelings of others to ourselves in order to establish a foundation for higher level social cognition. Figure 2-1 depicts the primary locations of mirror neurons in the brain and Table 2-5 details the functions of each.

FIGURE 2-1
Mirror Neurons in the Brain

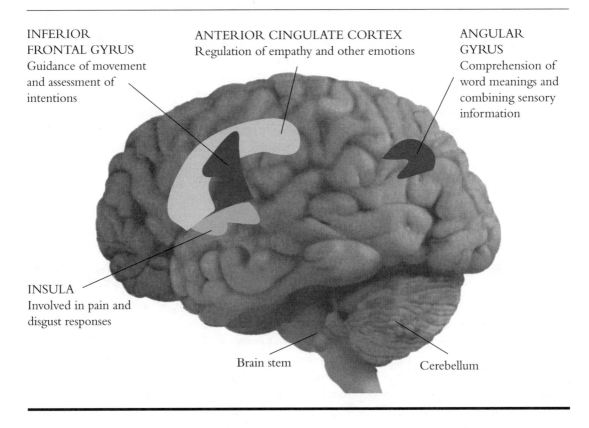

INFERIOR FRONTAL GYRUS
Guidance of movement and assessment of intentions

ANTERIOR CINGULATE CORTEX
Regulation of empathy and other emotions

ANGULAR GYRUS
Comprehension of word meanings and combining sensory information

INSULA
Involved in pain and disgust responses

Brain stem

Cerebellum

TABLE 2-5
Mirror Neurons and Social-Emotional Functioning

Angular Gyrus—mirror neurons allow for cross modal mapping of skills including the visual-spatial appreciation of language through metaphor and proverbs.

Anterior Cingulate Cortex—mirror neurons may allow for the shifting of attention inward to develop self awareness and introspection. Such awareness allows us to place psychological distance between ourselves and sense of self, thereby spawning the development of a *"theory of mind."*

Inferior Frontal Gyrus—mirror neurons may be involved in imitation of motor movement that forms the basic precepts allowing us to perceive another's intentions.

Anterior Insular Cortex—mirror neurons may be critical in developing empathy by allowing us to feel and interpret the perception of pain, whether experienced by ourselves or someone else.

2. Self Awareness: The field of cognitive neuropsychology has made impressive strides since the preeminent behavioral psychologist John Watson declared in 1913:

> *"Psychology as the behaviorist views it is a purely objective experimental branch of natural science. Introspection forms no essential part of its methods, nor is the scientific value of its data dependent upon the readiness with which they lend themselves to interpretation in terms of consciousness."*

It is beyond the scope of this chapter to detail the voluminous material put forth by philosophers and psychologists alike on the supremely intellectual challenge of understanding consciousness. However, one can say that cognitive neuroscience has led the charge to empirically understand the phenomena of conscious awareness as expressed through neuronal networks. As stated previously, the ability to share an affective experience with another may have its neural foundation embedded within mirror neurons, while *self awareness* is more closely linked with the maturation of the frontal lobes. According to Asendorpf and Baudonniere (1993), self awareness requires a capacity for secondary representation of the self or *cognitive referencing*, a phenomena that occurs around age two when children begin to develop psychological distance from themselves. During the preschool years children develop the ability to recognize both one's own perspectives and experiences and those of others, and this type of mental understanding may help to establish early self awareness skills (Decety & Jackson, 2004). According to Ruby and Decety (2004), when children are asked to adopt another person's perspective or to evaluate their own beliefs from a different vantage point, the right inferior frontal cortex is strongly activated. Beginning in preschool, most teachers foster a sense of self-awareness in children by constantly challenging them to consider the consequences of their actions on others. Essentially, the right hemisphere is being asked to take a critical examination of the self. In fact, right hemispheric damage is often associated with impairments in personal self evaluation, as well as autobiographical memory (Decety & Jackson, 2004). Still, the question must be asked: which neural mechanisms within the right hemisphere allows children to place psychological distance from their own psyche to create a mental state of self awareness?

According to Dehaene, Sergent, and Changeux (2003), there lies a distributed set of neurons in the right hemisphere with the capacity for very long-distance cortical connections that are capable of interconnecting multiple aspects of neural modules in a simultaneous fashion. These specialized networks of cells are called *spindle cells* and consist of a large projection of neurons found only in great apes, whales, and human beings (Goldberg, 2005). Spindle cells are thought to be involved in coordinating widely distributed neural activity involving both emotion and cognition. These cells may also be involved in higher level emotional attributions such as interpreting the emotion in another's eye gaze, attributing intentions to others, appreciating types of humor, and comprehending the moral reference point in stories (Decety & Jackson, 2004). According to Dehaene et al. (2003), the ability of a distributed set of neurons to forge long distance connections (spindle cells) allows multiple brain regions to cast their signals in a spontaneous rather than modular manner. Hence, spindle cells may be the anatomical underpinnings of consciousness and self-awareness at a neuronal level. In fact, spindle cell transmission tends to be underactivated, and may adversely impact consciousness and the development of a sense of self in disorders as adult schizophrenia and high functioning autism (Happe et al., 1996).

Spindle cells are primarily clustered in the anterior cingulate cortex and the insular cortex in the right hemisphere. Both of these regions have been documented to be an important area in self-awareness and mental-state attribution (Keenan et al., 2003). The *insular cortex* (often referred to as just the insula) lies deep within the lateral sulcus, a region that separates the temporal lobe and inferior parietal lobe. This brain region is relatively complicated and is required to decipher a variety of perceptive experiences. The insular cortex is well situated for the integration of information relating to the affective and reactive components of pain given that its circuitry is connected, in part, to fear avoidance. Ruby and Decety (2004) noted that when subjects were asked to adopt another person's perspective, or imagine another's feelings compared with their own perspective, the right hemisphere in the inferior parietal cortex was involved. Hence, the right inferior parietal cortex in conjunction with the prefrontal cortex may play a crucial role in empathy by maintaining a distinction (psychological distance) between the feelings and intentions of the self versus the feelings and intentions of another. At approximately 18 months of age, children begin to demonstrate an emerging awareness of others' emotions (Decety & Jackson, 2004).

> **KEY LEARNING POINTS:**
> **Spindle Cells**
>
> The development of the right hemisphere, specifcially the long distance neuronal connections known as *spindle cells*, may be critical in a child's ability to foster the capacity for self-awareness. Spindle cells are involved in coordinating widely distributed neural activity involving both emotion and cognititon, and are an important component in both self-awareness and mental-state attribution (Keenan et al., 2003). At approximately 18 months of age children begin to demonstrate an emerging awareness of other's emotions (Decety & Jackson, 2004).

Mental Flexibility: Once a child begins to attribute mental states and intentions from another's emotional vantage point, and also uses this information to guide and plan their own behavior, then the emergence of a *"theory of mind"* has begun. In fact, theory of mind may indeed represent the initial underpinnings of social-emotional executive functioning skills, as it allows children to play, guide, and emotionally regulate behavior. Therefore, self-awareness may be the initial step taken to split our psyche in half, though the actual evaluative and interpretive process represents a much higher type of cortical skill, namely, social-emotional executive functioning skills. As Barkley (2001) noted, the evolutionary importance of *executive functioning* skills may have been to generate sequential mind scripts that allow human beings to better adapt to their social environment. In other words, certain components of executive functioning may actually represent a cognitive capacity to manage emotional behavior for the pursuit of goal attainment. A critical aspect of managing emotional behavior includes explicit processing of the mental states of the self as well as others. Perhaps the ability to manage emotional behavior led to the evolutionary development of more cognitive executive functioning skills such as controlling one's impulses for future rewards, developing working memory skills to reinforce societal mores and values when in socially compromising situations, and crafting more adaptive responses when emotionally confronted or challenged. This notion was also consistent with Decety and Jackson's (2004) claim that the evolution of empathetic behavior also required some form of an active inhibitory mechanism to place the breaks on emotional impulsivity. Hence, the strategy of maximizing long-term outcomes over immediate needs may have offered an environmental advantage that allowed human beings to more readily adapt to their newfound social environment (Barkley, 2001).

The conceptual notion of *theory of mind* basically refers to the executive control capabilities of the human brain to coordinate certain representations of the self as if seen through the eyes of another. According to Rolls (2004), the *orbitofrontal* cortex is the region of the brain that ultimately drives a child not only to consider another person's affective state but also to ascribe an emotional valence or value judgment to another's feelings. This triggers a cognitive set of automatic social skill responses in order to respond appropriately to the situation. Therefore, effective social skill interactions require more than the isolated ability to share an affective state with another, or the ability to distinguish between the self versus other, or to have the mental flexibility to adopt another's frame of reference. Simply put, there must be a value judgment placed upon the ability to share and experience the emotional experiences of another through shared sensory perceptions. The *orbitofrontal cortex* has rich interconnections with the limbic regions of the brain, and plays a crucial role in ascribing a reward value on emotional stimuli that ultimately guides behavior through reinforcement contingencies (Rolls, 2004). Hence, it is the reward value itself derived from praise and positive encouragement that may well lead to following school rules and directions, earning extra privileges in character education programs, and receiving extra stickers for classroom cooperation. This behavior then becomes the representation of the *orbitofrontal cortex*. As Rolls (2004) noted, the *orbitofrontal cortex* is also involved in the rapid reversal of behavior (unlearning) by stimulus-reinforcement association, which in many ways allows for the inhibition of behavior as well.

Specific damage to the orbitofrontal cortex results in alterations of learned associations related to rewards and punishment, and may lead to maladaptive social skill behavior. For instance, children who have suffered a traumatic brain injury (TBI) involving the orbitofrontal cortex are less skilled in social problem solving situations, and are rated as being less socially competent and lonelier than healthy children (Yeates et al., 2007). In addition, children with TBI often display significant impairments in most areas of social-affective functioning including pragmatic language skills, understanding emotions, and the appreciation of mental states in others. Lastly, childhood TBI has been associated with adverse long-term social outcomes as well, even when controlling for variables such as group affiliation, sex, race, socioeconomic status, and IQ (Yeates et al., 2007). In summary, damage to the orbitofrontal cortex may fundamentally hinder the ability to make learned associations between social rewards and social punishers and thus alter a child's emotional landscape as it relates to their social skill interactions (Rolls, 2004).

KEY LEARNING POINTS: Theory of Mind

Theory of mind refers to the executive control capabilities of the human brain to coordinate certain representations of the self as if seen through the eyes of another. According to Rolls (2004), the *orbitofrontal cortex* is the region of the brain that ultimately drives a child not only to consider another person's affective state, but also to ascribe an emotional valence or value judgment to another's feelings. Damage to the *orbitofrontal cortex* may fundamentally hinder the ability to make learned associations between social rewards and social punishers (Rolls, 2004).

Vignette #2: *Madison has been invited to her best friend's house for a sleepover to celebrate her 8th birthday. Both Madison and her best friend Ruby are simply ecstatic at the notion of staying up late, eating hordes of junk food, giggling uncontrollably, and swapping stories about boys at school. To*

Madison's dismay, she arrived promptly in time for the party only to realize that Ruby had also invited another friend, Victoria, as well. Madison has never been fond of Victoria as she always seemed to belittle Madison in school, frequently competed for Ruby's friendship, and took an unwarranted sense of pride in showing off. Madison's initial impulse was to turn around and go home, angered by the thought of sharing her best friend Ruby with her arch enemy Victoria. This initial barrage of negativity fueling every pore of Madison's body was quickly confronted by an equally compelling directive; namely, Madison did not want to hurt Ruby's feelings. Madison and Ruby's eyes met and there was an affective sharing of emotional confusion and pain triggered primarily by **mirror neurons** *in the anterior insular cortex and inferior frontal cortex. Madison paused a moment to reflect upon Ruby's feelings, and realized that if she left the party in such an abrupt manner, Ruby may become devastated and have a very disappointing eighth birthday. Her ability to consider Ruby's emotional reference point reflected Madison's* **spindle cells** *in the right hemisphere providing her with the self-awareness to view her own feelings from another's perspective. Madison quickly managed a wry smile and grabbed hold of Ruby's hand, whirled around to take Victoria's hand, and promptly marched hand-in-hand toward the television set for an evening of childhood delight. Madison's* **orbitofrontal cortex** *determined that the best decision in this type of social encounter would simply be to make the best of it, a behavioristic response driven completely by the neural subcomponents of empathy.*

The Neurobiology of Temperament and Emotion

Behavioral aggression is certainly a complex phenomenon, with many learning paradigms, neural systems, and environmental stimuli all contributing to the subsequent behavioral output of a child. From an educational perspective, most teachers tend to agree that successful learning commences with the development of behavioral self-control in a classroom learning environment. As previously discussed, the development of empathy can help nurture a hierarchical set of behaviors leading to emotional wellness through appropriate social reciprocity and exchanges. After all, the recipe for most disruptive behavior disorders often consists of little concern or empathy for the needs of others, coupled with a rather impervious regard for behavioral consequences. Therefore, the development of *empathy* in children may very well be the single most important facet of affective processing, analogous to the development of *phonology* for effective reading or *number sense* to perform mathematics. Certainly, there is a constellation of factors contributing toward empathetic differences in children including the moral climate of the home environment, the quality and consistency of parent-child interactions, the social mores and values of the community, and the social reinforcement contingency used at home. However, some children seem born with the remarkable capacity for empathetic behavior, as if empathy was embedded within their DNA despite their environmental circumstances. Perhaps the individual temperamental make-up of each child may ultimately provide the emotional foundation from which empathy can truly emerge. After all, temperament is strongly related to most psychopathologies, especially those involving affective disturbances (Whittle et al., 2006).

Temperament refers to relatively stable, early-appearing individual differences in behavioral tendencies (Saudino, 2005). Beginning in the second century, the notion of temperament began to emerge amongst early scholars as individuals were classified into four types of emotional flavors. The *melancholic* temperament was sad and despondent; the *sanguine* temperament more positive and cheerful; the *choleric* temperament somewhat angry and hot-tempered; and the *phlegmatic* temperament more low key and easy-going. Each temperamental subtype was further correlated with a particular bodily fluid, e.g., blood, bile, or phlegm. More contemporary research highlighting the importance of temperament was conducted by Alexander Thomas and Stella Chess (1977). These researchers identified nine temperament factors such as quality of mood, adaptability, and activity level in their classic New York Longitudinal Study. Each temperament factor was combined to determine the degree of difficulty with which infants responded to their caregiver. Children classified as being difficult in temperament were deemed *at-risk* for maladaptive behaviors and conduct disorders (Thomas & Chess, 1977). Certainly, there has been rigorous debate in the literature regarding the specific behavioral dimensions most associated with temperament and, for that matter, the theoretical orientations of temperament itself (Fox, 2004). Nevertheless, factor analysis has yielded four factors that have consistently appeared in most studies of temperament; inhibition, reactivity, emotionality, and behavioral persistence (Fox, 2004).

Perhaps an appropriate analogy may come from music. In music, the tonal underpinnings used to create all songs, tunes, and jingles stem from just a small number of notes. Certainly, these notes can be arranged, combined, and rearranged in an infinite array of combinations, chord structures, and keys to create sounds from Rush to Beethoven to Hannah Montana. Similarly, there are four chemical bases of DNA that can also be arranged and rearranged in thousands of different combinations to create the music of life for every known creature, plant, or animal on the planet. Therefore, the notion of temperament is the foundation, the building blocks, the permanent constellation of behavioral traits from which emotionality, social exchanges, personality, and empathetic behavioral functioning may ultimately emerge.

1. Introversion vs. Extraversion: The brilliant Swiss psychiatrist Carl Jung was perhaps the first to recognize that certain core distinctions in temperamental make-up may actually reflect cortical arousal mechanisms to the flow of psychic energy in the brain. For instance, extraverts feel energized when interacting with large groups of people in social gatherings, and feel depleted of energy when left alone. Conversely, introverts feel more energized when directing their psychic resources toward their internal world of thoughts and ideas, while feeling a depletion of energy when surrounded by large groups of people or confronted by intense social situations. According to Jerome Kagan (2005), one of the foremost researchers in the area of human morality and temperament, most variations in temperament styles stem from genetic differences in the brain's arousal mechanisms. Some of the neurotransmitters in the brain that affect levels of arousal include norepinephrine, corticotrophin-releasing hormone, GABA, dopamine, serotonin, and opioids. Kagan (2005) viewed children who were inherently shy, extremely timid, and avoidant of unfamiliar people, objects, and situations as being inhibited and as having a more introverted affective style. Conversely, children who were more sociable in novel situations and who readily approached unfamiliar people and situations were deemed uninhibited, and therefore had a more extraverted affective style. Elliot and Thrash (2002) noted that extraverted children were not only more outgoing in their affective style, but they also had a more positive and outgoing demeanor. The *valence* of their emotional response, meaning the direction of a child's behavioral actions, was more of an *approach* response for children with an extraverted temperament. On the other hand, children with more *avoidant* temperaments were thought to be more introverted in their affective style, and often sought refuge from large social gatherings or personal encounters.

According to Elliot and Thrash (2002), introverted children tended have a more *avoidant valence* and demonstrated more negativity in their overall affective response style. Fox (2004) noted that in preschool children, there was more right sided or right frontal EEG activity in behaviorally inhibited children than in non-inhibited children. Because the right hemisphere tends to be architecturally wired to process more novel information (Goldberg, 2005), perhaps over-activation of this area results in a cognitive over-sensitivity to new or novel tasks. According to Fox (2004), the behaviorally inhibited child remains at-risk for maladaptive social behavior and psychopathology, due in part to heightened emotional reactivity and negative affect being associated with right frontal activity. Nevertheless, nurturing environments with consistent caregivers may have a profound impact on the behavioral manifestation of a particular temperament trait and, over time, actually alter one's brain circuitry (Fox, 2004). It is important to note that genes account for a robust 20% to 60% of the variability in temperament dimensions, while unique environmental influences account for up to 40% to 80% of the variance not explained by genetics (Saudino, 2005).

> **KEY LEARNING POINTS:**
> **Introversion vs. Extraversion**
>
> **INTROVERSION**—over-activation of the right prefrontal cortex may lead to an over-sensitivity to more novel situations and thus more avoidance in social situations.
>
> **EXTRAVERSION** —under-activation of the right prefrontal cortex.may lead to a lack of sensitivity in more novel social situations and thus greater social affiliation.

2. High Reactivity vs. Low Reactivity: Kagan (2005) deemed that variation in the excitability of the amygdala was primarily responsible for another stark dichotomy in affective styles, namely, reactivity. Reactivity basically refers to the emotional thermostat or relative intensity of a stimulus, and the degree with which it becomes registered before being further processed in other brain regions (e.g., prefrontal cortex). According to Fowles (2006), the pioneering work of Jeffrey Gray first established the amygdala as being the primary trigger for a neural network called the *"Behavior Inhibition System."* This system serves three primary functions when confronted with a threatening situation: namely, to suppress any ongoing behavior, to increase attention to the environment, and to intensify arousal and response speed. The amygdala consists of small bundles of nuclei located subcortically in the anterior portions of the temporal lobes. It is a phylogenetically old structure shaped like an almond, and primarily serves to code incoming sensory and/or cognitive information that has affective significance (LeDoux, 2003). The amygdala plays a role in the perception of threatening information, the appraisal of social signals that convey a threat, and the acquisition of fear conditioned responses (LeDoux, 2003). The basolateral regions of the amygdala are primarily responsible for modulating its overall excitability (Fudge et al., 2002). Therefore, the amygdala serves as the center piece for *"fear based"* learning by ascribing an emotional valence to sensory information. Interestingly, Gray and McNaughton (2000) attributed fear to the amygdala, though anxiety was attributed to a separate neural network in the brain and represented the emotional component of fear.

Nevertheless, not all fears are associated with an overactive amygdala. According to Pine (2007), lesions to the amygdala in primates produce rather substantial *reductions* to most types of conditioned fears due to an inability to register a threat appraisal from a stimulus. Pine (2007) reasoned that since amygdala activation becomes much more developed at earlier ages than the prefrontal cortex to which it is connected, perhaps the ability to overcome social fears in humans may only be possible once the prefrontal cortex matures.

From a temperamental perspective, emotional responses have now been defined in terms of two dimensions: (1) *valence*, which was previously discussed as being a behavioral response to either

KEY LEARNING POINTS: Reactivity

LOW REACTIVITY—a need for greater stimulation and excitement to trigger the amygdala. These children often develop into behaviorally outgoing and uninhibited children.

HIGH REACTIVITY—a need for minimal stimulation of the amygdala to activate the cerebral cortex. As infants, there may be more crying noted and these children run the risk of developing anxiety disorders.

approach or avoid a social situation, and (2) *reactivity,* which determines the emotional intensity of the stimulus. Therefore, children with low reactivity may be more active in their demeanor, and engage in more sensation seeking behaviors than children higher in reactivity. This is precisely what Kagan (2005) noted, as *low reactive* infants tend to be born with a relatively high amygdala set point. In other words, these children need far greater stimulation and excitement to activate their amygdala. The behavioral orientation of *low reactive* children tends to be relatively outgoing and uninhibited (Kagan, 2005). In addition, *low reactive* children may run the risk of failing to conform to community standards because they are far less sensitive to criticism and lack certain checks and balances to govern their behavior (Kagan & Snidman, 2004).

Conversely, *high reactive* infants are born with a relatively low amygdala set point and therefore need minimal stimulation to activate this brain region. These infants tend to have heightened motor activity and more frequent crying bouts when exposed to unfamiliar stimuli (Kagan, 2005). Perhaps babies with colic may be experiencing an over-active amygdala, although it should be noted that there is no proven cause of colic in infants. According to Kagan and Snidman (2004), children who are *high reactive* run the greatest risk of developing anxiety conditions or perhaps a social phobia in adolescence and adulthood. In summary, reactivity at either extreme can be counterproductive to the emotional adaptability of a child in school, as low reactive children crave stimulation and excitement leading to externalizing disorders, while high reactive children may have more internalizing disorders resulting from sensory overload.

3. Positive vs. Negative Affect: Most adults are capable of distinguishing between a vast array of emotions, but children tend to clump emotional impulses into two broad categories, good or bad. The cognitive interpretation of emotions represents a complex interaction between the emotional valence (*approach vs. avoidance in novel situations*) coupled with the sheer intensity of the emotion itself (*reactivity*). For instance, fear arises from an *avoidant* valence coupled with an intense or heightened state of arousal in the central nervous system (Posner, Russell, & Peterson, 2005). Nevertheless, the cognitive interpretation of fear as either being a pleasant or an unpleasant emotion is frankly in the eye of the beholder. For example, fear as defined by a roller coaster spiraling sideways and upside down at breathtaking speeds is quite enjoyable for some, while the fear of delivering a speech in front of a large audience is often unpleasant for others. Therefore, it is important to note that temperament predispositions correlate not with specific discrete emotions such as happy or sad, but rather with broad domains of emotionality to color the experiences of a child (Posner, Russell, & Peterson, 2005).

The neural circuitry of positive versus negative affect primarily involves the brain's reward processing network including the striatum, the amygdala, and the orbitofrontal cortex (Forbes & Dahl, 2005). The striatum is a part of the brain located underneath the cerebral cortex. It receives projections from most cortical areas and serves as the main entry gate into the basal ganglia. The striatum has a multitude of functions including motor and cognitive planning, mapping context to action, and most importantly, *detecting* the presence of reward-related goals. However, it is the orbitofrontal cortex that actually processes the magnitude or value of a reward as well as the expectation of the reward (Rolls, 2004). According to Forbes and Dahl (2005), the reward centers of the brain are primarily fueled by the dopamine neurotransmitter innervating the striatum, amygdala, and orbitofrontal cortex to provide a pleasant state or mood (*see Table 2-6*). The reward circuit tends to become more aroused during the anticipation of a reward, particularly in a region of the basal ganglia called the *nucleus accumbens*, than when a reward is actually received (Knutson et al., 2000). This holds much truth for children, especially around Christmastime when the emotional excitement awaiting Santa's arrival often trumps Christmas day itself. Unfortunately, reward systems are not always subject to full regulatory influence by the rational centers of our prefrontal cortex. Therefore, over-activation of the reward circuit may have implications for the development of substance use disorders, while under-activation of the reward circuit may be associated with internalizing disorders such as depression (Forbes & Dahl, 2005. Table 2-6 depicts the reward circuitry of the brain, with the orbitofrontal cortex being primarily responsible for assigning the overall reward value of the emotional stimulus. For most practitioners of cognitive behavioral therapy, the child's reaction and subsequent cognitive interpretation of the emotion becomes the primary change agent through therapy. Therefore, coloring the cognitive interpretation of a feeling serves as a top-down type of therapeutic technique to modify a negative affective experience into something more positive.

TABLE 2-6
Social Reward Circuitry of the Brain

BRAIN REGION	FUNCTION
Amygdala	• Appraisal of social signals and sensitivity to predicted reward value.
Hippocampus	• Triggers memory of desired goal.
Nucleus Accumbens	• Anticipates an upcoming reward
Striatum	• Detects the presence of rewards
Dorsolateral Prefrontal Cortex	• Represents goals related to rewards
Orbitofrontal Cortex	• Assesses the overall magnitude or reward value of the stimulus.

4. Behavioral Persistence: A common cry echoed among skilled parents, savvy educators, and insightful therapists is that success or failure should never be defined by eventual outcomes, but rather by the persistence, effort, and tenacity demonstrated in our pursuits. There have been various terms used in the literature, such as *persistence, fortitude, constraint,* or *industriousness,* to capture the

**KEY LEARNING POINTS:
Anterior Cingulate Cortex**

ANTERIOR CINGULATE CORTEX—provides constraint over emotion and cognition with decreased activation linked to a lack of task initiation, apathetic and unmotivated behavior, and anhedonia (Whittle et al., 2006).

diligent efforts displayed by children toward a goal directed activity. Nevertheless, *conation* is a term that has been used primarily in neuropsychology to refer to a child's ability to apply intellectual energy toward a specific task in order to achieve a desired goal (Reitan & Wolfson, 2000). Certainly, the ability to sharply focus attention, resist outside distractions, and thwart internal impulses remains paramount to the temperament trait of persistence. Therefore, most factor analytic studies of temperament view persistence as being a by-product of attention, and tend to cluster the cognitive construct of attention with the emotional trait of persistence into a unitary construct (Saudino, 2005). According to Whittle et al. (2006), the anterior cingulate cortex plays a key role in the regulation of both emotional and cognitive behavior. More specifically, the ventral portion of the anterior cingulate cortex appears to be strongly associated with task motivation, due in part to its strong connections with the amygdala. This brain region may in fact require a delicate balance or homeostasis in order to attain maximum performance from a student. Essentially, the anterior cingulate cortex functions to provide behavioral constraints over both emotion and cognition. For instance, activation of the anterior cingulate cortex has been reported in children with anxiety disorders (Allman et al., 2001) in addition to cognitive tasks involving response inhibition (Drevets & Raichle, 1998). Conversely, decreased activation of the anterior cingulate cortex, has been linked to lack of initiation, apathetic or unmotivated behavior, and anhedonia (Whittle et al., 2006).

SUMMARY

Affective neuroscience is unraveling new insights at a breathtaking speed, allowing better understanding of the neural underpinnings of emotional development. Too often, behavioral dysfunction is hastily explained as stemming from simplistic cause and effect paradigms such as poor parenting, undesirable peer influences, or simply a lack of a moral code. According to Susman (2006), complex human behaviors are the result of an interwoven constellation of psychobiological systems influenced by a multitude of environmental factors. Simply put, the neurobiological architecture of human emotion is far too complex to capture using a singular paradigm. After all, if the brain was wired together in such a simplistic manner, human beings would be too simple-minded to understand it (Dehaene, 2007). Nevertheless, current affective models are attempting to integrate the fundamental aspects of temperament with the behavioral expression of empathy. The neural building blocks of empathy involve a variety of factors such as affective sharing in another's emotional experiences, the ability to make a *self* versus *other* distinction, and the mental flexibility to adopt the emotional perspective of another. In addition, there must be a value judgment placed upon the ability to share and experience the emotional experiences of another in order to guide our behavior through reinforcement contingencies. Certainly, the temperamental makeup of a child, as defined by an approach or avoidant valence, degree of reactivity, quality of affect, and behavioral persistence, guides our emotional perceptions and colors our behavioral choices. One way to combat antisocial behavior may be to target early maladaptive emotional responses in order to enhance more empathetic responding (Susman, 2006).

Future research is beginning to bridge the gap between the fundamental neurobiological tenets of emotion with complex social exchanges in a multidimensional environment. For example, the *circumplex model* of affective functioning attempts to integrate affective states that arise from temperament systems, most notably *valence* (approach vs. avoidance responses) and intensity (high vs. low reactivity) (Posner, Russell, & Peterson, 2005). Figure 2-2 provides a graphic representation of the *circumplex model,* as each emotion represents as a linear combination of two temperamental dimensions to derive either a positive or negative affective state. Therefore, there are no discrete borders or separate neural pathways delineating the subtle nuances between emotions, but rather emotions arise primarily from the cognitive interpretations of core physiological experiences. According to Posner, Russell, and Peterson (2005), the prefrontal cortex is primarily responsible for integrating and modifying information gleaned from emotional systems, and to cognitively appraise these sensations as being positive or negative within varying situations and contexts. Therefore, emotional dysfunction can derive from either cognitive distortions and poor prefrontal appraisal capabilities, or, more simply, the faulty activation of the emotion itself (Posner, Russell, & Peterson, 2005). In summary, antisocial behavior and sociopathic behavior has often been defined as children lacking a social conscious with no moral compass to guide behavior. However, affective neuroscience is beginning to unveil the neural signature of behavioral dysfunction, which may ultimately stem from a relatively weak *behavioral inhibition system* coupled with a lack of empathy for others.

FIGURE 2-2
Circumplex Model of Affective States

(Posner, Russell, & Peterson, 2005)

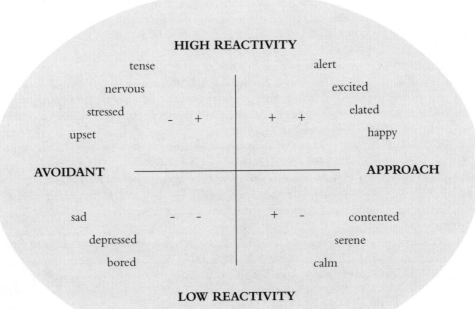

REFERENCES

Allman, J. M., Hakeem, A., Erwin, J. M., Nimchinski, E., & Hof, P. (2001). The anterior cingulate cortex: The evolution of an interface between emotion and cognition. *Annals of the New York Academy of Sciences, 935,* 107-117.

Asendorpf, J. G., & Baudonniere, P. M. (1993). Self awareness and other-awareness: Mirror self-recognition and synchronic imitation among unfamiliar peers. *Developmental Psychology, 29,* 88-95.

Barkley, R. (2001). The executive functions and self regulation: An evolutionary neuropsychological perspective. *Neuropsychology Review, 11*(1), 1-29.

Blair, C. (2002). School readiness. Integrating cognition and emotion in a neurobiological conceptualization of children's functioning at school entry. *American Psychologist, 57,* 111-127.

Cicchetti, D. & Posner, M.I. (2005). Cognitive and affective neuroscience and developmental psychopathology. *Development and Psychopathology, 17,* 569-575.

Cicerone, K. (2002). The enigma of executive functioning: Theoretical contributions to therapeutic interventions. In P. J. Eslinger (Ed.), *Neuropsychological interventions: Clinical research and practice.* New York: Guilford Press.

Dahl, R. E. (2001). Affect regulation, brain development, and behavioral/emotional health in adolescence. *CNS Spectrums, 6*(1), 60-72.

Decety, J., & Jackson, P. L. (2004). The functional architecture of human empathy. *Behavioral and Cognitive Neuroscience Reviews, 3*(2), 71-100.

Dehaene, S. (2007). A few steps toward a science of mental life. *Mind, Brain, and Education, 1*(1), 28-47.

Dehaene, S., Sergent, C., & Changeux, J. P. (2003). A neuronal model linking subjective reports and objective neurophysiological data during conscious perception. *Proceedings of the National Academy of Sciences of the United States of America, 100*(14), 8520-8525.

Drevets, W. C., & Raichle, M. E. (1998). Reciprocal suppression of regional cerebral blood flow during emotional versus higher cognitive processes: Implications for interactions between emotion and cognition. *Cognition and Emotion, 12*(3), 353-385.

Elliot, A. J., & Thrash, T. M. (2002). Approach-avoidance motivation in personality: Approach and avoidance temperaments and goals. *Journal of Personality and Social Psychology, 82,* 804-818.

Eronen, M., Tiihonen, J , & Hakola, P. (1996). Homicide behavior of females in Finland years 1980-1994. *Duodecim, 112*(14), 1281-1286.

Fields, R. D. (2008). White matter matters. *Scientific American,* 54-61.

Filley, C. M., Price, B. H., Nell, V., Antoinette, T., Morgan, A. S. , Bresnahan, S. J. , Pincus, J. H. , Gelbort, M. M., Weissberg, M. , & Kelly, J. (2001). Toward an understanding of violence: Neurobehavioral aspects of unwarranted physical aggression: Aspen neurobehavioral conference consensus statement. *Neuropsychiatry, Neuropsychology, and Behavioral Neurology, 14,* 1-14.

Forbes, E. E., & Dahl, R. E. (2005). Neural systems of positive affect: Relevance to understanding child and adolescent depression. *Development and Psychopathology, 17,* 827-850.

Fowles, D. C. (2006). Jeffrey Gray's contributions to theories of anxiety, personality, and psychopathology. In T. Conli (Ed.), *Biology of personality and individual differences,* (pp. 7-36). New York: Guilford Press.

Fox, N. A. (2004). Temperament and early experience form social behavior. *Annals of the New York Academy of Sciences, 1038,* 171-178.

Fudge, J. L., Kunishio, K., Walsh, P., Richard, C., & Haber, S. N. (2002). Amygdaloid projections to ventromedial striatal subterritories in the primate. *Neuroscience, 110,* 257-275.

Goldberg, E. (2005). *The wisdom paradox.* New York: Gotham Books.

Gray, J. A., & McNaughton, N. (2000). *The neuropsychology of anxiety: An enquiry into the functions of the septo-hippocampal system* (2nd ed.). Oxford: Oxford University Press.

Gunnar, M. R. & Quevedo, K. M. (2008). Early care experiences and HPA axis regulation in children: A mechanism for later trauma vulnerability. *Progressive Brain Research, 167,* 137-149.

Happe, F., Ehlers, S., Fletcher, P., Frith, U., Johansson, M., Gillberg, C., (1996). Theory of mind in the brain. Evidence from a PET scan study of Asperger syndrome. *Neuroreport, 8,* 197-201.

Jabbi, M., Swart, M., & Keysers, C. (2007). Empathy for positive and negative emotions in the gustatory cortex. *Neuroimage, 34*(4), 1744-53.

Johnson, M. K., Griffin, R., Csibra, G., Halit, H., Farroni, T., De Haan, M., et al. (2005). The emergence of the social brain network: Evidence from typical and atypical development. *Developmental and Psychopathology, 17,* 599-619.

Kagan, J. (2005). Human morality and temperament. Nebraska Symposium on Motivation. *Nebraska Symposium on Motivation, 51,* 1 -32.

Kagan, J., & Snidman, N. (2004). *The long shadow of temperament.* Cambridge, MA: Harvard University Press.

Keenan, J. P., Gallup, G.G., & Falk, D. (2003). *The face in the mirror: The search for the origins of consciousness.* New York: Harper-Collins.

Keysers, C., & Gazzola, V. (2006). Towards a unifying theory of social cognition. *Progress in Brain Research, 156,* 379-401.

Knutson, B., Westdorp, A., Kaiser, E., & Hommer, D. (2000). FMRI visualization of brain activity during a monetary incentive delay task. *Neuroimage, 12*(1):20-27.

LeDoux, J. E. (2003). The emotional brain, fear, and the amygdala. *Cellular and Molecular Neurobiology, 23,* 727–738.

Leone, P. E., & McLaughlin, J. J. (1995). Appropriate placement of students with emotional and behavioral disorders: Emerging policy options. In J. M. Kauffman, J. Lloyd, & T. Astuto (Eds.), *Issues in the educational placement of pupils with emotional and behavioral disorders.* Hillside, N.J.: Lawrence Erlbaum.

Moeller, T. G. (2001). Youth aggression and violence: *A psychological approach.* Hillside, N.J.: Lawrence Erlbaum Associates.

National Center for Educational Statistics: U.S. Department of Education: (2007). *Indicators of School Crime and Safety: 2007,* Washington, D.C: U.S. Department of Justice.

Pine, D. S. (2007) Research review: A neuroscience framework for pediatric anxiety disorders. *Journal of Child Psychology and Psychiatry, 48*(7), 631-648.

Posner, J., Russell, J. A., & Peterson, B. S. (2005). The circumplex model of affect: An integrative approach to affective neuroscience, cognitive development, and psychopathology. *Development and Psychopathology, 17,* 715-734.

Powell, K. B., & Voeller, K.S. (2004). Prefrontal executive function syndromes in children. *Journal of Child Neurology, 19,* 785-797.

Ramachandran, V.S., & Oberman, L.M. (2006). Broken mirrors: A theory of autism. *Scientific American, Nov; 295*(5): 62-9.

Reddy, L. A. (2001). Serious emotional disturbance in children and adolescents: Current status and future directions. *Behavior Therapy, 32,* 667-691.

Reitan, R. M., & Wilson, D. (2000). Conation: A neglected aspect of neuropsychological functioning. *Archives of Clinical Neuropsychology, 15*(5), 443-453.

Rolls, E. T. (2004). The functions of the orbitofrontal cortex. *Brain and Cognition, 55,* 11-29.

Ruby, P., & Decety, J. (2004). How do you feel versus how do you think she would feel? A neuroimaging study of perspective taking with social emotions. *Journal of Cognitive Neuroscience, 16,* 988-999.

Saudino, K. J. (2005). Behavioral genetics and child temperament. *Developmental and Behavioral Pediatrics, 26*(3), 214-223.

Susman, E. J. (2006). Psychobiology of persistent antisocial behavior: Stress, early vulnerabilities and the attenuation hypothesis. *Neuroscience and Biobehavioral Reviews, 30,* 376-389.

Swanson, J. W., Holser, C. E., and Ganju, V. K. (1990). Violence and psychiatric disorder in the community: Evidence from epidemiologic catchment area surveys. *Hospital Community Psychiatry, 41,* 761-770.

Thomas, A., & Chess, S. (1977). *Temperament and development.* New York, N.Y.: Bruner/Mazel.

Valliant, P. M. , Gristey, C. , Pottier, D. , & Kosmyna, R. (1999). Risk factors in violent and nonviolent offenders. *Psychological Reports, 85*(2), 675-680.

Watson, J. B. (1913). Psychology as the behaviorist views it. *Psychology Review, 20,* 158-177.

Whittle, S., Allen, N. B., Lubman, D. I., & Yucel, M. (2006). The neurobiological basis of temperament: Towards a better understanding of psychopathology. *Neuroscience and Biobehavioral Reviews, 30,* 511-525.

Wicker, B., Keysers, C., Plailly, J., Royet, J.P., Gallese, V., & Rizzolatti, G. (2003). Both of us   disgusted in my insula: The common neural basis of seeing and feeling disgust. *Neuron, 40*(3), 655-664.

Worling, J. R. (2001). Personality-based typology of adolescent male sexual offenders: differences in recidivism rates, victim-selection characteristics, and personal victimization behaviors. *Sex Abuse, 13(3)*, 149-166.

Yeates, K. O., Bigler, E. D., Dennis, M., Gerhardt, C.A., Rubin, K. H., Stancin, T., Taylor, H.G.,   Vannatta, K. (2007). Social outcomes in childhood brain disorder: A heuristic integration of   social neuroscience and developmental psychology. *Psychological Bulletin, 133*(3), 535-556.

CHAPTER 3

RIGHT HEMISPHERIC DISORDERS AND EMOTIONAL DISTURBANCE

Jed Yalof, Psy.D.

"Your vision will become clear only when you look into your heart. Who looks outside, dreams. Who looks inside, awakens."

—Carl Jung

INTRODUCTION

This chapter presents a summary of the research on and characteristics of right hemispheric disorders and emotional disturbances. To that end, emotional disturbance and its psychosocial correlates will be reviewed in relation to: (a) cortical functioning; (b) neurobiology; and (c) assessment and intervention strategies. The goal of the chapter is to make this information accessible to the educators, professional service providers, family members, and significant others who play an important role in the child's life.

Understanding the emotional world of children who struggle with right hemispheric disorders is crucial to the development of formulations and interventions. Nevertheless, emotion is neither easy to describe nor isolate from the related concepts of *affect, mood,* and *feeling.* A review of how emotion is described in standard diagnostic nomenclature illustrates this point. The *Diagnostic and Statistical Manual of Mental Disorders, 4th edition* (DSM IV_TR) does not define emotion as a separate term in its glossary, but instead discusses emotion under the definition of *affect* and describes emotion as a "…subjectively experienced feeling state" (p. 819). "Common examples of affect are sadness, elation, and anger" (p. 819). *Emotion* and *affect* are also related by virtue of affect referring to "…more fluctuating changes in emotional 'weather'" (p. 819). Moreover, emotion is described in relation to mood, where mood is described as a sustained and pervasive emotional climate variable (e.g., dysphoric, elevated, euthymic, expansive, or irritable). Thus, in the manner of an overlapping Venn diagram (Figure 3-1), feeling, affect and mood appear to share a relationship to emotion. In particular, "feeling" comprises the subjective emotional state, while "affect" is expressed behavior(s) associated with the feeling, and "mood" is viewed as being the more consistent emotional climate in which the affect manifests behaviorally (*DSM IV_TR, 2000*). An example of the relationship that exists among the concepts of feeling, emotion, affect, and mood following DSM terminology- might be expressed as follows: "I feel sad (emotion) today (affect), and am generally irritable (mood)."

FIGURE 3-1
Venn diagram illustrating the relationship between feelings, affect, mood and emotions.

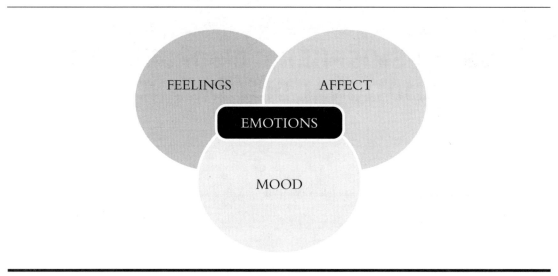

Frattaroli (2001), writing from the perspective of a psychoanalyst, discussed the subtle relationship among affect, feeling, and emotion in a different way. He defined affect as "…a purely physiological unconscious process or state–the biological component of an emotion" (p. 189). Emotion was defined as "…a complex conscious experience that is based on affect" (p. 189). Emotion involves both physiological arousal and an impulse to act, in addition to a feeling. Feeling represents "…a more subtle quality of awareness that can be introspectively distilled out from the physiological urgency of the emotional experience, and that does not impel toward action" (p. 189). Affect can occur without emotion (e.g., palpitations without awareness of anxiety). Emotion can be present without feeling (e.g., an impulse to act without awareness of feeling). Frattaroli (2001) also stated it was possible to experience feeling without the physical indices of affect or emotion (e.g., a pure feeling state without heightened arousal).

Palombo (2006), who has written extensively about the emotional experience of children presenting with a pattern of presumed right hemisphere cognitive deficits, also identified affect as a physiological state of arousal with variable "…feeling tone and physiological change" (p. 110). Palombo defined emotion in the following way: "*Emotion* is the mental representation and external behavioral manifestation of affects. Emotions may be appraised cognitively, linked to thoughts, and expressed behaviorally. The subjective experiences associated with affects/emotions are *feelings*; these are responses to internal or external stimuli that have a positive or negative valence and that have meaning to the person having the experience" (p. 110). Palmobo's definition included the idea that emotion can be related to biological change, subjective feeling, behavior, thought, and mental representation.

LeDoux (1998) added a definitive biological element to the description of emotion by stating that emotions are "…biological functions of the nervous system" (p. 12). LeDoux also sought to integrate longstanding questions about how best to define emotions. This debate included whether emotions were identified mainly on the basis of physical change, cognitive label in relation to social context, or conscious or unconscious appraisal of stimulus valence. LeDoux suggested the relationship between emotion and cognition as being "…best thought of as separate but interacting mental health functions mediated by separate but interacting systems" (p. 69).

> **KEY LEARNING POINTS:**
> **Defining Emotion**
>
> * Emotion involves both physical arousal and an impulse to act.
> * Emotion involves a subjective state of feeling.
> * Emotion is a mental representation that can be appraised cognitively.
> * Emotions are adaptive and biological parts of the nervous system.
> * Right hemisphere damage can heighten the risk for emotional disturbance secondary to misreading emotional cues.

Emotions are entwined clearly within the neuropsychology and neurophysiology of the brain-behavior matrix. The articulation of this relationship is essential because certain brain areas tend to be associated strongly with certain types of cognitive skills and also exercise varying degrees of influence over emotional functioning. For instance, the left hemisphere is more language-based, whereas the right hemisphere tends to be specialized for the processing and integration of novel learning, spatial cognition, and nonverbal information, such as voice tone, posture, and gesture. (e.g., Hale & Fiorello, 2004; Rourke, 1989; Rourke, 1995). Damage to the right hemisphere can lead to compromised sensoria, social perception, and behavioral maladjustment. Furthermore, such damage can also heighten the risk for emotional disturbance in children, which in turn affects adjustment in the educational, social, and (ultimately) vocational spheres. An informed neuropsychological understanding of emotional disturbances in relation to right hemisphere disorders can therefore shape assessment, clinical formulation, psychiatric diagnosis, educational classification, and various intervention strategies designed to support psychosocial adjustment for a right hemisphere damaged child.

Cortical Organization: An Overview

This section presents a brief overview of cortical organization as a foundation to understanding emotional disturbances that comprise both cortical (e.g., frontal, temporal, parietal, and occipital lobes) and subcortical structures (e.g., basal ganglia, thalamus, limbic system) in relation to right hemispheric disorders. The reader is also referred to other primary sources (e.g., Blumenfeld, 2002; Hale & Fiorello, 2004; Kolb & Wishaw, 2003; Salloway, Malloy, & Cummings, 1997; Teeter & Semrud-Clikeman, 1994) for a more extensive neuroanatomical-neurophysiological overview of cortical and subcortical structures and functions.

The cerebral cortex is the most evolved part of the brain. The cortex is the brain's external layering of gray matter that makes up "80%" of its size (Kolb & Wishaw, 2003, p. 62). The cerebral cortex is comprised of right and left hemispheres that are separated anatomically by the longitudinal fissure and connected by the corpus callosum, a white fibrous band of neurons that acts as an information conduit between both hemispheres. Neurocognitive functioning involves the interactive connections between and within hemispheres, and between the cortical and subcortical regions (e.g., Hale & Fiorello, 2004) The result is a transformation of sensory information into the planned, sequenced, and regulated behavior of language, judgment, perception, and emotionality.

FIGURE 3-2
Subdivisions of the Cerebral Cortex and the Relative Function of Each Lobe

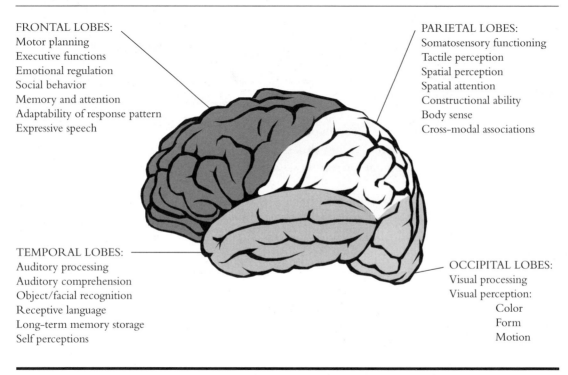

FRONTAL LOBES:
Motor planning
Executive functions
Emotional regulation
Social behavior
Memory and attention
Adaptability of response pattern
Expressive speech

PARIETAL LOBES:
Somatosensory functioning
Tactile perception
Spatial perception
Spatial attention
Constructional ability
Body sense
Cross-modal associations

TEMPORAL LOBES:
Auditory processing
Auditory comprehension
Object/facial recognition
Receptive language
Long-term memory storage
Self perceptions

OCCIPITAL LOBES:
Visual processing
Visual perception:
Color
Form
Motion

Within each hemisphere are four lobes (see Figure 3-2), designated primarily, but not solely, for specific neurocognitive functions. In fact, the four lobes work together to bring about the integration and comprehension of sensory information in a way that allows for thought and action. Hale and Fiorello (2004) summarized the four lobes and their primary functions as follows:

1. Frontal lobe structures have primary responsibility for motor (e.g., planning, sequencing, action) and executive functions (e.g., planning, strategizing, evaluation, monitoring, inhibitory, regulatory, working memory); with different frontal areas having responsibility for various tasks (e.g., Broca's area for expressive speech; orbitofrontal area for affect regulation).

2. Temporal lobe structures have primary responsibility for auditory processing and auditory comprehension (e.g., Wernicke's area), object recognition and representation, and longer-term memory storage. According to Hale and Fiorello, the connection between the temporal lobe and subcortical limbic system has important implications for "…attention, learning, memory, and emotion" (p. 59).

3. Parietal lobe structures have primary responsibility for somatosensory functioning (e.g., kinesthesia, touch, pain, pressure, temperature) as well as being critical to the functions of self-awareness, spatial perception and spatial attention, and multi-modal connections of different sensory inputs.

> **KEY LEARNING POINTS:**
> **Cerebral Cortex**
>
> - The cerebral cortex is the most evolved part of the brain.
> - The left hemisphere is usually dominant for language.
> - The right hemisphere is usually dominant for nonverbal processing.
> - Emotions are adaptive and biological parts of the nervous system.
> - The right hemisphere has more association areas, specializes in novel learning, and multi-modal processing.

4. Occipital lobe structures have primary responsibility for visual processing, including object recognition (e.g., contrast, color, form, motion, and location). In addition to these primary functions, there are complex cross-modality communications (e.g., between temporal-parietal-visual lobes) that allow for progressively sophisticated, sequential synthesis, and utilization of what was initially basic sensory information (e.g., a sound, an image, a felt sense of pressure) under the organizing direction of the frontal lobes (Goldberg, 2001; Luria, 1973).

Lastly, the right and left hemispheres are somewhat different in their function and organization (e.g., Goldberg & Costa, 1981; Teeter & Semrud-Clikeman, 1994). Teeter and Semrud-Clikeman (1994) summarized some of the basic differences between the right and left hemispheres, noting the right hemisphere has more association areas, tends to be more conducive to multi-modality processing and integration, and is more capable of processing novel information. Furthermore, because of its rich axonal connections, the right hemisphere can handle a higher level of informational complexity than the left hemisphere. The two hemispheres may be able to provide some degree of compensation for each other when particular functions are lost, such as when the language functions of a damaged left hemisphere can, under certain conditions, be taken up by the right hemisphere. However, this support is not without related volumetric sacrifice and cost to the right hemisphere's ability to perform its usual functions (Teeter & Semrud-Clikeman, 1994). Conversely, when right hemispheric structures have been damaged, there is the potential risk for a range of cognitive and emotional deficits that depend on its integrity.

The Neurobiology of Emotion

Emotional disturbances arising from right hemisphere dysfunctions are essentially outcome measures. That is, the emotional disturbance is a response to an underlying problem (e.g., nonverbal learning disability (NLD), neurological disease, brain injury). The neurobiological model that explains how sensory experience translates to emotion is useful across the varying types of right hemisphere disorders. How, then, is emotion processed neurobiologically?

Papez (1937) (as cited in Mega, Cummings, Salloway, & Malloy, 1997; also see Kolb & Wishaw, 2003) described a circuit for the internal and external experience of emotion, highlighting the relationship among subcortical limbic structures and their eventual connection to the frontal cortex (see Figure 3-3). Papez discussed circular communication between (1) the *mammillary bodies* in the hypothalamus (e.g., where emotion is initiated, also essential for basic functions such as sexuality, thirst, hunger), (2) the *anterior thalamus* (e.g., a relay station to the cortex for sensory input except smell), (3) the *cingulate gyrus* (e.g., involved in pain and anger regulation), where emotion was "…consciously perceived" (Mega et al., 1997, p. 4), and (4) the *hippocampus* (e.g., important for consolidation of long-term memory). Information flowed back to the mammillary bodies by way of the fornix bundle (e.g., group of axons). The *medial cingulate area* was considered to be the integration point between emotion and the frontal lobes. Kolb and Wishaw (2003) describe how an idea enters the circuit, is elaborated as an emotion, and stimulates the hypothalamus to release hormones that lead to a physical and emotional responses.

FIGURE 3-3

Major Subcortical Structures of the Limbic System

Illustration courtesy of Barbara Yalof, M.Ed.

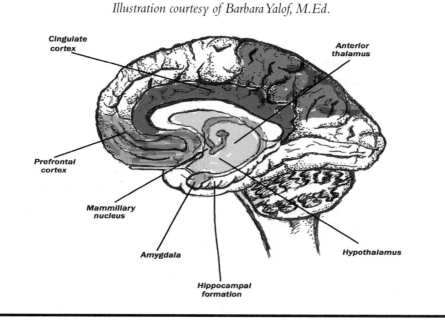

Since Papez's description of the limbic circuit, other subcortical areas, such as the *amygdala* (e.g., involved in major emotional activities, such as love, mood, and aggression; senses danger), have been integrated into the functioning of the limbic system (Mega et al., 1997). Damage to the limbic circuit can result in hypolimbic (e.g., primary affective disorders; Kluver-Bucy), hyperlimbic (e.g., mania, obsessive-compulsive), or dysfunctional (e.g., problems observing social decorum, anxiety-panic)

syndromes (Mega et al., 1997). Thus, limbic damage has significant consequences for emotional dysfunction and can impact cortical structures that play a role in integrating limbic system input.

What, however, is the nature of the relationship between the experience of emotion and the right hemisphere? According to Schore's (1994) neurodevelopmental model of attachment based on the role of the right hemisphere in mediating affect, the limbic system is more highly developed in the right hemisphere. Schore (1994) described the right hemisphere as essential for processing nonverbal communication of affect (e.g., tone, gesture, expressiveness, intensity) and elaborated upon the right hemisphere's neurochemical readiness (e.g., dopamine, opiod peptides, etc.) for maternal stimulation. Schore described events that lead to the maturation of the right orbitofrontal cortex, which he saw as crucial to the development of a positive attachment between child and caretaker. In addition, Schore posited the end of the first year as a very important imprinting period for the development of this bond. Schore (2003, p. 9) stated, "The child uses the output of the mother's emotional-regulating right cortex as a template for the imprinting of the hard-wiring of circuits in his own right cortex that will come to mediate his expanding affective capacities." Lastly, Schore (1994, 2003) also noted the right orbitofrontal cortex is associated with object tracking, appraisal of objects that have emotional significance, and self-regulation skills. Relational trauma impacts the development of the right hemisphere and quality of attachment between caretaker and child. Moreover, Schore (2003, p. 35) developed his position by describing how "…every type of early forming primitive disorder…(p. 35) is associated with compromised functioning in the right orbital prefrontal area (e.g., mania, unipolar depression, drug addiction, psychopathy, personality disorders) and stated (p.35), "Because the orbitofrontal system is centrally involved in the executive functions of the right cortex, these studies underscore the importance of the role of right hemisphere dysfunction in psychiatric disorders."

> **KEY LEARNING POINTS:**
> **Neurobiology of Emotion**
>
> - The limbic circuit processes emotion.
> - The right hemisphere has a strong connection to the limbic circuit.
> - The right orbitofrontal cortex is especially sensitive to nonverbal communication.
> - Dysfunctional attachment patterns and other forms of primitive psychopathology may be related to compromised functioning of the right orbitofrontal cortex.

Right Hemisphere Disorders

Ellen, age 11, was riding her bicycle in the local neighborhood, but forgot to wear her bicycle helmet as she rushed outside to join her friends. As she was riding down the street, her front tire hit a pebble and she was thrown from her bike, landing on her right side, with her forehead smacking hard against the pavement. She was not responding when her name was called. Her friends immediately contacted Ellen's mother, who called 911. Ellen was taken by ambulance to the hospital, where she remained unconscious for 4 days. A CAT scan revealed a right hemisphere, closed-head injury with frontal lobe hemorrhaging and diffuse axonal injury. Ellen recovered slowly, though she developed a left-hand fine-motor tremor, and manifested significant problems with novel learning, spatial tasks, judgment, interpersonal relations, regulating her feelings, and increased anxiety and agitation. She required extensive physical and occupational therapy, counseling, and special educational supports as part of her rehabilitation plan.

The role of the right hemisphere in affect regulation is important for appreciating the expected emotional co-variants of right hemisphere disorders. Neurodevelopmental deficits, neurological disease processes, or brain injury to the right hemisphere lead to various social-emotional problems; however, there is no prototypical presentation of right hemisphere disorders and emotional disturbances. Instead, there are general guidelines that qualify the presence of right hemispheric compromise (e.g., neuropsychological assessment, neuro-imaging) along the general dimensions of neuropsychiatric (e.g., Kaplan-Solms & Solms, 2000), and neurodevelopmental dysfunction (e.g., Stellern, Marlowe, Jacobs, & Cossairt, 1985; Yalof, 2006). Familiarity with various right hemispheric clinical presentations makes clear the intimate connection between the right hemisphere and emotional functioning. To illustrate this point, the following section is presented in two parts: (1) a review of the Nonverbal Learning Disabililty (NLD) syndrome as a general model for the way in which atypical right hemisphere performance signals particular kinds of emotional disturbances, and (2) a sampling of neuropsychiatric research on the emotional manifestations of right hemisphere brain damage.

Nonverbal Learning Disability Syndrome

The research of Rourke (e.g., 1985, 1989, 1995) has been highly instrumental in identifying a clustering of neuropsychological symptoms and syndromes associated with a particular type of cognitive and social-emotional profile that reflect NLD. Rourke's studies focused on the identification of a specific pattern of learning in children between the ages of 9-14 with a corresponding constellation of right hemisphere neurocognitive deficits. Rourke observed a characteristic pattern of intelligence test scores (WISC) in which verbal intelligence was superior to visual-spatial intelligence, and academic achievement on the Wide Range Achievement Test showed spelling and reading skills that were superior to arithmetic, with difficulty noted especially in the spatial alignment of numbers. Additionally, students demonstrating a nonverbal learning deficit also had more problems on tasks of complex psychomotor functioning, novel problem solving, hypothesis testing, and cognitive flexibility, and were at risk for both emotional difficulty of the internalizing type (e.g., anxiety, shyness, social isolation, and depression) and social-skill deficits.

Identification of this particular deficit patterns in the context of academic impairment led Rourke to categorize these students as NLD, a concept introduced initially by Johnson and Myklebust (1967). Embedded within the NLD profile was a vicious cycle in which demands on the right hemisphere for management of nonverbal stimuli lowered the threshold for academic problems and raised the bar for associated emotional complications, which, in turn, could reduce receptivity to the learning process and impede psycho-social adjustment.

NLD Deficit Model

Rourke organized the NLD profile into a model of primary, secondary, tertiary, and related disturbances in order to illustrate the manner in which disturbances to the "white matter" (Rourke, 1995) neuronal pathways (e.g., fiber tracts, more prevalent in right than left hemispheres) resulted in an identifiable neuropsychological and social-emotional deficit pattern. Primary deficits, under the aegis of the right hemisphere, involved tactile-perceptual, visual-spatial organization, novel learning, and complex motor skill. Secondary deficits built on the primary areas of disturbance involved tactile and visual attention, as well as exploratory behavior. Tertiary deficits included tactile and visual memory, abstract reasoning, and speech and language deficits. Rourke also identified verbal deficits in oral-motor praxis, prosody, phonology-semantics, content, pragmatics, and function.

That is, NLD youngsters had difficulty using language to secure positive reinforcement from the environment. Rourke further identified academic deficits associated with NLD (early grapho-motor, reading comprehension, mechanical arithmetic, mathematics, and science), and socioemotional deficits, which he described as adaptation to novelty, social competence, emotional stability, and activity level (Rourke, 1995, p. 7). NLD assets were in the auditory-verbal realm.

NLD Classification

NLD is not classified easily in the nomenclature of educational or mental health disorders. For example, neither DSM IV_TR (2000) nor the Individual with Disabilities Education Improvement Act (IDEIA) (2004) recognize NLD as a specific learning disability. However, the *Psychodynamic Diagnostic Manual* (PDM) does recognize NLD and analogizes it to the DSM IV_TR (2000) diagnosis of Learning Disability Not Otherwise Specified. In fact, Voeller (1991) discussed children exhibiting NLD as having a social-emotional learning disability, and focused on how their clinical presentation changes with development noting varying subtypes and differential diagnostic issues (e.g., communication disorders, pervasive developmental disorders, and possible co-morbid diagnoses, including conduct disorder, obsessive-compulsive disorder, and Fragile X for males) associated with the primary disability. Thus, children exhibiting disorders on the NLD spectrum are at heightened risk for displaying a pattern of emotional disturbance associated with a neuropsychological profile reflective of relative deficit in the right hemisphere. Emotional disturbance can present as depression, anxiety, inhibition, withdrawal, and anger.

Rourke (1995), in developing his NLD model, has evolved a classification system that views NLD as a spectrum disorder. Rourke was careful to qualify the difference between NLD as a neurodevelopmentally based syndrome presentation apparent during childhood and other neuropsychiatric conditions in which *NLD characteristics also have a syndrome presentation, but emerge in response to "...neurological disease, disorder or dysfunction"* (p. 6, italics in original). Tsatsanis and Rourke (1995) summarized categorically NLD spectrum disorders that shared white matter disease classification and NLD assets and deficits. Disorders were classified by symptom similarity to the prototypical profile into Level 1 ("virtually all"), Level 2 ("considerable majority"), and Level 3 ("many"). The prototypical profile included visual-spatial, complex psychomotor, and concept formation; poor mechanical arithmetic relative to reading and spelling; novel information; rigidity; and hyperactivity in early childhood followed by shyness, withdrawal, or immaturity. Classified as Level 1 were: "Callosal agenesis (uncomplicated), Asperger Syndrome, Velocardial syndrome, Williams syndrome, de Lange syndrome, Hydrocephalus (early, shunted), and Congenital hypothyroidism" (p. 486). Classified as Level 2 were: "Sotos syndrome, prophylactic treatment for acute lymphocytic leukemia (long-term survivors), Metachromatic leukodystrophy (early in disease progression), Turner syndrome, and Fetal alcohol syndrome (high-functioning)" (p. 486). Classified as Level 3 were: "Multiple sclerosis (early to middle stages), traumatic brain injury (diffuse white matter perturbations), toxicant-induced encephalopathies (affecting white matter), and Autism (high-functioning)" (p. 486).

Palombo (2006) commented on Rourke's work, including the need for more attention to the emotional dimension of social-emotional functioning. Palombo emphasized this area in his clinical work and identified social clumsiness, inappropriate behavior, difficulty establishing peer relations, rejection sensitivity, and poor social reciprocity. Furthermore, Palombo described how children exhibiting NLD characteristics have difficulty with emotional communication, reading facial expressions and feelings, gist, humor, and managing emotions (e.g., anxiety, depression, irritability, helplessness). Self-esteem problems and difficulty responding to emotional words were also noted, with an associated vulnerability to poor regulation of emotion, and decreased sense of self-cohesion and self-narrative. Additionally, Palombo (pp. 128-142) categorized NLD youngsters into four subgroups based upon social impairment deficits, using three domains of social impairment as discriminators for the different NLD subtypes (see Table 3-1). These three domains are: (1) "…impairments in complex and nonlinguistic perception leading to *social imperception*" (italics in original, p. 128) as the core NLD deficit; (2) social problems related to attention and executive level are secondary deficits and more variable; and (3) reciprocal social communication social interaction, and emotional functioning. Subtype I, as based on the above domains, had problems with complex nonverbal processing and developed social problems. Subtype II met criteria for the first subtype and also had problems with attention and executive functioning. Subtype III also met criteria for the first subtype and had additional impairment in social cognition (e.g., social reciprocity, communication, and emotional functioning). Subtype IV met criteria for the second type and had social cognition impairments similar to the third subtype.

TABLE 3-1
Summary of Palombo's NLD Subtypes

SUBTYPE I: Problems with complex nonverbal reasoning and processing.

SUBTYPE II: Subtype I criteria plus problems with attention and executive functioning.

SUBTYPE III: Subtype I criteria plus impaired social cognition.

SUBTYPE IV: Subtype II criteria plus impaired social cognition.

Theory of Mind

One additional area that has received attention in the NLD literature is Theory of Mind (ToM), or the ability to accurately and easily attribute states of mind to self and other. The ability to engage in what Frith (2004) termed "intuitive mentalising" (p. 678) is essential for adaptive functioning. Palombo (2006) discussed ToM deficits as central to understanding the social competence and social-emotional issues that characterize individuals who present with a NLD profile. Recently, Griffin et al. (2006) found that patients who incurred right hemisphere brain-injury had more difficulty with complex, ToM, second-order attributions (e.g., identifying presence or absence of deception) than a control group. Anatomical regions identified as most predictive of ToM deficits were the "…inferior frontal cortex…perhaps in conjunction with the insular/somatosensory cortex" (p. 214).

Extrapolating ToM to other research involving right hemisphere disorder finds support for its role in the interpretation of another person's state of mind. For example, Shamay-Tsoory, Tomer, and Aharon-Peretz (2005) found that individuals with unilateral right hemisphere or bilateral damage to the prefrontal region (especially the ventromedial (VM)area) had more difficulty detecting sarcasm than either controls or individuals with damage to posterior right or left regions. Sarcasm scores correlated significantly for right-sided VM area, but not for left sided VM area. There was no relationship between sarcasm performance and scores on measures of executive functioning. Heberlein, Adolphs, Pennebacker, and Tranel (2003) reported that damage to the right somatosensory cortex resulted in less spontaneous use of emotional and social process words than non-brain damaged controls when viewing a movie. Ostrove, Simpson, and Gardner (1990) noted patients with diffuse right hemisphere brain damage were more likely to attribute positive emotion to neutral situations than a control group, further suggesting that damage to the right hemisphere could affect the ability to make subtle, but important assessments of emotion in situations where external cues are ambiguous.

Brain Injury and Neuropsychiatric Sequela

Right hemispheric brain damage may be the result of penetrating or non-penetrating head injuries that create brain tissue tearing, compression, or shearing. These traumas occur in conjunction with the type of event that leads to the head injury, be that acceleration-dependent (e.g., acceleration, deceleration, rotation) or non-acceleration-dependent (e.g., crushing) (Snow & Hooper, 1994). Secondary medical considerations when evaluating head injuries include hypoxia, ischemia, cerebral edema, hemorrhage, cerebral atrophy and ventricular enlargement, and post-traumatic epilepsy (Snow & Hooper, 1994).

Differences have been observed in psychiatric presentations among individuals with penetrating and non-penetrating brain injuries. Borek, Butler, and Fleminger (2001) reviewed case notes of patients with non-penetrating head injuries. Their research noted significant associations between right hemisphere injury and hallucinations, depression, and apathy. Significant associations were also found between left hemisphere injury and lack of insight, confabulation, and aggression. Lishman (1968), four decades earlier, evaluated psychiatric symptoms of patients with penetrating head injury and found that the right hemisphere injuries showed more frequent occurrence of affective symptoms, behavior disorders, and somatic symptoms than the left hemisphere injuries. Lishman reported, "Among affective disorders, depression, irritability, and apathy show a right hemisphere preponderance" (p. 404). The following research elaborates on some of the aforementioned findings with respect to emotional disturbance relative to right hemisphere integrity.

Psychotic Ideation and Emotion

The four studies summarized below discuss psychotic ideation and right hemisphere disorder and their relationship to emotion. Walters, Harrison, Williamson, and Foster (2006) reviewed archived patient data and found that right-sided damage, more than left sided damage, was associated with left hemispace visual hallucinations (under the control of the right hemisphere) and negative emotional valence (e.g., fear). Second, Stewart and Brennan (2005) presented a case study of a male patient with right temporal lobe damage (e.g., resection of right superficial middle and inferior

---

KEY LEARNING POINTS: NLD

- NLD reflects a pattern of basic right hemisphere deficits in tactile-perceptual, visual-spatial organization, novel learning, and complex motor skill.
- NLD is associated with deficits in social perception, social interaction, social competence, theory-of-mind, and language pragmatics.
- NLD is often associated with depression, anxiety, and social withdrawal.
- NLD can be understood best on a spectrum that classifies educational, social-emotional, and neurological disorders.

KEY LEARNING POINTS:
Right Hemispheric Brain Injury

Right hemispheric brain injury is associated with:

- Psychotic Ideation and Emotional Distress
- Aggression
- Somatic Complaints
- Mania and Other Mood Disturbances
- Misreading of Facial Expression and Emotional Intent.

arteries) who developed auditory hallucinations associated with emotional outbursts, agitation, aggression, labile mood, and seizures (also see Borek, Butler, & Fleminger, 2001). Third, Mohr, Bracha, and Brugger (2003) found increased dopamine in the right hemispheres' of a non-clinical population correlated with magical ideation and neglect of right hemispace. Thus, spatial behavior and magical ideation were connected conceptually, and tied to the right hemisphere. Lastly, Ellis (1994) explored the role of the right hemisphere in relation to face recognition and memory deficits in patients with Capgras Delusion. In Caprgras Delusion, patients have delusional beliefs that a double has replaced a significant other (e.g., "You look like him, but you are not him!")

PTBI and Aggression

With respect to post-traumatic brain injury (PTBI) and aggression, Kim et al. (2007) noted the "frontal lesion" as a risk factor in their summary of research findings (p.109). Additionally, Wood and Liossi (2006) found that a group of aggressive patients did poorer on visual-spatial tasks, presumably a right hemisphere domain, and on verbal memory testing, presumably a left hemisphere domain, than non-aggressive patients at 1-2 years post-injury. Tateno, Jorge, and Robinson (2003) found more aggression in PTBI patients compared to patients without traumatic brain injury, and no difference between frequency of either right and left side lesions in PTBI group (the aggressive group had more diffuse lesions). Mychak, Kramer, Boone, and Miller (2001) found that patients diagnosed with right side frontotemporal dementia were more likely than left side patients to display socially undesirable behaviors, including aggression and criminal behavior. These researchers concluded that the right frontotemporal region played a role in mediating social behavior and discussed the role of the right hemisphere in emotional comprehension and expression. The right hemisphere affects the ability to appreciate emotional complexity and might play a role in suicidal behavior as a form of self-directed aggression. Rohlfs and Ramirez, in their review of aggression and brain asymmetry, cited Weinberg's work (2006, p. 292) and stated, "Weinberg (2000) suggested that suicidal patients showed a compensatory shift to left hemisphere information processing due to functional insufficiency of their right hemisphere. This shift would manifest a tendency to dissociation and other typical traits for suicidal people."

PTBI and Mood Disorders

A sampling of research is presented to show the relationship between mood disturbance and right hemisphere damage. Paradiso, Vaidya, Tranel, Kosier, and Robinson (2008) reported that post-stroke non-dysphoric depression, in which there is a reduced ability to report sad emotions, was associated with lesions in the right anterior hemisphere. The inability to report sad emotions was presumed reflective of impaired self-awareness in conjunction with right hemisphere brain damage. Kim et al. (2007) reviewed the literature from 1978-2006 on neuropsychiatric complications of PTBI, and found that having a right lateral hemispheric lesion increased the risk for depression with anxiety. In fact, depression was the only diagnostic category under which a right hemispheric lesion was identified specifically in the summary chart (p. 109). For PTBI mania, "non-dominant hemispheric lesion," "multifocal lesions," "frontal lesions," and orbitofrontal lesions" were cited in the summary chart, and "right temporal" lesions (p. 117), "small right white matter frontal contusion" (p. 118) and "bilateral orbitofrontal contusions" (p. 118) were referenced in the text.

Ruocco and Swirsky-Sacchetti (2007) found that among nonverbal measures, visual memory and visuo-spatial ability, both considered to be under the primary direction of the right-hemisphere, were associated negatively and significantly with self-defeating/masochistic as well as paranoid scales of the Millon Clinical Multiaxial Inventory. Narushima, Kosier, and Robinson (2003) noted that left hemisphere stroke was associated with severity of post-stroke depression more than right hemisphere stroke when assessed in relation to distance from the frontal pole six months after the stroke occurred; however, this finding did not rule-out an association between right hemisphere stroke and depressive symptoms. Min and Lee (1997) observed that a group of patients presenting with depressive, anxious, and somatic disorders were more likely to locate somatic complaints on the left side of their bodies. These results suggested that the right hemisphere has more involvement in emotional reactions, and that repression of conflict reflected a disconnection between the right hemisphere and the language based left hemisphere. Left side somaticizers scored higher than their right side counterparts on anxiety and depression measures, but not as high as patients with left and right side complaints; however, scores between groups were not statistically significant. Finally, Glosser and Koppell (1987) found that a group of children with right hemisphere and bilateral cognitive impairment had less anxiety and depression, but a greater tendency to somaticize, than children whose cognitive impairment was associated mainly with deficit on left hemispheric tasks. Taken together, these results suggested that children with a right hemisphere neurocognitive profile may be less able to identify dysphoric emotion and more prone to somatic displacement.

Facial Expression

Emotions are often expressed through facial expression. Schore (1994) described the infant's exquisite sensitivity to the mother's facial expression during the first year of life, and the readiness of the right hemisphere to mature (or regress) in response to this maternal input. Several studies are presented that support the right hemisphere's role in interpreting facial expression and emotion.

Kazandjian, Borod, and Brickman (2007) rated patient presentation of emotional monologues and found that patients with anterior right brain damage showed less intense facial expression than patients with left side brain lesions or right brain damaged patients with posterior lesions. These results supported the idea that the right hemisphere mediates facial emotion. Kohler, Barrett, Gur, Turetsky, and Moberg (2007) presented results that further supported the role of the right hemisphere in mediating facial expression. Kohler et al. (2007) found an overall relationship between schizophrenic patients' recognition of facial emotions and the ability to identify an odor presented through the right nostril. However, this relationship was not found for controls. Still, these results were supportive of literature suggestive of a right hemisphere preference for processing negative emotional stimuli (especially sad face expressions) and odor identification in schizophrenics.

Prodan, Orbelo, Testa, and Ross (2001) investigated upper and lower visual field processing of facial displays of emotion when stimuli were presented to the right and left hemispheres. These researchers hypothesized that lower half facial displays were processed by the left hemisphere because of the left hemisphere's specialization for various learned social emotions (e.g., pride, guilt, jealousy), whereas the right hemisphere was more sensitized to primary emotions (e.g., anger, fear). Adult volunteers viewed the lower half of facial displays unless instructed to look at the upper half, in which case only the right hemisphere was responsive to the upper half of facial emotion. The results were consistent with research indicating the right hemisphere is predominant in processing blended facial expressions of complex emotional states. Once again, blended facial expression identifies complex emotional states, and upper facial expression is likely to express the primary emotion. With prompting and cueing, the right hemisphere is more responsive to the upper visual field. Thus, the right hemisphere holds the key for identification of primary emotion and discerning emotional complexity expressed facially. Lastly, Anderson, Spencer, Fulbright, and Phelps (2000) found that epileptic patients with right temporal lobe resections, including 70-80% of the amygdala, were less able to process facial emotions than patients with left temporal resections or a control group. Patients with right temporal lobe damage were also less able to evaluate fearful faces correctly, pointing to the role of the right amygdala in processing fear, and the right temporal region in processing disgust and sadness as withdrawal emotions. Finally, right hemisphere damage was also associated with lower ratings in processing happiness as a facial expression. In summary, these studies are examples of research indicative of the right hemisphere's role in identifying particular emotional facial expressions.

Assessment and Intervention

Assessment of right hemisphere disorders takes many paths, depending upon the nature of the presenting problem. In fact, most interventions frequently involve a collation of multiple data points, including comprehensive history, neuropsychological assessment findings, and, when warranted, neuroimaging data. Intervention approaches often include educational strategies to remediate academic deficiencies, occupational therapy, speech therapy, vocational re-training, medication, and individual, family, and/or group counseling. In all instances, professionals are guided by diagnostic assessment findings.

Diagnostic assessment often varies depending upon the nature of referral. For example, a medical referral in response to a mild concussion, a brain injury, or neurological symptoms might necessitate neuroimaging studies that range from a skull X-ray or CT scan, to PET, SPECT, or fMRI as more sophisticated procedures that permit dimensional and detailed review of brain imagery, brain metabolism, and tissue integrity. The particular diagnostic procedure is related to the presenting problem, with risks and benefits of different techniques weighed accordingly. In fact, Sohlberg and Mateer (2001) presented a comprehensive review of the different types of medical diagnostic procedures utilized in response to medical referrals. A medical diagnostic assessment involves the examination of the patient's physical and neurological status (Blumenfeld, 2002). The comprehensive examination seeks to develop a diagnosis and treatment plan through the integration of presenting complaint with medical history, review of "head-to-toe" systems (Blumenfeld, p. 6), including family history, social and environmental history, medications and allergies, physical examination, and laboratory data.

Neuropsychological assessment refines the strengths and deficits of different skill domains. Groth-Marnat (2000) identified domains routinely evaluated during the course of neuropsychological assessment, including: intelligence, pre-morbid functioning, learning and memory, verbal-language and academic abilities, attention and orientation, concentration, visuo-constructive ability, executive and motor functioning, and emotional status. Furthermore, Groth-Marnat (2000) noted that neuropsychological assessment is a rich source of information for many patients, including those individuals who present with problems that involve neurological symptoms, post-injury rehabilitation, psychological functioning, vocational status, education, and the judicial system. Neuropsychological assessment, in conjunction with collateral information obtained from significant others (e.g., family, teachers, employers) in addition to a review of educational and medical records makes it clear that most children's areas of need are difficult to ascertain only by observation.

With respect to a neuropsychological approach to educational testing, Miller (2007) focused on the role of the school psychologist in providing evaluations that are grounded in an understanding of brain-behavior relationships. Miller (2007) stated, "An increasing number of children in the schools are affected with known or suspected neurological conditions" (p. 5). Miller (2007) also observed that children are more likely to return to school quickly rather than going through a rehabilitation period after being stabilized from a head injury. These children pose challenges both at home (see Sohlberg & Mateer, 2001 for a review of rehabilitation planning and family counseling strategies) and in school. Moreover, Miller (2007) noted an increasing number of children who required medication to help regulate behavior and mood, or who have chronic medical conditions, or have neurodevelopmental disorders, such as those found on the NLD spectrum (e.g., autism, Aspergers) required additional assistance at school. These children may require a range of school-based interventions, such as individual and/or group counseling, and speech-language and/or occupational therapies, in order to make progress toward educational objectives.

Lastly, Miller (2007) outlined assessment domains similar to the areas that Groth-Marnat (2000) emphasized, noting the value both of neuropsychological training and the utilization of neuropsychological measures in responding to questions about a student's academic difficulties. For example, careful and systematic evaluation of sensory-motor, attention, visual-spatial, language, memory-learning, executive, reasoning, social-emotional, and behavioral domains provides a comprehensive picture of the student and facilitates planning decisions relative to educational needs. Data from a thorough school neuropsychological assessment also permits a particularized intervention approach. The value of school neuropsychological assessment in evaluating, diagnosing, and intervening around specific academic problem areas has been elaborated in a series of books related to reading (Feifer & De Fina, 2000; Feifer & Della Toffalo, 2007), written language (Feifer & De Fina, 2002), and mathematics (Feifer & De Fina, 2005) as core educational areas that require special attention. Furthermore, Yalof and Abraham (2006) described the different types of personality tests that can be used in helping to quantify and quality the emotional problems of students when assessing for special education purposes.

CONCLUSION

The relationship between the right hemisphere and emotional functioning is intimate. The neurobiology of the right hemisphere is especially sensitized to emotional expression, and disorders of the right hemisphere, despite different causes and symptoms, increase the risk of emotional disturbance. Family members, medical professionals, psychologists, speech-language therapists, and educators each play a significant role in the diagnosis, formulation, and remedial-rehabilitative processes associated with an understanding of right hemisphere disorder and emotional disturbance.

REFERENCES

American Psychiatric Association. (2000). *Diagnostic and statistical manual of mental disorders* (4th ed. text revision). Washington, DC: Author.

Anderson, A. K., Spencer, D. D., Fulbright, R. K., & Phelps, E. A. (2000). Contributions of the anteromedial temporal lobes to the evaluation of facial emotion. *Neuropsychology, 14,* 526-536.

Borek, L. L., Butler, R., & Fleminger, S. (2001). Are neuropsychiatric symptoms associated with evidence of right brain injury in referrals to a neuropsychiatric brain injury unit? *Brain Injury, 15,* 65-69.

Blumenfeld, H. (2002). Neuroanatomy through clinical cases. Sunderland, MA: Sinauer.

Ellis, H. D. (1994). The role of the right hemisphere in the Capgras delusion. *Psychopathology, 27,* 177-185.

Feifer, S. G., & De Fina, P. A. (2000). *The neuropsychology of reading disorders: Diagnosis and intervention workbook.* Middletown, MD: School Neuropsychology Press.

Feifer, S. G., & De Fina, P. A. (2002). *The neurpsychology of written language disorders: Diagnosis and intervention.* Middletown, MD: School Neuropsychology Press.

Feifer, S. G., & De Fina, P. A. (2005). *The neuropsychology of mathematics: Diagnosis and intervention.* Middletown, MD: School Neuropsychology Press.

Feifer, S. G., & Della Toffalo, D. A. (2007). *Integrating RTI with cognitive neuropsychology: A scientific approach to reading.* Middletown, MD: School Neuropsychology Press.

Frattaroli, E. (2001). *Healing the soul in the age of the brain: Becoming conscious in an unconscious world.* New York: Viking.

Frith, U. (2004). Emanuel Miller lecture: Confusions and controversies about Asperger syndrome. Journal of Child Psychology and *Psychiatry, 45,* 672-686.

Glosser, G., & Koppell, S. (1987). Emotional-behavioral patterns in children with learning disabilities. *Journal of Learning Disabilities, 20 (6),* 365-368.

Goldberg, E. (2001). *The executive brain: Frontal lobes and the civilized mind.* New York: Oxford University Press.

Goldberg, E., & Costa, L.D. (1981). Hemispheric differences in the acquisition and use of descriptive systems. *Brain and Language, 14 (1),* 144-173.

Griffin, R., Friedman, O., Ween, J., Winner, E., Happé, F., & Brownell, H. (2006). Theory of mind and the right cerebral hemisphere: Refining the scope of impairment. *Laterality, 11,* 195-225.

Groth-Marnat, G. (2000). *Neuropsychological assessment in clinical practice: A guide to test interpretation and integration.* New York: Wiley.

Hale, J.B., & Fiorello, C. A. (2004). *School neuropsychology: A practitioner's handbook.* New York: Guilford.

Heberlein, A. S., Adolphs, R., Pennebaker, J. W., & Tranel, D. (2003). Effects of damage to right-hemisphere brain structures on spontaneous emotional and social judgments. *Political Psychology, 24,* 705-726.

Individuals with Disabilities Education Improvement Act of 2004, 20 U.S.C 1400 § *et seq.*

Johnson, D. J., & Myklebust, H.R. (1967). *Learning disabilities: Educational principles and practice.* New York: Grune & Stratton.

Kaplan-Solms, K., & Solms, M. (2000). *Clinical studies in neuro-psychoanalysis: Introduction to a depth neuropsychology.* Madison, CT: International Universities Press, Inc.

Kazandjian, S., Borod, J. C., & Brickman, A. M. (2007). Facial expression during emotional monologues in unilateral stroke: An analysis of monologue segments. *Applied Neuropsychology, 14,* 235-246.

Kim, E., Lauterbach, E. C., Reeve, A., Arciniegas, D. B., Coburn, K., Mendez, M., Rummans, T. A., & Coffey, E. D. (2007). Neuropsychiatric complications of traumatic brain injury: A critical review of the literature (A report by the ANPA Committee on Research). *The Journal of Neuropsychiatry and Clinical Neurosciences, 19,* 106-127.

Kohler, C. G., Barrett, F. S., Gur, R. C., Turetsky, B. I., & Moberg, P. (2007). Association between facial emotion recognition and odor identification in schizophrenia. *The Journal of Neuropsychiatry and Clinical Neurosciences, 19,* 128-131.

Kolb, B., & Wishaw, I. O., (2003). *Fundamentals of human neuropsychology* (5th ed.). New York: Worth.

LeDoux, J. (1998). *The emotional brain: The mysterious underpinnings of emotional life.* New York: Simon & Schuster.

Lishman, W.A. (1968). Brain damage in relation to psychiatric disability after head injury. *British Journal of Psychiatry, 114*, 373-410.

Luria, A. R. (1973). *The working brain: An introduction to neuropsychology*. New York: Basic Books.

Mega, M. S., Cummings, J. L., Salloway, S., & Malloy, P. (1997). The limbic system: An autonomic, phylogenetic, and clinical perspective. In S. Salloway, P. Malloy, & J. L. Cummings (Eds.), *The neuropsychiatry of limbic and subcortical disorders* (pp. 3-18). Washington, DC: American Psychiatric Press.

Miller, D. C. (2007). *Essentials of school neuropsychological assessment*. Hoboken, NJ: Wiley.

Min, S. K., & Lee, B. O. (1997). Laterality in somatization. *Psychosomatic Medicine, 59 (3)*, 236-240.

Mohr, C., Bracha, H. S., & Brugger, P (2003). Magical ideation modulates spatial behavior. *The Journal of Neuropsychiatry and Neurosciences, 15*, 168-174.

Mychak, P., Kramer, J. H., Boone, K. B., & Miller, B. L. (2001). The influence of right frontotemporal dysfunction on social behavior in frontotemporal dementia. *Neurology, 56*, S11-S15.

Narushima, K., Kosier, J.T., & Robinson, R. G. (2003). A reappraisal of poststroke depression, intra- and inter-hemispheric lesion location using metaanalysis. *The Journal of Neuropsychiatry and Clinical Neuroscience, 15*, 422-430.

Ostrove, J. M., Simpson, T., & Gardner, H. (1990). Beyond scripts: A note on the capacity of right hemisphere-damaged patients to process social and emotional content. *Brain and Cognition, 12*, 144-154.

Palombo, J. (2006). *Nonverbal learning disabilities: A clinical perspective*. New York: W.W. Norton.

Paradiso, S., Vaidya, J., Tranel, D., Kosier, T., & Robinson, R. G. (2008). Nondysphoric depression following stroke. *The Journal of Neuropsychiatry and Clnical Neurosciences, 20*, 52-61.

PDM Task Force (2006). *Psychodynamic diagnostic manual*. Silver Spring, MD: Alliance of Psychoanalytic Organizations.

Prodan, C. I., Orbelo, D. M., Testa, J.A., & Ross, E.D. (2001). Hemispheric differences in recognizing upper and lower facial displays of emotion. *Neuropsychiatry, Neuropsychological, and Behavioral Neurology, 14*, 206-212.

Rohlfs, P., & Ramirez, J. M. (2006). Aggression and brain asymmetries: A theoretical review. *Aggression and Violent Behavior, 11*, 283-297.

Rourke, B. P. (Ed.). (1985). *Neuropsychology of learning disabilities: Essentials of subtype analysis*. New York: Guilford.

Rourke, B. P. (1989). *Nonverbal learning disabilities: The syndrome and the model*. New York: Guilford.

Rourke, B. P. (Ed.). (1995). *Syndrome of nonverbal learning disabilities: Neurodevelopmental manifestations*. New York: Guilford.

Ruocco, A. C., & Swirsky-Sacchetti, T. (2007). Personality disorder symptomatology and neuropsychological functioning in closed head injury. *The Journal of Neuroropsychiatry and Clinical Neurosciences, 19 (1)*, 27-35.

Salloway, S., Malloy, P., & Cummings, J.L. (Eds.). (1997). *The neuropsychiatry of limbic and subcortical disorders*. Washington, DC: American Psychiatric Press.

Schore, A. N. (1994). *Affect regulation and the origin of the self: The neurobiology of emotional development*. Hillsdale, NJ: Erlbaum.

Schore, A. N. (2003). *Affect dysregulation and disorders of the self*. New York: Norton.

Shamay-Tsoory, S. G., Tomer, R., & Aharon-Peretz, J. (2005). The neuroanatomical basis of understanding sarcasm and its relationship to social cognition. *Neuropsychology, 19*, 288-300.

Snow, J. H., & Hooper, S. R. (1994). *Pediatric traumatic brain injury*. Thousand Oaks, CA: Sage.

Sohlberg, M. M., & Mateer, C. A. (2001). *Cognitive rehabilitation: An integrative neuropsychological approach*. New York: Guilford.

Stellern, J., Marlowe, M., Jacobs, J., & Cossairt, A. (1985). Neuropsychological significance of right hemisphere cognitive mode in behavior disorders. *Behavioral Disorders, 10*, 113-124.

Stewart, B., & Brennan, D.M. (2005). Auditory hallucinations after right temporal gyri resection. *The Journal of Neuropsychiatry and Clinical Neurosciences, 17 (2)*, 243-245.

Tateno, A., Jorge, R. E., & Robinson, R. G. (2003). Clinical correlates of aggressive behavior after traumatic brain injury. *The Journal of Neuropsychiatry and Clinical Neurosciences, 15*, 155-160.

Teeter, P. A., & Semrud-Clikeman, M. (1994). *Child neuropsychology: Assessment and interventions for neurodevelopmental disorders*. Boston: Allyn & Bacon.

Tsatsanis, K. D., & Rourke, B. P. (1995). Conclusion and future directions. In B. P. Rourke (Ed.), *Syndrome of nonverbal learning disabilities: Neurodevelopmental manifestations* (pp. 476-496). New York: Guilford.

Voeller, K. K. S. (1991). Social-emotional learning disabilities. *Psychiatric Annals, 21*, 735-741.

Walters, R. P., Harrison, D. W., Williamson, J. & Foster, P. (2006). Lateralized visual hallucinations: An analysis of affective valence. *Applied Neuropsychology, 13*, 160-165.

Wood, R. L., & Liossi, C. (2006). Neuropsychological correlates of aggression following traumatic brain injury. *Journal of Clinical Neuropsychiatry and Clinical Neurosciences, 18 (3)*, 333-341.

Yalof, J. (2006). Case illustration of a boy with nonverbal learning disorder and Asperger's features: Neuropsychological and personality assessment. *Journal of Personality Assessment, 87*, 15-34.

Yalof, J. & Abraham, P. (2006). Personality assessment in schools. In S.R. Smith, & L. Handler (Eds.), *The clinical assessment of children and adolescents: A practitioner's handbook* (pp. 19-35). Hillsdale, NJ: Erlbaum.

CHAPTER 4

EXECUTIVE FUNCTIONS AND EMOTIONAL DISTURBANCE

George McCloskey, Ph.D.
Joseph Hewitt, D.O.
Julie N. Henzel, M.A., NCSP
Eleazar Eusebio, M.A., Ed.S., NCSP

"If the human brain were so simple that we could understand it, we would be so simple that we couldn't."

—Emerson M. Pugh

This chapter will present an overarching model of executive functions that offers a framework for discussing the role of executive functions in cueing and directing perceptions, emotions, cognitions, and actions, and how executive functions relate to emotional disturbance. Also discussed in the chapter is the diagnosis of emotional disturbance from the perspective of executive function involvement, methods for assessing the executive function deficits of children experiencing emotional disturbance, and intervention strategies that address the executive function deficits of children demonstrating emotional disturbances.

Much more space than has been allotted for this chapter could be devoted to a discussion of exactly what constitutes emotions and emotional disturbance and the specific frontal lobe neural circuits representing executive functions that are thought to be involved in the various expressions of emotions and emotional disturbance in children. For the purposes of brevity, Table 4–1 provides a listing of research studies that have linked frontal lobe neural circuitry involving executive functions with specific emotional disorders. Interested readers should also examine the volume entitled *Frontal-subcortical circuits in psychiatric and neurological disorders* edited by Lichter and Cummings (2001). Many of the other chapters in this volume have devoted significant space to discussions of the type of research summarized in Table 4-1 and Lichter and Cummings. Rather than repeat or summarize the content presented in those chapters, this chapter extends the discussion further by examining the role of executive functions in emotional disturbance. Readers are provided with a brief description of an information processing model that integrates emotion with perception, cognition and action, and a comprehensive model of executive function capacities that cue and direct perception, emotion, cognition, and action. The remainder of the chapter discusses the implications of this comprehensive model of executive functions for the assessment and diagnosis of emotional disturbance and for the development of interventions that deal with the problems created by emotional disturbance.

TABLE 4-1
Evidence of Frontal Lobe/Executive Dysfunction in Select Mental Disorders

Disorder	Study	Sample Characteristics	Impairments Found	Evaluation Method
ADHD	Semrud-Clikeman et al., 2000	Males ages 8-18: ADHD (CT) (n = 10) group, control group (n = 11)	Inhibition and sustained attention; asymmetry of the head of the caudate, smaller volume of the left caudate head, and smaller volume of the white matter of the right frontal lobe	Direct assessments and MRI
	Willis & Weiler, 2005	Review of neuroimaging studies conducted with ADHD children since 1999	Most studies suggest abnormalities in frontal-striatal neurological substrates	EEG and MRI
	Hale et al., 2005	Children ages 6-16 with ADHD (n = 49)	Sustained attention, visual attention/discrimination, declarative verbal memory, working memory, behavior inhibition/regulation, mental flexibility, and set shifting	Direct assessments
	Hale et al., 2008	Children ages 6-12: ADHD group (n = 64), SLD group (n = 24), control group (n = 306)	Sustained attention, mental flexibility, and response inhibition; children with ADHD (CT) showed greatest impairment	Direct assessments
	Papadopoulos et al., 2005	Children in grades 4 and 6: attention/hyperactivity difficulties group (n = 49), control group (n = 49)	Formulating and executing plans, self-monitoring of performance	Computerized individual assessment, direct assessment
Unipolar Depression	Beyer & Krishnan, 2002	Review of volumetric imaging studies conducted between 1976-2001 involving patients with unipolar depression. Majority of studies were controlled.	Abnormalities of the frontal lobe (specifically in subgenual prefrontal cortex), basal ganglia (caudate and putamen), and cerebellum; possible abnormalities in the hippocampus/amygdala	CT and MRI

Disorder	Study	Sample Characteristics	Impairments Found	Evaluation Method
	Steingard et al., 2002	Adolescents: major depression (n = 19, mean age = 15.4), control group (n = 38, mean age = 14.6)	Decreased white matter/increased gray matter in frontal lobe	MRI
	Emerson et al., 2005	Males ages 9-11: anxious-depressed (n = 19), control (n = 9)	Set shifting, hypothesis testing, categorical problem-solving, visual-motor processing speed, visual attention	Direct assessments
	Ottowitz et al., 2002	Review of studies conducted between 1980-2001 with subjects under age 65 with major depression	Processing speed, planning, and problem-solving	Direct assessments
	Pardo et al., 2006	Adults 15-60 years: major depression (n = 9), control group (n = 14)	Processing speed (reaction time)	Direct assessment
	Landro et al., 2001	Adults: major depression group (n = 22), control group (n = 30)	Selective attention, working memory, verbal long-term memory, and verbal fluency	Direct assessments
Bipolar Depression (BD)	Ahn et al., 2007	Children ages 6-16: BD I group (n = 46), control group (n = 22)	Larger right nucleus accumbens in prepubertal subjects with BPD	MRI
	Caetano et al., 2005	Review of 19 neuroimaging studies with BD children/adolescents from 1966-2005	Various abnormalities in fronto-limbic structures and smaller amygdala volumes	MRI and MRS
	Quraishi & Frangou, 2002	Review of 42 controlled studies from 1980-2000 with BD adults ages 16-65	Verbal memory, planning, abstract concept formation, and set shifting; visuo-spatial memory (variable)	Direct assessments
	Pavuluri et al., 2006	Children ages 7-17: BD medicated group (n = 28), BD un-medicated group (n = 28), control group (n = 28)	Declarative verbal memory, sustained, attention, set shifting, processing speed, and working memory in medicated and un-medicated groups	Direct assessments
	Dickstein et al., 2004	Children ages 6-17: BD group (n = 21), control group (n = 21)	Attentional set-shifting and visuo-spatial memory	Direct assessments
	Doyle et al., 2005	Children ages 10-18: BD group (n = 57), control group (n = 46)	Sustained attention, working memory, and processing speed; near significance for problems with interference control, abstract problem solving, and verbal learning	Direct assessments
	McClure et al., 2005	BD group (n = 40) control group (n = 22)	Formulating socially appropriate responses to interpersonal	Direct assessments

Disorder	Study	Sample Characteristics	Impairments Found	Evaluation Method
			situations, recognizing facial affect, decreased response inhibition and flexibility	
Generalized Anxiety Disorder (GAD) and other anxiety disorders	Krain et al., 2008	Adolescents ages 13-17: GAD and/or social phobia group (n = 16), control group (n = 13)	Increased activation of frontal-limbic regions of the brain in anxiety-disordered subjects who reported higher intolerance of uncertainty on a task	fMRI, computerized individual assessment, and self-report rating scales
	Monk et al., 2006	Adolescents ages 9-17: GAD group (n = 18), control group (n = 15)	Abnormal activation in the ventrolateral prefrontal cortex in response to viewing angry faces	Computerized individual assessment and fMRI
	Vassa et al., 2007	Children/adolescents ages 9-20: anxiety group--social phobia, separation anxiety disorder, generalized anxiety disorder, anxiety disorder NOS, panic disorder, and/or OCD (n = 57), control group (n = 103)	Visual memory in subjects with social phobia	Direct assessments
	Dupuy et al., 2008	Adults ages 18-65: GAD + MDD group (n = 15), GAD only group (n = 17)	Intolerance of uncertainty, poorer problem orientation, and more cognitive avoidance in subjects with GAD + MDD than those with GAD only	Cognitive process self-report rating scales
	Erickson et al., 2007	College students: high general anxiety group (n = 40), control group (n = 40)	Objective interpretation of social interactions— (interpretation of peer impressions as overly negative or falsely positive)	Self-report measures in response to laboratory-created social interactions
	Easter et al., 2005	Children/adolescents: anxiety group—social phobia, separation anxiety disorder, and/or GAD group (n = 15); control group (n = 11)	Face/emotion correspondence	Direct assessment
	Bögels & Zigterman, 2000	Children/adolescents ages 9-18: anxiety group—primary diagnosis of separation anxiety disorder, social phobia, or GAD (n = 15); clinical group—primary diagnosis of ODD, ADHD, or CD (n = 15); control group (n = 15)	Anxiety group: objective interpretation of ambiguous situations (more negative orientation), self-efficacy for coping	Direct assessment
Tourette's Syndrome (TS)	Marsh et al., 2007	Child TS group (n = 32), adult TS group (n = 34), child/adult control group (n = 70)	Inhibition, regulation, processing speed; abnormalities of frontostriatal regulatory circuits	Direct assessment and fMRI

Disorder	Study	Sample Characteristics	Impairments Found	Evaluation Method
	Amat et al., 2006	Children: TS group (n = 62), control group (n = 32)	Behavioral regulation, impulsivity, compulsions	MRI
	Channon, et al., 2003	Children ages 9-18: TS group (n = 29), control group (n = 21)	Inhibition, set shifting; more severe impairments in comorbid ADHD	Direct assessment
	Storch et al., 2007	Children ages 8-17: TS or chronic tic disorder (n = 59)	Sustained attention, set shifting, and planning	Direct assessment
	Mahone et al., 2001	Children ages 6-16: TS group (n = 46), control group (n = 28)	Disinhibition and intrusions	Direct assessment
Obsessive Compulsive Disorder (OCD)	Viard et al., 2005	Adolescents/young adults: OCD group (n = 12), control group (n = 15)	Abnormal reactions in the parietal, temporal precuneus region	fMRI
	Maltby et al., 2005	OCD group (n = 14), control group (n = 14)	Excessive activation in rostra, caudal and frontal striatal regions, caudate, and thalamus. Posterior cingulate were also hyperactive among OCD patients.	fMRI
	Penadés et al., 2005	OCD with non-comorbid depression group (n = 35), control group (n =33)	Organizational encoding in non-verbal memory, inference control, set shifting, and organizational strategies	Direct assessment
	Chamberlain et al., 2007	OCD group (n = 20), control group (n = 20)	Spatial working memory, executive planning, visual pattern recognition memory, and cognitive inflexibility	Direct assessment
	Bannon et al., 2006	OCD group (n = 40), control group (n = 20)	Inhibition and set shifting	Direct assessment
	Shin et al., 2004	OCD group (n = 20)	Visuo-construction	Direct assessment
Autism Spectrum Disorder (ASD) and Pervasive Developmental Disorder NOS (PDD NOS)	Kleinhans et. al, 2008	ASD group (n = 14), control group (n = 14)	Reduced hemispheric differentiation, atypical functional and frontal structural asymmetries	fMRI Direct assessment and fMRI
	Allen & Courchesne, 2003	Adolescents/adults: ASD group (n = 8), control group (n = 8)	Reductions in activation of cerebral cortex, particularly in the parietal lobes	fMRI
	Wang et al., 2006	Children ages 7-17: ASD group (n = 18), control group (n = 18)	abnormalities in the neural circuitry of the prefrontal and temporal regions	Parent-report measures on autistic symptoms and executive dysfunction
	Thede & Coolidge, 2007	Children ages 5-17: ASD group (n = 23), control group (n = 31)	Decision making, meta-cognitive problems, and social appropriateness	Direct assessment

Disorder	Study	Sample Characteristics	Impairments Found	Evaluation Method
	Winsler et. al, 2007	Children ages 7-18: ASD group (n = 33), ADHD group (n = 21), control group (n = 28)	Set shifting, cognitive inflexibility, perseverative errors	Direct assessment
	Joseph et al., 2005	Children: autism group (n = 37), control group (n = 31)	Working memory, planning, and inhibitory control	Direct assessment
	Hala et al., 2005	Children: autism group ages 5-15 (n = 13), control group ages 5-7 (n = 13)	Set shifting, inhibition, central coherence, source monitoring	Direct assessment
	Kleinhans et al., 2005	Adolescents/adults with ASD (n = 12)	Cognitive switching and initiation of lexical retrieval strategies	Direct assessment
	Williams et al., 2004	Review of 21 studies of children with ASD (n = 281)	Initiation and visuo-motor integration	Direct assessment
	Verte et al., 2006	Children ages 6-13 with PDD NOS (n = 25)	Inattention, hyperactivity, and impulsivity	Direct assessment and fMRI
Conduct Disorder (CD) and Oppositional Defiant Disorder (ODD)	Banich et al., 2007	Adolescent males ages 14-18: Conduct problems group (n = 12), control group (n = 12) {lit. labels them substance and conduct problems (scp)	Activated parahippocampal regions bilaterally, posterior regions, right-sided medial prefrontal areas, and subcortical regions including the thalamus and caudate, attentional problems	Direct assessment
	Pajer et al., 2008	Adolescent girls ages 15-17: CD group (n = 52), control group (n = 41)	Visuo-spatial and executive function	Direct assessment
	vanGoozen et. al, 2004	Children ages 7-12: ODD group (n = 15), ODD/ADHD group (n = 26), control group (n = 36)	Set shifting, regulating behavior under motivational inhibitory controls; increased response perseveration	Direct assessment
	Speltz et al., 1999	Preschool boys ages 3-5: CD group (n = 80), control group (n = 80)	Motor planning and verbal fluency	Direct assessment
	Barkley et. al, 2001	Individuals ages 12-19: ODD/ADHD group (n = 101), control group (n = 39)	Inattention, inhibition; working memory	Direct assessment
	Thorell & Wahlstedt, 2006	Children ages 4-6 with ODD and comorbid ADHD (n =201)	Inhibition, working memory, and verbal fluency	Direct assessment

Information Processing and Emotions

To appreciate the role of executive functions in emotional disturbance requires an information processing framework that places emotions in a workable context. Within such a framework, it is helpful to specify four general domains of functioning: *sensation/perception* (referred to here as perception), *emotion, cognition*, and *action*. In the flow of information from the outside world, sensations related to the environment or to the internal physical or mental states of the person are translated into perceptions. These sensation-generated perceptions are the catalyst for the generation of emotions, which precede both cognition (i.e., thought processes involved in creating mental representations and making meaning out of the emotion-laden perceptions) and action. Because emotions usually follow perception but precede cognition, the "feeling of what is happening" typically precedes thought or action related to the environmental event (Damasio, 1999; Hardcastle, 1999; Panksepp, 1998; Whalen, Rach, Etcoff, McInerney et al., 1998; Ledoux, 1996).

Although sensations and perceptions precede emotional reaction, the prevailing emotional state of the individual preceding new sensations and perceptions greatly influences what specific information in the environment is sensed and perceived and how it is processed. In other words, a general emotional tenor precedes sensations and perceptions which then influence or alter the emotional state which then influences the cognitions and actions related to the original sensations and perceptions. Figure 4-1 provides a visual representation of this information processing framework. In the diagrams, emotional state is represented as a backdrop on which all perception, cognition, and action occurs; and which, in turn, influences changes in the emotional state, which then in turn further influences new perceptions, cognitions and actions (Adolphs & Damasio, 2000; Hardcastle, 1999).

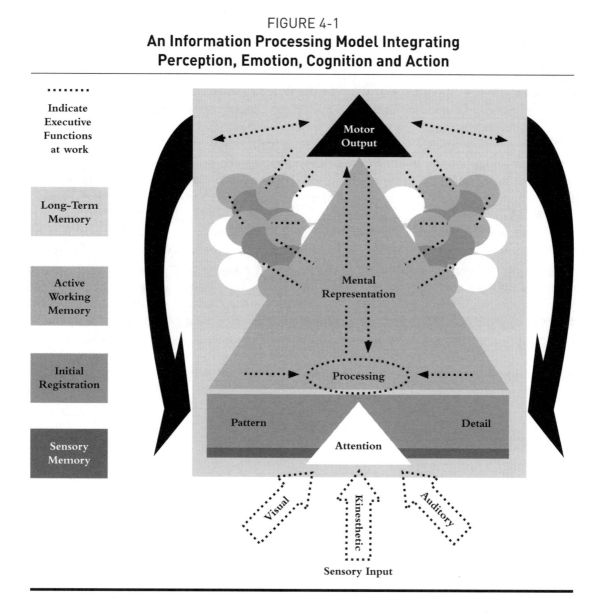

FIGURE 4-1
**An Information Processing Model Integrating
Perception, Emotion, Cognition and Action**

While in one sense emotions precede cognition and action, there is a flow of information in both directions; for example, while emotions precede and therefore influence cognition, cognition, in turn, can influence emotions. In this manner, cognition can alter the influence of emotions in the experiencing of new sensations and perceptions. The interaction of emotion and cognition is a continuous process, with each one influencing the other to varying degrees. The idea of taking control of one's emotions, or taking a more "rational" approach to the experiencing of emotions and their influence on cognition and actions, is often viewed in a rather simplistic conception of cognition controlling emotion. Although such a conception may be accurate in a very general way, it is necessary to understand the modular nature of cognition, such that when cognition exerts control over emotion, it is important to specify what aspect of cognition is doing the exerting.

The Role of Executive Functions in Information Processing

We can have cognitions about our emotions and have emotions about our cognitions, but to exert control over either of these requires an additional set of capacities—those that enable self-direction. These capacities represent the executive functions. When executive functions are being used effectively, a person can exert control over perceptions, emotions, thoughts, and actions as well as the interactions among all four, and maintain a state of functioning that is more likely to be judged as normal. When executive functions are not being used effectively, one of the consequences may be what we refer to as emotional disturbances or emotional disorders. To have a clear understanding of the role that executive function difficulties play in emotional disturbance, it is necessary to have a multidimensional perspective of executive function capacities and to specify the various components in such a multidimensional model.

A Comprehensive Model of Executive Functions

The term executive functions can be viewed as an overarching neuropsychological construct that is used to represent a set of mental capacities that are responsible for cueing, directing, and coordinating multiple aspects of perception, emotion, cognition, and action (Gioia, Isquith, Guy, & Kenworthy, 1996; McCloskey, Perkins, & VanDivner, 2009). The operational definition of executive functions used to guide the construction of this chapter is represented by five interconnected concepts:

1. executive functions are multiple in nature; they do not represent a single, unitary trait;
2. executive functions are directive in nature, i.e., they are mental capacities that are responsible for cueing and directing the use of other mental capacities;
3. executive functions cue and direct other mental capacities involving perception, emotion, cognition, and action;
4. executive function use can vary greatly across four arenas of involvement: intrapersonal, interpersonal, environment, and symbol system use; and
5. executive function use is reflected in the activation of neural networks within some portion of the frontal lobes (McCloskey, Perkins, & VanDivner, 2009).

Although the term executive functions is becoming more readily recognized by professionals and lay persons, the general metaphorical comparison of executive functions to the CEO of the brain or the conductor of the brains orchestra (Brown, 2006; Goldberg, 2001; Gioia, Isquith & Guy, 2001; Wasserstein & Lynn, 2001) represents an oversimplification of the concept, such that it reduces its clinical utility and increases the likelihood that it will join the ranks of other popular neurospeak clichés.

To avoid such oversimplification, it is better to view the multiple facets of executive functions as constituting a collection of "co-conductors," each responsible for a separate aspect of the overall production of the orchestra, but each responsible for its separate contribution to the whole while working—ideally—in a highly collaborative manner with the others to ensure the desired outcomes.

Stuss and Alexander (2000) have very effectively addressed this complex nature of executive functions and their neural substrate correlates in the human frontal lobes:

"We emphasize that there are specific processes related to different brain regions within the frontal lobes. There is no frontal homunculus, no unitary executive function. Rather, there are distinct processes that do converge on a general concept of control functions. The idea of a supervisory system is very applicable, if the emphasis is on a system constructed of multiple parts. From a clinical viewpoint, the position that there is no homunculus suggests that there is not a single frontal lobe syndrome with point-to-point correspondence to a homunculus." (p. 291)

With the perspective presented by Stuss and Alexander in mind, executive functions can be thought of as a set of directive capacities that are responsible for a person's ability to engage in purposeful, organized, strategic, self-regulated, self-aware, goal-directed processing of perceptions, emotions, thoughts, and actions. As a collection of directive capacities, executive functions cue the use of other mental capacities such as reasoning, language, and visuospatial representation, and memory resources.

While various researchers and clinicians have identified and described the functions of many different directive capacities, and integrated some of these into partial models of executive function control (e.g., Barkley, 1997, 2005; Denckla, 1996; Freeman, 2000; Miller, 2001; Taylor, 1998; Stuss & Alexander, 2000), there has not been much in the way of efforts to provide a comprehensive model of executive functions until recently (McCloskey, Perkins, & VanDivner, 2009).

This section briefly discusses the overarching theoretical model of executive function control processes developed by the lead author (McCloskey, 2004) that will be used to guide the discussion of executive functions and emotional disturbance in the remainder of this chapter. The holarchical, developmental model visually represented in Figures 4-2 and 4-3 builds on the conceptual and empirical work from multiple disciplines (Barkley, 1997, 2005; Denkla, 1996; Freeman, 2000; Miller, 2001; Stuss & Alexander, 2000; Wilber, 1977, 1979, 1995, 2000). This model is proposed as a way to help conceptualize and organize the interplay of the multiple executive capacities that involve frontal lobe neural functions. As shown in Figures 4-2 and 4-3, the model is structured into five holarchically organized tiers representing different levels of specificity of executive function capacity. Each tier is discussed briefly below.

FIGURE 4-2
Co-Conductors in a Holarchical Model of Executive Functions

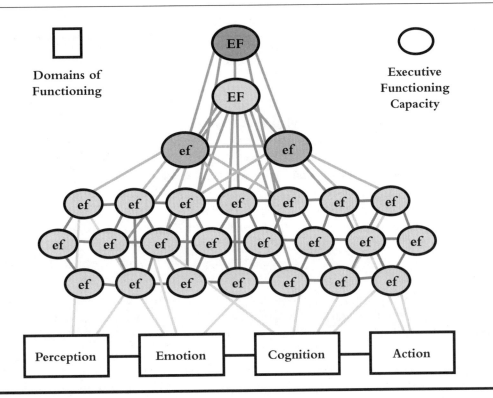

FIGURE 4-3
The McCloskey Model of Executive Functions

V. Trans-self Integration
Sense of source, Cosmic consciousness

IV. Self Generation
Mind-Body Integration, Sense of Spirit

III. Self Control

Self Realization
Self Awareness
Self Analysis

Self Determination
Goal Generation
Long-Term Foresight/Planning

II. Self Control: Self Regulation

Perceive	Modulate	Sustain	Interrupt Stop
Focus Select	Inhibit	Hold	Foresee Plan (Short-Term)
Initiate	Gauge	Manipulate	Shift Flexible
Organize	Generate	Associate	Balance
Store	Retrieve	Pace	Executive (Behavior Syntax)
Time	Monitor Check	Correct	

Sensation/Perception Cognition Emotion Action

I. Self Control: Self Activation
Awaken, Attend

Self-activation

The *self-activation* tier involves the process of awakening or "ramping up" of executive function capacities after a prolonged nonconscious state such as deep sleep (Balkin et al., 2002). The less than optimal state of perceiving, feeling, thinking and acting that is usually associated with the process of self-activation is referred to as sleep inertia. Although sleep inertia typically resolves within the first 5 to 20 minutes after awakening, it can take much longer for some persons to reach a state in which they feel "awake" and ready to function. The longer this state of sleep inertia persists, the more likely it is that the less than optimal direction of daily functioning will be viewed as problematic. While executive function control at this lowest tier typically is mediated nonconsciously in the form of a gradual return to wakefulness, some forms of habituated cueing can be activated to assist with the transition to a full waking state, or to reduce the effects of prolonged sleep inertia.

Self-regulation

The *self-regulation* tier is comprised of a large number of executive functions capacities responsible for cueing, directing and coordinating functioning within the domains of sensation and perception, emotion, cognition, and action. Whether consciously or nonconsciously activated, the neural networks engaged in the use of these executive functions are responsible for the self-regulated aspects of control that get us through our day-to-day routines. The model of executive functions presented here explicitly identifies 23 self-regulation capacities that are used to varying degrees and in varying combinations to direct and cue our perceiving, thinking, feeling, and acting most of the time. Table 4-2 provides a brief description of each of the 23 self-regulation executive functions.

TABLE 4-2
Brief Definitions of the 23 Self Regulation Executive Function Capacities

Perceive—The Perceive function cues the use of sensory and perception processes to take information in from the external environment or "inner awareness" to tune into perceptions, emotions, thoughts, or actions as they are occurring.

Initiate—The Initiate function cues the initial engagement of perceiving, feeling, thinking, or acting.

Modulate/Effort—The Modulate function cues the regulation of the amount and intensity of mental energy invested in perceiving, feeling, thinking, and acting.

Gauge—The Gauge function cues identification of the demands (perceptual, emotional, mental, physical) of a task or situation and cues the activation of the perceptions, emotions, thoughts, or actions needed to effectively engage the task or situation.

Focus/Select—The Focus/Select function cues the direction of attention to the most relevant specifics (perceptions, emotions, thoughts, and/or actions) of a given environment, situation, or content while downgrading or ignoring the less relevant elements.

Sustain—The Sustain function cues sustained engagement of the processes involved in perceiving, feeling, thinking, or acting.

Stop/Interrupt—The Stop/Interrupt function cues the sudden, immediate discontinuation of perceiving, feeling, thinking, or acting.

Inhibit—the Inhibit function cues resistance to, or suppression of, urges to perceive, feel, think, or act on first impulse.

Flexible/Shift—the Flexible/Shift function cues a change of focus or alteration of perceptions, emotions, thoughts or actions in reaction to what is occurring in the internal or external environments.

Hold—the Hold function cues activation of the necessary cognitive processes required to maintain information in working memory and continues cueing these processes until the information is manipulated, stored, or acted on as desired.

Manipulate—the Manipulate function cues the use of working memory or other cognitive processes for the manipulation of perceptions, feelings, thoughts, or actions that are being held in mind or being accessed in the environment.

Organize—the Organize function cues the use of routines for sorting, sequencing, or otherwise arranging perceptions, feelings, thoughts, and/or actions, to enhance or improve the efficiency of experience, learning, or performance.

Foresee/Plan (Short-term)—cues the anticipation of conditions or events in the very near future, such as the consequences of one's own actions, or cues the engagement of the capacities required to identify a series of perception, feelings, thoughts, and/or actions, and the likely or desired outcome that would result from carrying them out in the very near future.

Generate—the Generate function cues the realization that a novel solution is required for the current problem, and cues the activation of the resources needed to carry out the required novel problem-solving.
Associate—the Associate function cues the realization that associations need to be made between the current problem situation and past problem situations and cues the activation of the resources needed to carry out the required associative problem-solving routines.

Balance—the Balance function cues the regulation of the trade-off between opposing processes or states (e.g., pattern vs detail; speed vs accuracy; humor vs seriousness) to enhance or improve experiencing, learning, or performing..

Store—the Store function cues the movement of information about perceptions, feelings, thoughts and actions from the mental processing environment of the present moment into "storage" for possible retrieval at a later time.

Retrieve—the Retrieve function cues the activation of cognitive processes responsible for finding and retrieving previously stored information about perceptions, feelings, thoughts and actions. The more specific the demands or constraints placed on the retrieval task, the greater the requirements for precision of retrieval cues.

Pace—the Pace function cues the awareness of, and the regulation of, the rate at which perception, emotion, cognition, and action are experienced or performed.

Time—the Time function cues the monitoring of the passage of time (e.g., cueing the engagement of the mental functions that enable a person to have an internal sense of how long they have been working) or cues the use of time estimation routines (e.g., cueing the engagement of mental functions that enable a person to have an internal sense of how long something will take to complete, or how much time is still left in a specific period of time).

Execute—the Execute function cues the orchestrating of the proper syntax of a series of perceptions, feelings, thoughts, and/or actions, especially in cases where automated routines are being accessed or are initially being developed.

Monitor—the Monitor function cues the activation of appropriate routines for checking the accuracy of perceptions, emotions, thoughts, or actions.

Correct—the Correct function cues the use of appropriate routines for correcting errors of perception, emotion, thought, or action based on feedback from internal or external sources.

The 23 self-regulation executive functions are distinct from one another and also are not uniform in their degree of control capacity; a person's effectiveness with each one can vary greatly. A person might be very effective at using the focus/select cue to direct attention to a stimulus, but be very ineffective in the use of the sustain cue when it would be advantageous to maintain attention to the stimulus for an extended period of time.

The diagrams in Figure 4-2 and 4-3 represent the various domains of function with separate boxes for perception, emotion, cognition and action. The distinct separation of the four domains is meant to highlight the fact that self-regulation, in the context of these domains, is not uniform, but rather is highly dissociable; the extent of control exerted by a specific self-regulation capacity can vary greatly within each of the four domains (and within multiple subdomains within each domain). A person may be able to exert effective executive function control in one domain (or sub-domain) but not in another. The result is a profile of self-regulation executive functions that vary individually by domain of function. For example, a person might be very effective in the inhibition of perceptions, emotions, and thoughts, but not actions, while at the same time being very effective with flexibly shifting perceptions and actions but not emotions and thoughts. Moreover, a profile could be generated indicating the degree of effective use of each of the 23 self-regulation capacities within each of the four domains (and within multiple subdomains) of perception, emotion, cognition, and action.

Although the concept of domains of function helps to clarify the nature of many executive control difficulties, it cannot explain all of the variation that is observed in the daily use of self-regulation executive functions. An additional concept, referred to here as Arenas of Involvement, represents a critical dimension for increasing understanding of the full range of variability in engagement of self-regulation capacities. *Arenas of Involvement* acknowledge that executive control can vary greatly depending on whether the person is attempting to exert control of self in relation to their own internal states (i.e., control within the Intrapersonal Arena); control of self in relation to others (i.e., control of self within the Interpersonal Arena); control of self in relation to the environment around them (i.e., control of self in the Environment Arena); or control of self in relation to engagement of the culturally-derived symbol systems used to process and share information (i.e., control of self in the Symbol System Arena). A brief description of the nature of executive function involvement in each arena is provided below.

The intrapersonal arena. The intrapersonal arena refers to a child's use of self-regulation capacities to cue and direct perceptions, feelings, thoughts, and actions in relation to themselves, i.e. how the child perceives him/herself, feels about him/herself, thinks about him/herself, and acts toward him/herself. The effective use of executive functions in the intrapersonal arena enables a person to avoid addictions, self-mutilation, and other self-destructive habits and patterns of perception, emotion, thought, and action that can reduce the quality of life. Conversely, the effective use of executive functions in this arena drives the daily engagement of purposeful, positive behavior, a positive sense of self, self-control and self-discipline.

The interpersonal arena. The interpersonal arena refers to a child's use of self-regulation capacities to cue and direct perceptions, feelings, thoughts, and actions in relation to the perceptions, feelings, thoughts, and actions of other persons. The overall result of the effective engagement of executive functions in this arena is the ability to interact appropriately with others as circumstances dictate; to appreciate and deal with the perspectives of others; to generate a theory of mind that enables a person to understand, infer, and predict the motivations, needs, and desires of others; and to find ways to balance the needs of the self with the needs of others.

The environment arena. The environment arena refers to a child's use of self-regulation capacities to cue and direct perceptions, feelings, thoughts, and actions in relation to their surroundings. The overall result of the effective engagement of executive functions in relation to environmental surroundings is the ability to carry out daily functioning in a manner that utilizes natural and man-made resources to produce the desired outcomes and to avoid "accidents" by anticipating the impact and consequences of one's own actions in, and on, the physical environment.

The symbol system arena. The symbol system arena refers to cueing and regulating a person's perceptions, feelings, thoughts, and actions relating to the processing of information transmitted through symbol systems. The overall result of the effective engagement of executive functions in relation to symbol systems is the ability to effectively direct self-expression through reading, writing, and speaking one or more languages; to direct work with the conceptual bases of mathematics, science and other formal systems of thought and knowledge; to direct the use of symbol system communication tools such as computers; and to enhance learning and performance in all of these areas.

As is the case with domains of functioning, Arenas of Involvement are dissociable; a child may experience executive control difficulties in one or more of the arenas while demonstrating very effective control in one of more of the other arenas. Also, dissociation of specific self-regulation capacities also can be evidenced within a single arena of involvement and for a single domain of functioning. For example, a child might effectively use some self-regulation capacities to direct cognition domains within the Interpersonal Arena while being very poor with the use of other self-regulation capacities to direct cognition within that same arena. Figure 4-4 demonstrates the full dissociable nature of executive functions, illustrating a possible combination of executive function strengths and weaknesses for a single self-regulation function (Inhibit) within a single domain of functioning (Emotion) across the four arenas of involvement. The diagram shows a child that is able to direct the inhibition of emotion very effectively dealing with others and adequately when dealing with feelings about him or herself, but who has great difficulty directing the inhibition of emotions relative to academic work (e.g., feelings of frustration with reading, writing, and math) as well as with situations that arise in the environment (e.g., feelings of anger about a broken toy).

FIGURE 4-4
Examples of Variations in Cueing Capacity Strength for the Inhibit Self Regulation Executive Function for the Perception Domain of Functioning Within the Four Arenas of Involvement

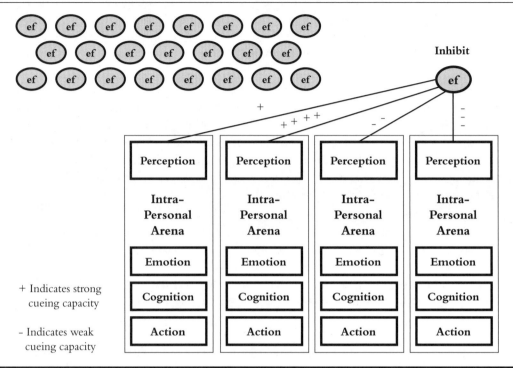

Self-Realization and Self-Determination

The third tier of the model specifies self-control processes that extend beyond basic self-regulation. Two subdomains are distinguished at this level: self-realization and self-determination as described below.

Self-realization. Although it may seem otherwise, being able to direct, cue and coordinate the use of self-regulation executive capacities does not require a person to be consciously aware of what they are doing or how they are doing it. It is possible for a person with only a vague sense of moment to moment occurrences to nonconsciously make use of executive function capacities to self-regulate perceptions, feelings, thoughts and actions without engaging in any form of self-realization. Engagement of specific neural circuits involving portions of the frontal lobes is necessary for a person to be aware of themselves in a reflective manner and/or to become aware of the self-regulation capacities they may or may not be utilizing nonconsciously, and/or to take conscious control of the use of self-regulation capacities (Johnson, Baxter, Wilder, Pipe, et al., 2002; Morin, 2004). Frequent and sustained use of these neural pathways leads to greater self-control in relation to the increasing sense of self and an increasing awareness of the capacity for conscious self-regulation of the 23 self-regulation capacities that are typically accessed nonconsciously.

Engagement of self-awareness functions for prolonged periods of time supports the emergence of the capacity for self-analysis. Self-analysis involves sustained and enhanced reflection on one's control, or lack of control, of perceptions, emotions, thoughts, and actions, thereby yielding judgments about the adequacy or inadequacy of one's functioning in these domains. Over time, these reflections and judgments can lead to a more nuanced idea of "who I am," i.e., a sense of self as defined by "what and how well I perceive, feel, think, and do." This increased awareness of self may or may not be accompanied by an increased capacity for becoming aware of how others react to "what I perceive, feel, think and do." Increased reflection from the point of view of the self in relation to others has the potential for adding multiple dimensions to the process of defining "who I am." Through greater exertion of executive control at this tier, self-analysis can be used to develop a sense of personal strengths and weaknesses and how they impact daily functioning.

Self-determination. To act in a self-determined manner requires the engagement of specific neural circuits involving portions of the frontal lobes that enable goal setting and long-term planning (Luria, 1980). Engagement of these circuits makes it possible for a person to develop foresight and to formulate plans that extend beyond the brief time span of the short-term-oriented executive function of Plan that was identified as one of the 23 specific self-regulation capacities listed in Table 4-2.

The executive function capacity for self-determination enables the development of personal goals as well as the capacity for evaluation of the adequacy of self-regulation efforts—and the perceptions, emotions, cognitions and actions they direct—in moving toward or achieving self-selected goals and/or carrying out self-selected plans. Long-term goal development reflects an appreciation of the potential benefits of ignoring or refusing lesser rewards while working toward greater rewards likely to be derived at a much later point in time. The self-determination capacities that generate, maintain, monitor and revise long-term goals and plans must compete with more immediately experienced short-term desires and urges that can lead a person away from the long-term vision. The better developed one's self-determination capacities, the more likely it is that they will be engaged to effectively suppress desires for immediate gratification that are likely to be incompatible with the self-determined long-term goals.

The relationship between higher-tier Self-Determination and lower-tier Self-Regulation executive functions is similar to that between higher-tier Self-Realization and lower-tier Self-Regulation functions in the sense that no self-determined goal or self-desired outcome is necessary for effective lower-tier daily self-regulation to occur. Consequently, it is possible for a person to engage in day-to-day functioning without ever engaging in any act of self-determination beyond responding to fleeting inner urges or external demands imposed in the immediate moment.

While not required for day-to-day self-regulation, self-determination functions can greatly influence how lower-tier self-regulation functions are used to direct day-to-day perceptions, feelings, thoughts and actions in a manner to that of Self-Realization capacities. A person can live their entire life with no personal goals or plans, following instead the goals and plans set out for them by others, and in a manner that leads to great success through the effective application of lower-tier self-regulation executive capacities. Conversely, self-determination executive functions can be greatly enhanced by the effective use of lower-tier self-regulation capacities. It is not necessary, however, to have developed all 23 self-regulation executive functions to a high degree in order to successfully execute a self-determined plan or achieve a self-determined goal. The better developed a person's self-determination capacities, the more likely they are to find ways to make the most of the self-regulation functions they might possess—whether great or few. When self-determination capacities are poorly developed, any self-regulation deficiencies that may be present are likely to create obstacles to the carrying out of long-term plans, many of which may be ill-advised or poorly formulated to begin with due to the poor self-determination capacities. Even in the case of exceptional self-determination capacities, it is possible that the number and severity of self-regulation deficits is so great as to make it highly unlikely that the person will ever achieve the goals they envision or carry out the long-term plans that they are capable of devising unless the lower-tier self-regulation functions of others are enlisted to aid in the process.

Self-Generation

The previous tiers have addressed how we exert control over the perceptions, feelings, thoughts and actions of our daily lives and develop capacities for extending control beyond the immediate moment through self-reflection, foresight, goal-setting and planning. At some point in life however, a person may begin to pose questions about the nature of human existence and the meaning of life— questions that seem to be taken for granted by many people. The propensity to pose these questions represents the next tier of executive control identified in this model as the Self-Generation capacity. Pursuit of the answers to Self-Generation questions often leads to spiritual paths, the development of a personal philosophy of life, or the need for self-generation of a set of principles that are used to guide perceptions, thoughts, feelings and actions. On a collective level, engagement of this executive capacity cues and directs efforts to grapple with the most difficult aspects of the codes of ethical behavior, systems of justice, and modes of communal existence. There are a number of compelling reasons for including the Self-Generation tier in a comprehensive model of executive functions. Research in the neurosciences clearly shows that posing self-generative questions and grappling with ethical dilemmas co-occur with the activation of neural circuits heavily dependent on specific areas of the frontal lobes (Greene, Nystrom, Engell, Darley, & Cohen, 2004; Greene, Sommerville, Nystrom, Darley, & Cohen, 2001; Newberg, Alavi, Baime, Mozley, et al., 1997; Newberg, Alavi, Baime, Pourdehnad, et al., 2001; Newberg, D'Aquili, & Rause, 2001; Vaitl, Gruzelier, Jamieson, Lehmann, et al., 2005). The engagement of Self-Generation capacities can have a tremendous impact on how a person engages all of the lower tier executive functions and can serve as a higher source of intentional direction for many, even all, aspects of a person's life.

Like all other self-control executive functions, Self-Generation capacities can emerge independently of the other executive function capacities and utilized to some degree regardless of the state of development of the other executive capacities. While a person might spend a great deal of time developing a highly refined philosophy of life intended to guide daily functioning, they might be unable to effectively use self-regulation capacities in a manner that enables the realization of long-term goals or consistent behavior patterns associated with the overarching philosophy. In a similar manner, while a person might be greatly invested in understanding the meaning of life or determining ethical principles for guiding human behavior, they might be lacking in self-awareness of personal strengths and weaknesses related to self-regulation and emotional functioning. Conversely, a person might direct his or her life in a coherent and meaningful manner with great personal insight and great success in achieving personal goals through well developed self-regulation functions, and yet never question the meaning of it all, i.e., never activating neural circuits that are involved with engaging self-generation capacities.

Trans-Self Integration

Beyond posing questions about the meaning or purpose of life and existence lies the capacity to realize at a much deeper level the truth of the assertion that human existence is merely an illusion—

a state created by our physical brains. With this insight often comes a desire to see past the illusion of self to get a glimpse of what might lie beyond the limits of human perception. These efforts to experience "ultimate truth" or the "reality beyond reality" often lead to what some mystic traditions refer to as unity consciousness.

As in the case of Self-Generation, there are compelling reasons for including Trans-Self Integration in a comprehensive model of executive functions. Neuroscience research has indicated that the ability to experience the phenomenological state of egolessness or unity consciousness is directly linked to neural circuits heavily dependent on areas of the frontal lobes (Benson, Malhotra, Goldman, Jacobs, & Hopkins, 1990; Newberg, D'Aquili, & Rause, 2001; Herzog, Lele, Kuwert, Langen, et al., 1990; Newberg, Alavi, Baime, Moxley, et al, 1997; Newberg, Alavi, Baime, et al, 2001). As with Self-Generation capacities, the experiencing of a trans-self integral experience can have a tremendous impact on how a person engages all of the executive capacities at lower tiers, as it can serve as an ultimate source of intentional direction for many, or possibly all, aspects of the person's life. In dealings with children and young adults, the likelihood of encountering an individual who has advanced their frontal lobe activation to this degree is quite low but certainly not impossible.

Executive Function Tiers and Emotional Disturbance
As noted in the earlier discussion of human information processing, it is important to recognize that the self-control capacities of all tiers within the model will be influenced to some degree by a child's prevailing emotional state. Negative mood states associated with depression, anxiety, and other emotional disturbances can have a great impact on how a child perceives, feels, thinks, and acts, thereby influencing the child's capacity for self-control at all levels. Negative-mood-influenced processing can make it much harder for a child to self-activate in order to get out of bed in the morning; much more difficult to effectively self-regulate daily functioning; much less likely to ignore, or to obsess over, self-awareness and self-reflection; much more likely to arrive at negative or nihilistic answers to self-generation questions; and much more likely to lose oneself completely in the process of contemplating the state of "no one" or "no thing." Without proper treatment, executive function difficulties at one or more tiers that cause, or are the result of, emotional disturbance will have a negative impact on the quality of life of the child, family members, friends, teachers and others with whom the child may come in contact.

Development of Executive Functions
The multi-tier framework of the Executive Function Model presented here represents a developmental holarchy (Koestler, 1964, Wilber, 1995) rather than a hierarchy. The tier structure is not meant to represent a hierarchical progression of neuropsychological development where one level must be completed before advancement to the next level is possible and where all movement progresses in a single direction from one tier to the next higher tier. Rather, the tier structure represents a developmental holarchy that is a more fluid, dynamic model where no rigid constraints are placed on the processes of movement among tiers. In a holarchical arrangement, a child can progress from a lower tier to a higher tier without mastering all of the capacities represented at the lower tier. In addition, development at a lower tier can continue to progress after the child has moved on to develop capacities at one or more higher tiers; a child can develop highly refined capabilities at higher tiers while still demonstrating substantial deficiencies in functioning at one or more lower tiers. Within such a holarchical structure, increased self-awareness and self-analysis can inform and enhance the use of self-regulation capacities, but they are not required for the use of self-regulation

capacities. Conversely, development of a sense of self and an awareness of what a person can, and cannot, do can be greatly enhanced by the effective use of self-regulation executive functions, but is not necessarily dependent on the effective development of any or all of the 23 specified self-regulation executive functions for its emergence of refinement; it is possible for a child to be very deficient in the use of one or more self-regulation executive functions and be painfully self-aware of these deficiencies. It must be acknowledged, however, that some self-regulation deficiencies can make it extremely difficult to develop self-awareness or to engage in self-reflection. For example, a person who is exceptionally poor at inhibiting impulsive perceiving, feeling, thinking, or acting, and who cannot sustain attention to perceptions, feelings, thoughts, or actions for more than a few seconds likely will find it extremely difficult to engage in any prolonged form of self reflection or self analysis.

Development of any executive control capacity is a slow, gradual process. Intra-individual variation is an important consideration in the development of executive functions. For a specific child, the development of self-regulation executive functions does not necessarily progress at the same rate. One capacity can be more or less developed than any other at any given point in time. Even when one or more self-regulation capacities are well developed in a child, this does not guarantee that all other self-regulation functions will be developed to a similar level for that child. For any given child, the specific profile of executive function strengths and weaknesses can show large variations.

Although most individuals show growth in executive function capacities over time, the developmental trajectory (i.e., the rate of growth over time) of each executive function capacity is variable from person to person. At the same age, different individuals can vary considerably in their level of development of any specific executive capacity. Using the *Inhibit* cue as an example, some 2-year olds are relatively proficient at using the *Inhibit* cue across different arenas of involvement, while other 2-year olds are nearly incapable of doing so in any of the arenas. In developmental continuum terms, some 2-year olds are able to demonstrate use of the *Inhibit* cue as effectively as the average 4-year-old, yet other 2-year olds may have a capacity for use of the *Inhibit* cue that more closely resembles that of the average 1-year-old. Such inter-individual variation is observable at all ages for all executive capacities.

Executive Functions and Emotional Disturbance

The need for a comprehensive model of executive functions when discussing emotional disturbance might be apparent to readers at this point. While problems that are classified as emotional disturbance typically have an emotional component to them, most, if not all, emotional disturbances also involve perceptions, thoughts and actions. In the case of clinical depression, for example, while emotions are negatively impacted, perceptions, thoughts, and actions as well as physiological well-being also can be negatively impacted. The discussion of executive control in relation to emotional disturbance, therefore, needs to address a person's capacity for self direction in relation to all four domains, not just the domain of emotion.

Additionally, as Ken Wilber (1977, 1979, 2000) has elucidated so effectively, emotional disturbances can be focused at different tiers of development of consciousness, thereby necessitating an understanding of the different levels of self-control as well as different approaches to treatment based on the level of consciousness and self-control at which the problems are occurring. For individuals who are accessing neural networks related to self-generation capacities, depression is likely to be experienced in a very different way than for a person who has not ventured beyond the level of self-realization and self-determination; likewise, a person whose perceptions, emotions, thoughts and actions are completely focused exclusively on day-to-day functioning will experience depression very differently than persons who are engaged in the development of self-control at the higher tiers.

Considering the multiple components of the comprehensive model presented here, it is suggested that executive function difficulties related to emotional disturbance can vary by:

1. The specific executive functions affected
2. The developmental tiers of self-control affected
3. The domains of functioning affected
4. The arenas of involvement affected
5. The chronological age of the child

Although a term such as *executive dysfunction* could be offered to describe difficulties with self-control of functioning related to emotional disturbance, such a diagnostic category currently does not appear in any widely agreed upon mental health diagnostic schema. The most recent version of the DSM (DSM-IV-TR, 2000), for example, offers no category such as Executive Dysfunction, Dysexecutive Function Syndrome, or any such category label that represents executive function difficulties although such a diagnostic category likely is being considered for inclusion in future editions of the DSM.

Although there could be some merit in the development of a separate diagnostic category for executive function-based emotional disorders, the greatest challenge to the creation of such a category is the fact that the diagnostic criteria of most of the existing clinical conditions specified in the DSM include difficulties with one or more of the executive function capacities specified in the comprehensive model presented here. In many ways, the DSM can be thought of as a *behavioral user's guide to all the things that can go wrong with the frontal lobes.* A number of researchers and clinicians share such a perspective (Arnsten & Robbins, 2002; Goldberg, 2001; Lichter & Cummings, 2001; Miller & Cummings, 2006; Pennington, Bennetto, McAleer, & Roberts, 1996; Stuss & Knight, 2002), especially when frontal lobe functions are operationally defined as all executive capacities in combination with working memory processes. Arnsten and Robbins (2002) succinctly articulated such a view, stating:

> "Deficits in PFC [prefrontal cortex, aka frontal lobe] function are evident in every neuropsychiatric disorder (indeed, the term "psychiatric problem" seems synonymous with PFC dysfunction). Abilities carried out by the PFC can also become impaired in so-called "normal" individuals under conditions of uncontrollable stress, fatigue, and with advancing age." (p. 51; text within [ ] added for clarification).

It is important not to interpret statements such as this as implying that executive function difficulties are the sole cause of all emotional disorders listed in DSM. Additionally, it cannot be inferred that frontal lobe dysfunction is only found in these disorders, as some individuals will present with executive difficulties that impact emotional functioning in the absence of a specific diagnosis. What is very clear, however, is that executive function difficulties are associated in some way with all emotional disorders as well as with nearly every other type of mental disorder catalogued by the DSM.

Take as an example, Generalized Anxiety Disorder (GAD). GAD involves neural circuits routed through a number of subcortical structures classified as part of the limbic system, with the paths of these circuits also passing through various areas of the frontal lobes (Krain, Hefton, Pine, Ernst, et al., 2006; Krain, Gotiner, Hefton, Ernst, et al., 2008; Stein, Westenberg, Herman, Liebowitz, 2002). While dysfunction of the portion of the neural circuit traveling through the limbic system might be the root cause of a person's anxiety disorder, the disruption of the subcortical portion of the circuit can impact frontal lobe functions including those involved with self-control. This results in disruption in the effective use of one or more executive function capacities while the person is in a state of anxiety. Concomitantly, the list of diagnostic criteria for GAD includes difficulty *controlling* worry, difficulty concentrating, irritability, and sleep disturbance. All of these symptoms are likely to involve difficulties with the engagement of various executive function capacities as a result of the experiencing of anxiety (e.g., difficulties with cueing the *inhibition* of, or *interruption* of, anxious feelings and thoughts about self, others, the environment, and/or symbol systems; difficulties with cueing the *focusing* and *sustaining* of attention to important perceptions, feelings, thoughts and actions related to self, others, the environment, and/or symbol systems; difficulties with cueing the *modulation* of perceptions, emotions, thoughts and/or actions in relation to self, others, the environment and/or symbol systems).

Of great importance to the understanding of the relationship between executive functions and emotional disturbance are the concepts of *domains of functioning* and *arenas of involvement*. Consider the example of the behavioral difficulties experienced by children diagnosed with Oppositional Defiant Disorder (ODD) or Conduct Disorder (CD) in contrast with Autistic Spectrum Disorders (ASDs). ODD and CD clearly reflect multiple self-regulation and self-realization deficits; an important feature of both diagnoses is that the deficits be manifested in a specific arena of involvement—the *Interpersonal Arena*—but can affect all four domains of functioning: perception, emotion, cognition, action. The control difficulties of children with accurate diagnoses of CD or ODD will be evident in the difficulties these children have with the cueing and direction of perceptions, emotions, thoughts and/or actions when they are interacting with others. These difficulties are often accompanied by difficulties with self-analysis and self-awareness. Although difficulties may be exhibited at other tiers or in other arenas, they do not constitute the core difficulties represented in the DSM criteria for these disorders.

The Autism Spectrum Disorders (ASDs) also include executive function deficiencies related to the *interpersonal arena*. Although the executive function difficulties of those with ASDs also typically involve all four of the domains of *perception, emotion, cognition,* and *action*, the difficulties with self-analysis and self awareness associated with ASDs are much more severe and accompanied by severe deficits in self-determination.

Just as DSM diagnostic categories focused on emotional functioning problems may involve difficulties with the effective cueing and directing of perception, thought and action as well as emotion, diagnostic categories that focus on cognitive functioning problems may involve difficulties with the effective cueing and directing of emotions as well as perceptions, thoughts and actions. Take for example the case of ADHD. The DSM criteria for ADHD clearly specify executive function difficulties involving the self-regulation cues of Inhibit, Modulate, Focus/Select, and Sustain. Although the wording of the diagnostic criteria emphasizes the effect of executive function difficulties on perception, cognition and action, these difficulties also can be observed in relation to emotional functioning for some children.

Considering the discussion above, it is our perspective that simply including a new diagnostic category for executive function difficulties in future revisions of the DSM will not sufficiently address the central role that executive function difficulties play in most of the existing DSM diagnostic categories. The new edition of the DSM, therefore, would have greater clinical utility if it were to incorporate a new axis that could be used to identify specific executive function difficulties experienced by an individual in addition to any clinical diagnoses that might be assigned. The inclusion of an Executive Function Axis in the next edition of the DSM would encourage careful delineation of the specific executive function difficulties exhibited by a child, regardless of the specific diagnostic label's assigned, and would avoid the rather onerous and limiting task of creating a taxonomy of executive function difficulties thought to be associated with each of the existing DSM categories.

Following this line of reasoning, the pervasiveness of executive function difficulties of one type or another associated with most of the emotional and mental disorders experienced by children makes clear the need to carefully identify the specific nature of the executive function difficulties exhibited by each child so that appropriate interventions can be identified and implemented. Assessment and intervention efforts related to the executive function difficulties associated with diagnosed emotional disorders will be the central focus of the remaining sections of this chapter.

This discussion of emotional disturbance and executive functions in this section has focused on the DSM criteria used in clinical settings. In school settings, emotional disturbance is defined in a much more general manner. Jacobs and Decker (2007) have provided the federal definition along with some commentary on the criteria there in:

> "i. The term means a condition exhibiting one or more of the following characteristics over a long period of time and to a marked degree that adversely affects a child's educational performance:
>
> A. An inability to learn that cannot be explained by intellectual, sensory, or health factors.
> B. An inability to build or maintain satisfactory interpersonal relationships with peers and teachers.
> C. Inappropriate types of behavior or feelings under normal circumstances.
> D. A general pervasive mood of unhappiness or depression.
> E. A tendency to develop physical symptoms associated with personal or school problems.
> ii. The term includes schizophrenia. The term does not apply to children who are socially maladjusted, unless it is determined that they have an emotional disturbance. (34 C.F.R. § 300.8) . . ." (p.135)

In clarifying their discussion of this definition, Jacobs and Decker (2007) noted that an *inability to learn* (criteria A) refers to children who are so disturbed that they cannot learn. Children with emotional difficulties that interfere with their academic performance would not meet this criteria. *Inability to build satisfactory interpersonal relationships* (criteria B) refers to children who are not able to enter into or maintain relationships with peers or teachers. This excludes children who simply associate with undesirable peer groups or who are unpopular. *Inappropriate types of behavior* (criteria C) refers to behaviors that are odd, bizarre, or unusual, not simply those that are disturbing teachers or classmates. *Pervasive moods of unhappiness or depression* (criteria D) must be observable. Finally, criteria E refers to fears or physical symptoms that are marked and displayed over a significant period of time. (p. 135).

Upon initial review, the attempt to describe all forms of emotional disturbance in a single categorical statement may seem problematic. In actuality, such a broadly worded definition opens the door for shifting the focus away from the diagnostic label or labels that may be assigned to a child and onto the specific emotional and behavioral difficulties being experienced by the child and the intervention efforts that will be used to address these difficulties.

Assessment of Emotional Disturbance From an Executive Function Perspective

Although a number of formal assessments of executive function are currently available (e.g., the *Wisconsin Card Sorting Test* [WCST; Heaton et al., 1993], the *Rey Complex Figure* [RCF; Meyers & Meyers, 1995], the NEPSY-II [Korkman, Kirk, & Kemp 2007], the *Delis-Kaplan Executive Functions Scale* [D-KEFS; Delis et al., 2001], the *Behavioral Assessment of Dysexecutive Syndrome in Children* [BADS-C; Wilson et al., 1996]), their focus and scope are very limited in that they all:

1. make use of a norm-referenced, individually-administered format that directly assesses the child's use of executive function capacities to direct task performance;
2. focus assessment on executive function direction of information processing capacities only within the domains of perception, cognition, and action; and
3. focus only on the use of executive function capacities in the symbol system arena.

The fact that current assessments targeting executive functions have focused almost exclusively on the role of executive functions in cueing and directing perception, cognition, and action only within the symbol system arena, makes these tasks of limited value in the assessment of executive function difficulties associated with emotional disturbance. While this focus on the Symbol System arena is a good fit with the direct formal methods that dominate assessment practices in clinics and schools, it greatly limits the clinical utility of these measures when evaluating the executive function capacities of a child exhibiting emotional difficulties.

The expectation of some professionals that executive function measures focused on perception, cognition, and action within the symbol system arena could be appropriate for effective identification of executive function strengths and weaknesses of children exhibiting emotional difficulties has in fact produced somewhat misleading findings in the research literature. In the case of conduct disorder, for example, several research studies consistently have shown abnormal patterns of frontal lobe neural activation in conduct disordered persons (Avila, Cuenca, Felix, & Pacet, 2004; Baving, Laucht, & Schmidt, 2000; Blake & Grafman, 2004; Clark, Prior, & Kinsella, 2000; Demekis, 2003; Oosterlaan, Scheres, & Sergeant, 2005). Psychometrically-oriented research studies using symbol system measures of executive functions, however, have failed to consistently identify specific executive function deficits in the performance of individuals diagnosed with conduct disorder (Demekis, 2003; Feifer & Rattan, 2007; Oosterlaan, Scheres, & Sergeant, 2005; Avila, Cuenca, Felix, & Pacet, 2004).

This lack of consistent findings has much to do with the use of symbol system assessments to identify executive function deficits in children and adults whose primary executive function problems were not manifested in their engagement with symbol systems, but rather in their functioning in the interpersonal arena. In keeping with the comprehensive model of executive functions presented earlier, there is no good reason to expect that individuals with self-regulation executive difficulties in the interpersonal arena would also manifest such difficulties in the intrapersonal, symbol system, or the environment arenas. A lack of such expectancy, however, does not preclude the possibility of additional executive function difficulties in other arenas manifesting as co-morbidities for these individuals. In fact, the research studies cited here reported executive function deficits with symbol system content for some of the persons in these studies along with reported intrapersonal executive function deficits that led to the diagnosis of conduct disorder in the first place (Avila, Cuenca, Felix, & Pacet, 2004).

Behavior rating scales offer an alternative to the individually-administered direct assessment techniques mentioned above. Rating scales offer parents, teachers, and the child the opportunity to offer their perceptions of the frequency of occurrence of behaviors thought to be indicative of executive function difficulties. Currently, the Behavior Rating Inventory of Executive Functions (BRIEF) is the only series of executive function rating scales that are appropriate for use with school-age children (BRIEF, Gioia et al., 1996; BRIEF-Preschool Version, Gioia et al., 1996; BRIEF-Self-Report Version, Guy, Isquith, & Gioia, 1996). These scales provide scores that reflect parent and teacher report and child self-report ratings of the frequency of a child's ineffective use of executive capacities based on personal recollections of behavior during the most recent six month period.

The BRIEF rating scales offer norm-referenced documentation of parent, teacher, and self appraisals of executive function deficits as they manifest within 8 eight self-regulation sub-categories: Inhibit, Shift, Emotional Control, Working Memory, Plan/Organize, Organization of Materials, and Monitor. Items are dispersed across the four arenas of involvement, but not in a systematic manner resulting in uneven arena coverage within each executive function sub-category. A set of norm-referenced rating scales is currently in development that will enable clinicians to more effectively identify specific executive function strengths and weaknesses within the context of the comprehensive model of executive functions introduced earlier in this chapter (*McCloskey Executive Functions Scales* [MEFS], 2009).

Given the complex nature of executive functions, it should not be surprising to readers that assessment of these capacities requires a multidimensional approach. As indicated earlier in this section, competent assessment of executive function capacities requires a comprehensive framework. Such a framework extends assessment beyond the narrow focus of individually-administered norm-referenced measures and parent, teacher, and child rating scales to ensure that a multifaceted perspective is taken when assessing a child's use, or disuse, of executive function capacities.

In cases where emotional disturbance is suspected or clearly present, the purpose of the assessment of executive functions is not to determine whether a diagnostic label of executive dysfunction should also be assigned to the child. Rather, assessment should clearly identify the specific executive function problems being demonstrated by the child, specify any existing executive function strengths, and identify potential interventions that can draw on strengths while addressing specific problems and concerns. Discussing assessment of executive functions in this manner is consistent with the previously offered theoretical perspective. The purpose for the elaboration of 23 distinct self-regulation executive functions shown in Table 4-2 is to define self-regulation in enough detail to enable the development of intervention plans that can help children overcome their emotional difficulties by obtaining greater access to these important self-regulation capacities.

Use of executive function capacities can vary greatly depending on domains of functioning and arenas of involvement. The multiplicity of factors that can contribute to variability in the demonstration of executive functions necessitates a multidimensional, multimethod approach to assessment. The assessment methods employed should attempt to determine the effectiveness of executive functions for the cueing and directing of perceiving, feeling, thinking, and acting in relation to self (interpersonal), others (interpersonal), the world (environmental) and the cultural tools of communication (symbol system).

Different approaches and methods, including individually-administered norm-referenced tests and behavior rating scales, can be applied in the assessment of executive function capacities. Table 4-3 provides general descriptions of these assessment approaches and methods along with a matrix that lists specific examples of assessment tools based on the various combinations of method and approach. Although each method x approach category can provide valuable information about a child's use of executive function capacities, collection of data only from a single category cannot produce an adequate assessment of executive functions. Ideally, a truly multidimensional assessment would gather data using one or more techniques in each category. Resources are available to assist clinicians with informal assessment approaches such as the Executive Function Structured Interview (EFSI), the Executive Function Structured Interview for Children (EFSI-C), the Executive Function Student Observation Form (EFSO), the Executive Function Classroom Observation Form (EFCO) available in McCloskey, Perkins, & VanDivner (2009).

TABLE 4-3
Approaches and Methods for the Assessment of Executive Functions

Assessment Approach	Assessment Method	
	Formal Methods use of interviews, records reviews, and observation and interpretation methods that employ predetermined comparison standards	**Informal Methods** use of interviews, records reviews, and observation and interpretation methods that do not employ predetermined comparison standards
Indirect Approaches collection of information using methods that do not involve direct contact with the child	Behavior Rating Scales Parent Behavior Rating Scales Teacher Behavior Rating Scales Self-Report Rating Scales (e.g., BRIEF, MEFS)	Interviews of Parents, Teachers (EFSO) Review of School Records Process-Oriented Interpretation of Parent and Teacher Ratings and Self Reports
Direct Approaches collection of information through direct interaction with, or observation of, the child or his or her work products	Individually-Administered Standardized Tests (e.g., D-KEFS, NEPSY-II, WCST, BADS-C)	Child Interview Systematic and Nonsystematic Behavioral Observations (EFSO and EFCO) Process-Oriented Interpretation of Standardized Test Administration and Classroom Work Samples

Functional Behavior Assessment and Executive Functions

Current best practices advocate the use of functional behavior assessment (FBA) techniques to plan interventions for students exhibiting emotional and behavior disorders (O'Neill, Horner, Albin, Sprague, et al., 1997; Knoster & McCurdy, 2002; Rutherford, Quinn, & Mathur, 2007). FBA techniques identify setting events and antecedents that trigger problem behaviors, describe the negative behaviors to be changed, specify positive replacement behaviors, and document the consequences that exist for both positive and negative behaviors. Once these elements are identified, interventions can be planned that alter the event settings and antecedents thereby avoiding the occurrence of problem behaviors. The FBA approach emphasizes the external structuring of consequences to encourage the occurrence of positive behaviors and avoidance of negative ones. It is important to recognize that FBA approaches emphasize interventions wherein external control is employed to obtain and maintain acceptable behaviors. FBA experts have been clear on this point (O'Neill et al., 1997):

> "Behavior support plans are designed to alter patterns of problem behavior. The process by which this is done, however, involves change in the behavior of family, teachers, staff, or managers in various settings. Plans of behavior support define what we will do differently. It is the change in our behavior that will result in improved behavior of the focus person." (p. 65).

FBAs and the resulting behavior support plans attempt to affect change in as efficient and effective a manner as possible and as quickly as possible. FBAs do not explain or provide an understanding of the root causes of why the setting events or antecedents cause the behaviors that lead to consequences that are as undesirable from the perspective of the child as they are from the perspective of parents and teachers. Nor do they focus on intervention strategies for enabling the child to transition from external control conditions to internal self-regulation. While strict behaviorists might argue that it is unnecessary to speculate about causal issues, parents, teachers, and students themselves seek such explanations in their efforts to make sense of things.

The limitations of traditional FBA can be overcome when a functional assessment incorporates knowledge of executive functions and their development, making it clear that the origin of the problem behaviors lie in brain functions over which the child does not have conscious control. Understanding the nature of brain function helps parents, teachers, and students realize that the behaviors being exhibited by children with emotional and behavior problems are not conscious, premeditated acts, defiantly carried out in the presence of a clear awareness of the consequences they will produce. Rather, all involved can be better served by realizing that the problem behaviors are the result of inadequate activation of executive function capacities necessary for regulating perceptions, feelings, thoughts and actions. The underlying message to all needs to be that the problem behaviors associated with emotional and behavioral disorders are not simply a matter of personal choice or a means to achieve desired consequences. Acknowledgement of the neuropsychological origins of the problem behaviors provides parents, teachers, and school staff with a conceptual framework that promotes understanding and compassion in efforts to help the child rather than engendering negative insinuations about the child's character and moral fiber.

Informed by knowledge of executive functions, the functional assessment model can be revised as in Figure 4-5. In this model, executive function difficulties resulting in ineffective regulation of perceptions, feelings, thoughts and actions lead to undesired behavioral responses to setting events and/or antecedents thereby producing undesired consequences. Whereas traditional FBA is viewed as an A–B–C (Antecedents-Behaviors-Consequences) model, executive-driven functional assessment can be viewed as an A-[EF/PETA]-B-C (Antecedents-[Executive Function Miscueing of Perceptions, Emotions, Thoughts, Actions]-Behavior-Consequences) model. Clinicians interested in exploring executive function assessment issues and methods in more detail can consult *Assessment and Intervention for Executive Function Difficulties* (McCloskey, Perkins, & VanDivner, 2009) and *Essentials of Executive Function Assessment* (McCloskey, 2009).

FIGURE 4-5
An Executive-Driven Functional Assessment Model

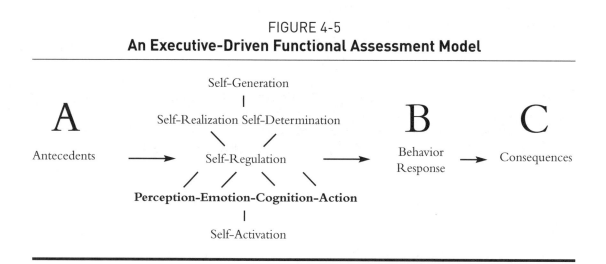

Interventions for Executive Function Difficulties Associated With Emotional Disturbance

In the last section, we discussed how a comprehensive model of executive functions can be used to guide assessment of executive function difficulties. In a similar manner, the model can be used to guide intervention efforts with children exhibiting executive function difficulties associated with emotional disturbance. The multiple tiers conception of self-control can help to identify the nature of the executive function difficulties being exhibited. The tiers of the model also offer a general guideline for the kind of intervention techniques that are most likely to produce the desired results given the nature of the executive function difficulties that arise at each of the levels. What follows is a brief discussion of interventions related to each tier of the model.

Self-Activation

Many children experience difficulties with Self-Activation capacities, finding it hard to awake for school in the morning. Such self-activation difficulties can be greatly exacerbated by emotional problems. Mood disorders and sleep disturbances almost always have some impact on self-activation capacities (DSM, 2000). Given the pervasiveness of these difficulties, it is surprising that few intervention techniques have been proposed or researched (Millman, 2005). Although undocumented to this date, the lead author of this chapter has had some success with stimulus-response conditioning to produce the engagement of automated, non-consciously controlled behavior routines immediately upon awakening. Such routines enable the child to start the process of awakening without allowing the "noise" (e.g., centers responsible for "telling" you to go back to sleep when the alarm clock sounds) produced by areas of the brain not directly associated with the awakening of frontal lobe self-regulation capacities.

Self-Regulation

Children who have relatively little in the way of Self-Regulation executive function capacities to engage in internally-generated self-control appear to respond best to strict behavior modification techniques (O'Neill et. al, 1997). In such cases, external control methods based on behavior modification techniques are most likely to produce the desired behavior changes. It must be acknowledged, however, that such external control techniques do not make the child aware of the specifics of the external control regimen, nor do they make the child aware of the executive function capacities needed to self-regulate and self-correct the difficulties. These techniques manage the child's behavior without the child being aware of the overall plan for management. Additionally, there usually are no self-regulation goals in the behavior plans when such techniques are being applied; the goals tend to be focused on the desired behavior changes irrespective of the means by which those behavior changes are obtained.

In some cases where emotional disturbance results from, or causes, an extreme lack of self-regulation capacity, pharmacological interventions are used to treat the symptoms of the emotional disturbance. It is important to recognize that pharmacological intervention is itself a form of external control imposed on the child who at that point in time is demonstrating little or no capacity for self-regulation. As an extreme form of external control, pharmacological intervention shares many of the limitations of strict behavior modification techniques. The use of medication to deal with emotional problems does not necessarily make the child more aware of their self-regulation difficulties associated with their emotional problems and does not teach the child how to increase the self-regulation capacities needed to begin to take control of the emotional problems that led to the use of medication in the first place. It is important to note that while pharmacological interventions are not specifically designed to increase a child's awareness of self-regulation capacities needed to correct undesired perceptions, emotions, thoughts and actions, they sometimes have exactly this effect on a child. The lead author of this chapter has observed cases in which the use of stimulant medication for only a brief period of time "awakened" the child to what the mental state of increased self-regulation of attention "feels like," thereby increasing the child's capacity to self-regulate in order to produce the same mental state without the use of the medication. In such cases, it appears that the use of medication dramatically increases personal awareness of what self-regulation capacities are and nonconsciously provides the child with the tools necessary to increase self-regulation at will.

Self-Realization and Self-Determination

School-age children whose Self-Regulation capacities are less well-developed than same-age peers, but who nonetheless are able to demonstrate some degree of internally generated self-control, are more likely to benefit from interventions that focus on making the child aware of their self-regulation and emotional control difficulties and teach them strategies for increasing self-regulation of perceptions, emotions, thoughts and actions. Therapeutic techniques that emphasize this approach include problem-solving models such as Myrna Shure's I Can Problem Solve program (Shure, 1992) and cognitive behavior therapy (Friedburg & McClure, 2002); Mennuti & Christner, 2006). Although these techniques can be very effective with a wide age range of children, the younger the child, the more likely it is that frequent prompts will need to be provided to cue the child to make use of the problem-solving strategies that they have learned.

Older school-age children who are developing greater Self-Realization and Self-Determination capacities may be good candidates for use of a mindfulness-based cognitive behavior therapy (CBT) approach to increasing self-regulation capacities (Kelly, 2005; Segal, Williams, & Teasdale, 2002; Singh et al., 2007; Wasserstein & Lynn, 2001). Like traditional CBT, mindfulness-based CBT techniques teach strategies for increasing self-control of perceptions, emotions, thoughts and actions. In addition to teaching these strategies, mindfulness-based approaches also focus on increasing self-awareness, i.e., increasing the child's capacity to think about and reflect on their own perceptions, emotions, thoughts and actions. Children who are able to increase such self-awareness capacities are more likely to be able to monitor their perceptions, emotions, thoughts and actions on a daily basis and realize when they need to make use of the CBT problem-solving routines they have been taught. The crucial component of this approach is increasing the child's capacity to become self-aware of their own perceptions, emotions, thoughts and actions, and aware of the strategies that can be used to alter unwanted perceptions, emotions, thoughts and actions. It is important to note the parallel between this therapeutic approach and the "spontaneous" creation of awareness observed in some children who use medication for a very short period of time. In both situations, the key element is increased awareness of what self-regulation is and how to engage it effectively. In the case of exposure to medication, conscious awareness is unintentionally generated from a nonconscious source; in the case of mindfulness-based CBT, conscious awareness is intentionally generated from a conscious source—the therapeutic regimen.

Self-Generation

Relatively older children have the potential to start to activate neural networks accessing the Self-Generation capacities that enable them to ask and ponder the larger questions about the meaning of existence. When a child begins to engage these self-generation capacities to produce such questions, the answers that they begin to generate can be greatly influenced by their emotional states. As noted earlier, negative mood states associated with depression, anxiety, and other emotional disturbances can have a great impact on how a child perceives, feels, thinks, and acts. Negative-mood-influenced nihilistic answers to self-generation questions can lead to a child believing that there really is no purpose or meaning to life, thereby releasing them of the need to be concerned for their own well-being or the well-being of others, sometimes with harmful repercussions that can be as extreme as suicide and murder. In some cases, the use of medications may be necessary to effectively treat severe depression, anxiety and other mood disorders. Additionally, therapeutic techniques focused at the Self-Regulation and Self-Awareness levels may be used to externally control behaviors related to mood disorders or help the child learn to gain greater capacity for internal self-regulation. It is important to note, however, that pharmacologic and other therapeutic techniques aimed at dealing with lower levels of self-control will not address directly any associated problems at the self-generation level. At some point, a dialogue will need to be established to address the questions emanating from the child's accessing of self-generation capacities. While some choose to turn to religious doctrines to engage this dialogue, there are secular therapeutic approaches that can be modified for use with children, such as Victor Frankl's *Logotherapy* (Frankl, 1984, 1988; Pattakos, 2008) and Roberto Assagioli's *Psychosynthesis* (Assagioli, 1976).

Trans-Self-Integration

Although there are few school-age children who push their frontal lobes to this farthest reach of self-regulation capacity, the possibility of encountering the rare case certainly exists. Traditionally considered a spiritual path involving deep meditation, mainstream scientific exploration of therapeutic techniques in this area is lacking. Well-adjusted persons seeking this path often learn techniques such as transcendental meditation from a spiritual guide. The quest for trans-self integration, however, represents only the positive route of this deepest of frontal lobe neural network activation patterns. When an individual experiencing emotional disturbance attempts to access this path, the negative routes traversed can lead to disastrous results, as evidenced by the aberrant behavior and, in the worst of cases, the individual and mass suicides, of cult members who "see the light" in the teachings of charlatans and misguided gurus. Individuals at greatest risk of negative outcomes of trans-self integration activation are those suffering from Dissociative Disorders and possibly Adjustment Disorders. Although these disorders are typically not encountered or diagnosed until adulthood, clinicians should be aware of the warning signs that could indicate precursors to, or the presence of, such disorders.

Conceptualizing Intervention Efforts

When the role of executive function difficulties in problem behaviors exhibited by a child with emotional disorders is acknowledged, the ultimate goal of any intervention should be to increase the child's capacity for internally directed self-regulation. From a neuropsychological perspective, intervention efforts can be grounded in three key concepts:

1. Executive function difficulties associated with emotional disturbance are the result of sub optimal brain function.
2. Sub-optimal brain function can be altered through intervention.
3. Intervention can activate the use of intact brain function.

When dealing with a child with emotional problems, it is important for parents, teachers and others not to attribute the child's difficulties to character flaws or consciously chosen states of mind, such as laziness, lack of motivation, apathy, irresponsibility, or stubbornness. Rather, it must be understood that the observed behaviors are rooted in brain functions that most likely are not a matter of conscious choice, and that the child most likely does not possess the skill to immediately alter these brain functions. Resisting the urge, therefore, to blame the child for choosing their emotional state while recognizing the executive function difficulties demonstrated by the child should lead to clearer statements indicating perceptions, emotions, thoughts or actions that can be changed from negative to positive through intervention.

In the absence of clear evidence that a child was born with severe brain damage or has suffered a severe traumatic brain injury since birth, it is best to approach intervention efforts thinking that a child possesses the neural capacity to alter current brain function states. An optimistic stance enables the clinician to develop an intervention plan with the goal of positive change eventually guided by internal self-regulation rather than simply managing a sub-optimal negative state of functioning through external control. If the executive difficulties are the result of disuse of existing neural capacities, then an intervention plan focused on positive behavior change goals will be based on teaching the child how to activate these neural networks, either consciously or nonconsciously, to achieve the positive goals.

Although the ultimate goal of intervention should be to increase the child's capacity for internally directed self-regulation, we recognize that selection of a specific intervention approach will be dictated by the conditions of the present moment rather than the ultimate future goal.

Conceptualizing interventions, therefore, will likely require the need to balance applications of external control with the generation of internal control. In many instances, intervention will need to start with the external control techniques and gradually move to teaching strategies that will lead to greater internal self-regulation. Effective interventions require careful monitoring of progress during the intervention period to enable the practitioner, parents, and school staff to make the necessary adjustments for moving from external control to internal self-regulation.

Factors Impacting Intervention Efforts

It is critical to acknowledge that the effectiveness of any intervention attempt will depend greatly on the executive function capacities of the practitioner and those most closely associated with the child—especially family members. Through modeling and coaching, these individuals play an essential role in helping the child develop greater self-regulation capacities. Practitioners that rely heavily on the use of rewards and punishment assume, either implicitly or explicitly, that the child already possesses the executive function capacities required to achieve the desired goals, and that failure to achieve goals is a matter of conscious choice, a lack of desire or motivation, or both. It is important to acknowledge that rewards and punishments can be very effective elements of an intervention, as they serve as a source of consistent, frequent feedback about the effectiveness of performance, thereby enabling engagement of the proper level of self-regulation required for achieving goals. Unfortunately, the executive function difficulties of many children make it difficult, and in some cases nearly impossible, for them to sufficiently or consistently cue themselves to achieve goals, even when motivation to do so is high. If rewards or punishment are to be used as part of an intervention program, progress should be monitored closely as modifications may be required. When such programs are not working, it may be necessary to eliminate the rewards and punishments and redesign the intervention rather than concluding that the child is not capable or responding positively to intervention efforts.

Clinicians also need to keep in mind that externally administered rewards and punishments are still forms of external control. As such, they do not teach children to become consciously aware of, reflect on, and internalize self-regulation capacities. While rewards and/or punishments can play a role in the external control phase of an intervention program, the ultimate goal of internally-directed self-regulation will require the child to be consciously engaged in learning how to develop and use executive function capacities. When using external control techniques, it is important to keep in mind that, given the fact that the executive function difficulties children experience are not of their own choosing, some leeway is needed when applying consequences for behaviors that violate rules. Although we do not advocate that all rules be suspended when dealing with children with executive function difficulties, we do believe that the consequences should be of a reasonable nature and not overly harsh. This point is especially relevant when considering Manifest Determination issues and outcomes related to the behavior of students with diagnosed emotional disturbances and associated executive function difficulties.

The limited space of a chapter does not really allow for a detailed discussion of the development of executive functions over time as well as the impact of maturational delays on the self-regulation difficulties of children experiencing emotional disturbance. Delays in the development of executive functions in disorders such as ADHD have been found to correspond with delays in the development of frontal cortex (Kelly, DiMartino, Uddin, Shehzad, et al., in press; Rubia, 2007; Shaw, Eckstrand, Blumenthal, Lerch, et al., 2007). Delays in maturation certainly can have a slowing effect on progress toward intervention goals; on the positive side, however, passage of time in itself can be a powerful intervention mechanism when the problem is simply one of maturational delay. When children are faced with overly aggressive expectations for brain maturation, time may be the key ingredient needed for achieving the desired levels of self-direction. Recognition of the effects of maturation on the development of self-regulation capacities does not mean adopting a wait and see approach to dealing with executive function-related emotional problems. Rather, energy and effort should be put into developing and implementing interventions in the present moment that attempt to produce positive changes in the suspected areas of difficulty. By engaging intervention efforts, practitioners and parents are providing the child with knowledge of self-regulation processes that can be tapped when increases in neural development make increased use of executive capacities possible. Even in the case of children with more substantial developmental delays, it is possible that the most effective element of the intervention program is that more time has passed, thereby allowing the child's brain to begin to put into practice the self-regulation routines that were being taught in the intervention.

Consideration of executive function maturation naturally leads to a discussion of grade retention of students demonstrating executive function difficulties related to emotional disturbance. The research completed to date (Jimerson, 2001) suggests that grade retention is beneficial only for a small subset of students. Although the characteristics of this subset are not well established, we strongly suspect that

Intervention Planning and Implementation

For the purposes of planning and implementation interventions that address executive function difficulties, the following general guidelines are offered:

1. Provide the child with as rich an "executive function environment" as possible, i.e., parents and teachers can model the effective use of executive function; an absence of positive modeling and/or the presence of negative modeling likely will reduce the effectiveness of intervention efforts.
2. Initiate efforts with the perspective that the executive function difficulties the child exhibits are the result of nonconscious disuse of existing self-regulation capacities that can be made conscious to the child and activated through intervention efforts.
3. Build the child's awareness of executive functions, most specifically, those needed to achieve desired intervention goals.
4. Teach the child how and when to activate the use of the needed executive capacities with the ultimate goal being internalization of the self-regulation routines needed for effective functioning.
5. In the case of lack of responsiveness to internalized self-regulation intervention, or when assessment data indicate the need, develop and apply, as needed, interventions involving external control. Monitor the use of external control interventions closely to determine when to begin the gradual transition to intervention efforts focused on developing internal self-control.
6. Maintain and model attitudes of hope, perseverance, and patience throughout all intervention efforts.
7. Maintain, and foster in others, reasonable expectations for behavior change and the application of sensible and reasonable consequences for unacceptable behavior that may arise before or during intervention efforts.

slow maturation of multiple executive functions is among their key characteristic features. In the absence of clear evidence regarding exactly which students would benefit from retention however, we believe that retention cannot be supported as a general intervention practice for students exhibiting executive function difficulties associated with emotional problems.

Intervention Strategies

Detailed discussion of specific intervention strategies for executive function difficulties is beyond the scope of this chapter. Readers interested in learning more about specific intervention strategies are referred to sources such as McCloskey, Perkins, & VanDivner (2009), Greene (2001) and Greene & Albon (2006), Shure (1992) Friedburg & McClure, (2002), and Mennuti & Christner (2006). As indicated throughout this section, intervention strategies can be ordered along a continuum from strict external control to self-directed efforts at internalizing greater self-regulation capacity through self-help efforts. A general outline of the kinds of strategies most frequently researched and applied for the purposes of increasing either internal or external control are shown in Table 4-4.

TABLE 4-4
Internally and Externally Oriented General Intervention Strategies for Executive Function Difficulties

Intervention Strategies for Developing Internal Control.
> Increasing Awareness
> Modeling Appropriate Use of Executive Functions
> Teaching Specific Executive Functions as Skills
Routines
> Using Verbal Mediation
> Using Verbal or Nonverbal Labeling
> Teaching the Use of Internal Feedback
> Establishing Self-Administered Rewards
Intervention Strategies for Maintaining External Control.
> Pharmacological Treatment
> Structuring the Environment
> Structuring Time
> Externalizing Cues for Effective Processing
> Providing Feedback
> Providing Rewards
> Aligning External Demands With Internal Desires

The Executive Function-Driven Model of Functional Assessment and Intervention

Earlier in this chapter, we discussed the concept of executive-driven functional assessments and how incorporating an understanding of executive function difficulties and the intervention approaches for dealing with these difficulties can help to expand behavioral support plans beyond their current limited emphasis on external control substitutes. The expanded EF-driven A-[EF/PETA]-B-C model that was presented for assessment can also be used to ensure that interventions focus not just on behaviors, but on the perceptions, feelings, thoughts and actions that lead to the behaviors and the executive control capacities that cue and direct all of these. The EF-driven A-[EF/PETA]-B-C assessment/intervention model increases awareness of the brain-based nature of the difficulties that the child is experiencing, which in turn is more likely to lead to a more sympathetic approach to dealing with the resulting behavior difficulties.

It is important to note that the EF-driven model of FBA focuses on self-regulation rather than maintenance of external control as the ultimate goal of intervention efforts. We fully acknowledge, however, the fact that in school settings, the executive function difficulties of children experiencing emotional problems range from very mild to very severe, necessitating a full range of intervention options. These options vary along a continuum from maintaining strict external control through a carefully monitored behavior support plan within a very restricted educational setting at one end of the continuum, to increasing internal control through increased awareness and skill-building at the other end of the continuum. Whatever the source and expression of emotional problems, whatever the desired outcomes, and whatever path intervention efforts take, we believe that adopting an EF-driven A-[EF/PETA]-B-C assessment/intervention model will ensure sensible and humane treatment of the child along the way.

SUMMARY

This chapter presented an overarching model of executive functions that offered a framework for discussing the role of executive functions in cueing and directing perceptions, emotions, cognitions, and actions, and how executive functions relate to emotional disturbance. Also discussed was the diagnosis of emotional disturbance from the perspective of executive function involvement, methods for assessing the executive function deficits of children experiencing emotional disturbance, a functional behavior assessment model that incorporates the concept of executive functions, and intervention strategies that address the executive function deficits of children demonstrating emotional disturbances at various levels within the McCloskey Model of Executive Functions.

REFERENCES

Adolphs, R. & Damasio, A. R. (2000). Neurobiology of emotion at a systems level. In J.C. Borod (Ed.), *The neuropsychology of emotion* (pp. 194-213). New York: Oxford University Press.

American Psychiatric Association (2000). *Diagnostic and statistical manual of mental Disorders, Fourth Edition, Text Revision (DSM-IV-TR)*. Washington, D.C.: Author.

Arnsten, A. F. T., & Robbins, T. W. (2002). Neurochemical modulation of prefrontal cortical functioning in humans and animals. In D. T. Stuss & R. T. Knight (Eds.), *Principles of frontal lobe function* (pp. 31-50). New York: Oxford University Press.

Assagioli, R. (1976). *Psychosynthesis: A manual of principles and techniques.* New York: Penguin Books.

Avila, C., Cuenca, I., Felix, V., & Parcet, M. (2004). Measuring impulsivity in school-aged boys and examining its relationship with ADHD and ODD ratings. *Journal of Abnormal Child Psychology, 32(3)*, 295-305.

Balkin, T. J., Braun, A. R., Wesensten, N. J., Jeffries, K., Varga, M., Baldwin, P., et al. (2002). *The process of awakening: A PET study of regional brain activity patterns mediating the re-establishment of alertness and consciousness.* Brain, *125(10)*, 2308-2319.

Barkley, R. A. (1997, 2005). *ADHD and the nature of self-control.* New York: Guilford Press.

Baving, L., Laucht, M., Schmidt, M. H. (1999). Atypical frontal brain activation in ADHD: preschool and elementary school boys and girls. *Journal of the American Academy of Child and Adolescent Psychiatry, 38(11)*, 1363-1371.

Benson, H., Malhotra, M. S., Goldman, R. F., Jacobs, G. D., & Hopkins, P. J. (1990). Three case reports of the metabolic and electroencephalographic changes during advanced Buddhist meditation techniques. *Behavioral Medicine, 16*, 90-95.

Blake, P., & Grafman, J. (2004). The neurobiology of aggression. *The Lancet, 364*, 12-14.

Brown, T. E. (2006). Executive Functions and Attention Deficit Hyperactivity Disorder: Implications of two conflicting views. *International Journal of Disability, Development and Education, 53 (1)*, 35-46.

Clark, C., Prior, M., & Kinsella, G. (2000). Do executive function deficits differentiate between adolescents with ADHD and oppositional defiant/conduct disorder? A neuropsychological study using the six elements tests and Hayling sentence completion test. *Journal of Abnormal Psychology, 28*, 403-415.

Damasio, A. (1999). *The feeling of what happens: Body and emotion in the making of consciousness.* San Diego, CA: Harcourt Inc.

Delis, D. C., Kaplan, E., & Kramer, J. H. (2001). *Delis-Kaplan executive function system.* San Antonio, TX: The Psychological Corporation.

Demakis, G. J. (2003). A meta-analytic review of the sensitivity of the Wisconsin Card Sorting Test to frontal and lateralized frontal brain damage. *Neuropsychology, 17(2)*, 255-264.

Denckla, M. B. (1996). A theory and model of executive function: A neuropsychological perspective. In G. R. Lyon & N. A. Krasnegor (Eds.), *Attention, memory, and executive function* (pp. 263-278). Baltimore: Paul H. Brookes.

Feifer, S. G., & Rattan, G. (2007). Executive functioning skills in male students with social-emotional disorders. *International Journal of Neurosciences, 117(11)*, 1565-1577.

Frankl, V. E. (1988). *The will to meaning: Foundations and applications of Logotherapy.* New York: Plume.

Frankl, V. E. (1984). *Man's search for meaning.* New York: Washington Square Press.

Freeman, W. J. (2000). *How brains make up their minds.* New York: Columbia University Press.

Friedburg, R. D., & McClure, J. M. (2002). *Clinical practice of cognitive therapy with children and adolescents: The nuts and bolts.* New York: Guilford Press.

Gioia, G. A., Isquith, P. K., & Guy, S. C. (2001). Assessment of executive functions in children with neurological impairment. In R. Simeonsson & S. L. Rosenthal (Eds.), *Psychological and developmental assessment: Children with disabilities and chronic conditions* (pp. 317-356). New York: Guilford Press.

Gioia, G. A., Andrews Epsy, K., & Isquith, P. K. (1996). *Behavior Rating Inventory of Executive Function – Preschool Version: Professional Manual.* Lutz, FL: Psychological Assessment Resources, Inc.

Gioia, G. A., Isquith, P. K., Guy, S. C., & Kenworthy, L. (1996). *Behavior Rating Inventory of Executive Function: Professional Manual.* Lutz, FL: Psychological Assessment Resources, Inc.

Goldberg, E. (2001). *The executive brain: Frontal lobes and the civilized mind.* New York: Oxford University Press.

Greene, J. D., Nystrom, L. E., Engell, A. D., Darley, J. M., & Cohen, J. D. (2004). The neural bases of cognitive conflict and control in moral judgment. *Neuron, 44(2)*, 389-400.

Greene, J. D., Sommerville, R. B., Nystrom, L. E., Darley, J. M., & Cohen, J. D. (2001). An fMRI investigation of emotional engagement in moral judgment. *Science, 293*, 2105-2108.

Greene, R. W. (2001). *The explosive child: A new approach for understanding and parenting easily frustrated, chronically inflexible children.* New York: Perennial.

Greene, R. W., & Albon, J. S. (2006). *Treating explosive kids: The collaborative problem-solving approach.* New York: Guilford Press.

Guy, S. C., Isquith, P. K., & Gioia, G. A. (1996). *Behavior Rating Inventory of Executive Function – Self-Report Version: Professional manual.* Lutz, FL: Psychological Assessment Resources, Inc.

Hardcastle, V. G. (1999). It's O.K. to be complicated: The case of emotion. In R. Nunez & W. J. Freeman (Eds.), *Reclaiming cognition: The primacy of action, intention and emotion* (pp. 237-250). Thorverton, UK: Imprint Academic.

Heaton, R. K., Chelune, G. J., Talley, J. L., Kay, G. G., & Curtiss, G. (1993). *Wisconsin Card Sorting Test.* Lutz, FL: Psychological Assessment Resources, Inc.

Herzog, H., Lele, V. R., Kuwert, T., Langen, K. J., Kops, E. R., & Feinendegen, L. E. (1990). Changed pattern of regional glucose metabolism during Yoga meditative relaxation. *Neuropsychobiology, 23*, 182-187.

Jacobs, S. & Decker, D. D. (2007). Ethical-legal issues in the education of pupils with disabilities under IDEA. In S. Jacob and T. S. Hartshorne (Eds.), *Ethics and law for school psychologists, 5th Edition* (pp. 117-174). Hoboken, NJ: John Wiley & Sons

Jimerson, S. R. (2001). Meta-analysis of grade retention research: Implications for practice in the 21st Century. *School Psychology Review, 30*, 3, 420-437.

Johnson, S. C., Baxter, L. C., Wilder, L. S., Pipe, J. G., Heiserman, J. E., & Prigatano, G. P. (2002). Neural correlates of self-reflection. *Brain, 125(8)*, 1808-1814.

Kelly, A. M. C., DiMartino, A., Uddin, L. Q., Shehzad, Z., Gee, D. G., Reiss, P.T., Marguilies, D. S., Castellanos, F. X., & Milham, M. P. (In press). Development of anterior cingulated functional connectivity from late childhood to early adulthood. *Cerebral Cortex*, doi: 10.1093/cercor/bhn117.

Knoster, T. P., & McCurdy, B. (2002). Best practices in functional behavioral assessment for designing individualized student programs. In A. Thomas & J. Grimes (Eds.), *Best practices in school psychology IV* (pp.1007-1028). Bethesda, MD: National Association of School Psychologists.

Koestler, A. (1964). *The act of creation.* New York: Dell.

Korkman, M., Kirk, U. & Kemp, S. (2007). *NEPSY—Second edition.* San Antonio, TX: Harcourt Assessment.

Krain, A. L, Hefton, S., Ernst, M., Pine, D. S., Ernst, M., et al. (2006). A functional magnetic resonance imaging examination of developmental differences in the neural correlates of uncertainty and decision-making. *Journal of Child Psychology & Psychiatry, 47(10)*, 1023-1030.

Krain, A. L, Gotimer, K., Hefton, S., Ernst, M., Castellanos, F. X., Pine, D. S., et al. (2008). A functional magnetic resonance imaging investigation of uncertainty in adolescents with anxiety disorders. *Biological Psychiatry, 63(6)*, 563-568.

Ledoux, J. (1996). *The emotional brain: The mysterious underpinnings of emotional life.* New York: Simon & Schuster.

Lichter, D. G., & Cummings, J. L. (Eds.). (2001). *Frontal-subcortical circuits in psychiatric and neurological disorders.* New York: Guilford Press.

Luria, A. R. (1980). *Higher cortical functions in man* (2nd Ed.). New York: Basic Books.

McCloskey, G. (2004). Unpublished manuscript.

McCloskey, G. (2009). *McCloskey Executive Functions Scales.* Unpublished manuscript.

McCloskey, G., Perkins, L. A., & VanDivner, B. R. (2009). *Assessment and intervention for executive function difficulties.* New York: Routledge Press.

Mennutti, R. B., Freeman, A., & Christner, R. W. (Eds.) (2006). *Cognitive-behavioral interventions in educational settings.* New York: Routledge.

Meyers, J. E., & Meyers, K. R. (1995). *Rey complex figure test and recognition trial.* San Antonio, TX: Harcourt Assessment.

Miller, E. K. (2001). An integrative theory of prefrontal cortex function. *Annual Review of Neuroscience, 24*, 167-202.

Miller, B. L. & Cummings, J. L. (Eds.) (2006). *The human frontal lobes, second edition: Functions and disorders (science and practice of neuropsychology series).* New York: Guilford Press.

Millman, R. P. (2005). Excessive sleepiness in adolescents and young adults: causes, consequences, and treatment strategies. *Pediatrics, 115*, 1774-1786.

Morin, A. (2004). A neurocognitive and socioecological model of self-awareness. *Genetic, Social, and General Psychology Monographs, 130(3)*, 197-223.

Newberg, A., Alavi, A., Baime, M., Mozley, P. D., & D'Aquili, E. (1997). The measurement of cerebral blood flow during the complex task of meditation using HMPAO-SPECT imaging. *Journal of Nuclear Medicine, 38*, 95.

Newberg, A. B., Alavi, A, Baime, M., Pourdehnad, M., Santanna, J., & d'Aquili, E. G. (2001) The measurement of regional cerebral blood flow during the complex cognitive task of meditation: A preliminary SPECT study. *Psychiatry Research: Neuroimaging* 106: 113-122.

Newberg, A., d'Aquili, E. & Rause, V. (2001). *Why God won't go away: Brain science and the biology of belief.* New York: Ballantine Books.

O'Neill, R. E., Horner, R. H., Albin, R. W., Sprague, J.R., Storey, K., & Newton, J.S. (1997). *Functional assessment and program development for problem behavior: A practical handbook.* (2nd Ed.) Pacific Grove, CA: Brooks/Cole Publishing Co.

Oosterlaan, J., Scheres, A., & Sergeant, J. A. (2005). Which executive functioning deficits are associated with AD/HD, ODD/CD, and comorbid AD/HD+ODD/CD? *Journal of Abnormal Child Psychology, 33*, 69-85.

Panskepp, J. (1998). *Affective neuroscience: The foundations of human and animal emotions.* New York: Oxford University Press.

Pattakos, A. (2008). *Prisoners of our thoughts: Victor Frankl's principles of discovering meaning in life and work.* New York: Berrett Koehler Publishers.

Pennington, B. F., Bennetto, L., McAleer, O., & Roberts, R. J. (1996). Executive functions and working memory: theoretical and measurement issues. In G. R. Lyon & N. A. Krasnegor (Eds.), *Attention, memory, and executive function* (pp. 327-348). Baltimore: Paul H. Brookes.

Rubia, K. (2007). Neuroanatomic evidence for the maturational delay hypothesis of ADHD. *Proceedings of the National Academy of Sciences, 104*(50), 19663-19664.

Rutherford, R. B., Quinn, M. M., Mather, S. R. (2007). *Handbook of research in emotional and behavioral disorders.* New York: Guilford Press.

Segal, Z. V., Williams, J. M. G., & Teasdale, J. D. (2002). *Mindfulness-based cognitive therapy for depression: a new approach to preventing relapse.* New York: Guilford Press.

Shaw, P., Eckstrand, K., Sharp, W., Blumenthal, J., Lerch, J. P., Greenstein, D., Clasen, L., Evans, A., Gieddi, J., & Rapoport, J .L. (2007). Attention-deficit/hyperactivity disorder is characterized by a delay in cortical maturation. *Proceedings of the National Academy of Sciences, 104*(49), 19649-19654.

Shure, M. B. (1992). *Cognitive problem solving program.* Champaign, IL: Research Press.

Siegel, D. J. (2007). *The mindful brain: Reflections and attunement in the cultivation of well-being.* New York: W. W. Norton & Co.

Singh, N. N., Lancioni, G. E., Winton, A. S., Adkins, A. D., Wahler, A. G., Sabaawi, M., & Singh, J. (2007). Individuals with mental illness can control their aggressive behavior through mindfulness training. *Behavior Modification, 31*(3), 313-328.

Stein, D. S., Westenberg, H. G. M., Liebowitz, M .R. (2002). Social anxiety disorder and generalized anxiety disorder: Serotonergic and dopaminergic neurocircuitry. *Journal of Clinical Psychiatry, 63*(6), 12-19.

Stuss, D. T. & Alexander, M. P. (2000). Executive functions and the frontal lobes: A conceptual view. *Psychological Research, 63*, 289-298.

Stuss, D. T. & Knight, R. T. (Eds.). (2002). *Principles of frontal lobe function* (pp. 109-126). New York: Oxford University Press.

Taylor, J. G. (1998). Towards the networks of the brain: From brain imaging to consciousness. *Neural Networks, 12*(7-8), 943-959.

Vaitl, D., Gruzelier, J., Jamieson, G. A., Lehmann, D., Ott, U., Sammer, G., et al. (2005). *Psychobiology of altered states of consciousness. Psychological Bulletin, 131*, 98-127.

Wasserstein, J., & Lynn, A. (2001). Metacognitive remediation in adult ADHD. Treating executive function deficits via executive functions. *Annals of the New York Academy of Science, Jun 931*, 376-84.

Whalen, P. J., Rauch, S. L., Etcoff, N. L., McInerney, S. C., Lee, M. B., Jenike, M. A. (1998). Masked presentations of emotional facial expressions modulate amygdala activity without explicit knowledge. *The Journal of Neuroscience, 18*, 411-418.

Wilber, K. (1977). *Spectrum of consciousness.* Wheaton, IL: Quest Books.

Wilber, K. (1979). *No boundary: Eastern and western approaches to personal growth.* Boston: Shambhala Publications, Inc.

Wilber, K. (1995). *Sex, ecology, spirituality: The spirit of evolution.* Boston: Shambhala Publications, Inc.

Wilber, K. (2000). *Integral psychology.* Boston: Shambhala Publications, Inc.

Wilson, B. A., Alderman, N., Burgess, P., Emslie, H., & Evans, J. J. (1996). *Behavioral assessment of the dysexecutive syndrome (BADS).* Lutz, FL: Psychological Assessment Resources, Inc.

TABLE 1 REFERENCES

Ahn, M. S., Breeze, J. L., Makris, N., Kennedy, D. N., Hodge, S. M., Herbert, M. R., et al. (2007). Anatomic brain magnetic resonance imaging of the basal ganglia in pediatric bipolar disorder. *Journal of Affective Disorders, 104*(1-3), 147-154.

Allen, G. & Courchesne, E. (2003) Differential effects of developmental cerebellar abnormality on cognitive and motor functions in the cerebellum: An fMRI study of autism. *American Journal of Psychiatry, 160*(2), 262-273.

Amat, J. A., Bronen, R. A., Saluja, S., Sato, N., Zhu, H., Gorman, D., et al. (2006). Increased number of subcortical hyperintensities on MRI in children and adolescents With Tourette's syndrome, obsessive-compulsive disorder, and attention deficit hyperactivity disorder. *The American Journal of Psychiatry, 163*(6), 1106-1108.

Banich, M. T., Crowley, T. J., Thompson, J., Thompson, L. L., Jacobson, B. Ll, Liu, X., et al. (2007) Brain activation during the Stroop task in adolescents with severe substance and conduct problems: A pilot study. *Drug and Alcohol Dependence, 90*(2-3), 175-182.

Bannon, S., Gonzalvez, C. J., Croft, R. J., & Boyce, P. M. (2006). Executive functions in obsessive-compulsive disorder: State or trait deficits? *Australian and New Zealand Journal of Psychiatry, 40*(11-12), 1031-1038.

Barkley, R. A., Edwards, G., Laneri, M., Fletcher, K., & Metevia, L. (2001). Executive functioning, temporal discounting, and sense of time in adolescents with attention deficit hyperactivity disorder (ADHD) and oppositional defiant disorder (ODD). *Journal of Abnormal Child Psychology, 29*(6), 541-556.

Beyer, J. L. & Krishnan, K. R. R. (2002). Volumetric brain imaging findings in mood disorders. *Bipolar Disorders, 4*(2), 89-104.

Bögels, S. M. & Zigterman, D. (2000). Dysfunctional cognitions in children with social phobia, separation anxiety disorder, and generalized anxiety disorder. *Journal of Abnormal Psychology, 28*(2), 205-211.

Caetano, S. C., Olvera, R. L., Glahn, D., Fonseca, M, Pliszka, S., & Soares, J. C. (2005) Fronto-limbic brain abnormalities in juvenile onset bipolar disorder. *Biological Psychiatry, 58*(7), 525-531.

Chamberlain, S. R., Fineberg, N. A., Blackwell, A. D., Clark, L., Robbins, T. W., & Shahakian, B. J. (2007). A neuropsychological comparison of obsessive-compulsive disorder and trichotillomania. *Neuropsychologia, 45*(4), 654-62.

Channon, S., Pratt, P., Robertson, M. M. (2003). Executive function, memory, and learning in Tourette's syndrome. *Neuropsychology, 17*(2), 247-254.

Dickstein, D. P, Treland, J. E., Snow, J., McClure, E. B., Mehta, M. S., Towbin, K. E., et al. (2004). Neuropsychological performance in pediatric bipolar disorder. *Biological Psychiatry, 55*(1), 32-39.

Doyle, A. E., Wilens, T. E., Kwon, A., Seidman, L. J., Faraone, S. V., Fried, R., et al. (2005). Neuropsychological functioning in youth with bipolar disorder. *Biological Psychiatry, 58*(7), 540-548.

Dupuy, J. B. & Ladouceur, R. (2008). Cognitive processes of generalized anxiety disorder in comorbid generalized anxiety disorder and major depressive disorder. *Journal of Anxiety Disorders, 22*(3), 505-514.

Easter, J., McClure, E. B., Monk, C. S., Dhanani, M., Hodgdon, H., Leibenluft, E., et al. (2005). Emotion recognition deficits in pediatric anxiety disorders: Implications for amygdala research. *Journal of Child and Adolescent Psychopharmacology, 15*(4), 563-570.

Emerson, C. S., Mollet, G. A., & Harrison, D. W. (2005). Anxious-depression in boys: An evaluation of executive functioning. *Archives of Clinical Neuropsychology, 20*, 539-546.

Erickson, T. M. & Newman, M. G. (2007). Interpersonal and emotional processes in generalized anxiety disorder analogues during social interaction tasks. *Behavior Therapy, 38*(4), 364-377.

Hala, S., Rasmussen, C., Henderson, A.M. E. (2005). Three types of source monitoring by children with and without autism: The role of executive function. *Journal of Autism and Developmental Disorders, 35*(1), 75-89.

Hale, J. B., Fiorello, C. A., & Brown, L. (2005). Determining medication treatment effects using teacher ratings and classroom observations of children with ADHD: Does neuropsychological impairment matter? *Educational and Child Psychology, 22*(2), 39-59.

Hale, J. B., Reddy, L. A., Decker, S. L., Thompson, R., Henzel, J. N., & Teodori, A, et al. (2008). *Validation of a 15-minute executive function and behavior rating screening battery for children with ADHD.* Manuscript submitted for publication.

Jacobs, S. & Decker, D. D. (2007). Ethical-legal issues in the education of pupils with disabilities under IDEA. In S. Jacob and T. S. Hartshorne (Eds.), *Ethics and law for school psychologists, 5th Edition* (pp. 117-174). Hoboken, NJ: John Wiley & Sons.

Joseph, R. M., McGrath, L. M., & Tager-Flusberg, H. (2005). Executive dysfunction and its relation to language ability in verbal school-age children with autism. *Developmental Neuropsychology, 27*(3), 361-378.

Kleinhans, N. M., Akshoomoff, N., & Delis, D. C. (2005). Executive functions in autism and Asperger's disorder: Flexibility, fluency, and inhibition. *Developmental Neuropsychology, 27*(3), 379-401.

Kleinhans, N. M., Muller, R., Cohen, D. N., & Courchesne, E. (2008). Atypical functional lateralization of language in autism spectrum disorders. *Brain Research, 1221*(24), 115-125.

Krain, A. L, Gotimer, K., Hefton, S., Ernst, M., Castellanos, F. X., Pine, D. S., et al. (2008). A functional magnetic resonance imaging investigation of uncertainty in adolescents with anxiety disorders. *Biological Psychiatry, 63*(6), 563-568.

Landro, N. I., Stiles, T. C., & Sletvold, H. (2001). Neurological function in nonpsychotic unipolar major depression. *Neuropsychiatry, Neuropsychology, & Behavioral Neurology, 14*(4), 233-240.

Mahone, E. M., Koth, C. W., Cutting, L., Singer, H. S., & Denckla, M. B. (2001). Executive function in fluency and recall measures among children with Tourette syndrome or ADHD. *Journal of the International Neuropsychological Society, 7*(1), 102-111.

Maltby, N., Tolin, D. F., Worhunsky, P., O'Keefe, T. M., & Kiehl, K. A. (2005). Dysfunctional action monitoring hyperactivates frontal-striatal circuits in obsessive-compulsive disorder: an event-related fMRI study. *Neuroimage, 24*(2), 495-503.

Marsh, R., Zhu, H., Wang, Z., Skudlarski, P., Peterson, B. S. (2007). A developmental fMRI study of self-regulatory control in Tourette's syndrome. *American Journal of Psychiatry, 164*(6), 955-966.

McClure, E. B., Treland, J. E., Snow, J., Schmajuk, M., Dickstein, D. P, Towbin, K. E., et al. (2005). Deficits in social cognition and response flexibility in pediatric bipolar disorder. *American Journal of Psychiatry, 162*(9), 1644-1651.

Monk, C. S., Nelson, E. E, McClure, E. B., Mogg, K., Bradley, B .P., Leibenluft, E., et al. (2006). Ventrolateral prefrontal cortex activation and attentional bias in response to angry faces in adolescents with generalized anxiety disorder. *American Journal of Psychiatry, 163*(6), 1091-1097.

Ottowitz, W. E., Dougherty, D. D., & Savage, C. R. (2002). The neural network basis for abnormalities of attention and executive function in major depressive disorder: Implications for application of the medical disease model to psychiatric disorders. *Harvard Review of Psychiatry, 10*(2), 86-99.

Pajer, K., Chung, J., Leininger, L., Wang, W., Gardner, W., Yeates, K. (2008). Neuropsychological function in adolescent girls with conduct disorder. *Journal of the American Academy of Child and Adolescent Psychiatry, 47*(4), 416-425.

Papadopoulos, T. C., Panayiotou, G., Spanoudis, G., & Natsopoulos, D. (2005). Evidence of poor planning in children with attention deficits. *Journal of Abnormal Child Psychology, 33*(5), 611-623.

Pardo, J. V., Pardo, P. J., Humes, S. W., & Posner, M. I. (2006). Neurocognitive dysfunction in antidepressant-free, non-elderly patients with unipolar depression: Alerting and covert orienting of visuospatial attention. *Journal of Affective Disorders, 92*, 71-78.

Pavuluri, M. N., Schenkel, L. S., Aryal, S., Harral, E. M., Hill, S. K., Herbener, E.S., et al. (2006). Neurocognitive function in unmedicated manic and medicated euthymic pediatric bipolar patients. *American Journal of Psychiatry, 163*, 286-293.

Penades, R., Catalan, R., Andres, S., Salamero, M., & Gastto, C. (2005). Executive function and nonverbal memory in obsessive-compulsive disorder. *Psychiatry Research, 133*(1), 81-90.

Quraishi, S. & Frangou, S. (2002). Neuropsychology of bipolar disorder: A review. *Journal of Affective Disorders, 72*, 209-226.

Semrud-Clikeman, M., Steingard, R. J., Filipek, P., Biederman, J., Bekken, K., & Renshaw, P. F. (2000). Using MRI to examine brain-behavior relationships in males with attention deficit disorder with hyperactivity. *Journal of the American Academy of Child & Adolescent Psychiatry, 39*(4), 477-484.

Shin, Y., Ha, T. H., Kim, S.Y., & Kwon, J. S. (2004). Association between EEG alpha power and visuospatial function in obsessive-compulsive disorder. *Psychiatry and Clinical Neurosciences, 58*(1), 16-20.

Speltz, M.L., DeKlyen, M., Calderon, R., Greenberg, M.T., & Fisher, Philip, A. (1999). Neuropsychological characteristics and test behaviors of boys with early onset conduct problems. *Journal of Abnormal Psychology, 108*(2), 315-325.

Steingard, R. J., Renshaw, P. F., Hennen, J., Lenox, M., Bonella Cintron, C., Young, A. D., et al. (2002). Smaller frontal white matter volumes in depressed adolescents. *Biological Psychiatry, 52*(5), 413-417.

Storch, E. A., Lack, C. W., Simons, L. E., Goodman, W. K., Murphy, T. K., & Geffken, G. R. (2007). A measure of functional impairment in youth with Tourette's syndrome. *Journal of Pediatric Psychology, 32*(8), 950-959.

Thede, L. L. & Coolidge, F. L. (2007). Psychological and Neurobehavioral Comparisons of Children with Asperger's disorder versus high-functioning autism. *Journal of Autism and Developmental Disorders, 37*(5), 847–854.

Thorell, L. B. & Wahlstedt, C. (2006). Executive functioning deficits in relation to symptoms of ADHD and/or ODD in preschool children. *Infant and Child Development, 15*(5), 503-518.

Vasa, R. A., Roberson-Nay, R., Klein, R. G., Mannuzza, S., Moulton, J. L. III, Guardino, M. et al. (2007). Memory deficits in children with and at risk for anxiety disorders. Depression and Anxiety, 24(2), 85-94.

Verté, S., Geurts, H. M.., Roeyers, H., Oosterlaan, J., & Sergeant, J. A. (2006). Executive functioning in children with an autism spectrum disorder: Can we differentiate within the spectrum? *Journal of Autism and Developmental Disorders, 36*(3), 351–372.

van Goozen, S. H. M., Cohen-Kettenis, P. T., Snoek, H., Matthys, W., Swaab-Barneveld, H., & van Engeland, H. (2004). Executive functioning in children: a comparison of hospitalised ODD and ODD/ADHD children and normal controls. *Journal of Child Psychology and Psychiatry, 45*(2), 284-292.

Viard, A., Flament, M. F., Artiges, E., Dehaene, S., Naccache, L., & Cohen, D. (2005). Cognitive control in childhood-onset obsessive–compulsive disorder: a functional MRI study. *Psychological Medicine, 35*(7), 1007–1017.

Wang, A. T., Lee, S. S., Sigman, M., & Dapretto, M. (2006). Neural basis of irony comprehension in children with autism: the role of prosody and context. *Brain: A Journal of Neurology, 129*(4), 932-943.

Williams, J. H. G., Whiten, A., Singh, T. (2004). A systematic review of action imitation in autistic spectrum disorder. *Journal of Autism and Developmental Disorders, 34*(3), 285-299.

Willis, W. G. & Weiler, M. D. (2005). Neural substrates of childhood attention-deficit/hyperactivity disorder: Electroencephalographic and magnetic resonance imaging evidence. *Developmental Neuropsychology. 27*(1), 135-182.

Winsler, A., Abar, B., Feder, M. A., Schuun, C. D., & Rubio, D. A. (2007). Private speech and executive functioning among high-functioning children with autistic spectrum disorders. *Journal of Autism and Developmental Disorders, 37*(9), 1617–1635.

CHAPTER 5

FRONTAL LOBE DYSFUNCTION, PSYCHOPATHOLOGY, AND VIOLENCE

Ann Marie Leonard-Zabel, Ph.D.
Steven G. Feifer, D.Ed.

"Not all aggressive children are violent, and not all violent children display long-standing patterns of aggression. The more risk factors that a child has the more likely it is the child will display violence."

—(Bloomquist & Schnell, 2002)

According to the National Center for Educational Statistics (2007), there are a growing number of children and adolescents exhibiting aggressive and violent behavior in our schools. In today's society, why are more children and youth lacking the ability to show empathy and compassion for others, and instead engaging in more risky and delinquent behaviors? These are questions that pose major challenges not only for parents and teachers, but the criminal justice system as well. Children who manifest psychological and behavioral difficulties at such an early age are especially worrisome since these issues can affect academic and cognitive functioning, and also impact later social competence (Bloomquist & Schnell, 2002; Rosenthal & Bond, 1990).

Perhaps our discussion should begin by defining what the terms *aggression* and *violence* actually mean. Aggression can be defined as the deliberate attempt to harm another individual, physically or socially, or in some cases to destroy an object. On the other hand, violence can be defined as *"a destructive physical aggression intentionally directed at harming other persons or things."* (Bartol & Bartol, 2008, p. 143). Although there is no single nosology of aggression, Barratt, Stanford, Kent, and Felthous (1997) delineated three specific subtypes of aggressive acts:

1. *Premeditated Aggression*—consciously executed or planned aggressive acts for individual benefit or gain. For example, serial killers, planned acts of revenge, and many of the aforementioned school-wide shootings tend to reflect carefully thought out plots.
2. *Medically Related Aggression*—aggression as a symptom of a defined medical condition. For instance, children with temporal lobe epilepsy tend to have more difficulty with behavioral adjustment and adaptive behavior skills than peers (Culhane-Shelburne, Chapieski, Hiscock, & Glaze, 2002).
3. *Impulsive Aggression*—aggression resulting from a quick response to a stimulus that results in an agitated state and culminates in a specific act void of reason or interpersonal communication. This type of aggression often plagues students with emotional and behavioral disorders in school, hindering both academic and social skill development.

For discussion purposes, this delineation of aggression may serve as a common focal point for both mental health professionals and educators in order to examine the various triggers of discordant behavioral functioning in children. According to Loeber and Stouthamer-Loeber (1998), acts of aggression can manifest themselves through distinctive behavior patterns, emotions, cognitions, and social-emotional development. For instance, overt aggression involves direct confrontation with victims, administration of physical harm, or threats of physical harm. Overt aggression tends to decrease with age, and anger is usually an important ingredient in most overt acts of aggression. On the other hand, covert aggression usually involves indirect confrontation with victims. In fact, covert aggression relies on concealment, dishonesty, or sneaky acts of behavior, and is similar to passive-aggressive behavior; these behaviors tend to increase with age (Bartol & Bartol, 2008). Table 5-1 lists several overt and covert aggressive acts of aggression:

TABLE 5-1
Overt and Covert Aggressive Acts

Overt Actions
- Anger with a high level of arousal and violence.
- Lack of social finesse for coming up with nonaggressive solutions.
- Aggression begins early, especially in boys.

Covert Actions
- Less emotional and includes crimes such as fraud, larceny, and theft.
- Relies on cognitive capabilities, such as planning ability and deceitfulness.
- Has well-learned strategies to escape punishment.

In recent years, the study of childhood aggression and violence has focused on the impact of several neurodevelopmental risk factors affecting a variety of social emotional skills. These have included the ability to exercise self-control, emotional regulation, respect for others, the ability to comprehend differences between right and wrong, rule abiding behavior, and the development of insight in order to appreciate another person's perspective or point of view (Brownlie et al., 2004). Today, mental health practitioners are beginning to acknowledge the possible biological causes of aggression such as heredity, low arousal levels resulting in sensation seeking behaviors, high testosterone levels, neurological disorders such a brain tumors, encephalopathy, and substance abuse.

The aim of this chapter is to provide psychologists, educators, and mental health practitioners with a fundamental knowledge base of the relationship between frontal lobe dysfunction, psychopathology, and violent behavior. Further, a summary of functional neuroanatomy as well as the neuropsychological correlates involved in aggressive and violent behavior connected to brain-based psychopathology will be reviewed. Lastly, the implementation of generally accepted individualized assessment methods to guide practice with possible approaches to intervention are presented.

The brain is a complex organ relying on its component parts to work in harmony with one another so the child can function and develop adequately. Perhaps the most important region of the brain involved in the modulation of behavior is the frontal lobes. The frontal lobes are situated in the most anterior region of the brain, and encompass the primary motor cortex, the premotor cortex, Broca's area, and the prefrontal cortex (see Figure 5-1).

Three major brain systems exist related to aggressive and violent behaviors, including two regions of the frontal lobes—namely, the prefrontal cortex, and the cingulate system, as well as a third region housed within the temporal lobe (Amen, 2005). The prefrontal cortex is crucial to emotional regulation, and encompasses approximately one-third of the cerebral cortex. According to Grafman (1994) the prefrontal cortex is the last region of the brain to fully mature or myelinate. The prefrontal cortex has numerous neural connections with other regions of the brain as well as the deep structures of the limbic system. Due to its involvement with so many neuropsychological disorders, the prefrontal cortex plays a major role as the supervisor within the brain system.

> **KEY LEARNING POINTS:**
> **Aggression and Violence**
>
> - Aggression is the deliberate attempt to harm another individual or in some cases destroy an object. There are three main subtypes, and can be manifested in either an overt or covert form.
> - Violence involves destructive physical aggression intentionally directed at harming another person or object.
> - Mental health practitioners are exploring the biological causes of aggression and violence.

FIGURE 5-1

The Frontal Lobes Encompass the Primary Motor Cortex, the Premotor Cortex, Broca's Area, and the Prefrontal Cortex

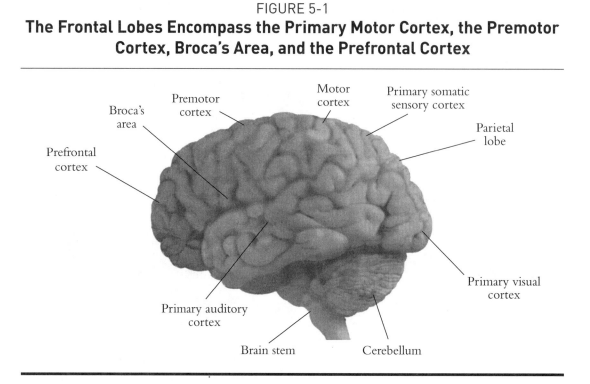

The prefrontal cortex is extremely important for the control and regulation of affect. In fact, the ability to compare and contrast present and past experiences is a result of prefrontal lobe connections to the associated regions of the brain involving the occipital, parietal, and temporal lobes. The use of insight and judgment, focus, impulse control, forethought, organization, and empathy are all functions of the prefrontal cortex (Siegel, 1999).

It is important to distinguish among the specific roles of the prefrontal cortex in both hemispheres of the brain. For instance, the left prefrontal cortex is primarily the verbal side of the brain where analysis and synthesis of incoming information occurs. It is the left prefrontal cortex that connects words to emotional experience and encoding memory. Beginning at approximately four years of age, the left prefrontal cortex with good executive decision-making and interpretive functions, starts to predominate over other areas of the brain (Siegel, 1999). On the other hand, the right prefrontal cortex tends to specialize in nonverbal functions. The right prefrontal cortex is vital to the retrieval of memory and spatial recognition skills, both of which are important for adequate nonverbal problem-solving skills (Siegel, 1999). Table 5-2 provides a condensed breakdown of the functions of the left and right prefrontal cortex areas vital to adequate brain-based emotional responses:

TABLE 5-2
Role of the Left and Right Prefrontal Cortex Areas

(Siegel, 1999)

Left Prefrontal Cortex		Right Prefrontal Cortex	
Analyze information	Synthesize information	Recognize people by their faces	Recognize meaning of facial expression
Plan and prepare to execute plans, including motoric plans	Analyze obstacles and assess failures and improvise solutions to attain goals	Recognize and interpret others' emotions via tone (melody) of voice, posture, and gesture	Reacting appropriately to negative implications of tone or gesture associated to specific looks or tones
Interpret experience and modulate emotional states	Controlling impulses and deciding how best to meet needs	Coordinate emotional relevance with information about previous life experience	Assist in interpreting stimuli and coordinating the feeling of risk states

Dysfunction in the prefrontal cortex often results in a variety of cognitive and emotional conditions including a short attention span, impulsivity, procrastination, disorganization, poor judgment, lack of empathy and insight (Amen, 2005). In addition, impairment in the prefrontal cortex often involves increased apathy, lowered activity level leading to poor internal supervision, and perseveration.

Clearly, these are all areas that can significantly hinder effective academic and social skills development in school. Additional difficulty with the prefrontal cortex can impact problem-solving ability leading to a lack of insight as well as organization and planning. Interpersonal as well as intrapersonal problems may also be present, as some children become extremely critical of others despite the fact that they may lack critical insight into their own behavior (Tranel, 1992). The frontal lobes, especially the prefrontal cortex, are sensitive and vulnerable to injury, which can result in devastating effects leading to chaotic, disorganized, asocial, and criminal behavior (Goldberg, 2001). Table 5-3 lists several behavioral conditions that can exist with a compromised prefrontal cortex.

KEY LEARNING POINTS:
Brain Systems Related to Aggression and Violence

- The prefrontal cortex, cingulate system, and the temporal lobes are the main brain regions related to aggression and violence.
- The prefrontal cortex is sensitive to injury, and because of its supervisory role in the cortex, it can lead to devastating life effects including antisocial and criminal behavior.

TABLE 5-3
Behavioral Conditions Associated With a Compromised Prefrontal Cortex

(Amen, 2005)

Mood Disorders
Antisocial Personality Disorder
Borderline Personality Disorder
Attentional Disorders
Oppositional Defiant Disorder
Traumatic Brain Injuries–Mild, Moderate, Severe
Depression
Schizophrenia
Conduct Disorder
Executive Functioning
Obsessive Compulsive Disorder

One behavioral condition that can pose devastating effects on academic learning and scholastic functioning is Traumatic Brain Injury (TBI). Some of the more common incidences resulting in TBI can include whiplash injuries, acceleration injuries, deceleration injuries, blunt force, sports, falls, and car accidents. These injuries can lead to subtle neurocognitive deficits, or in some cases can be devastating and lead to major cognitive problems in attention, memory, executive functioning, fatigue, irritability, anger, and labile temperament (Amen, 2005; Zilmer, Spiers, & Culbertson, 2008). Mild head trauma often goes medically unnoticed. In fact, the medical community may not know the true neuropsychological detriments of such an injury over time. Nevertheless, mild head trauma can lead to shearing, stretching, and even cell death impacting the essential building blocks of the central nervous system (CNS). In addition, head injuries are cumulative in effect, meaning that repeated blows to the head can lead to significant information processing deficits as well as cognitive decline (Zilmer, Spiers, & Culbertson, 2008).

Perhaps at no other time during human development does the brain undergo more changes than during adolescence. With the advent of new technologies, scientists have discovered that adolescent brains are much less developed than previously thought (American Bar Association, 2004). Using magnetic resonance imaging (MRI), a noninvasive methodology that allows scientists to safely scan children over time, subtle nuances in brain development can be tracked and documented (Goldberg, 2001). MRI studies have revealed the typical teenage brain produces an intense volume of gray matter, which is the primary brain tissue involved in cognition. Then, a period of "pruning" occurs as the adolescent brain discards gray matter at a rapid rate to help stimulate health and growth during development. The pruning process allows the brain to devise the most optimum neural pathways needed for cognition, and then ensures these pathways through the development of white matter (myelination). The white matter serves as insulation for the brain's neural circuitry, making the operation of the brain more efficient and precise while also speeding up neural connectivity in an exponential fashion (Sowell et al., 1999).

Sowell and colleagues (1999) found that the frontal lobes undergo far more changes during adolescence than in any other period of development. Since the frontal lobes are the last region of the brain to become fully myelinated, adolescents may not be able to reason as well as adults and thus over-rely on emotional decision making. In a study on brain development using volumetric imaging, Reiss and colleagues (1996) reported that maturation of the frontal lobes was correlated with measures of cognitive functioning. This may explain why some adolescents take a much more risky approach to life without really examining the consequences of their actions.

Children and youth sometimes exhibit delinquent behaviors that involve unlawful acts committed against persons and property, as well as drug/alcohol offenses and offenses against the public order (Bartol & Bartol, 2008). Delinquency is defined as "behavior against the criminal code committed by an individual who has not reached adulthood, as defined by state and/or federal law" (Bartol & Bartol, 2008, p. 26). Delinquency is further defined according to age ranges involving two major domains: child delinquency and juvenile delinquency. Table 5-4 explains the criteria for both:

**KEY LEARNING POINTS:
Impact of Brain-Based
Influences on Behavior**

- Whiplash injuries, acceleration injuries, deceleration injuries, blunt force, sports, falls and car accidents can lead to cognitive problems with attention, memory, and executive functioning skills impacted by fatigue, irritability, and labile temperament.
- Specific neuropsychological risk factors associated with antisocial behavior and delinquency have included faulty executive functioning skills, poor verbal abilities, and limited working memory skills.
- Focal orbitofrontal injuries may be associated with increased aggression as children may become stuck in a state of constantly feeling threatened, and automatically respond to stimuli in an aggressive fashion.

TABLE 5-4
Delinquency Defined According to Age Ranges

(Loeber, Farrington, & Petechuk, 2003)

Childhood Delinquency
- Between ages 7 and 12
- Attract the attention of mass
- Makes up 9 percent of all juvenile arrests.

Juvenile Delinquency
- Between ages 13 and 17
- Major contributors are media especially after certain vandalism, drug use, and violent crime. thievery, and violence.

According to Bartol and Bartol (2008), mental health practitioners need to develop an understanding of the neuropsychological and social developmental risk factors associated with delinquency. The social risk factors include poverty (must be accompanied by other factors in order to be an indicator), early peer rejection, association with antisocial peers, inadequate preschool child care, inadequate after-school care, and school failure. Parental and family risk factors include single family households (must be accompanied by multiple factors in order to be at risk), lax parental style, parental psychopathology, physical and emotional abuse or neglect, domestic violence, substance abuse, and antisocial siblings. Liu, Riane, Venables, and Mendeck (2004) reported that neuropsychological deficits in combination with social family risk factors are often found in persistent, serious, violent offenders.

In terms of specific neuropsychological risk factors associated with antisocial behavior and delinquency, most studies have focused on cognitive and language deficiencies, as well as faulty executive functioning skills (Morgan & Lilienfeld, 2000). Moffitt (2003) noted that risk factors also involved attributes such as a troublesome temperament, inadequate self-regulation skills, and poor interpersonal and social skills. With respect to language and executive functioning skills, Moffit and Lynam (1994) concluded that students with poor *executive functioning* skills and lower verbal abilities were prone to committing deviant acts for three possible reasons. First, these students had difficulty learning from environmental consequences, and may not comprehend the negative impact of their behavior on others. In other words, low verbal ability contributes to a *present vs. future oriented* cognitive style that fostered irresponsible behavior. Second, these students had relatively poor working memory skills, a skill primarily mediated by verbal rehearsal mechanisms. These cognitive deficits rendered them vulnerable to forgetting abstract ideas about ethical values and future rewards when confronted with a compromising situation. Lastly, students with poor *executive functioning* skills may have difficulty adapting their behavior to the constant changing of social circumstances, especially school related ones involving verbal adroitness. Stuss and Levine (2002) added a fourth reason by noting that verbal retrieval skills also allow students to both rehearse and develop alternative strategies for uncompromising situations. In essence, verbal abilities are essential toward developing behavioral self-control.

Brower and Price (2001) suggested that high rates of neuropsychiatric abnormalities reported in persons with violent and criminal behavior suggest an association between aggressive dyscontrol and brain injury impacting the frontal lobes. More specifically, the area of the prefrontal cortex that is closely connected to the limbic system and known as the *"paralimbic"* area is the orbitofrontal cortex. The orbitofrontal cortex is involved in mood regulation and stabilization of behavior especially when regulating impulsive behaviors. This brain region basically functions as a higher-level decision making mechanism fueled by emotional feelings engendered from previous experiences (Dolan, 1999). When the orbitofrontal cortex is damaged, or these experiences are overwhelmingly negative, children may become stuck in a state of constantly feeling threatened, and automatically respond to stimuli in an aggressive fashion. Thus, children brought up in households with inconsistent parenting, turbulence and violence, or unpredictable reinforcement contingencies may be more prone to reactive aggression. Rolls (1997) surmised that the orbitofrontal cortex is indeed responsible for the rapid learning and execution of a behavioral response based upon reward contingencies in the environment. In summary, focal orbitofrontal injury is particularly associated with increased aggression (Brower & Prince, 2001). However, there is no single study that has reliably demonstrated a characteristic pattern of frontal lobe dysfunction predictive of violent crime. Still, damage to the orbitofrontal cortex has been associated with poor impulse control, explosive and aggressive outbursts, inappropriate verbal lewdness, jocularity, and lack of sensitivity (Duffy and Campbell, 2004).

A second brain region related to aggressive and violent behaviors is the *anterior cingulate gyrus*, an area once thought to be independent from the limbic system. Originally, the limbic system was considered to be deep within the bowels of the brain involving archaic structures such as the amygdala, hippocampus, thalamus, and the hypothalamus. Now, the limbic system, deemed the *"emotional processing center"* of the brain, has been expanded to include not only the orbitalfrontal cortex but also the *anterior cingulate gyrus* as well. The *anterior cingulate gyrus* and the orbitofrontal cortex are thought to be the connecting areas between the prefrontal cortex and the limbic system, and function to modulate emotional processing (Wehrenberg & Prinz, 2007). Figure 5-2 displays the various brain regions comprising the emotional centers of our brain.

FIGURE 5-2
The Limbic System of the Brain

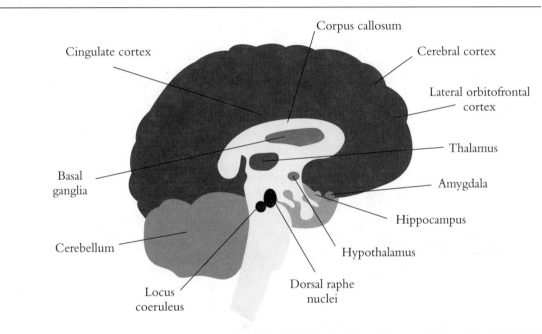

The anterior cingulate gyrus is important due to its responsibility for shifting attention to appropriate stimuli. According to Carter (1998), the anterior cingulate helps the brain divert its conscious energies either toward internal cognitive events, or to external cognitive stimuli. A helpful analogy is that of an *attention general* in the brain making an executive decision as to which events require conscious attention, and which will be overlooked. In fact, Carter (1998) noted that an under-active anterior cingulate cortex that focused too much attention on internal events was evident in schizophrenic patients, thus explaining some of their difficulty separating their own thoughts from outside voices. Certainly, impairment in this region can produce a wide variety of peculiar emotional responses, most of which seem related to an inability to appreciate and interpret emotions (LeDoux, 1996). The anterior cingulate cortex contributes toward inhibiting aggression and creating a sense of social self-awareness (Lapierre, Braun, & Hodgins, 1995). Table 5-5 lists several facets of anterior cingulated functioning.

TABLE 5-5
Role and Functioning of the Anterior Cingulate Gyrus

(Amen, 2000)

- Known as the brain's gear shifter.
- Responsible for cognitive flexibility.
- Able to see problem solving options.
- Able to go from one idea to the next easily.
- Responsible for a child being cooperative with others.
- Allows one to go with the flow of life.
- Rich connections with amygdala allow for shifting of attention toward more emotionally significant events.

A vital role of the anterior cingulate gyrus is to modulate the ability to shift between cognition and emotion. The ease with which children develop new solutions to both verbal and nonverbal problems is due to the ease and flexible nature in which the anterior cingulate gyrus transfers this information. When the anterior cingulate gyrus is healthy and working well, behavioral qualities of cooperation and adaptability emerge. These attributes are crucial for the development of higher ordered emotional skills such as negotiation and conflict resolution. When a child can seamlessly move from one idea to another with relative ease, the appropriate amount of neural activity is utilized by the anterior cingulate gyrus (Siegel, 1999). However, when the anterior cingulate gyrus is dysfunctional or has suffered an injury, there may be a variety of behaviors manifested within the individual. Behavioral difficulties that may occur due to faulty workings of the anterior cingulate are described in Table 5-6.

KEY LEARNING POINTS:
Aggression and the Brain

- A vital function of the anterior cingulated gyrus is the ability to shift between cognition and emotion swiftly and easily.
- A healthy anterior cingulate gyrus produces qualities of cooperation and adaptability, which are vital for social development, especially in the areas of negotiation and conflict resolution.
- Damage or insult to the temporal lobes may produce memory struggles, mood instability, auditory and visual illusions, dark thoughts, and social problems.
- There is a delicate balance between the amygdala, an area of the brain responsible for fear based learning, and the appropriate modulation of behavior by higher level brain regions in the prefrontal cortex.

TABLE 5-6
Behavior Difficulties Associated With the Anterior Cingulate Gyrus

(Amen, 2000)

Behavior	Feeling	Functioning
Unable to change gears	Worries	Affects attention
Inflexible behavior and attitude	Obsesses	Oppositional
Holds grudges for a long time	Compulsions	Addictive behaviors
Argumentative attitude and behavior	Somatic Issues	Chronic Pain

A third region of the brain related to aggressive and violent behaviors is the temporal lobe. Cognitive and behavioral difficulties that can manifest with an impaired temporal lobe include memory difficulties, mood instability, irritability, auditory and visual illusions, and periods of anxiety. In addition, there may be periods of confusion, dark thoughts, social problems, learning difficulties, and hyper-religiosity as well. Specific conditions affected by the temporal lobes include memory loss associated with decreased activity in the medial temporal lobes, anxiety, dissociation, involved depression, temporal lobe epilepsy, aggression, and suicide. There is also research to suggest that left temporal lobe involvement may be primarily responsible for aggression and violence. (Amen, 2005; Zilmer, Spiers, & Culbertson, 2008). A synopsis of the brain-based psychosocial functions of the temporal lobe is listed in Table 5-7.

KEY LEARNING POINTS:
Summary of Psychopathy Research

- Research findings have demonstrated that the diagnostic label of psychopathy in juveniles is closely linked to conduct disorder, with increased levels of delinquency and ongoing police involvement.
- Research findings on hemispheric asymmetry suggest that criminal psychopaths have striking inconsistencies with verbalized thoughts, feelings and intentions, presumably modulated by the left hemisphere.

TABLE 5-7
Temporal Lobe Functions

(Amen, 2000)

Understanding Language	Ability to Read Faces	Initiator of Long Term Memory
Word Retrieval	Ability to Read Social Cues	Visual Learning
Verbal Information	Emotional Stability	Auditory Learning
Rhyming and Musical Ability	Mood Stabilizer	Recognizing Problems

Lastly, an important neurological structure housed deep within the temporal lobes also responsible for problems with emotional processing is the amygdala. The amygdala is an almond-shaped cluster of neurons in the limbic system of the brain responsible for fear, anger, and disgust emotions. Keihl (2006) found that psychopaths exhibited low amygdala activity in comparison to the typical population especially during an emotional processing task. This finding suggested that the relationship between the amygdala and learning may emerge as a significant factor toward understanding the psychopath's emotional behavior. In fact, there appears to be a delicate balance between the amygdala and the appropriate modulation of behavior by higher level brain regions in the prefrontal cortex. Too little activation of the amygdala compromises fear-based learning, thus creating what some may deem as a *"sociopathic"* personality, characterized by the inability to appropriately process and learn from negative emotions. As Moeller (2001) noted, some aggressive youngsters may experience cortical under-arousal and a weak inhibitory system, which in turn may lead to fearlessness, thrill-seeking behavior, and problems learning from punishment. Conversely, over-activation of the amygdala leaves students in a hyper-aroused emotional state, and subsequently renders students vulnerable to aggressive and maladaptive response patterns. Their aggression is often reactive and impulsive in nature, and characterized by chronic agitation and behavior dysfunction. As Blair (2002) surmised, the degree with which children differ in their propensity to experience positive or negative emotions, as well as the intensity or degree with which emotions are experienced, is highly relevant to the development of higher order self-regulation skills.

Psychopathology

The term *"psychopath"* is often used to describe an individual who demonstrates a discernible cluster of maladaptive features hindering psychological and interpersonal development that clearly distinguishes them from the population norm (Bartol & Bartol, 2008). Certainly, there is evidence that psychopathic behavior has its roots in the neuropsychological architecture of the social brain. However, there appears to be serious shortcomings regarding the research conducted on psychopathy in children and adolescents. A major problem in the psychological literature is the identification of psychopathy itself. If indeed psychopathy exists in young children, it may be difficult to reliably measure because of the constant changes in the developmental patterns across the life span. "Many clinicians and researchers have resisted any trend to search for psychopathy in juveniles, noting the features of the adult psychopath may simply represent normal adolescent development" (Bartol & Bartol, 2008, p. 203). After all, adolescents can appear callous, self-centered, impulsive, display an eagerness for sensation-seeking behaviors, are not good at planning, and lack foresight ability for long-range goals.

Clouding the above definitional issue is the fact that current research findings have suggested the diagnostic label of *"juvenile psychopathy"* is similar to the diagnostic label of *"conduct disorder,"* only with higher levels of delinquency and police involvement (Murrie et al., 2004; Salekin et al., 2003). According to Blair et al. (2006), only 25 percent of juveniles with conduct disorder demonstrate psychopathic tendencies. Skilling, Quinsey and Craig (2001) also examined the prevalence rates of psychopathic traits in children. These researchers found that only 4.3 percent of a sample of more than a thousand boys from grades 4 to 8 could be classified as psychopathic. However, Daderman and Kristiannson (2003) suggested up to 59 percent of the violent juvenile sample they examined exhibited psychopathic behaviors. Lastly, Campbell, Porter, and Santor (2004) reported that only 9 percent of their research sample of incarcerated adolescent offenders could be classified as psychopaths. The variability in these research findings may be attributed to age of onset of behavioral problems, level of aggression, as well as persistent violent offending histories.

Hemispheric Functions

When reviewing the relationship between hemispheric asymmetry and behavioral dysfunction, Hare and McPherson (1984) hypothesized that criminal psychopaths often demonstrated an unusual relationship between their left and right hemispheres in both language processing and in emotional arousal states. For instance, additional research on hemispheric asymmetry by Hare (1998) and Lorenz and Newman (2002) suggested that criminal psychopaths had striking inconsistencies with their verbalized thoughts, feelings, and intentions. Specifically, most criminal psychopaths had deficiencies in linguistic processing, and did not rely upon verbal sequential operations to the extent that the typical normative population typically does. Furthermore, both Hare (1998) and Lorenz and Newman (2002) found that as language tasks increased in complexity, nonpsychopathic individuals relied heavily on the left hemisphere to process information, whereas psychopaths relied more on the right hemisphere.

There has also been research to suggest that psychopaths were less accurate than nonpsychopaths at reading emotional expressions displayed on faces (Kosson et al., 2002). For instance, Kosson et al. (2002) noted that psychopaths appeared less accurate than nonpsychopaths in facial emotional recognition, especially under conditions requiring left-hemispheric processing. Lorenz and Newman (2002) postulated that psychopaths exhibited an emotional paradox, meaning they were able to demonstrate typical appraisal of emotional cues and situations in the abstract, such as verbal discussions, but were deficient utilizing emotional cues to guide their judgments and behavior when living out their lives. Further research by both Lorenz and Newman (2002) and Bernstein et al. (2002) postulated this deficiency may be due to left hemispheric processing deficits. On the other hand, research from both Day and Wong (1996) and Silberman and Weingartner (1996) suggested that psychopaths also presented with impairments in the right hemisphere, which may prevent them from experiencing emotions when compared to the typical normative population.

There are many ways school neuropsychologists can utilize individualized assessment practices to guide possible approaches to intervention beyond cognitive and achievement tools. Some of the tools that may prove beneficial when exploring or measuring the range of psychopathology, personality, and social-emotional impact include the Trauma Symptoms Checklist for Children (TSCC ages 8-

16, Psychological Assessment Resources, Inc.), Trauma Symptoms Checklist for Young Children (TSCC ages 3-12, Psychological Assessment Resources, Inc.), the Minnesota Multiphasic Personality Inventory for Adolescents (MMPI-A, ages 14-18, Pearson Publications), Adolescent Psychopathology Scale-Long Form (ages 12-19, Psychological Assessment Resources, Inc.), the Hare Psychopathology Checklist: Youth Version (PCI:YV ages 12-18, Multi-Health Systems, Inc.), the Jesness Inventory Revised (JI-R ages 8+, Multi-Health Systems, Inc.), and the Antisocial Process Screening Device (APSD ages 6-13, Multi-Health Systems, Inc.).

When evaluating risk and need factors as well as the child's copying style and personality, the following assessment tools may prove helpful with diagnostic findings: the Adolescent & Child Urgent Threat Evaluation (ACUTE ages 8-18, Psychological Assessment Resources, Inc.), The Youth Level of Service/Case Management (YSL/CMI ages 12-17, the Structured Assessment of Violence Risk in Youth (SAVRY ages 12-18, Psychological Assessment Resources, Inc.), and the Coping Inventory for Stressful Situations: Adolescent (CISS ages 13-18, Multi-Health Systems, Inc.).

In conclusion, school neuropsychologists can begin to use their knowledge of brain-based behaviors to suggest, as part of the child's collaborative team, effective educational and behavioral interventions for students with neurological or neuropsychological difficulties involving frontal lobe dysfunction, psychopathology, and violence.

A final thought to remember when working with children and youth who present as aggressive and/or violent: "Treat people as if they were what they ought to be and you help them to become what they are capable of being." (By Johann von Goethe, poet 1749-1832)

REFERENCES

Amen, D. (2005). *The Brain and Behavior*. Mind Works Press.

American Bar Association (2004, January). *Adolescence, Brain Development and Legal Culpability*. Washington, DC.

Bartol, C. A. & Bartol, A.M. (2008). *Criminal Behavior A Psychosocial Approach* (8th ed.). Upper Saddle River, NJ: Pearson Education, Inc.

Barratt, E. S., Stanford, M. S., Kent, T.A.., & Felthous, A. (1997). Neuropsychological and psychophysiological substrates of impulsive aggression. *Biological psychiatry, 41*(10), 1045-1061.

Bernstein, A., Newman, J.P., Wallace, J.F., & Luh, K.E. (2000). Left hemisphere activation and deficient response modulation in psychopaths. *Psychological Science, 11*, 414-418.

Blair, C. (2002). School readiness. Integrating cognition and emotion in a neurobiological conceptualization of children's functioning at school entry. *American Psychologist, 57*, 111-127.

Blair, R.J., Perchardt, K.S., Budhani, S., Mitchell, D.G.V., & Pine, D. S. (2006). The development of psychopathy. *Journal of Child Psychology and Psychiatry, 47*, 262-275.

Bloomquist, M.L., & Schnell, S.V. (2002). *Helping children with aggression and conduct problems: Best practices and interventions*. New York, NY: Guilford Press.

Brower, M.C. & Price, B.H. (2001). Neuropsychiatry of frontal lobe dysfunction in violent and criminal behaviour: a critical review. *J. Neurol Neurosurg Psychiatry, 71*, 720-726 (December).

Brownlie, E.B., Beitchman, J.J., Escobai, M., Young, A., Atkinson, L., Johnson, C., Wilson, B., & Douglas, L. (2004). Early language impairment and young adult delinquent and aggressive behavior. *Journal of Abnormal Child Psychology, 32*, 453-349.

Campbell, M.A., Porter, S., & Santor, D. (2004). Psychopathic traits in adolescent offenders: An evaluation of criminal history, clinical, and psychosocial correlates. *Behavioral Sciences & the Law, 22*, 23-47.

Carter, R. (1998). *Mapping the Mind*. Berkeley: University of California Press.

Culhane-Shelburne, K , Chapieski, L., Hiscock, M., & Glaze, D. (2002). Executive functions in children with frontal and temporal lobe epilepsy. *Journal of the International Neuropsychological Society, 8*, 623-632.

D'Amato, R.C., Fletcher-Janzen, E., Reynolds, C.R. (2005). *Handbook of school neuropsychology*. Hoboken, NJ: Wiley & sons, Inc.

Daderman, A.M., & Kristiansson, M. (2003). Degree of psychopathology: Implications for treatment in male juvenile delinquents. *International Journal of Law and Psychiatry, 26*, 310-315.

Dahlberg, L.L., & Potter, L.B. (2001). Youth violence:Developmental pathways and prevention challenges. *American Journal of Preventive Medicine, 20*(1s), 3-14.

Day, R., & Wong, S. (1996). Anomalous perceptual asymmetries for negative emotional stimuli in the psychopath. *Journal of Abnormal Psychology, 105*, 648-652.

Dolan, R. J. (1999). On the neurology of morals. *Nature Neuroscience, 2*(11), 927-929.

Duffy J.D., & Campbell, J.J. III. (1994). The regional prefrontal syndromes: a theoretical and clinical overview. *Journal Neuropsychiatry Clinical Neuroscience, 6*, 379-387.

Goldberg, E., (2001). *The executive brain: Frontal lobes and the civilized mind*. New York, NY: Oxford University Press.

Hare, R.D. (1998). Emotional processing in psychopaths. In D.J. Cooke, R.D., Hare, & A. Forth (Eds.). *Psychopathy:Theory, research, and implications for society*. The Netherlands: Kluwer Academic Publishers.

Hare, R.D., & McPherson, L.M. (1984). Violent and aggressive behavior by criminal psychopaths. *International Journal of Law and Psychiatry, 7*, 35-50.

Keihl, K.A. (2006). A cognitive neuroscience perspective on psychopathy: Evidence for paralimbic system dysfunction. *Psychiatry Research, 142*, 17-128.

Kosson, D.S., Suchy, Y., Mayer, A.R., & Libby, J. (2002). Facial affect recognition in criminal psychopaths. *Emotion, 2*, 3998-411.

Lapierre, D., Braun, C. M. J., & Hodgins, S. (1995). Ventral frontal deficits in psychopathy: Neuropsychological test findings. *Neuropsychologia, 33*(2), 139-151.

LeDoux, J. (1996). *The emotional brain*. Simon & Schuster: New York.

Liu, J., Raine, A., Venables, P.H., & Mendick, S.A. (2004). Malnutrition at age 3 years and externalizing behaviors at ages 8, 11, and 17 years. *American Journal of Psychiatry, 161*, 2005-2013.

Loeber, R., Farmington, D.P., & Petechuk, D. (2003, May). *Child Delinquency: Early intervention and prevention. Child Delinquency Bulletin Series*. Washington, DC: U.S. Department of Justice, Office of Juvenile Justice and Delinquency Prevention.

Loeber, R., & Stouthamer-Loeber, M. (1998). Development of juvenile aggression and violence: Some common misconceptions and controversies. *American Psychologist, 33*, 242-259.

Lorenz, A.R., & Newman, J.P. (2002). Deficient response modulation and emotion processing in low-anxious Caucasian psychopathic offenders: Results from a lexical decision task. *Emotion, 2*, 91-104.

Moeller, T. G. (2001). *Youth aggression and violence: A psychological approach*. New Jersey: Lawrence Erlbaum Associates.

Moffitt, T.E. (2003). Life-course-persistent and adolescent-limited antisocial behavior: A 10-year research review and research agenda. In B.B. Lahey, T.E. Moffitt, and A. Caspi (Eds.), *Causes of conduct disorder and juvenile delinquency*. New York: Guilford.

Moffitt, T. E., & Lynam, D. Jr. (1994). The neuropsychology of conduct disorder and delinquency: Implications for understanding antisocial behavior. *Progress in Experimental Personality and Psychopathology Research*, 233-262.

Morgan, A. B. , & Lilienfeld, S. O. (2000). A meta-analytic review of the relation between antisocial behavior and neuropsychological measures of executive functions. *Clinical Psychology Review, 20*(1), 113-136.

Murrie, D.C., & Cornell, D.G., Kaplan, S., McConville, D., &Levy-Elkon, A. (2004). Psychopathy scores and violence among juvenile offenders: A multi-measure study. *Behavioral Sciences & Law, 22*, 49-67.

National Center for Educational Statistics: U.S. Department of Education: (2007). *Indicators of School Crime and Safety: 2007*, Washington, D.C: U.S. Department of Justice.

Rosenthal, M., & Bond, M.R. (1990). Behavioral and psychiatric sequelae. In M. Rosenthal, M. Bond, E.R. Griffith, & J.D. Miller (Eds.), *Rehabilitation of the adult and child with traumatic brain injury* (pp.179-192). Philadelphia: Davis.

Reiss, A.L., et al. Brain development, gender and IQ in children, a volumetric imaging study. *Brain, 119*(1996).

Rolls, E.T. (1997). The orbitofrontal cortex. *Philosophical Transactions of the Royal Society B, 351*, 1433-1443.

Salekin, R.T., Zeigler, T.A., Larrea, M.A., Anthony, V.L., & Bennett, A.D. (2003). Predicting psychopathology with two Millon Adolescent psychopathy scales. The importance of egocentric and callous traits. *Journal of Personality Assessment, 80*, 154-163.

Siegel, D. J. (1999). *The developing mind: How relationships and the brain interact to share who we are.* New York, NY: Guilford Press.

Silberman, E.K., & Weingartner, H. (1996). Hemisphere lateralization of functions related to emotion. *Brain and Cognition, 5*, 322-353.

Skilling, T.A., Quinsey, V.L., & Craig, W.M. (2001). Evidence of a tax on underlying serious antisocial behavior in boys. *Criminal Justice and Behavior, 28*, 450-470.

Stowell, E.R., Thompson, P.M., Holmes, C.J., Jerigan, T.L., and Toga, A.W. (1999). In vivo evidence for post-adolescent brain maturation in frontal and striatal regions. *Nature Neuroscience 10.*

Stuss, D.T., & Levine, B. (2002). Adult clinical neuropsychology: lesson from studies of the frontal lobes. *Annual Review of Psychology, 53*, 401-433.

Tranel, D. (1992). Functional neuroanatomy: Neuropsychological correlates of cortical and subcortical damage. In S.C. Yudofsky & R.E. Hales (Eds.), *The American Psychiatric Press textbook of neuropsychiatry* (2nd ed., pp. 57-88). Washington, DC: American Psychiatric Press.

Wehrenberg, M. & Prinz, S.M. (2007). *The anxious brain: The neurobiological basis of anxiety disorders and how to effectively treat them.* New York, NY: W.W. Norton and Company.

Zilmer, E. A., Spiers, M. V., Culbertson, W. C. (2008). *Principles of neuropsychology* (2nd Ed.). Belmont, CA: Thomson Wadesworth Publishers.

CHAPTER 6

MOOD AND ANXIETY DISORDERS IN CHILDREN

Steven G. Feifer, D.Ed.

"Students do not care what we know, until they know that we care."
—Robert Brooks

According to the National Center for Educational Statistics (2007), the proportion of children receiving special education services under the category of *"emotional disturbance"* has remained relatively constant over the past 30 years, hovering at approximately one percent (see Table 6-1). The general malaise of this special education category represents a sharp contrast to most other educational disabilities such as *"learning disabled"* and *"autism"* which have increased drastically over the years. Furthermore, children diagnosed as having an *"emotional disorder"* in public education is disproportional to the increased number of children being diagnosed as having *emotional conditions* by private clinicians. For instance, the rate of diagnosing pediatric bipolar disorder in outpatient clinical settings has doubled in the past five years (Leibenluft & Rich, 2008), and virtually quadrupled in community hospitals throughout the United States (Case et al., 2007). This incongruity in diagnostic epidemiology is further compounded by the fact that the educational nomenclature has remained relatively constant regarding the criteria for an emotional disturbance. Currently, students categorized as having an emotional disturbance, as defined under the Individuals with Disabilities Education Act (2004), are as follows:

TABLE 6-1
National Center for Educational Statistics (2007)

Children 3 to 21 Years old Served in Federally Supported Programs for the Disabled, by Type of Disability: Selected Years, 1976-77 Through 2005-06

Type of disability	1976–77	1980–81	1990–91	1994–95	1995–96	1996–97	1997–98	1998–99	1999–2000	2000–01	2001–02	2002–03	2003–04	2004–05	2005–06
						Number served (in thousands)									
All disabilities	**3,694**	**4,144**	**4,710**	**5,378**	**5,572**	**5,737**	**5,908**	**6,056**	**6,195**	**6,296**	**6,407**	**6,523**	**6,634**	**6,719**	**6,713**
Specific learning disabilities	796	1,462	2,129	2,489	2,578	2,651	2,727	2,790	2,834	2,868	2,861	2,848	2,831	2,798	2,735
Speech or language impairments	1,302	1,168	985	1,015	1,022	1,045	1,060	1,068	1,080	1,409	1,391	1,412	1,441	1,463	1,468
Mental retardation	961	830	534	555	571	579	589	597	600	624	616	602	593	578	556
Emotional disturbance	**283**	**347**	**389**	**427**	**437**	**446**	**454**	**462**	**469**	**481**	**483**	**485**	**489**	**489**	**477**
Hearing impairments	88	79	58	64	67	68	69	70	71	78	78	78	79	79	79
Orthopedic impairments	87	58	49	60	63	66	67	69	71	83	83	83	77	73	71
Other health impairments	141	98	55	106	133	160	190	220	253	303	350	403	464	521	570
Visual impairments	38	31	23	24	25	25	26	26	26	29	28	29	28	29	29
Multiple disabilities	—	68	96	88	93	98	106	106	111	133	136	138	140	140	141
Deaf-blindness	—	3	1	1	1	1	1	2	2	1	2	2	2	2	2
Autism	—	—	—	22	28	34	42	53	65	94	114	137	163	191	223
Traumatic brain injury	—	—	—	7	9	10	12	13	14	16	22	22	23	24	24
Developmental delay	—	—	—	—	—	—	2	12	19	178	242	283	305	332	339
Preschool disabled	†	†	390	519	544	555	565	568	581	†	†	†	†	†	†
Number served as a percent of total enrollment															
All disabilities	**8.3**	**10.1**	**11.4**	**12.2**	**12.4**	**12.6**	**12.8**	**13.0**	**13.2**	**13.3**	**13.4**	**13.5**	**13.7**	**13.8**	**13.8**
Specific learning disabilities	1.8	3.6	5.2	5.6	5.8	5.8	5.9	6.0	6.0	6.1	6.0	5.9	5.8	5.7	5.6
Speech or language impairments	2.9	2.9	2.4	2.3	2.3	2.3	2.3	2.3	2.3	3.0	2.9	2.9	3.0	3.0	3.0
Mental retardation	2.2	2.0	1.3	1.3	1.3	1.3	1.3	1.3	1.3	1.3	1.2	1.2	1.2	1.2	1.1
Emotional disturbance	**0.6**	**0.8**	**0.9**	**1.0**	**1.0**	**1.0**	**1.0**	**1.0**	**1.0**	**1.0**	**1.0**	**1.0**	**1.0**	**1.0**	**1.0**
Hearing impairments	0.2	0.2	0.1	0.1	0.1	0.1	0.1	0.2	0.2	0.2	0.2	0.2	0.2	0.2	0.2
Orthopedic impairments	0.2	0.1	0.1	0.1	0.1	0.1	0.1	0.1	0.2	0.2	0.2	0.2	0.2	0.2	0.1
Other health impairments	0.3	0.2	0.1	0.2	0.3	0.4	0.4	0.5	0.5	0.6	0.7	0.8	1.0	1.1	1.2
Visual impairments	0.1	0.1	0.1	0.1	0.1	0.1	0.1	0.1	0.1	0.1	0.1	0.1	0.1	0.1	0.1
Multiple disabilities	—	0.2	0.2	0.2	0.2	0.2	0.2	0.2	0.3	0.3	0.3	0.3	0.3	0.3	0.3
Deaf-blindness	—	#	#	#	#	#	#	#	#	#	#	#	#	#	#
Autism	—	—	—	0.1	0.1	0.1	0.1	0.1	0.1	0.2	0.2	0.3	0.3	0.4	0.5
Traumatic brain injury	—	—	—	#	#	#	#	#	#	#	#	#	#	#	0.1
Developmental delay	—	—	—	—	—	—	#	#	#	0.4	0.5	0.6	0.6	0.7	0.7
Preschool disabled	†	†	0.9	1.2	1.2	1.2	1.2	1.2	1.2	†	†	†	†	†	†

IDEA Definition of an Emotional Disturbance

"...a condition exhibiting one or more of the following characteristics over a long period of time and to a marked degree that adversely affects a child's educational performance—

    A. An inability to learn that cannot be explained by intellectual, sensory, or health factors.

    B. An inability to build or maintain satisfactory interpersonal relationships with peers and teachers.

    C. Inappropriate types of behavior or feelings under normal circumstances.

    D. A general pervasive mood of unhappiness or depression.

    E. A tendency to develop physical symptoms or fears associated with personal or school problems." [Code of Federal Regulations, Title 34, Section 300.7(c)(4)(i)]

There are numerous factors at play which may account for the paradoxical relationship between the substantial increases of emotional conditions in youth, compared with those students actually receiving special education services for an emotional condition. First, school systems abide by multidisciplinary team decisions meaning that non-mental health professionals, except for the school psychologist, are making decisions about the presence of an emotional disability. Second, unlike the DSM-IV-TR criteria, educational disabilities have an embedded "out clause"; namely, the diagnostic category of *"Other Health Impaired"*, which is an umbrella term used to categorize any health related disability often requiring the use of medication management. As noted in Table 6-1, the use of this diagnostic category has more than doubled in the past decade to a robust 1.2 percent of all students aged 3-21. Third, there continues to be much confusion and lack of consensus regarding the definition of most mood and anxiety disorders, especially *bipolar disorder*.

Bipolar Disorder in Children

According to Leibenluft and Rich (2008), the primary disagreement regarding the diagnosis of bipolar disorder in children centers on the criteria of mania. By definition, bipolar disorder generally refers to severe and abrupt mood swings ranging from mania to depression. However, there remains much confusion regarding the distinction between discrete mood episodes in children versus severe and chronic irritability. According to the DSM-IV-TR (2000), bipolar I is diagnosed when a full manic episode occurs for more than seven days with symptoms resulting in marked impairment of function. Conversely, bipolar II is diagnosed when a manic episode lasts under four days with noticeable symptoms, though not necessarily severe impairment in functioning. The symptomology for mania often includes periods of grandiosity, decreased need for sleep, pressured speech, racing thoughts, increased distractibility, and excessive pleasure seeking or risky behavior. This definition has been criticized primarily on the grounds that mania cannot be clinically differentiated from

KEY LEARNING POINTS:
Defining Bipolar Disorder

Bipolar I—diagnosed when a full manic episode occurs for more than seven days with symptoms resulting in marked impairment of function

Bipolar II—diagnosed when a manic episode lasts under four days with noticeable symptoms, though not necessarily severe impairment in functioning.

Severe Mood Dysregulation—characterized by more chronic irritability, hyperarousal, and hyper-reactivity to negative stimuli.

attention deficit disorder, and that cycling of moods can also occur rapidly throughout the day (Geller et al., 2007). According to Leibenluft and Rich (2008), caution should be taken before diagnosing a child under the age of 6 with bipolar disorder due, in part, to the co-morbidity of *attention deficit disorder* (up to 70%), *oppositional defiant disorder* (up to 80%), and *anxiety disorders* (up to 78%) in bipolar youth. Therefore, perhaps a more accurate diagnosis for children who do not meet the criteria for bipolar disorder due to manic episodes whose cycles are relatively brief, should be *severe mood dysregulation*, as characterized by more chronic irritability, hyper-arousal, and hyper-reactivity to negative stimuli (Leibenluft & Rich, 2008).

It is interesting to note that the co-morbidity of anxiety can often assist clinicians in differentiating the various behavioral manifestations of bipolar disorder (Dickstein et al., 2005). For instance, children with co-morbid anxiety disorders often have a significantly earlier onset of bipolar disorder and more psychiatric hospitalizations. In other words, the anxiety disorder may compound a child's ability to effectively cope and manage their bipolar condition. Conversely, children with severe mood dysregulation who also have a co-morbid anxiety disorder are not significantly more impaired than children with severe mood dysregulation without a co-morbid anxiety disorder (Dickstein et al., 2005). Therefore, severe mood dysregulation may be a separate strand or distinct phenotype from bipolar disorder, both in its core symptomology as well as susceptibility to being influenced by other anxiety related conditions. Perhaps pediatric studies of bipolar disorder need to evaluate the presence of anxiety in order to plot an appropriate course of treatment in children.

Neural Underpinnings of Bipolar Disorder

One of the more remarkable feats of affective neuroscience is to sift through a myriad of brain characteristics such as myelination, synaptic density, dendritic branching, pruning of neurons, and brain electro-chemical activity, all of which systematically change during childhood, and develop specific biological markers for dysfunctional behavior (Immordino-Yang & Fischer, 2007). Neuroimaging studies of bipolar disorder in adults have noted general brain atrophy in the right hemisphere, though pediatric populations have yielded inconsistent results (Kloos et al., 2008). Some of the preliminary findings are noted in Table 6-2:

TABLE 6-2
Key Brain Regions in Bipolar Disorder

1. *Amygdala*—Smaller amygdala size is a consistent neuroanatomic finding in children with bipolar disorder (DelBello et al., 2006). The amygdala is a phylogenetically old structure housed within the temporal lobes, and primarily serves to code incoming sensory and/or cognitive information that has affective significance (LeDoux, 2003). The amygdala plays a role in the perception of threatening information, the appraisal of social signals that convey a threat, and the acquisition of fear conditioned responses (LeDoux, 2003). The basolateral regions of the amygdala are primarily responsible for modulating its overall excitability (Fudge et al., 2002).

2. *Hippocampus*—Adult studies of bipolar disorder have yielded relatively normal hippocampal size and volume, yet some studies in children have suggested smaller hippocampal volume is evident in depression (Caetano et al., 2005). The hippocampus lies in close proximity to the amygdala and is primarily responsible for consolidating new memories and retrieving older ones.

3. *Cingulate Gyrus*—The anterior portion of the cingulate gyrus provides constraint over emotion and cognition. It does this by decreasing activation associated with: a lack of task initiation, apathetic and unmotivated behavior, and anhedonia (Whittle et al., 2006). Numerous studies have noted the left anterior cingulate in bipolar patients being significantly smaller in volume (Drevets et al., 1997; Kaur et al., 2005).

4. *Basal Ganglia*—Recent studies have suggested bipolar children have an enlarged right nucleus accumbens, an area housed within the basal ganglia (Ahn et al., 2007). The nucleus accumbens has rich interconnections with the limbic system, and plays a central role in the reward circuit of the brain (Kloos et al., 2008). It is a region of the brain highly sensitive to dopamine, a neurotransmitter involved with desire, and when over-stimulated, may lead to manic types of behaviors.

Many of the structural brain abnormalities in bipolar disorder involve critical frontal-subcortical circuitry that clearly impacts neurocognitive functioning. According to Adler et al. (2006) bipolar children typically perform well on standardized intelligence test measures of verbal and nonverbal problem solving skills. Nevertheless, there are often significant deficits on executive functioning tasks that are mediated by the prefrontal cortices. For instance, bipolar children typically have difficulty on a variety of attention tasks, as well as tasks involving declarative memory and working memory (Adler et al., 2006). In addition, Beardon, Hoffman, and Cannon (2001) found evidence of decreased performance on the Wisconsin Card Sort Test, a task requiring children to learn from environmental feedback and avoid perseveration of mistakes. Lastly, Feifer and Rattan (2007) also noted that children with emotional conditions requiring special education services scored extremely low on ratings of *Emotional Control* and *Shifting Attention* as measured by the *BRIEF,* an executive functioning rating scale.

Additional studies of adolescents with bipolar disorder have pinpointed specific deficits in the prefrontal lobes that are associated with executive functioning skills. For instance, the ventral prefrontal cortex, an area of the brain responsible for cognitive set shifting, decision making, and adapting behavior on the basis of emotional significance may have profound disturbances in bipolar children thereby hindering their ability to adapt to reward parameters (Blumberg et al., 2003). According to Leibenluft and Rich (2008), the ventral prefrontal cortex has rich interconnections with the amygdala, and deviations in this circuitry may prevent children from altering their behavior to changing reward contingencies. Consequently, bipolar children may adopt a rather inflexible response style lending to mood disturbances. Therefore, the following executive functioning skills may be compromised with bipolar children:

TABLE 6-3
Cognitive and Emotional Skills Compromised in Bipolar Disorder

Emotional Perception
     Task Initiation
     Focus Attention
     Sustain Attention
     Response Inhibition
          Cognitive Flexibility
          Working Memory
          Planning
          Task Organization
          Retrieval Fluency
          Time Management
          Task Execution
          Self Monitoring
               Modulating Effort
               Emotional Regulation
               Persistence of Effort

Reactive Aggression and Bipolar Disorder

Clinicians and researchers interested in the brain-behavioral manifestations of bipolar disorder are beginning to converge on a rather profound theoretical precept: namely, bipolar disorder may be more dimensional, rather than categorical; and as a result, they will most likely fall within a behavioral spectrum (Leibenluft & Rich, 2008). Clearly, this re-conceptualization of bipolar disorder as being dimensional remains counter-intuitive to the categorical model of mood disorders as outlined in the DSM-IV-TR. Nevertheless, affective neuroscience has allowed researchers to better understand the intrinsic properties of psychiatric conditions based upon specific brain structures, rather than just over-relying on behavioral characteristics to define a construct. For instance, according to Rich et al. (2006) bipolar children often misinterpret neutral faces, and rate them as more hostile and fear producing. Furthermore, bipolar children often require extremely intense displays of a particular facial expression to identify a specific emotion (Rich et al., 2006). Why do bipolar children exhibit such emotional limitations by misinterpreting facial cues and reacting in such an aggressive fashion with their moods and behavior? A behaviorist might look at specific negative reinforcement contingencies supporting maladaptive emotional responses (i.e., an abusive parent, poor structure at home, lack of social role models, etc.), and focus treatment on specific environmental variables. However, affective neuroscience acknowledges the role of the environment in shaping behavior, but primarily focuses treatment on how core emotions are mapped on to higher brain regions. Oftentimes, inefficient perceptions result in inefficient mapping, especially when reactive aggression is involved with bipolar youth.

Blair (2004) defined *reactive aggression* as hostile behavior initiated without regard for any potential goal, but rather a response to sheer frustration. In school, failing an academic test and blaming the teacher or hostility toward a peer for making a snide remark are primary examples of frustration that may lead to *reactive aggression*. It stands to reason that bipolar youth are especially vulnerable to *reactive aggression*, no matter the environmental contingencies involved. Nevertheless, it is important to distinguish *reactive aggression* from *instrumental aggression* which is defined as goal directed aggression such as robbing, stealing, or sexual advances, accompanied by a general lack of empathy or remorse for the victim (Blair, 2001). The discussion here is primarily tailored to *reactive aggression* in bipolar youth.

The neural circuitry which modulates reactive aggression is sometimes referred to as a *fear-based circuit*, and becomes initiated at lower brain levels by the hypothalamus and the periaqueductal gray, which jointly cause one to freeze when confronted by an environmental threat (Blair, 2001). If the threat continues, the amygdala, a central component of the limbic system, becomes activated and the classic *fight or flight* decision response comes into play. If flight is impossible, the brain will activate a reactive aggressive response as mediated by both the orbitofrontal cortex and ventromedial cortex (Blair, 2001). Damage to the orbitofrontal or ventromedial prefrontal cortex is associated with an increased display of *reactive aggression* in both children and adults (Blair et al., 2004). However, *reactive aggression* is also activated by intense environmental threats, or through repeated accumulations to past threats (Blair et al., 2004). Therefore, children who are physically or sexually abused, or have repeated exposure to threatening events and conditions may be at more risk to demonstrate *reactive aggression*. Hence, environmental contingencies may spawn the potential for reactive aggression, but neural networks in the brain must also be primed to respond in such a fashion as well.

According to Blair (2004), the orbitofrontal cortex is heavily involved in modulating *reactive aggression*, due in part to its strong connectivity with emotional brain circuits such as the amygdala. The orbitofrontal cortex basically functions as a higher-level decision making mechanism fueled by emotional feelings engendered from previous experiences (Dolan, 1999). When this brain region is damaged, or these experiences are overwhelmingly negative, children may become stuck in a state of feeling constantly threatened, and will automatically respond to stimuli

KEY LEARNING POINTS: Emotional Mapping and Reactive Aggression

- Bipolar children often misinterpret neutral faces, and rate them as more hostile and fear producing, and often require intense displays of facial expression to identify a particular emotion (Rich et al., 2006).

- Damage to the orbitofrontal or ventromedial prefrontal cortex is associated with an increased display of reactive aggression in both children and adults (Blair et al., 2004).

- Rolls (2004) surmised that the orbitofrontal cortex is heavily involved in modulating reactive aggression, due in part, to its strong connectivity with emotional brain circuits, such as the amygdala.

- Poor emotional mapping of emotional circuitry to the orbitofrontal cortex may lead to faulty perceptions of emotion, emotional inflexibility, and reactive aggression. This may be a primary neurobehavioral deficit with bipolar disordered children.

in an aggressive fashion. Perhaps this is why bipolar children often misinterpret neutral faces and rate them as more hostile, with a consequent response of aggressive hostility toward them. In essence, basic core emotions have projections to higher brain regions (orbitofrontal cortex) that interpret the data in either an adaptive or maladaptive manner. Thus, children brought up in households with inconsistent parenting, turbulence and violence, or unpredictable reinforcement contingencies may be more prone to *reactive aggression*. In summary, children may be at risk for reactive aggression due to an inability of the orbitofrontal cortex to effectively modulate reward valences in *fear-based* learning circuits (Rolls, 2004).

Treatment Contingencies for Bipolar Disorder

Since multiple neural systems are involved in bipolar disorder (see Table 6-2), there tends to be a wide variety of treatment algorithms, especially given the numerous co-morbid symptoms also associated with this disorder. Still, an attempt to rectify the affective instability in children should be at the core of any treatment regimen. According to Leibenluft and Rich (2008), an appropriate treatment algorithm should first focus upon stabilization of emotions through medication management, then re-teach the child proper adaptive responses to emotional challenges through therapy. Treatment programs should not only include cognitive behavioral therapy, but also include a family-focused therapeutic component (Leibenluft & Rich, 2008). Most social dysfunctions can be addressed through activities that promote social skill building, interpersonal problem solving, and role playing specific strategies and techniques. As noted by Leibenluft and Rich (2008), therapeutic success with a bipolar child is best achieved by improving the child's knowledge of the disorder, providing appropriate strategies and skills to regulate mood and behavior, fostering and promoting more pro-social peer interactions, and enhancing communication patterns within the family unit. All of these techniques are essentially re-teaching higher brain regions to develop more adaptive responses and more efficient mapping of core emotional stimuli. Table 6-4 outlines ten key counseling strategies and techniques to address bipolar disorder with children.

TABLE 3-4
Ten Counseling Strategies for Children With Bipolar Disorder

1. **Listen to your body**
   Goal: Child will learn to read the physiological clues of various emotions.
   Activity: Draw an outline of a person. Ask questions such as *"What does your heart do when you get angry?"* Next, draw a symbolic representation of the emotion (i.e., *"My heart beats fast—so I may draw drums," "How does your head feel when you are mad?", "My head hurts so I may draw a band-aid," "What do your feet feel like when you are angry?", "My feet feel like running so I may draw tennis shoes."*

2. **A to Z with Feelings**
   Goal: Child will learn to identify their current emotional state.
   Activity: Have a poster with feeling words from A to Z and corresponding faces. Have the child learn to appropriately identify current and past feeling states on the poster.

3. **Feelings Go-Fish**
   Goal: Child will identify situations that correspond with various feelings.
   Activity: Using a deck of cards with feelings faces and words (available from Childswork/Childsplay), play a game of Go-Fish. When a match is made, the child must verbalize and elaborate upon a feeling.

4. **Slow it Down**

   Goal: Child will learn to become aware of the physiological signs present in their own body and learn to slow down.

   Activity: Ask the child to run in place or engage in another form of cardiovascular exercise until their heart is beating fast. Compare the current feeling to the feelings associated with mania. Next, choose another exercise, but perform the activity in slow motion. Discuss how this can be used to control the fast feelings in the body.

5. **Music Selections**

   Goal: Child will match their feelings with music to help alter moods.

   Activity: Using a favorite music selection of the child, ask the child to verbalize their feelings while a particular song is playing. Create a catalogue of songs with emotions, and then compile a list of music that helps maintain a positive mood state.

6. **Mood Journals**

   Goal: Child will learn to notice specific triggers resulting in mood changes.

   Activity: Have the child keep an emotions journal that includes sleep, diet, and exercise habits as well any noteworthy events each day. In the journal, document all emotions associated with each activity. The child can write or draw in the journal as well. After approximately one week, begin to review the journal with the child to chart and catalogue activities with specific mood changes (i.e., lack of sleep induces depressive feelings).

7. **Feelings menu**

   Goal: The child will create a menu of healthy behaviors to assist during times of euphoria and/or feelings of anger or depression.

   Activity: Create a feelings menu with heading such as *tired, high energy, angry, irritable*, etc. Under each label develop a list of safe options that can happen when that feeling occurs. The child can illustrate the menu as well. Next, engage in a restaurant play activity with the child ordering and then acting out the menu item chosen.

8. **Reading faces**

   Goal: The child will learn to read other emotions and body language.

   Activity: Choose comic books with very animated characters, such as *Calvin and Hobbes*. Remove the words and captions from the comic strips and ask the child to guess the emotions of the characters based on their facial expressions and body language. Try the same activity by showing videos of cartoon with no sound and ask the child to identify the cartoon characters' feelings.

9. **Bowling**

   Goal: The child will learn to correlate specific feelings with behaviors.

   Activity: Write one feeling word on the bottom of each plastic bowling pin. After each roll, the bowler selects one of the pins that have been knocked down. Next, have the child describe an incident that conjures up the feeling on the bowling pin.

10. **Paint a metaphor**

    Goal: Child will gain an understanding of how multiple feelings can often blur together and rapidly change.

    Activity: Using paint or modeling clay, ask the child to match a color with an emotion (i.e. *red is happy, blue is sad, black is angry*, etc.). Next identify a specific event (i.e. *teacher not calling on you in class or a friend who chooses to play with someone else at recess*) and ask the child to paint the color that matches their feelings for each scenario. Keep naming events or scenarios until the paper is completely covered in wet paint. Then have the child take their brush and create a trail through the wet paint noticing the myriad of colors on the brush. Lastly, talk about how multiple feelings often accompany any endeavor, and the dangers of dwelling on just the negative ones.

---

*Strategies provided by Darci D. Feifer, M.Ed., LCPC

Pediatric Anxiety Disorders

The overlap of bipolar disorder with other psychiatric conditions such as ADHD, depression, and anxiety disorders is very common, and poses quite a challenge for most clinicians. Investigations into the developmentally distinct patterns of bipolar disorder have focused upon age of onset as well determining whether the core symptomalogy is more chronic or episodic (Wozniak, 2005). Pediatric anxiety disorders often co-occur with bipolar disorder, with most epidemiological studies estimating that approximately 10% of all children have some sort of anxiety impairment (Pine, 1994). Therefore, a detailed discussion of the various subtypes of anxiety disorders is needed in order to better distinguish anxiety conditions from bipolar disorder. According to Reinblatt and Riddle (2007), most anxiety conditions fall under the subtypes of generalized anxiety disorders (GAD), separation anxiety disorders (SAD), and social phobias (SoP). These anxiety subtypes tend to overlap with about 40% of children having at least two of these conditions, and 20% of children having all three (Reinblatt & Riddle, 2007). It is important to emphasize that anxiety is a normal adaptive response built into our emotional configuration. However, when fears become excessive, debilitating, and unreasonable, significant problems can occur. For example, as the following vignette shows, it is the psychological perception of the anxious feeling itself that ultimately dictates a child's behavioral response:

Vignette #1: *Brendan had always been a thrill seeker, and held a special affinity for speed and heights. Whether climbing the largest tree in the neighborhood, or racing his bicycle the fastest, or attempting to jump his skateboard over unthinkable distances, he craved the thrilling sensation of each attempt. However, these feeble neighborhood stunts were no match for what awaited Brendan at Cedar Point Amusement Park, namely, the Millennium Force roller coaster. Standing some 310 feet high and reaching breathtaking speeds of more than 90 miles per hour, the Millennium Force is simply the tallest and fastest steel structured roller coaster in North America. Brendan was enthralled at the opportunity to take his speed and height passion to yet another exhilarating level. What could make such an adventurous trip to the amusement park even more extraordinary? Of course, having his best friend Sam accompany him.*

Sam had always been a rather shy and behaviorally inhibited child, although he took an early liking to Brendan's adventuresome side and their friendship immediately flourished. Now happily ensconced in Middle School, the boys set out for their spine-tingling adventure to the park. First stop, the Millennium Force. As the luminous steel structure awaited them, Sam became flooded with anxiety and panic, characterized by a rapid heart-beat, sweaty palms, a dry throat, and choppy breathing. He was paralyzed with fear, though he felt obligated to accompany Brendan and not be viewed as a coward in his friend's eyes. Reluctantly, he joined Brendan in the first car of the coaster, and smiled sheepishly while the steel car elevated upward in a slow, methodical fashion toward its pinnacle in the clouds above. Sam was now feeling overwhelmed by an intense fear of dying and was beginning to tremble outwardly when he noticed Brendan was quietly grinning with a rather serene facial expression. It appeared as if a sudden calm had transfixed Brendan and he was completely at peace with the world. Suddenly, gravity ceased to exist as the boys were in a complete free fall diving toward the ground before the coaster engaged in a series of twirls, twists, loops, and falls before the ride finally came to an abrupt end in about 90 seconds. Brendan screamed with unbridled joy and exclaimed, "Let's do that again," while Sam chirped, "Not so fast, buddy, I think I am going to be sick!"

TABLE 6-5
Pediatric Anxiety Disorders

Generalized Anxiety Disorder (GAD): Children with GAD go through school filled with exaggerated worry and tension. These children often anticipate disaster and are overly concerned about health issues. This disorder rarely occurs in isolation, and most children often complain of fatigue, frequently request to use the bathroom, experience muscle tension, and are often uncomfortable in school.

Separation Anxiety Disorder (SAD): Children with SAD become extremely distressed when separated from a parent, and may refuse to be separated from important attachment figures. In addition, children with SAD may be afraid to sleep alone, worry excessively their parents may die, and often develop school refusal.

Social Phobia (SoP): Children with social anxiety disorder, or what is often referred to as social phobia, have a persistent fear of social performance that may be humiliating or embarrassing. These fears tend to become excessive and unreasonable, and result in the avoidance of social situations. Academic impairments, limited social skills, and restricted peer relationships often occur as well.

There are two noteworthy points illustrated by the aforementioned vignette. First, children respond differently when reacting to their own internal emotionally-based cues. For instance, Sam had always been a reserved and shy child, tended to worry frequently, had difficulty concentrating in school, and struggled sleeping through the night. In many respects, he met the clinical criteria for a Generalized Anxiety Disorder (GAD) since the focus of his anxiety was not tied into a fear of being embarrassed (Social Phobia) or a fear of being away from home (Separation Anxiety). Instead, he exhibited a pervasive feeling of apprehension and worrisome thoughts across most situations. Clearly, Sam expressed much worry and self-doubt when standing in line and anticipating the experience of an awe-inspiring activity such as the Millennium Force. However, his fear heightened to unprecedented levels while sitting in the coaster as it slowly climbed to the top of the track. There is compelling evidence that children with Generalized Anxiety Disorder (GAD) may have elevated amygdala activity at the core of their disorder, especially when their attention is constrained to their own internal emotional states (McClure et al., 2007). In fact, Sam was alone in his thoughts while the coaster elevated upward, and focused completely on the unsettling feelings and events occurring internally in his body. Therefore, amygdala hyperactivity may be a pathological feature associated with GAD and elevated fear levels.

Second, although amygdala circuitry may play a prominent role in the behavioral responses to threatening stimuli, a number of other brain structures also play a pivotal role in the modulation and interpretation of emotional behavior; namely, the orbitofrontal cortex and anterior cingulate cortex (Easter et al., 2005). The *orbitofrontal cortex* is housed within the frontal lobes and has rich interconnections with the limbic regions of the brain. This brain region plays a crucial role in ascribing a reward value on emotional stimuli which ultimately guides behavior through reinforcement contingencies (Rolls, 2004). Hence, Sam *interpreted* the anxious feelings and sensations he was experiencing as having a rather negative reward value; thereby fostering urgent thoughts of needing to escape the situation in order to relieve his tension. Conversely, Brendan, whose happy-go-lucky temperament seemed diametrically opposed to Sam's inhibited one, interpreted any anxious feelings and sensations as sheer excitement and utter joy, which only reinforced his craving for thrills and adventures. Granted, Brendan does not meet the criteria for GAD, although his raw feeling of emotion may have been every bit as intense as Sam's, just cognitively interpreted in a different manner. Figure 6-1 illustrates the various brain structures involved with generalized anxiety disorders.

FIGURE 6-1

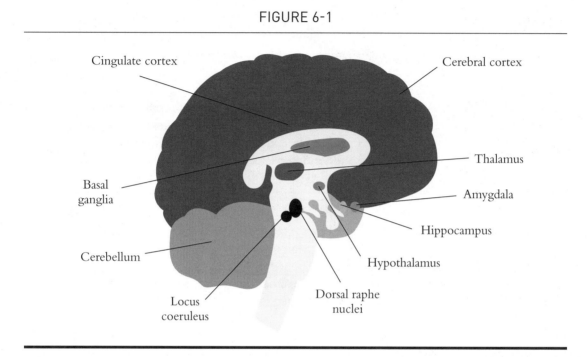

Most children and adults with anxiety disorders tend to put a negative spin or bias toward labeling emotions in a maladaptive manner (Easter et al., 2005). The reason for this bias may lie in a particular region of the frontal lobes called the *anterior cingulate cortex*. The *anterior cingulate cortex* functions as the brain's gear shifter, and allows children to shift between cognition and emotion in order to develop a more adaptive response to emotionally significant events (Allman et al., 2001). For instance, over-activation of the anterior cingulate cortex has been reported in children with anxiety disorders as well as cognitive tasks involving response inhibition (Drevets & Raichle, 1998). Therefore, deficits in the anterior cingulate cortex may be tantamount to having cognitive blinders that preclude children from developing a range of cognitive interpretations to ease unsettling feelings of fear and anxiety. This may leave children stuck in an emotional web of confusing perceptions, feelings, and emotions. Cognitive behavioral therapy (CBT) coupled with relaxation training may be especially helpful for children with anxiety disorders, especially if the source of their anxiety stems in part from amplified amygdala activity triggering or cueing the frontal regions of the brain (Khalid-Khan et al., 2007; McClure et al., 2007).

Social Anxiety Disorder
Social anxiety disorder, or what is often referred to as Social Phobia (SoP), is currently the third most prevalent psychiatric disorder in the adult community, with a mean onset age of approximately 15 years

old (Kessler et al., 1994). The core symptom of this disorder is a persistent fear of any social performance situation that may lead to a humiliating or embarrassing experience. Children with this disorder often have great impairment in their academic performance, social skills, peer relationships, and family encounters (Khalid-Khan et al., 2007). To the untrained eye, social anxiety disorder may be misinterpreted as just a bad case of shyness, which a child may ultimately outgrow. After all, children classified by age two as being behaviorally inhibited have a two-fold increase in the likelihood of developing a social phobia (Schwartz et al., 1999). However, other studies have cautioned that most shy children do not develop an anxiety disorder, let alone social phobia, and most adolescents with anxiety disorders have never been rated as shy (Mancini et al., 2005; Prior et al., 2000). Social anxiety disorder basically has two distinct sub-classifications. *Generalized* social anxiety disorder refers to children who experience anxiety and fear across most social situations, whereas *non-generalized* social anxiety involves specific social or performance-based situations, such as fear of public speaking (Khalid-Khan et al., 2007). Often, the distress is manifested by physical symptoms such as blushing, sweaty palms, abdominal discomfort, heart palpitations, and trembling in performance situations. According to Reinblatt and Riddle (2007), *selective mutism* is also a manifestation or severe variant of social anxiety disorder, as children are hypersensitive to being evaluated or judged when drawing attention to themselves by speaking.

Social anxiety disorder is a viciously cyclical disorder involving not one but rather two fears, modulated by at least two specific brain regions. The initial fear is a stress reaction often completely disproportional to and somewhat exaggerated by the situation at hand. As previously mentioned, the amygdala is the primary brain region that modulates fear processing and also functions to generate a behavioral response to fear (Goossens et al., 2007). Still, it is far too simplistic to attribute social anxiety disorder to an overactive amygdala that triggers the sympathetic nervous system into producing a physiological fear response. The more debilitating fear is actually the second fear, which is a consciously experienced sense of panic expressed directly toward magnifying the first fear. In other words, the child becomes completely overwhelmed by the feeling of panic, and consequently becomes more fearful of the fear itself than the actual situation from which the fear arose. Therefore, the first fear is reflexive in nature and triggered conditionally by an environmental stimulus. In a school situation, this may include being called upon unexpectedly in class, or being asked to solve a difficult math problem on the board, reading aloud in front of others, or giving an unexpected oral presentation. The initial flood of

KEY LEARNING POINTS:
Generalized Anxiety Disorder

- Generalized Anxiety Disorder (GAD) may have elevated amygdala activity at the core of the disorder, especially when attention is constrained to our own internal emotional states (McClure et al., 2007).
- The *orbitofrontal cortex* is housed within the frontal lobes and plays a crucial role in ascribing a reward value on emotional stimuli which ultimately guides behavior through reinforcement contingencies (Rolls, 2004).
- The *anterior cingulate cortex* primarily functions as the brain's gear shifter, and allows children to shift between cognition and emotion in order to adopt a more adaptive response to emotionally significant events (Allman et al., 2001).
- Cognitive behavioral therapy (CBT) coupled with relaxation training may be especially helpful for children with anxiety disorders.

KEY LEARNING POINTS:
Social Anxiety Disorder

- Social anxiety disorders have two distinct sub-classifications. *Generalized* social anxiety disorder refers to children who experience anxiety and fear across most social situations. *Non-generalized* social anxiety involves specific social or performance-based situations, such as fear of public speaking (Khalid-Khan et al., 2007).

- Social anxiety disorder is a viciously cyclical disorder involving not one but rather two fears, modulated by at least two specific brain regions.

- The amygdala is the primary brain region for fear processing and also functions to generate a behavioral response to fear (Goossens et al., 2007). It is the principal brain region activated during the initial fear, which is primarily reflexive.

- The second fear functions to keep the first fear alive and occurs at a more cerebral, than reflexive level, through automatic negative thoughts (ANTS). Higher level brain regions such as the orbitofrontal cortex and anterior cingulate cortex, both of which have rich interconnections with the amygdala, comprise the second fear circuit (Goossens et al., 2007).

- Medication management of anxiety disorders should begin with SSRI's to address the first fear system. Cognitive behavior therapy can assist children in reducing automatic negative thoughts by addressing the second fear system (Mancini et al., 2005).

adrenaline occurs automatically, as a conditioned response, and usually cannot be consciously controlled. However, the second fear can be controlled. The second fear functions to keep the first fear alive and occurs at a cerebral rather than reflexive level. For instance, automatic negative thoughts (ANTS) flood the child's psyche by echoing statements such as "What if I turn red and humiliate myself?", "What if I stop breathing and pass out?", "What if I lose control of my bladder?", or "What if I make a fool of myself and all of my friends start to laugh?" The first fear may be sudden, automatic, and unforgiving, but it is the cognitive interpretation of this fear which fortifies it. Hence, the initial fear may arise from subcortical brain structures such as the amygdala, but higher level brain regions in the orbitofrontal cortex and anterior cingulate cortex, both of which have rich interconnections with the amygdala, comprise the second fear circuit (Goossens et al., 2007).

Interestingly, when the reaction to the initial flash of fear is acceptance, rather than attempting to fight the fear, then both fears tend to diminish quickly. For instance, Blair et al. (2008) examined the neural responses to generalized social phobia and noted that both the medial prefrontal cortex, a vital area in the cognitive representation of the self, and the amygdala were clearly involved in the pathophysiology of social anxiety disorder. Therefore, the initial fear (amygdala) in conjunction with the child's cognitive interpretation of the fear (medial prefrontal cortex) dictated an appropriate adaptive behavioral response to the fear. In summary, as affective neuroscience continues to shed light on the neural architecture of fear, there is evidence for multiple neural systems modulating different elements of the human fear response.

Lastly, social phobia has also been associated with abnormal processing of angry faces, because angry faces often convey a sense of disapproval (Kolasssa & Miltner, 2006). According to Easter et al. (2005), children and adults with anxiety disorders have a relative bias toward labeling facial emotions as being overly negative. This may, in part, be due to deficient information processing, which misperceives neutral faces and emotions as being threatening and therefore heightens social concerns. There is some inconsistency in the research pertaining to emotional perception and anxiety, though some social phobics tend to show right hemispheric abnormalities in the initial stages of processing angry faces (Kolassa & Miltner, 2006). Therefore, the initial visual perception of faces may be modulated by more right hemispheric mechanisms consistent with the first fear response. However, higher level affective perception, regardless of emotional valence, tends to be associated with left amygdala and left anterior cingulate activity, which is consistent with the second fear based system (Killgore & Yurgelun-Todd, 2004). Regardless, cognitive behavioral therapy (CBT) has emerged as the primary means to treat anxiety disorders by replacing or discarding automatic negative thoughts associated with the second fear system (Mancini et al., 2005). According to Reinblatt and Riddle (2007), medication management of anxiety disorders should begin with Selective Serotonin Reuptake Inhibitors (SSRIs) to dampen the initial flash of fear associated with the first fear system, then cognitive behavior therapy to address the negative cognitions associated with the second fear system.

Obsessive Compulsive Disorder

Anxiety disorders should be conceived as encompassing a wide spectrum of behavioral manifestations, as most do not necessarily have clear and distinct behavioral boundaries between each

---

KEY LEARNING POINTS:
Obsessive Compulsive Disorder

- OCD occurs in 2% to 4% of the pediatric population, has a mean onset range between 7 and 12 years old, and has a slight male predominance of 3:2 male-to-female ratio (Geller, 2006).
- The frontostriatal systems (connections between the basal ganglia and the frontal lobes) tend to be implicated in OCD with children.
- The caudate nucleus connects to the orbitofrontal cortex and often triggers this brain region when something may be wrong leading to obsessions (Carter, 1998).
- The putamen has connections with posterior regions of the frontal cortex around the premotor strip, and may be implicated in compulsory types of behaviors (Carter, 1998).

---

condition. Similar to autistic spectrum disorders, most anxiety conditions occur in an assortment of ranges and degrees of impairment, especially obsessive compulsive disorder (OCD). According to Geller (2006), OCD occurs in 2% to 4% of the pediatric population, has a mean onset range between 7 and 12 years old, and has a slight male predominance of a 3:2 male-to-female ratio. By definition, OCD is an anxiety disorder characterized by recurrent, unwanted thoughts (obsessions) and repetitive behaviors to help rid these thoughts (compulsions). These behaviors may include constant hand washing to eradicate germs (contamination), counting certain objects over and over again for fear of losing them (hoarding), or constant reassurance checking with parents (fear of loss). Unfortunately, performing these rituals brings about only temporary relief from the crippling fear and anxiety. Likewise, not performing these rituals usually spells an increase in anxiety. As noted in Table 6-6, OCD spectrum disorders may manifest themselves through a variety of behavioral peculiarities.

KEY LEARNING POINTS: Post-Traumatic Stress Disorder

- PTSD develops in response to exposure to a traumatic experience such as direct physical or sexual abuse, witnessing the abuse of a loved one, or witnessing an event involving death or serious injury.

- There are three responses to trauma that children often experience: 1) re-experiencing the trauma through repetitive play or flashbacks, 2) avoidance of stimuli associated with the trauma, and 3) persistent symptoms from trauma that increases arousal and interferes with school functioning (Najjar et al., 2008).

- The hippocampus, a key memory center of the brain, and the cerebullar vermis, both contain a high density of glucocorticoid receptors that are stimulated by stress (Anderson et al., 2002). .

- Alterations to the amygdala and cerebellular vermis in severely maltreated children may result in impulsive violence as these children tend to attribute hostility to situations that are relatively benign, have increased levels of fear, and develop overly negative self perceptions (Ayoub & Rappolt-Schlichtmann, 2007).

TABLE 3-6
Obsessive Compulsive Disorders

(Geller, 2006)

Trichotillomania (pulling out hair)
Onychophagia (nail biting)
Chronic Skin Picking
Pathological Gambling
Eating Disorders
Religious/Moral Obsessions
Hoarding/Saving Compulsions
Sexual Obsessions/Paraphilias
Contamination/Cleanliness
Self-Mutilating/Cutting
Aggressive/Harm Obsessions (fear of death or loss of loved one)

As noted by Geller (2006), only 15% of pediatric obsessions and compulsions have a clear precipitating factor or specific stressor identified. In fact, the actual trigger for this broad constellation of behaviors is most likely neurophysiological in nature, and primarily resides in the corpus striatum of the human brain (Carter, 1998). The corpus striatum represents a large subsection of the basal ganglia, which is the largest subcortical structure in the brain located near the thalamus beneath the frontal lobes. As Geller (2006) noted, the frontostriatal systems (connections between the basal ganglia and the frontal lobes) tend to be implicated in OCD with children. Specifically, the corpus striatum is comprised of two main structures, the caudate nucleus and the putamen. According to Carter (1998), the caudate nucleus connects to the orbitofrontal cortex and often triggers this particular brain region when something may be wrong. Like most frontostriatal pathways, this system is particularly sensitive to the neurotransmitter dopamine. Therefore, neurochemical dysfunctions may result in the caudate nucleus literally becoming stuck in its triggering mechanism that something is wrong (obsessions). Conversely, the second main structure of the basal ganglia is the putamen, which has connections with posterior regions of the frontal cortex around the premotor strip controlling motor functions (Carter, 1998). Once again, this frontostriatal system is particularly sensitive to dopamine, with neurochemical dysfunction possibly leading to uncontrolled motoric responses taking the form of Tourette's Syndrome or other compulsory types of behaviors.

In terms of treatment, there are therapeutic benefits obtained through the co-administration of both dopamine blockers and SSRIs in OCD patients. In fact, Anafranil was the first serotonin reuptake inhibitior researched for the treatment of childhood OCD and the only tricyclic antidepressant with an FDA indication for pediatric OCD (Reinblatt & Riddle, 2007). SSRIs have essentially replaced tricyclic antidepressants as a first-line medication for most pediatric anxiety disorders (Reinblatt & Riddle, 2007). Still, the question begs as to whether treatment for OCD should involve solely medication management, or perhaps other forms of therapeutic approaches. The Pediatric OCD Treatment Study (2004) evaluated the efficacy of cognitive behavioral therapy alone, or using medication management in the treatment of OCD. This was one of the first studies to demonstrate the effectiveness of utilizing both cognitive behavioral therapy and medication management to produce the most efficacious outcomes for children.

Post-Traumatic Stress Disorder

There is a current re-conceptualization in the literature pertaining to Post-Traumatic Stress Disorder (PTSD). By definition, PTSD is an anxiety-based syndrome that develops in response to exposure to some traumatic experience. For children, this may involve direct physical or sexual abuse, witnessing the abuse of a loved one, or witnessing an event involving death or serious injury. As noted in the DSM-IV-TR, there are three responses to trauma that children often experience: 1) re-experiencing the trauma through repetitive play or flashbacks, 2) avoidance of stimuli associated with the trauma, and 3) persistent symptoms stemming from trauma that increases arousal and interferes with school functioning (Najjar et al., 2008). There is evidence that SSRIs may be useful in adult PTSD, but to date, there are no randomized placebo-based studies to support the use of psychopharmacological agents with children and adolescents (Reinblatt & Riddle, 2006). Perhaps one reason PTSD has been so difficult to study empirically is that most children exposed to trauma often present with functional impairment and distress, but do not meet the full criteria for the disorder (Najjar et al., 2008). In fact, many children employ certain adaptive responses that mask the disorder, or simply do not appreciate the danger they are facing, such that repeated, chronic, exposure to trauma is merely deemed as being the "norm." However, a closer look at the neural mechanisms involved with trauma may shed some light on the developmental nature of this disorder as well.

Certainly, trauma can affect the development of trust, emotional regulation, and social skills in children, in addition to hindering school adaptation (Najjar et al., 2008). There is emerging evidence from the neuropsychological literature that suggests exposure to severe stress early in life leads to atypical neurodevelopmental pathways being formed (Ayoub & Rappolt-Schlichtmann, 2007). These neural pathways may be very adaptive for the current stressful experience that child is facing, but relatively maladaptive for the more benign environment a child encounters in school. Neuroimaging studies have yielded a number of differences in the brains of maltreated children including a 17% smaller corpus callosum, attenuation of the left neocortex, cerebellum, amygdala, and hippocampus, and enhanced electrical activity of the limbic system (Ayoub & Rappolt-Schlichtmann, 2007).

Furthermore, the hippocampus, a key memory center in the brain, also appears to be particularly sensitive to stress, due in part, to the high density of glucocorticoid (cortisol) receptors in this area (Gould & Tanapat, 1999). Therefore, specific memory deficits or complete alterations in memory are often seen in PTSD due, in part, to cortisol neurotoxicity from chronic and severe stress (Ayoub & Rappolt-Schlichtmann, 2007). As previously noted, a hyperactive amygdala is one of the neural signatures of anxiety. Conversely, an underactive amygdala often results in a lack of social inhibition and failure to perceive a potential threat in the environment (Wismer Fries & Pollack, 2007). It is conceivable that a hyperactive amygdala may indeed develop through repeated and chronic exposure to stress. In essence, the amygdala is adapting to its environment by being hypervigilant and overly protective. This in turn, triggers the release of many stress hormones, including cortisol, which then stimulates two areas of the brain dense with glucocorticoid receptors, namely, the hippocampus and cerebellular vermis. The cerebellular vermis, a narrow structure that links the hemispheres of the cerebellum, functions to inhibit limbic system activity (Anderson et al., 2002). The net result of this chemical chain reaction is an overactive emotional or limbic response, unable to be regulated by prefrontal cortical activity. Simply put, alterations to the amygdala and cerebellular vermis in severely maltreated children may result in impulsive violence as these children tend to attribute hostility to situations that are relatively benign, have increased levels of fear, and develop overly negative self-perceptions, which is especially evident for physically abused girls. (Ayoub & Rappolt-Schlichtmann, 2007). Therefore, the brain is not necessarily impaired by early trauma, but merely develops alternative pathways to adapt to chronic stress by being hypervigilant and overprotective in a stressful environment. Nevertheless, such vigilance becomes counterproductive in a more benign or safe environment such as school.

Bottom-Up vs. Top-Down Anxiety Disorders

It is important to reiterate that adaptive behavioral responses to threats ultimately involve our highest decision making centers in the brain, namely, the prefrontal cortex. How the prefrontal cortex chooses to interpret a particular threat essentially determines the appropriateness of a particular response. For instance, there is evidence to suggest that maltreated children often exhibit higher levels of dissociation than their non-abused counterparts, due to a relatively poor adaptive response to a threat (Macfie et al., 2001). In other words, some children simply dissociate or block out specific memories of the trauma from common memory. Conversely, other children who come from similar stressful environments and are subjugated to malice and maltreatment do not exhibit any unusual emotional or behavioral manifestations due to their ability to appropriately adapt to fear and distress. In essence, lower brain centers involved in stress such as the amygdala, hippocampus, and cerebellular vermis are modulated by higher centers of the brain; the prefrontal cortex (Ayoub & Rappolt-Schlichtmann, 2007). In many ways, fear and anxiety are mapped out in a particular neural code to the prefrontal cortex in an analogous manner to reading or any other learned endeavor. In the case of reading, atypical phonological processing in the early years leads to inefficient neural mappings between letters and sounds in the later years, which subsequently results in faulty automatic word recognition skills (Noble & McCandliss, 2005). In the case of anxiety, atypical neural mappings in the younger years caused by high levels of stress hormones (cortisol) may lead to faulty neural mappings by higher brain centers, and thus skew bio-behavioral response patterns (Ayoub & Rappolt-Schlichtmann, 2007).

According to Berkowitz et al. (2007), neuroimaging studies repeatedly show abnormalities in the prefrontal cortex in anxious individuals. In fact, due to atypical neural mappings, PTSD, panic attacks, and phobias all seem to be characterized by relative *under-activity* of the prefrontal cortex (Berkowitz et al., 2007). There is evidence to suggest that the right ventrolateral prefrontal cortex specifically modulates the amygdala's response to threat and fear, and the prefrontal cortex's failure to match the intensity of a hyperactive amygdala leads to many anxiety based disorders (Monk et al., 2008). Therefore, perhaps certain classes of anxiety disorders (i.e., PTSD, panic attacks, and phobias) should not be conceptualized as distinct categorical conditions, but rather should be viewed along a spectrum. The spectrum of anxious behaviors basically manifests from a hyperactive amygdala coupled with an underactive prefrontal cortex. In essence, these types of anxiety disorders should be conceptualized in more of a <u>bottom-up</u> fashion, since the neural flow stems from a subcortical or bottom region of the brain (amygdala) to an under-active top portion of the brain (prefrontal cortex) unable to cope with the emotion.

Conversely, disorders such as generalized anxiety disorder and obsessive-compulsive disorder may be more <u>top-down</u> types of anxiety disorders, and often characterized by chronic *over-activity* of the prefrontal cortex leading to worry and self-doubt (Berkowitz et al., 2007). According to Pine (2008), cognitive behavioral therapy is the most effective form of treatment for more top-down types of anxiety disorders, especially when children learn how to manage their own fears. One of the major goals of cognitive behavioral therapy is to identify and monitor thoughts, assumptions, beliefs, and behaviors that fuel anxious thoughts and feelings, and replace them with more realistic and helpful ones. Though SSRIs are highly effective for treating anxiety, cognitive behavioral therapy is equally as effective, or in some cases can surpass medication (Pine, 2008). Table 6-7 illustrates specific techniques to assist children in both identifying and changing thought patterns which fuel their anxious condition.

One final note: if the amygdala and hippocampus work together and mistakenly pair a specific memory to a specific fear outside the auspices of conscious control by the prefrontal cortex, then a myriad of phobias or irrational fears may emerge. The levels of irrationality go beyond the scope of

KEY LEARNING POINTS:
Top Down vs. Bottom-up Anxiety Disorders

- Bottom-Up Anxiety Disorders: PTSD, Panic Attacks, and Phobias repeatedly show atypical neural mapping characterized by relative under-activity of the prefrontal cortex and over-activity of subcortical regions of the brain such as the amygdala (Berkowitz et al., 2007).

- Top-Down Anxiety Disorders: Disorders such as generalized anxiety disorder and obsessive-compulsive disorder may be more top-down types of anxiety disorders, and are characterized by over-activity of the prefrontal cortex leading to worry, doubt, and fear (Berkowitz et al., 2007).

- Four specific treatments of anxiety disorders include:
  1) SSRIs may be the most effective treatment for bottom-up disorders which occur outside of conscious control (Reinblatt & Riddle, 2007).
  2) Exposure therapy and systematic desensitization can quiet an overactive amygdala in more "bottom-up" types of anxiety disorders (Goossens et al. 2007)
  3) Children with strong interpersonal attachments to caregivers can develop far greater resiliency to stress than children with insecure attachments (Adams et al., 2007).
  4) Cognitive behavior therapy is equally as effective, or in some cases, can surpass medication (Pine, 2008).

this chapter, but the types of phobias that may be triggered could include anything from: the fear of the number 13 (Triskadekaphobia), the color purple (Porphyrophobia), kissing (Philematophobia), puppets (Pupaphobia), tombstones (Placophobia), or hundreds of other possible entities. Fortunately, there is evidence to show that direct treatment, called exposure therapy, which involves systematic desensitization to specific fears can indeed quiet the amygdala and successfully overcome these fears (Goossens et al., 2007).

TABLE 6-7
Seven Cognitive Behavioral Strategies for Children With Anxiety Disorders

Learning to tackle anxiety is a multi-step process. The following strategies should assist clinicians in accomplishing four fundamental treatment goals:

1. Understanding the anxiety.
2. Calming the physical symptoms.
3. Creating a plan to use when anxiety creeps begins to emerge.
4. Revise the plan as needed.

1. **Empty chair**
   Goal: Child will try to gain insight into the source of their own anxiety.
   Activity: Child will talk to an *"empty chair"* or a stuffed animal to explain the anxiety. The stuffed animal can ask questions about the anxious moments.

2. **Count it away**
   Goal: To calm the sympathetic nervous system and learn how to cope with unpleasant bodily sensations.
   Activity: Child will identify a relaxing scene by either drawing a picture in detail or verbalizing an image in their minds. Next, ask the child to count backwards slowly from ten. Upon reaching zero, teach the child to visualize the relaxing scene. This exercise may need to be repeated until a state of relaxation occurs.

3. **Distraction**
   Goal: To calm the sympathetic nervous system and modulate levels of stress.
   Activity: Child will count items in their present environment (i.e. ceiling tiles, buttons, trees, cracks on the sidewalk, etc.) and avoid ruminating on their own bodily sensations. Without constantly acknowledging the body's response, the initial burst of fear often diminishes quickly.

4. **Map it to the absurd**
   Goal: Teach the child to create humor from the anxious state.
   Activity: First, the child will identify the anxiety producing event and then readily acknowledge what may happen if the worst case scenario actually occurred. Next, repeatedly ask the child *"what if"* following every statement until reaching a point of relative absurdity. For instance: *"I am worried about being late to basketball practice because everyone will stare at me when I come in. If everyone stares at me, I will turn red, feel self-conscious, and probably fall flat on my face and get a bloody nose. If I get a bloody nose, then it will drip all over the floor and then the coach will make me mop it up. If I mop up all the blood, I will be too tired to participate in practice. If I am too tired, then I will be thrown off the team. If I get thrown off the team, then I will never be able to play basketball again, etc…"*

5. **Magical Medallions**

   Goal: Child will use a symbolic item to help them self-soothe.

   Activity: Have the child use clay to create a medallion. The child can draw symbols on the medallion and paint it. This could also become a family supported exercise by having caretakers add a symbol on the medallion that would remind the child of their positive attachment with their caregiver. The child can then rub the medallion whenever anxious moments occur.

6. **Throw the anxiety away**

   Goal: To provide the child a sense of control over their anxious feelings.

   Activity: Ask the child to make a list of what creates anxiety. Each idea needs to be on a separate strip of paper. After the list is created, ask the child what should be done to get rid of these worrisome thoughts (i.e., offer ideas like throwing them in the garbage, keeping them in the therapists' office, tearing them up into little pieces etc.). Once the thought is discarded, replace with more positive and adaptive cognitions.

7. **Talk until the bell beeps**

   Goal: Child will learn to verbalize their anxious feelings.

   Activity: Begin talking specifically about the anxiety and suddenly begin to time the child, usually in 30 second intervals. The child then switches topics and begins to talk about something more enjoyable and entertaining until the timer beeps. Praise the child for having such wonderful control over their fears and anxious thoughts.

---

*Strategies provided by Darci D. Feifer, M.Ed., LCPC

SUMMARY

In conclusion, there is a myriad of anxiety-based conditions that can plague children and lead to academic and social skill difficulties. Perhaps affective neuroscience can assist both in redefining anxiety disorders in terms of either *bottom-up versus top-down* conditions, as well as serve as a catalyst toward more effective treatments. It should be noted that there is evidence that children with strong interpersonal attachments to caregivers can develop far greater resiliency to stress and anxiety than children with insecure attachments. For example, insecure toddlers often show elevated cortisol responses and anxious behavior to stressful events, even with their attachment figure present (Nachmias et al., 1996). According to Adams et al. (2007), positive, stable, warm, and caring home environments conducive to strong attachments between children and their caregivers is essential toward lowering cortisol levels and diminishing stress and anxiety. Conversely, less effective parenting as defined by lower levels of warmth, poor structure and routine, and lack of involvement is associated with dysfunctional cortisol patterns and greater stress and anxiety (Adams et al., 2007). The theme of resiliency and the necessity for both parents and teachers to develop strong interpersonal attachments in an unconditional manner will be featured in later chapters. Clearly, for children, the ability to appropriately match a behavioral response to a given context is the hallmark of healthy emotional functioning.

REFERENCES

Adam, E. K., Klimes-Dougan, B., & Gunnar, M. R. (2007). *Social regulation of the adrenocortical response to stress in infants, children, and adolescents.* In D. Coch, G. Dawson, & K. W. Fischer: Human behavior, learning, and the developing brain: atypical development, (p. 264–304) New York: Guilford Publications.

Adler, C. M., DelBello, M. P., & Strakowski, S. M. (2006). Brain network dysfunction in bipolar disorder. *CNS Spectrums, 11*(4), 312-320.

Ahn, M.S., Breeze, J. L., Makris, N., Kennedy, D. N., Hodge, S. M., Herbert, M. R., Seidman, L. J., Biederman, J., Caviness, V.S., & Frazier, J.A. (2007). Anatomic brain magnetic resonance imaging of the basal ganglia in pediatric bipolar disorder. *Journal of Affective Disorders, 104*, 147-154.

Allman, J. M., Hakeem, A., Erwin, J. M., Nimchinsky, E., & Hof, P. (2001). The anterior cingulate cortex. The evolution of an interface between emotion and cognition. *Annals of the New York Academy of Sciences, 935*, 107-117.

American Psychiatric Association (2000). *Diagnostic and statistical manual of mental disorders*, Fourth Edition, Text Revision (DSM-IV-TR). Washington, D. C.: Author.

Anderson, C., Teicher, M., Polcari, A., & Renshaw, P. (2002). Abnormal T2 relaxation time in the cerebellar vermis of adults sexually abused in childhood: Potential role of the vermis in stress-enhanced risk for drug abuse. *Psychoneuroendocrinology, 27*(1-2), 231-244.

Ayoub, C. C., & Rappolt-Schlichtmann, G. (2007). *Child maltreatment and the development of alternate pathways in biology and behavior.* In D. Coch, G. Dawson, & K.W. Fisher: Human behavior, learning, and the developing brain: atypical development, (p. 305-330) New York: Guilford Publications.

Beardon, C. E., Hoffman, K. M., & Cannon, T. D. (2001). The neuropsychology and neuroanatomy of bipolar affective disorder: a critical review. *Bipolar Disorder, 3*, 106-150.

Berkowitz, R. L., Coplan, J. D., Reddy, D. P., & Gorman, J. M. (2007). The human dimension: how the prefrontal cortex modulates the subcortical fear response. *Reviews in the Neurosciences, 18*(3-4), 191-207.

Blair, K., Geraci, M., Devido, J., McCaffrey, D., Chen, G., Vythilingam, M., Ng, P., Hollon, N., Jones, M., Blair, R. J., & Pine, D. S. (2008). Neural response to self and other referential praise and criticism in generalized social phobia. *Archives of General Psychiatry, 65*(10), 1176-1184.

Blair, R. J. (2001) Neurocognitive models of aggression, the antisocial personality disorders, and psychopathy. *Journal of Neurology and Neurosurgical Psychiatry, 71*, 727-731.

Blair, R. J. (2004) The roles of the orbital frontal cortex in the modulation of antisocial behavior. *Brain and Cognition, 55*, 198-208.

Blair, R..J., Mitchell, D. G.V., & Peschardt, K. (2004) *The psychopath: Brain & behavior.* Blackwell: Oxford, U.K.

Blumberg, H. P., Martin, A., Kaufman, J., Leung, H. C., Skudlarski, P., Lacadie, C., Fulbright, R. K., Gore, J. C., Charney, D. S., Krystal, J. H., & Peterson B. S. (2003). Fronto-striatal abnormalities in adolescents with bipolar disorder: preliminary observations from functioning MRI. *American Journal of Psychiatry, 160*(7), 1345-1347.

Caetano, S.C., Olvera, R. L., Glahn, D., Fonseca, M., Pliszka, S., & Soares, J. C. (2005). Fronto-limbic brain abnormalities in juvenile onset bipolar disorder. *Biological Psychiatry, 58*, 525-531.

Carter, R. (1998). Mapping the Mind. Berkeley: University of California Press.

Case, B. G., Olfson, M., Marcus, S. C., & Siegel, C. (2007). Trends in the inpatient mental health treatment of children and adolescents in US community hospitals between 1990 and 2000. *Archives of General Psychiatry, 64*(1):89-96.

DelBello, M.P., Adler, C.M., & Strakowski, S. M. (2006). The neurophysiology of childhood and adolescent bipolar disorder. *CNS Spectrums, 11*, 298-311.

Dickstein, D. P., Rich, B.A., Binstock, A.B., Pradella, A.G., Towbin, K.E., Pine, D.S., & Leibenluft, E. (2005). Comorbid anxiety in phenotypes of bipolar disorder. *Journal of Child and Adolescent Psychopharmacology, 15*(4), 534-548.

Dolan, R. J. (1999). On the neurology of morals. *Nature Neuroscience, 2*(11), 927- 929.

Drevets, W. C., Price, J. L., Simpson, J. R. Jr., Todd, R. D., Reich, T., Vannier, M., & Raichle M . E . (1 9 9 7) . Subgenual prefrontal cortex abnormalities in mood disorders. *Nature, 386*, 824-827.

Drevets, W. C., & Raichle, M. E. (1998). Reciprocal suppression of regional cerebral blood flow during emotional versus higher cognitive processes: implications for interactions between emotion and cognition. *Cognition and Emotion, 12*(3), 353-385.

Easter, J., McClure, E. B., Monk, C. S., Dhanani, M., Hodgdon, H., Leibenluft, E., Charney, D. S., Pine, D. S., & Ernst, M. E. (2005). Emotion recognition deficits in pediatric anxiety disorders: implications for amygdala research. *Journal of Child and Adolescent Psychopharmacology, 15*(4), 563-570.

Feifer, S.G., & Rattan, G. (2007). Executive functioning skills in male students with social-emotional disorders. *International Journal of Neuroscience, 117*, 1565-1577.

Fudge, J. L., Kunishio, K., Walsh, P., Richard, C., & Haber, S. N. (2002). Amygdaloid projections to ventromedial striatal subterritories in the primate. *Neuroscience, 110*, 257-275.

Geller, D. A. (2006). Obsessive-compulsive and spectrum disorders in children and adolescents. *Psychiatric Clinics of North America, 29*, 353-370.

Geller, B., Tillman, R., & Bolhofner, K. (2007). Proposed definitions of bipolar I disorder episodes and daily rapid cycling phenomena in preschoolers, school-aged children, adolescents, and adults. *Journal of Child and Adolescent Psychopharmacology, 17*(2), 217-222.

Goossens, L., Sunaert, S., Peeters, R., Griez, E. J., & Schruers, K. R. (2007). Amygdala hyper-function in phobic fear normalizes after exposure. *Biological Psychiatry, 62*(10), 1119-1125.

Gould, E., & Tanapat, P. (1999). Stress and hippocampal neurogenesis. *Biological Psychiatry, 46*(11), 1472-1479.

Immordino-Yang, M . H. & Fischer, K. (2007). *Dynamic development of hemispheric biases in three cases: Cognitive/hemispheric cycles, music, and hemipherectom.* In D. Coch, K.W. Fischer, and G. Dawson, Human behavior and the developing brain: Typical development, (p. 77) New York: Guilford Press.

Individuals with Disabilities Education Improvement Act of 2004. (PL No. 108-446, 20 USC 1400).

Kaur, S., Sassi, R. B., Axelson, D., Nicoletti, M., Brambilla, P., Monkul, E. S., Hatch, J. P., Keshavan, M. S., Ryan, N., Birmaher, B., & Soares, J. C. (2005). Cingulate cortex anatomical abnormalities in children and adolescents with bipolar disorder. *American Journal of Psychiatry, 162*, 1637-1643.

Kessler, R. C., McGonagle, K. A., Zhao, S., Nelson, C. B., Hughes, M., Eshleman, S., Wittchen, H. U., & Kendler, K. S. (1994). Lifetime and 12 month prevalence of DSM III-R psychiatric disorders in the United States. Results from the National Comorbidity Survey. *Archives of General Psychiatry, 51*(1), 8-19.

Khalid-Khan, S., Santibanez, M. P., McMicken, C., & Rynn, M. A. (2007). Social anxiety disorder in children and adolescents: epidemiology, diagnosis, and treatment. *Pediatric Drugs, 9*(4), 227-237.

Killgore, W. D., & Yurgelun-Todd, D. A. (2004). Activation of the amygdale and anterior cingulated during nonconscious processing of sad versus happy faces. *Neuroimage, 21*(4), 1215- 1223.

Kloos, A., Weller, E. B., & Weller, R. A. (2008). Biological basis of bipolar disorders in children and adolescents. *Current Psychiatry Reports, 10*, 98-103.

Kolassa, I. T., & Miltner, W. H. (2006). Psychophysiological correlates of face processing in social phobia. *Brain Research, 1118*(1), 130-141.

LeDoux, J. E. (2003). The emotional brain, fear, and the amygdala. *Cellular and Molecular Neurobiology, 23*, 727-738.

Leibenluft, E. & Rich, B.A. (2008). Pediatric bipolar disorder. *Annual Review of Clinical Psychology,* (4), 163-187.

Macfie, J., Cicchetti, D., & Toth, S. (2001). The development of dissociation in maltreated preschool-aged children. *Development and Psychopathology, 13*, 233-234.

Mancini, C., Van Ameringen, M., Bennett, M., Patterson, B. & Watson, C. (2005). Emerging treatments for child and adolescent social phobia: a review. *Journal of Child and Adolescent Psychopharmacology, 15*(4), 589-607.

McClure, E. B., Adler, A., Monk, C. S., Cameron, J., Smith, S., Nelson, E. E., Leibenluft, E., Ernst, M., & Pine, D. S. (2007). fMRI predictors of treatment outcome in pediatric anxiety disorders. *Psychopharmacology, 191*, 97-105.

Monk, C.S., Telzer, E. H., Mogg, K., Bradley, B. P., Mai, X., Louro, H. M., Chen, G., McClure-Tone, E. B., Ernst, M., & Pine, D. S. (2008). Amygdala and ventrolateral prefrontal cortex activation to masked angry faces in children and adolescents with generalized anxiety disorder. *Archives of General Psychiatry, 65*(5), 568-576.

Nachmias, M., Gunnar, M. R., Mangelsdorf, S., Parritz, R., & Buss, K. A. (1996). Behavioral inhibition and stress reactivity: Moderating role of attachment security. *Child Development, 67*(2), 508-522.

Najjar, F., Weller, R. A., Weisbrot, J., & Weller, E. B. (2008). Post-traumatic stress disorder and its treatment in children and adolescents. *Current Psychiatry Reports, 10*, 104-108.

National Center for Educational Statistics: U.S. Department of Education: (2007). *Digest of Educational Statistics,* Washington, D.C: U.S. Department of Justice.

Noble, K. G., & McCandliss, B. D. (2005). Reading development and impairment: Behavioral, social, and neurobiological factors. *Developmental and Behavioral Pediatrics, 26*(5), 370-376.

Pediatric OCD Treatment Study (POTS) Team (2004). Cognitive-behavior therapy, sertraline, and their combination for children and adolescents with obsessive-compulsive disorders: the Pediatric OCD Treatment Study (POTS) randomized controlled trial. *Journal of the American Medical Association, 292*, 1969-1976.

Pine, D. S. (1994). Child-adult anxiety disorders. *Journal of the American Academy of Child and Adolescent Psychiatry, 33*, 280-281.

Pine, D. S. (2008, October 24th). Presentation given at The Lab School of Washington's 13th Annual Research Conference: *Stress & Learning: Anxiety and Coping*, Bethesda, Md.

Prior, M., Smart, D., Sanson, A., & Oberklaid, F. (2000). Does shy-inhibited temperament in childhood lead to anxiety problems in adolescence? *Journal of the American Academy of Child and Adolescent Psychiatry, 39*(4), 461-468.

Reinblatt, S. P. & Riddle, M. A. (2007). The pharmacological management of childhood anxiety disorders: a review. *Psychopharmacology, 191*, 67-86.

Rich, B. A., Vinton, D. T., Roberson-Nay, R., Hommer, R. E., Berghorst, L. H., McClure, E. B., Fromm, S. J., Pine, D. S., & Leibenluft, E. (2006). Limbic hyper-activation during processing of neutral facial expressions in children with bipolar disorder. *Proceedings of the National Academy of Sciences of the United States of America, 103*(23), 8900-8905.

Rolls, E. T. (2004). Convergence of sensory systems in the orbitofrontal cotex in primates and brain design for emotion. *The anatomical record. Part A, Discoveries in molecular, cellular, and evolutionary biology, 281*(1), 1212-1225.

Schwartz, C. E., Snidman, N., & Kagan, J. (1999). Adolescent social anxiety as an outcome of inhibited temperament in childhood. *Journal of American Academy of Child and Adolescent Psychiatry, 38*(8), 1008-1015.

Whittle, S., Allen, N. B., Lubman, D. I., & Yucel, M. (2006). The neurobiological basis of temperament: Towards a better understanding of psychopathology. *Neuroscience and Biobehavioral Reviews, 30*, 511-525.

Wismer Fries, A. B., & Pollak, S. D. (2007). *Emotion processing and the developing brain*. In D. Coch, K. W. Fischer & G. Dawson, *Human behavior, learning, and the developing brain: Typical development*, (p. 329-361) New York: Guilford Publications.

Wozniak, J. (2005). Recognizing and managing bipolar disorder in children. *Journal of Clinical Psychiatry, 66*(1), 18-23.

CHAPTER 7

PSYCHOPHARMACOLOGY, DEPRESSION, AND ALTERNATIVE TREATMENT MODALITIES

Gurmal Rattan, Ph.D.

"Every heart sings a song, incomplete, until another heart whispers back. Those who wish to sing always find a song. At the touch of a lover, everyone becomes a poet."

—Plato

Rationale

The surge in psychotropic medications to children has grown significantly since the past decade (Jensen, Bhartara, Vitiello, Hoagwood, Feil, & Burke, 1999). A national sample of commercially insured pediatric patients from 1998 to 2002 showed that antidepressants increased from 160 per 10,000 in 1998 to 240 per 10,000 in 2002 (Delate, Gelenberg, Simmons, & Motheral, 2004). These researchers also found that antidepressant use among girls was higher (68%) than boys (34%) and that the overall trend indicated a continuing use of psychotropic medications. In fact, the use of psychotropic medications for mental health issues accounted for 17% of total prescription costs and surpassed the cost for other health related pediatric conditions such as: antibiotics, asthma, skin problems, and allergies (see DuPaul & Carlson, 2005).

More recently, Division 16 of the American Psychological Association (APA) established a Task Force on Psychopharmacology, Learning, and Behavior in the early 1990's (Kubiszyn, 2005). This

I would like to thank Dr. James Lenze for his consultation on the graphic designs and a very hardy thanks to my graduate assistants, Susan Faber and Gregory Boerio for their invaluable assistance with this chapter. Lastly, a special thanks to Tina Rattan for her editorial assistance.

task force identified areas of opportunities, issues, controversy, while a further review in 1995 surveyed school psychologists' attitudes and interest for training in psychopharmacology (Kubiszyn & Carlson, 1995). A similar task force in 2002 assessed salient issues in child psychopharmacology, policy, research practice, and the new role opportunities. From these task forces, it becomes evident that psychotropic prescription use and its effects on children's emotions (Herranz, Armijo, & Arteaga, 1988), intelligence (Handen et al., 1992, Phelps, Brown, & Power, 2002), interpersonal and academic performance (Wilens et al., 2003) are apparent. The important role for school psychologists to assess the efficacy of psychotropic medication is clearly discussed by DuPaul and Carlson (2005). For example, these authors state that the school psychologist could collaborate with the physician at the outset and establish a protocol using timelines, baseline data, rating scales, and academic/emotional/behavioral/interpersonal diagnostic assessment data in order to elevate the effectiveness of medication. Moreover, knowledge of pharmacokinetics could prove to be a useful tool in delineating the adverse side effects (e.g., attention, concentration, irritability, nausea) on children's learning and behavior when reporting this information to both teachers and parents. In fact, research investigating the teacher's perception of psychotropic medication suggested that teachers had only a moderate degree of influence in the use of medication (Singh, Epstein, Luebke, Singh, 1990). These latter researchers assessed the perceptions of 146 teachers on the role that various professionals had on both the initiation and discontinuation of medications. For the most part, the teachers viewed the physician and the school psychologist to be most influential in evaluating the effects of drugs while the teachers viewed themselves as playing a more subservient role. Of particular interest, however, was that teachers categorically felt that their training related to drug treatment was inadequate and that there was a further need for training. Therefore, the school psychologist becomes an instrumental resource to the teacher and parent alike. Moreover, the information gathered by the school psychologist can be used to determine if and when a combined drug, behavioral, or cognitive intervention may be the most appropriate in addition to providing information to the physician for possible dosage adjustments.

With the increasing use of off-label psychotropic medications to treat children, the increase in polypharmacy, and the myriad of medical, legal, educational, and psychological issues associated with the effects of psychotropic drugs on learning and behavior (Kubiszyn, 2005), the school psychologists may not always be prepared given the lack of training in the biological basis of behavior and medication-based evaluations. This is confounded by the fact that very few training programs currently provide the Level I training in basic psychopharmacology as set forth by the American Psychological Association (see DuPaul & Carlson, 2005). To that end, this chapter is intended to be used by school psychologists, teachers, and allied professionals to help provide information for parents and other consumers in a user-friendly manner when delineating the principles of pharmacokinetics and its effects on learning and behavior. The first part of the chapter will focus on the mechanisms involved in psychopharmacology while the latter part of the chapter will discuss drugs used for depression along with alternate treatment modalities.

Background

When the etiology of emotional disturbance is examined, neurobiological factors can clearly be one source of variation. With over 100 billion neurons with their associated 100 trillion synaptic connections, it is easy to see where problems can arise. Neurons are normally destroyed through the process of necrosis (ne-kro´sis) (cells exploding through inflammation) or apoptosis (ap´op-toh´sis) (cells wasting away) in an attempt to keep the brain operating at maximum efficiency. However, bad signals or programming cause good neurons to be inadvertently destroyed. As discussed later in the text, certain aberrations in gene products (e.g., ion channels, enzymes, transport carriers, receptors, transcription factors, genes) can also contribute to factors that result in emotional disturbance (see Julien, 2001; Stahl, 2000, 2008). Add to this the fact that at age 6, one can find the highest concentration of synapses. However, about 50% of these synapses are eliminated throughout the teenage years. If the wrong neurons are pruned, it may well lead to Attentional Deficit Hyperactivity Disorder (ADHD) along with other neurodevelopmental disorders. With such pruning and the extensive loss of neurons, it is clear to see that when a teenager exercises extremely poor judgment, the parent or guardian responds in frustrated manner with, "What were you thinking—have you lost your mind ?!?". This last statement is correct based on the neurophysiology of brain since one-half of the synaptic connections from age 6 have been destroyed.

Psychopharmacology is an investigation of how drugs affect the brain and subsequent behavior. Pharmacokinetics on the other hand, examines the components of how drugs are absorbed, distributed, metabolized, and excreted throughout the system. A terrific book that provides an exhaustive but clear and easy to read text with numerous illustrations is by Stephen Stahl (2008).

DRUG PRIMER

GABA and Glutamate

There are three general categories of neurons that respond to drug actions. They consist of the Glutamate (gloo-tuh-meyt), GABA (gab-uh), and the monoamines (mon-oh-ah-meen). It is the monoamines that are involved in mood and behavior and will receive greater coverage below. The Glutamate neurons are universally excitatory in nature and are very fast acting (usually milliseconds). For example, these types of neurons can create panic attacks, seizures, and related symptoms due to the excessive amount of calcium that enters the cell.

Examples of drugs that can be used to treat such disorders consist of Neurotin—used for epilepsy, and Lamotrigine—used for epilepsy and bipolar disorder. On the other hand, the GABA neurotransmitters are universally inhibitory, and like the Glutamate, are very fast acting to produce a sedating effect by increasing the conductance of chloride into the cell. Drugs such as Xanax or Valium produce this fast calming effect.

As noted in Figure 7-1 below, the mechanism to activate the GABA or Glutamate neurons requires that these neurotransmitters be lodged in their respective receptor sites located at the top of the neuron. Once these neurotransmitters bind to their respective sites, the channel opens to allow the chloride to enter into the GABA cell and the calcium to enter into the Glutamate cell. Picture A in Figure 7-1 shows that the GABA neurotransmitter has lodged on to its receptor site and therefore opens

> **KEY LEARNING POINTS:**
> **Three Neurons That Respond to Drug Action**
>
> 1. **GABA**—fast acting neurotransmitters that produce a sedating or inhibitory effect by allowing chloride to enter the cell.
> 2. **Glutamate**—fast acting neurotransmitters that produce an excitatory effect by allowing calcium to enter the cell.
> 3. **Monoamines**—slower acting neurotransmitters involved with mood and behavior regulation. The monoamines consist primarily of serotonin, dopamine, and norepinephrine.

the cell to increase the sedating effects. In contrast, the Glutamate neurotransmitter has not lodged on to its receptor site and the channel is barely open. The consequent excitatory effects of the calcium ions then are minimal. This would change extremely quickly if the Glutamate neurotransmitter was to bind with its receptor site.

Another concept associated with these types of neurons is the allosteric (al-*uh*-**ster**-ik) effect that occurs when other sites are occupied by their respective neurotransmitters. For example, the binding sites for the GABA consist of: 1) picrotoxin (pik-*ruh*-**tok**-sin)—this is used as a stimulant, especially in treating barbiturate poisoning, 2) alcohol, 3) barbiturate (bahr-**bich**-er-it)—this is an anticonvulsant site, 4) Benzodiazepine (ben-zoh-dahy-**az**-*uh*-peen) (BZ)—this site is used as a muscle relaxant. There are also some minor sites associated with BZ such as omega 1 which are used in the treatment of insomnia. These sites behave allosterically, that is, they can increase the channel opening and allow a greater amount of chloride into the cell thereby enhancing the sedating effects, or they can close the channel to reduce the sedating effects. However, as allosteric modulators, they can only do this if the GABA neurotransmitter is first lodged at its receptor site. Without the GABA neurotransmitter in place, there can be no net increase or decrease in the channel opening or closing than what would be provided strictly by the GABA or Glutamate neurotransmitters binding with their respective sites. The Glutamate site works in the same allosteric method described for the GABA.

FIGURE 7-1

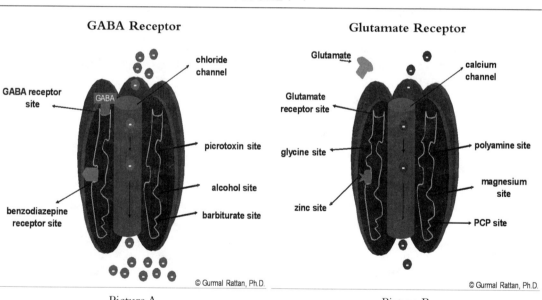

Picture A   Picture B

Figure 7-1. For Picture A, the GABA neurotransmitter is lodged in its receptor site which opens the channel to increase the sedating effects resulting from the chloride ions. With the addition of the BZ neurotransmitter binding to its receptor site, it significantly increases the flow of chloride ions thereby enhancing the effects of sedation via allosteric modulation. The Glutamate receptor in Picture B is at its resting state. Without the binding of the Glutamate neurotransmitter to its receptor site, there is no increase of calcium ions regardless of any of the other neurotransmitters (e.g., zinc) binding to their respective sites.

Monoamines

The third type of neurotransmitter is referred to as the monoamine neurotransmitter and consists primarily of the serotonin (ser-*uh*-**toh**-nin) (5HT), norepinephrine (nawr-ep-*uh*-**nef**-rin) (NE), and dopamine (**doh**-*puh*-meen) (DA) neurotransmitters in addition to various neuropeptides (nur-oh-pep-tahyds) such as Sumatriptan or Rizatriptan. The monoamine neurotransmitters have slower onset stimulation times which may take from hours to days to develop but will have consequent therapeutic effects that last for days to weeks. Given the prevalence of the monoamines (e.g., Zoloft, Prozac, Wellbutrin, Strattera), they will be examined in greater detail.

The cellular configuration of the monoamines consists of a 7 transmembrane region with a binding site in the center. The 7 transmembrane is a part of the superfamily of receptors that involve a second-messenger system. The process involves a series of complex procedures from the neurotransmitter binding with the receptor, to a subsequent binding with a G-protein linked receptor. This is then followed by a synthesis of a second messenger system. It is this configuration that produces a cascading effect that eventually leads to a gene action and a synthesis of the necessary gene products. Examples of gene products consist of: receptors, ion channel, peptides, enzymes, neurotrophic growth factors, transcription factors, and reuptake carriers. For example, the gene may get a signal that there are too many receptors, and as a result, it down-regulates or reduces the number of receptors. A large number of receptors may result if there are too little neurotransmitters available for binding. Once the number of neurotransmitters increases, then a signal gets sent out via the mediation process of gene action to reduce the number of receptors. Alternatively, if there are insufficient neurotransmitters and the cell wants to capture existing neurotransmitters in the synapse, it may up-regulate or increase the number of receptors. However, if a drug blocks receptors from binding with the available neurotransmitters for an extended amount of time, an artificial up regulation may occur in its effort to capture existing neurotransmitters. Such is the case in the nigrostriatal (n-ahy-groh-strahy-ey-t'l) pathways of the dopamine system where the dopamine D2 receptor is continually blocked to reduce psychotic symptoms (see later discussion). This excessive blockage results in tardive dyskinesia (dis-ki-**nee**-*zhuh*) which is a disorder characterized by hyperkinetic movements such as: constant chewing, tongue protrusions, limb movements. The work provided by these genes is invaluable in meeting changing environmental needs. However, given their complex nature of operations, the gene may get a bad signal and produce too much or too little of the necessary products. As a result, this may be one source underlying the etiology of problems ranging from learning disorders, attentional disorders, memory problems, to psychopathology and the like.

Serotonin

The production of serotonin or 5–hydroxytryptamine (5- hahy-droxee-trip-tah-mahyn, 5HT) is a result of the precursor tryptophan (**trip**-*tuh*-fan) which is pumped into the cell. Through enzymatic action, the tryptophan is converted into 5-hydroxytryptophan (5HTP) before it is then converted into the serotonin neurotransmitter or 5HT. Serotonin has nine postsynaptic receptors in addition to two presynaptic receptors. The postsynaptic serotonin receptors as noted in Figure 7-2 consist of: 5HT1A, 5HT1B/D, 5HT2A, 5HT2C, 5HT3, 5HT4/5, 5HT6, 5HT7, 5HTX/Y/Z (see Stahl, 2008). The two presynaptic receptors located at the axon terminal, the 5HT1B/D autoreceptor and alpha 2 heteroreceptor serve to regulate release of 5HT. The 5HT1B/D is controlled by serotonin, and stimulation of this receptor by 5HT will stop release of the serotonin neurotransmitter while the alpha 2 heteroreceptor serves the same function if stimulated; but in this case, the alpha 2 heteroreceptor is

KEY LEARNING POINTS: Serotonin

- Tryptophan is a precursor for serotonin (5HT) production.
- Serotonin has nine postsynaptic receptors and two presynaptic receptors.
- Norepinephrine regulates the release of serotonin by stimulating the alpha 2 heteroreceptor.
- The cell bodies of serotonergic neurons are located in the raphe nuclei with projections to the frontal cortex (mood), the basal ganglia (motor skills), the limbic region (anxiety), the hypothalamus (appetite), the brain stem (sleep), spinal cord (sexual behavior), and the gut (appetite).
- Shortage of serotonin is associated with: anxiety, panic, phobias, posttraumatic stress disorder, obsessions, compulsions, or eating disorders.

stimulated by the NE neurotransmitter. The interesting point here is that norepinephrine alpha 2 heteroreceptor is located on the serotonin cell, yet it is the NE neurotransmitter that acts to regulate release of serotonin by stimulating this receptor. In addition, there is also a 5HT1A autoreceptor located on the somatodendritic region of the serotonin neuron which, when stimulated by 5HT, turns off release of the serotonin neurotransmitter. In addition to the above mechanisms, there are also two enzymes which act to regulate 5HT, the MAO which is located inside the cell, and the COMT which is located outside the cell in the synapse. Both of these enzymes serve to destroy excess neurotransmitters. The last mechanism is the serotonin transporter pump which transports 5HT back into the presynaptic cell thereby reducing the amount of neurotransmitters available in synapse. As you can see, there are numerous methods by which drugs can increase or decrease the amount of serotonin in the system. As illustrated in Figure 7-2, a Selective Serotonin Reuptake Inhibitor (SSRI), such as Prozac, is used to block further reuptake of serotonin back into the presynaptic cell, while an antagonist such as Remeron can be used to block the alpha 2 presynaptic heteroreceptor and thereby enable the continual release of serotonin into the synapse.

FIGURE 7-2
Serotonin Receptor

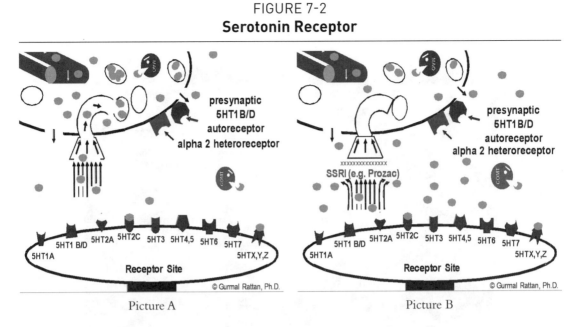

Picture A   Picture B

Figure 7-2. Picture A shows the relatively small amount of serotonin in the synapse when the reuptake pump is operating. In Picture B, Prozac, an SSRI is preventing the pump from removing the excess serotonin. As a result, it is hypothesized that the greater amount of neurotransmitters in the synapse and their subsequent binding with the receptors create the therapeutic effects to alleviate depression.

Serotonergic Projection Area

The cell bodies for the serotonergic neurons are contained in the raphe (**rey**-fee) nucleus which is located in the brain stem and has projections throughout the brain (see Figure 7-3). The serotonin neurons can be found in numerous locations, for example: the frontal cortex regulates mood; those in the basal ganglia regulate motor movements such as obsessions and compulsions; those in the limbic region are involved in anxiety and panic; those in the hypothalamus regulate appetite and eating behaviors; those in the brain stem regulate sleep and vomiting; those in the spinal cord regulate sexual behavior such as orgasm and ejaculation; and those in the gut regulate appetite. The theory behind affective problems suggests that a shortage of serotonin can result in depression, and this may well be the basis for a host of problems such as anxiety, panic, phobias, posttraumatic stress disorder, obsessions, compulsions, or eating disorders (Stahl, 2000). The serotonin deficiency is supported by the fact that the above disorders also respond to serotonin even without an underlying depression.

FIGURE 7-3
Serotonin Pathways

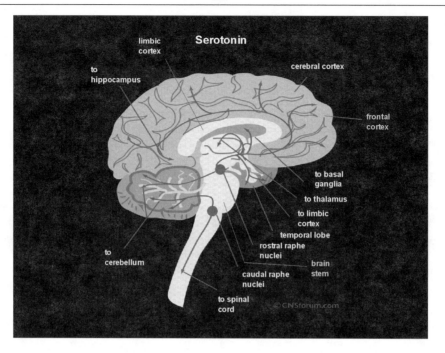

Figure 7-3. The above shows the projections sites for Serotonin and the raphe nuclei which contains the cell bodies for this neurotransmitter.

Norepinephrine

Norepinephrine (NE) neurotransmitters are produced by the infusion of tyrosine (**tahy**-*ruh*-seen), an amino acid, into the norepinephrine receptor cell. Three enzymes act upon the tyrosine in a sequence to convert this amino acid into the NE neurotransmitter. The first enzyme is tyrosine hydroxylase (TOH) which converts tyrosine into DOPA, while the DOPA decarboxylase (DDC) enzyme then acts to convert DOPA into the dopamine (DA) neurotransmitter. In the last stage, the remaining enzyme, dopamine beta hydroxylase (DBH) converts DA into the NE neurotransmitter. The interesting thing here is that DA is its own neurotransmitter, yet it is a precursor to the production of NE. The NE neurotransmitter is destroyed by several processes. The two enzymes which destroy NE are the monoamine oxidase (MAO) and catechol-O-methyl transferase (COMT) enzymes. In addition, NE can also be transported back into the cell by the norepinephrine transporter pump thereby reducing the amount of NE in the synapse. Drug action can focus on preventing NE returning back to the cell and/or blocking the MAO and COMT from destroying excess NE.

The norepinephrine neuron consists of seven postsynaptic receptor sites: alpha 1, postsynaptic alpha 2A, alpha 2B, alpha 2C, and beta 1, beta 2, beta 3 receptors (see Stahl, 2008). There is also a presynaptic alpha 2 autoreceptor which is attached to the presynaptic norepinephrine cell and acts as a regulator. When the alpha 2 autoreceptor is stimulated by NE or the norepinephrine neurotransmitter, it shuts down further release of NE into the synapse. As discussed later in this chapter, the alpha 2 autoreceptor is the site of drug action where a drug can serve as an antagonist (e.g., Remeron) to block the norepinephrine receptor from being stimulated by NE. As a net result of this blocking action, NE continues to be released into the synapse to provide the necessary therapeutic action. Alternatively, drugs can also act as an agonist to stimulate the autoreceptor and stop NE release. When there is too much norepinephrine, symptoms such as anxiety and panic attacks may result. These symptoms are mediated by the alpha 1 and beta 1 receptors in the amygdala and may be reduced by adrenergic blockers such as Prazosin (Stahl, 2008).

Depression may result when there is too little norepinephrine in the synapse. Picture A in Figure 7-4 shows a relative depletion of norepinephrine in the synapse. The reuptake transporter pump, represented by the funnel, pumps NE back into the cell, while the MAO inside the cell and the COMT outside the cell are destroying excess norepinephrine. As a result, there may be too little NE to bind with the receptors and produce a desired therapeutic effect. To that end, selective Norepinephrine Reuptake Inhibitors (NRI) such as Strattera block the funnel thereby keeping more NE into the presynaptic cell as noted in Picture B. Another method to keep more NE in the synapse is associated with the presynaptic alpha 2 autoreceptor. The role of this autoreceptor is to maintain homeostasis, such that if there is too much NE in the synapse, a NE neurotransmitter would bind to this receptor site and turn off or reduce further release of this neurotransmitter in order to prevent over firing. As noted above, if an alpha 2 antagonist such as Remeron is administered, it blocks the NE from binding with the alpha 2 autoreceptor thereby preventing norepinephrine from being shut off. As a result, the dual mechanisms of blocking the reuptake pump with an NRI along with an alpha 2 antagonist increase the amount of NE available for binding with the postsynaptic receptors to produce the desired therapeutic effect.

FIGURE 7-4
Norepinephrine Receptor

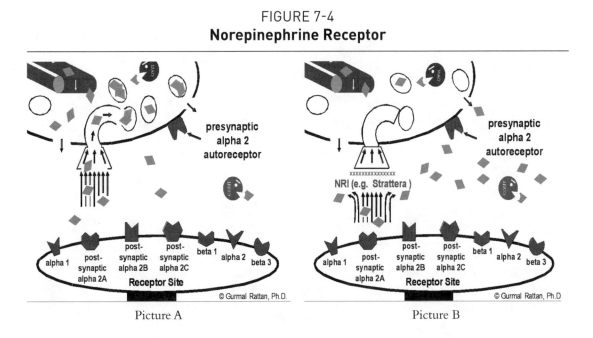

Picture A   Picture B

Figure 7-4. Picture A shows a relative depletion of NE while picture B shows the positive effects of Strattera, an NRI in blocking the reuptake of NE and thereby reducing depression.

KEY LEARNING POINTS:
Norepinephrine

- Three enzymes act upon tyrosine to convert this amino acid into norepinephrine.
- Dopamine is a precursor to norepinephrine.
- Monoamine oxidase (MAO) and catechol-O-methyl transferase (COMT) are enzymes that destroy norepinephrine.
- Alpha 2 autoreceptors shut down the release of norepinephrine when stimulated.
- Remeron is a drug that acts as an agonist to stimulate the alpha 2 autoreceptor and stop the release of norepinephrine.
- Strattera is an example of a selective Norepinephrine Reuptake Inhibitor (NRI) that blocks the reuptake of NE thereby keeping more NE in the synapse.
- Cell bodies for noradrenergic neurons are located in the locus coeruleus.
- A shortage of NE is associated with the following problems: concentration, working memory, response speed, psychomotor slowing, fatigue, and anxiety.

Noradrenergic Pathways

The cell bodies for the noradrenergic neurons are contained in the locus coeruleus (si-roo-lee-uhs) pathways which reside in the brain stem and project throughout the brain (see Figure 7-5). The beta 1 receptors in the frontal lobe regulate mood, while the alpha 2 receptors in the frontal lobe regulate attention, concentration, working memory, and response speed. Projections to the limbic region regulate behaviors such as: emotions, agitation, and energy; the latter which manifests as fatigue and psychomotor slowing. The norepinephrine neurons located in the cerebellum are thought to regulate motor movement such as tremors while those in the brainstem regulate cardiovascular functions such as blood pressure and heart rate via beta 1 receptors. Additionally, in the urinary tract area, the norepinephrine neurons regulate bladder functions via the alpha 1 receptor. In short, the locus coeruleus regulates cognition, mood, emotions, and movement. Behavioral disorders associated with norepinephrine deficiency are thought to result in problems with: concentration, working memory, response speed, psychomotor slowing, fatigue, and anxiety. These symptoms can also accompany disorders associated with depression, ADHD, schizophrenia, and Alzheimer's disease.

FIGURE 7-5
Noradrenergic Pathways

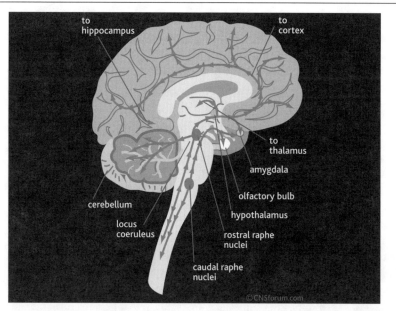

Figure 7-5. The above picture shows the projections sites for NE and the locus coeruleus which contain the cell bodies for the norepinephrine neuron.

Dopamine

The production of the dopamine neurotransmitter, not surprisingly, consists of the same two enzymes that are used to make the NE neurotransmitter, the TOH which produces DOPA and DDC which produces DA. Like the NE, dopamine neurotransmitters are destroyed by the same two enzymes that destroy the NE; the MAOs and the COMT.

The dopamine neuron is comprised of five postsynaptic receptor sites: D1, D2, D3, D4, and D5. Of these, the one most commonly associated with psychiatric disorders is the D2 receptor. The dopamine cell also has a presynaptic autoreceptor which works to regulate release of DA in the same manner that exists for the serotonin and norepinephrine neurons as described above.

As noted in Figure 7-6, dopamine behaves in a similar fashion to the other monoamines. Picture A shows a relative depletion of dopamine in the synapse. The reuptake transporter pump, represented by the funnel, pumps dopamine back into the cell, while the MAO inside the cell and the COMT outside the cell are destroying excess dopamine. As a result, there may be too little DA to bind with the receptors and produce a desired therapeutic effect. To that end, Dopamine Reuptake Inhibitors (DRI) such as Concerta block the funnel, thereby keeping more dopamine in the presynaptic cell as noted in Picture B. Dopamine also has its own presynaptic autoreceptor to shut down further release of DA in order to prevent over firing of these receptors. As with the serotonin and norepinephrine neurons, drugs can act as antagonists to increase DA in the synapse or as agonists to stop further release.

KEY LEARNING POINTS:
Four Dopamine Pathways

- Dopamine neurons are comprised of 5 receptor sites, with psychiatric disorders usually associated with the D2 receptor.
- Monoamine oxidase (MAO) and catechol-O-methyl transferase (COMT) are enzymes that destroy dopamine.
- Dopamine pathways consist of four major areas:

1. **Mesolimbic pathways**—too *much* DA in this region leads to positive symptoms of schizophrenia such as delusions, hallucinations, and disorganized speech
2. **Mesocortical pathways**—too *little* DA leads to negative symptoms of psychoses such as: cognitive symptoms (e.g., verbal fluency, executive functioning problems) and emotional blunting (e.g., affective flattening, loss of pleasure)
3. **Nigrostriatal pathways**—too *little* DA leads to movement disorders in the extrapyramidal system
4. **Tuberoinfundibular pathways**—too *little* DA leads to breast secretions in males and females

Side note: Atypical antipsychotics (e.g., clozapine, risperidone, olanzapine, quetiapine and ziprasidone) consist of serotonin-dopamine antagonists (SDA) that help maintain therapeutic levels of DA in the mesolimbic region while increasing DA in the mesocortical, nigrostriatal, and tuberoinfundibular pathways.

FIGURE 7-6
Dopamine Receptor

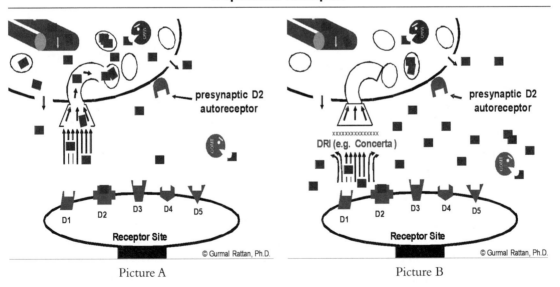

Picture A   Picture B

Figure 7-6. Picture A shows a relative depletion of dopamine while Picture B shows the positive effects of Concerta, a DRI in blocking the reuptake of DA and thereby reducing depression.

Dopamineric Pathways

The dopamine pathways are comprised of four major areas: 1) mesolimbic, 2) nigrostriatal, 3) mesocortical, and 4) tuberoinfundibular (see Figure 7-7).

The mesolimbic (me-so-**lim**-bik) pathways have projections from the midbrain to the nucleus accumbens, with the latter region being responsible for regulating the pleasurable behaviors of euphoria associated with drug use. The mesolimbic area is also targeted by antipsychotic drugs in order to reduce the positive symptoms of psychoses such as delusions, hallucination, and disorganized speech. This is a result of too much DA in this pathway which is responsible for these behaviors. When the older conventional antipsychotics (e.g., Haloperidol) were used, they blocked dopamine everywhere in the brain. Besides producing immediate unwanted side effects such as dry mouth, blurred vision, cognitive blunting, weight gain, drowsiness, decreased blood pressure and the like, these conventional drugs also resulted in a deficiency of DA in the mesocortical, nigrostriatal, and tuberoinfundibular pathways. Deficiency of DA in these latter pathways created its own series of problems. The mesocortical pathway has projections from the midbrain to the limbic region and is responsible for the emotional and cognitive problems in addition to social isolation and apathy issues. The constant blockage of dopamine in the mesocortical pathway has led to an increase of negative symptoms of schizophrenia, such as emotional blunting (e.g., affective flattening, alogia— reduced fluency in thought and speech, anhedonia (an-hee-**doh**-nee-*uh*)—loss of pleasure, and attentional problems) and cognitive symptoms (e.g., verbal fluency, serial learning, and executive functioning problems). The nigrostriatal pathway has projections from the substantia nigra to the basal ganglia and is part of the extrapyramidal system (i.e., the basal ganglia, substantia nigra, cerebellum, and interconnecting pathways). Normally, dopamine inhibits acetylcholine activity; however, with the prolonged blockage of dopamine by the conventional antipsychotics, acetylcholine remains unchecked. It is this increased acetylcholine level (or a depletion of dopamine) that is responsible for the extrapyramidal symptoms (EPS) associated with movement disorders such as Parkinson's, rigidity, bradykinesia (bray-dee-ki-**nee**-zha) (slow movements), and tremors. Anticholinergic (an-ti-koh-*luh*-**nur**-jik) drugs, such as Cogentin, are used to block the acetylcholine receptors to reduce EPS. This not withstanding, however, the dopamine starved receptors up-regulate in the nigrostriatal pathway and with this constant up-regulation, it can lead to tardive dyskinesia (e.g., constant chewing, tongue protrusion). Conversely, too much dopamine can lead to chorea (jerky movements of arms, legs, face) and tics. The tuberoinfundibular pathways regulate prolactin secretion with projections from the hypothalamus to the anterior pituitary gland. Here, extended blockage of the D2 dopamine receptor can lead to breast secretions in both males and females. As a very quick summary, a normal functioning brain has its own mechanisms to maintain homeostasis, however, the injection of antagonist or agonist for an extended period of time can off set this balance and create unwanted and sometime hideous side effects as referenced above.

The relatively newer atypical antipsychotics (e.g., clozapine, risperidone, olanzapine, quetiapine and ziprasidone) have been used to increase the amount of dopamine in the mesocortical, nigrostriatal, and tuberoinfundibular pathways to reduce the adverse symptoms listed above, while maintaining therapeutic levels of dopamine in the mesolimbic pathways to reduce the positive symptoms of schizophrenia. The atypical antipsychotics drugs accomplish this by blocking the serotonin 5HT2A receptors which are located on the dopamine cell. When the 5HT2A receptors are stimulated by serotonin, they inhibit dopamine release. Conversely, when the 5HT2A receptors are blocked, dopamine is freely released. The atypical antipsychotics are referred to as serotonin-dopamine antagonist (SDA) and operate by blocking the 5HT2A receptors to enable further release of DA into the synapse. PET scan studies have shown that a 10-20% reduction of dopamine blockage in the nigrostriatal pathways via the atypicals are sufficient to reduce ESP and tardive dyskinesia (Stahl, 2000, 2008) while the atypical antipsychotics also improve cognitive functioning and reduce negative symptoms in the mesocortical pathways. The improved functioning must be weighed by the numerous side effects (see Stahl, 2008).

FIGURE 7-7
Dopamineric Pathways

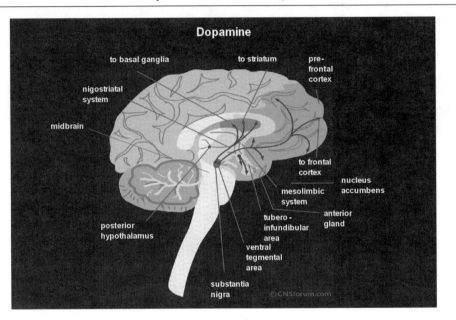

Figure 7-7. The cell bodies for dopamine are contained in the following pathways: 1) mesolimbic, 2) nigrostriatal 3) mesocortical, and 4) tuberoinfundibular

Agonist Spectrum
The following is a discussion of the agonist spectrum since drugs generally either speed up or slow down the system. To that end, drugs can behave in a complex manner to accomplish their goals. The components of the agonist spectrum work like a rheostat setting where a channel of the GABA or Glutamate neurons can range from being fully opened to being fully closed. Similarly, the G protein-linked receptors can range from fully activating the second messenger system in order to produce a gene response to fully inactivating this system (see section on monoamines). Very briefly, an inverse agonist can turn off the system completely, a partial agonist can turn the system on slightly, and finally, the agonist can turn on the system fully (see Figure 7-8). It is important to understand that the agonist spectrum operates in a range like a rheostat setting versus a simple on-off setting. Another important concept is the set point for a partial agonist. Each drug that serves as a partial agonist has a unique set point such that it is only able to turn on the system to a certain level, and it will not open up or turn on the system any further by increasing the dosage. The mechanisms underlying the drug action can take on the following characteristics:

Agonist: A drug that behaves as an agonist will fully open the ion-channel for the GABA or Glutamate receptors or fully activate a second messenger system associated with the G protein-linked receptor to create a therapeutic effect. An agonist will, therefore, fully open a channel or activate a second messenger system if the two receptor systems are at rest. While this may provide the most potent effect, over firing of neurons can create their own set of problems (e.g., anxiety with too much NE).

Partial Agonist: A drug that is a partial agonist is able to partially open a channel that is at its normal resting state and partially close an ion-channel that is fully open. A partial agonist can, therefore, boost a deficient neurotransmitter or block an excessive neurotransmitter. For example, Buspirone (BuSpar) is a 5HT1A partial agonist and acts by up-regulating presynaptic receptors and is also used as an anxiolytic agent and a serotonin receptor agonist.

Antagonist: A drug that behaves as an antagonist has no active properties of its own and should not be confused as being the opposite of an agonist. The antagonist role is to place the ion-channel or G protein-linked receptor back to its normal resting position. To that end, if the channel is fully open (agonist) or the G protein-linked receptor is fully activated (agonist), the antagonists will close the receptor systems and return them to their normal resting position. Likewise, if the above systems are fully closed or inactivated (inverse agonist), the antagonist will open the system and return them to their normal resting positions. Additionally, the antagonist can also serve to block a receptor from being stimulated as described below with the alpha 2 antagonist. For example, the antagonist Flumazenil reverses the effects of benzodiazepine, a full agonist for the GABA receptor, as a way to reverse the anesthetic effects in cases of overdose. Alternatively, as a blocker, Remeron is an alpha 2 antagonist that is associated with the G protein-lined receptor system. Here, Remeron blocks both the presynaptic alpha 2 autoreceptors located on the norepinephrine cell and the presynaptic alpha 2 heteroreceptors located on the serotonin cell. By blocking these receptor sites, it maintains an uninterrupted flow of NE and 5HT respectively, which would have otherwise been discontinued if they had been stimulated by the NE neurotransmitter. The key role for the antagonist, then, is to maintain homoeostasis in the system since too much or too little neuronal firing can create pathological behavior.

Inverse Agonist: A drug that behaves as an inverse agonist fully closes an ion-channel by completely blocking any conductance of chloride into the GABA channel. This has the net effect of creating anxiety. Drugs used to reverse this effect include Alprazolam (Xanax), a benzodiazepine class of drugs that are used to treat behaviors such as anxiety disorders and panic attacks.

FIGURE 7-8
Agonist Spectrum

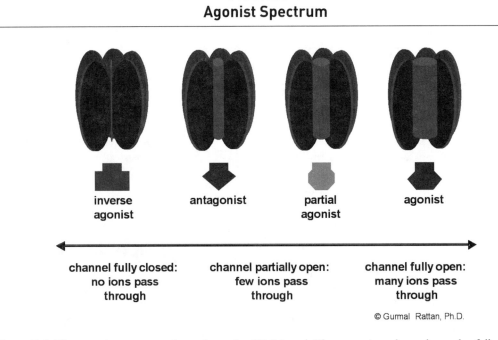

© Gurmal Rattan, Ph.D.

Figure 7-8. The agonist spectrum shows how the GABA and Glutamate ion channels can be fully opened (agonist) or fully closed (inverse agonist) based on the binding of the GABA and Glutamate neurotransmitters to their respective receptors and the subsequent allosteric effects of drug action.

Monoamine Oxidase Inhibitors

The purpose of the monoamine oxidase (MAO) is to destroy excess neurotransmitters that exist in the cell and turn them into inactive metabolites. There are two types of MAOs, type A and B. The A type is related to depression, while type B is related to neurodegenerative disorders. It is type A that is most utilized with emotional disorders, especially for the serotonin and norepinephrine neurotransmitters. The early history of MAOs in the 1960's produced irreversible MAO inhibitors. By inhibiting the MAOs, the excess neurotransmitters remained in the cell and were able to be released to create the therapeutic effect of reducing depression. Certain foods and beverages that are consumed contain tyramines which are a precursor to the production of norepinephrine. Normally, these foods are metabolized by the MAOs; however, when the MAOs are destroyed by the irreversible MAO inhibitors (e.g., Nardil), the tyramines released by such foods remain unprocessed. It is believed that these tyramines trigger release of NE, such that too much NE firing resulted in potential vasoconstriction, high blood pressure, intracerebral hemorrhage, and possibly death. In fact, 10 mg of dietary tyramines may be sufficient to raise blood pressure (Stahl, 2008). With the newer reversible MAO inhibitor (e.g., Aurorix), the MAOs continue to destroy excess neurotransmitters. However, when the tyramines are ingested, they displace the MAO inhibitors and allow the excess neurotransmitters to be destroyed. Examples of foods high in tyramines are: smoked, aged, or pickled meat or fish; sauerkraut; aged cheeses (e.g., swiss, cheddar, blue, stilton); yeast extracts; fava beans; beef or chicken liver; aged sausages (e.g., bologna, pepperoni, salami); game meats (e.g., venison, rabbit); and red wines (e.g., chianti, sherry) (see Northwestern Memorial Hospital, 2007).

Tricyclics

The tricyclics (tri-cy-clic) (TCA) were named because of their three ring structure. They were developed in the 1950s and 1960s along with other antipsychotic drugs and were initially thought to provide a tranquilizing effect for schizophrenia. Although their structure was similar to phenothiazine, an antipsychotic drug, the TCAs did not prove useful for this purpose. However, the TCAs proved to be potent serotonin (e.g., clomipramine) and norepinephrine (e.g., desipramine) reuptake inhibitors with minor reuptake properties for dopamine. As such, TCAs have been found to be an effective therapy for depression, attention, mood disorders, receptiveness to learning, and increased social functioning. The above notwithstanding, the TCAs also came with numerous and, in many cases, intolerable side effects. For example, the TCAs would also block the antihistamine (HI) site on the histamine receptor to cause weight gain and drowsiness; block muscarinic cholinergic receptors to cause dry mouth, blurred vision, drowsiness, and constipation; and block the alpha adrenergic receptor to cause dizziness, decreased blood pressure, and drowsiness. Some signs of *overdose* may include: confusion, disturbed concentration, transient visual hallucinations, and vomiting. Moreover, the TCAs could also block the sodium channels in the heart and brain to result in cardiac arrest and seizures in overdose situations (Stahl, 2000, 2008). Given the rather debilitating side effects, the TCAs were replaced by the selective serotonin reuptake inhibitors (SSRIs) described below. However, TCAs are still co-administered with an SSRI for treatment resistant patients who do not respond to an SSRI as a sole therapy. The TCA's potency, in part, comes from its blocking or antagonist effects on the 5HT2A receptor. It is by blocking the 5HT2A receptor that simultaneously creates stimulation of the 5HT1A receptor; it is this latter event which provides the potency of the therapeutic effects (see discussion on SARIs below). The TCAs are still used in third world countries given the relatively lower cost of the drug. However, given the noxious and sometimes fatal outcome, TCAs have been removed as a first line defense.

Selective Serotonin Reuptake Inhibitors (SSRI)

The simplest therapeutic approach to reduce depression starts with a *monotherapy* or a single action mechanism. Here, the Selective Serotonin Reuptake Inhibitors (SSRIs) block the reuptake of excess

---

**KEY LEARNING POINTS:
SSRIs - Side Effects- Potential Benefits**

SSRIs:
Fluoxetine – Prozac
Sertraline – Zoloft
Paroxetine – Paxil, Apropax, Seroxat
Fluvoxamine – Luvox, Ferverin, Dumirox, Floxyfral
Citalopram – Celexa, Cipramil, Serostat, Cipram
Escitalopram – Lexapro, Cipralex

Side effects: Examples of side effects generally consist of: nausea, difficulty sleeping, drowsiness, anxiety, nervousness, tremors, dry mouth, diarrhea, decreased sexual drive. Signs of overdose include: dizziness, agitation and tremor, convulsions, delirium, and hallucinations.

Potential benefits: The positive aspects of SSRIs are their potential to increase concentration, attention, mood, receptiveness to learning, and interpersonal skills (Stahl, 2000, 2008). The attached appendix in the back of this chapter provides greater coverage of drugs, their associated psychopharmacological mechanisms, side effects, and contraindications.

neurotransmitters into the presynaptic neuron. It should be noted that the SSRIs are not a pure reuptake of serotonin exclusively. There are other minor actions that consist of norepinephrine reuptake (NRI), dopamine reuptake (DRI), serotonin 2C agonist action, along with other factors involved in the processing of the drug through the cytochrome P450 enzymes system (e.g., 1A2, 2D6, and 3A4 enzymes).

When examining the process more closely and by way of a very simple summary, the monoamine hypothesis states that depression is caused by too few neurotransmitters. However, with SSRI treatment, there are ample neurotransmitters available shortly after treatment begins, but the symptoms do not remit until much later. The neurotransmitter hypothesis states that the constant depletion of 5HT has caused a pathological up-regulation of receptors at both the pre and postsynaptic receptors. Once treatment begins, there is a flurry of 5HT which first appears at the somatodendritic end of the serotonin neuron before making its way to the synapse near the axon terminal. This increased level of 5HT then sends signals via the genome to down-regulate the receptors at the somatodendritic area. The effect of the increased neurotransmitters also acts to down-regulate and desensitize the 5HT1A autoreceptor that is located on the cell body of the serotonin neuron. Remember, the autoreceptor's role is to turn off release of 5HT when stimulated. However, in this case, with the flurry of neurotransmitters and genome action, the 5HT1A receptors have both down-regulated and become desensitized, thereby having the net effect of disinhibiting 5HT. This, in short, allows an ample supply of serotonin neurotransmitters to reach the axon terminal for potential release into the synapse. The time frame for treatment of the above process correlates with the general eight week time frame it takes to see the positive results of drug treatment. This time frame also corresponds to the body's tolerance of the side effects. Approximately 2/3 of the individuals respond to treatment while 1/3 respond to placebo. The long term response rate may vary with their compliance to the drug regimen since 1/3 of individuals do not refill their prescription after the first supply of medication (Stahl, 2008).

Norepinephrine Reuptake Inhibitor (NRI)
The NRI has shown to be more effective than SSRIs for depression associated with: fatigue, apathy, concentration, memory, and slow response speed on information processing tasks. Reboxetine, an NRI, has shown efficacy in improving the energy level involved in performing motoric and cognitive tasks, and shown improvement in social functioning. The NRI can be used when serotonin has proved to be ineffective in reducing depression.

Serotonin norepinephrine reuptake inhibitors (SNRI)
Another mechanism for the approximately 1/3 of individuals who do not respond to antidepressants is to increase the therapeutic potency by combining the reuptake of both 5HT and NE. The resulting Serotonin Norepinephrine Reuptake Inhibitor (SNRI) creates a more synergistic property such that the two together are more potent than each taken separately (see Figure 7-9). This mechanism involves the 5HT and NE separately producing a gene expression to enhance the therapeutic efficacy. An example of such a dual action mechanism can be seen in Venlafaxine (Effexor) which can reduce both depression and anxiety. An example of an SNRI drug includes Duloxetine (Cymbalta). Side effects generally consist of: nausea, dry mouth, constipation or diarrhea, and sexual side effects (see appendix for more details).

FIGURE 7-9

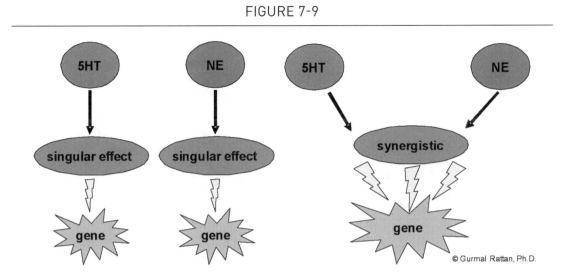

© Gurmal Rattan, Ph.D.

Figure 7-9. This figure shows the potency of the synergism when 5HT and NE are combined to produce a more potent therapeutic effect than when each is stimulated individually.

Alpha 2 Antagonist

To increase NE, an alpha 2 antagonist mechanism can be used to block the presynaptic alpha 2 autoreceptor located on the norepinephrine cell. Similarly, to increase 5HT, the alpha 2 antagonist can also block the norepinephrine presynaptic alpha 2 heteroreceptor located on the serotonin cell. As discussed previously, the alpha 2 receptor's role is to shut off release of either NE on the norepinephrine neuron or 5HT on the serotonin neuron to prevent either from over firing. By blocking these receptors with an antagonist, it disinhibits the neurotransmitters from shutting off, or more simply, it "turns on" or enables both 5HT and NE neurotransmitters to keep flowing. (Stahl, 2008) describes the above mechanism as "cutting the brake cable."

With the increased NE neurotransmitters available in the synapse given the alpha 2 antagonist action described above, the resulting surge of NE neurotransmitters then enables NE to also stimulate the alpha 1 receptor located on the somatodendritic cell of the serotonin neuron. This latter mechanism then acts as an accelerator, like "stepping on the gas" (Stahl, 2008) to further increase the release of 5HT. An example of such a drug that utilizes the mechanisms of alpha 2 antagonisms is Mirtazapine (Remeron) which is used for panic disorders and generalized anxiety disorders. In Figure 7-10, the NE neurotransmitter is stimulating the alpha 1 somatodendritic receptor on the serotonin cell in Picture A to accelerate 5HT release. Similarly, in Picture B, the alpha 2 antagonist blocks the alpha 2 heteroreceptor that is also located on the serotonin cell in order to keep 5HT flowing into the synapse. The net result of both actions produces a flurry of 5HT being released from the serotonin cell. In summary, an alpha 2 antagonist serves two functions: 1) it disinhibits 5HT and NE (or keeps it "turned on" by "cutting the brake cable"), that is, by blocking the norepinephrine alpha 2 autoreceptor and serotonin alpha 2 heteroreceptor, and 2) because of the alpha 2 antagonistic activity on the norepinephrine cell, the increased NE can then stimulate the serotonin somatodendritic alpha 1 receptors and thereby accelerates release of 5HT ("stepping on the gas"). Examples of alpha 2 antagonists that can increase both 5HT and NE include: Mirtazapine, Risperidone, Mianserin,

Quetiapine, and Clozapine. For refractory individuals who do not respond to the increase of neurotransmitters via blockage of the reuptake pumps as noted by SNRI (e.g., Venlafaxine), the additional mechanism of increasing 5HT and NE by the alpha 2 antagonist action clearly increases the therapeutic efficacy. The polypharmacy of combining Mirtazapine with an SNRI appears to have distinct advantages. As an added note, Mirtazapine has also been referred as a Noradrenergic and Specific Serotonin Antidepressant (NaSSA). With its alpha 2 antagonistic properties for the serotonin neuron, 5HT is released to all serotonin receptors. In doing so, however, Mirtazapine is also able to simultaneously block serotonin 2A, 2C, and 3 receptors while stimulating the 5HT1A receptor. The net effect is a reduction of depression and anxiety without the side effects (e.g., sexual, GI, nausea, sleep) except for weight gain.

FIGURE 7-10
Alpha 2 Antagonism

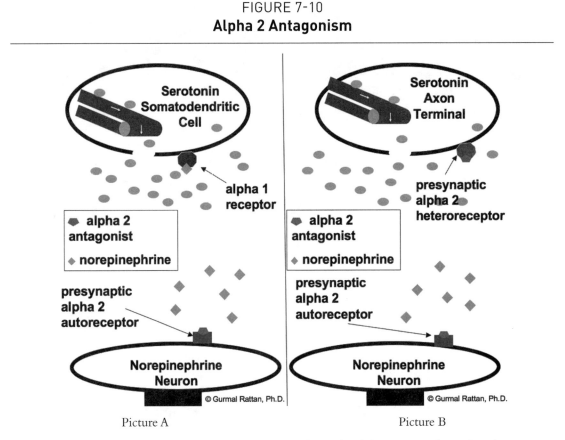

Picture A   Picture B

Figure 7-10. Picture A shows the NE neurotransmitter stimulating the alpha 1 receptor located on the serotonin somatodendritic neuron and the alpha 2 antagonist blocking the presynaptic alpha 2 autoreceptor located on the norepinephrine neuron. Picture B shows the alpha 2 antagonist blocking both the presynaptic alpha 2 heteroreceptor located on the serotonin axon terminal and the presynaptic alpha 2 autoreceptors located on the norepinephrine neurons. The effect of the NE stimulating the alpha 1 receptor in Picture A accelerates the release of 5HT ("stepping on the gas") while the actions of the alpha 2 antagonists in both pictures enables the continued release of 5HT ("cutting the brake cable"—see Stahl, 2008) to be maintained. The net result from the above actions provides a significant increase of 5HT into the synapse.

Serotonin 2A Antagonists/Reuptake Inhibitors (SARI)

In this category of drugs, the therapeutic actions of the drugs are produced by three behaviors: 1) primarily blocking the 5HT2A with additional blockage of the 5HT2C receptors (antagonist properties), 2) stimulating the 5HT1A receptor (agonist properties), and 3) reuptake inhibitors of 5HT. The mechanism that makes this class of drugs effective is the result of the phenomena of "intramolecular polypharmacy" (Stahl, 2008) whereby the blockage of the 5HT2A receptor enables stimulation of the 5HT1A receptor (see Figure 7-11). In normal situations in which the 5HT2A receptor is stimulated, the result is to inhibit the 5HT1A receptor from being stimulated. However, when the 2A receptor is blocked, this inhibiting effect is removed. It is, therefore, the removal of this inhibition of the 5HT1A receptor or rather the stimulation of the 5HT1A receptor coupled with the 5HT2A blockage and the 5HT reuptake inhibition that creates the therapeutic effects. However, a moderately high dose of SARI drugs, such as Trazodone (Desyrel, Molipaxin) is required for the above action. The advantage of the SARIs is that it has antidepressant properties without the sexual dysfunctions, insomnia, and anxiety often associated with other antidepressants.

FIGURE 7-11
Range of Therapeutic Effects

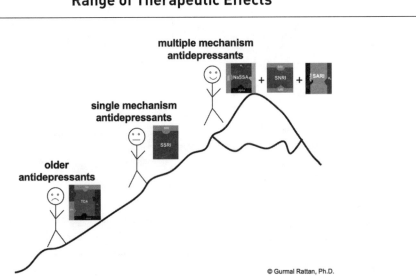

Figure 7-11. The above figure illustrates the range of therapeutic effects from: 1) the older antidepressants (e.g., TCA) with their hideous side effects, 2) the single mechanism of SSRI with relatively fewer side effects, to 3) the more potent therapeutic effects of NaSSA, SNRI, and SARI with their relatively minor side effects.

Pharmacokinetics – CYP450

Another important aspect of understanding the mechanism of drug action is pharmacokinetics (fahr-ma-koh-kih-ne-tiks). Very simply, pharmacokinetics deals with how the body absorbs, distributes, metabolizes, and excretes the drug (see Figure 7-12). To that end, the hepatic and gut use a system called the cytochrome (cy-to-chrome) P450 (CYP450) enzyme system. Here, the drug is absorbed through the gut wall into the liver in order to separate out the active ingredients before it is excreted. However, not all of the active ingredients of the drug are processed before it exits the body. Of the 30 CYP450 enzyme systems, five are involved with processing antidepressants and mood stabilizers, specifically, the 1A2, 2D6, 2C9, 2C19, and 3A4 enzyme systems. The interesting note about these systems is the genetic polymorphism or the variability in processing the efficacy of these systems as a function of race. As Stahl (2000) points out, 5-10% of Caucasians poorly metabolize the 2D6 system, while 20% of Japanese and Chinese and 3-5% of Caucasians poorly metabolize the 2C19 enzyme system. The clinical significance of the above suggests that dosages will need to be adjusted according to race to prevent toxic effects from developing.

FIGURE 7-12

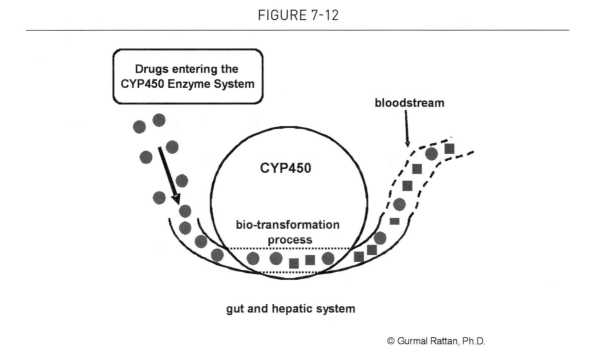

© Gurmal Rattan, Ph.D.

Figure 7-12. The CYP450 enzyme system above shows the transformation of a drug into active and inactive metabolites as it gets processed in the gut and hepatic system. The squares leaving the CYP 450 system represent active or processed drugs, while the circles represent the unprocessed or inactive metabolites.

Another issue is the interaction between specific drugs and their effects on the processing efficiency of the CYP450 system. For example, the SSRI Fluvoxamine (e.g., Luvox, Ferverin, Dumirox, and Floxyfral) is a substrate of the CYP450 1A2 enzyme system and it inhibits or reduces the metabolism of the 1A2 system. Therefore, if other drugs are also substrates of the 1A2 system (e.g., TCA - Clomipramine, Imipramine), then the dosage of these latter drugs must be lowered or blood levels will rise to cause toxic side effects (e.g., seizures). An inhibitor, therefore, reduces the efficiency of the drug metabolism, such that a lower dose is required to prevent toxic side effects.

The CYP450 2D6 is a substrate of several SSRIs (e.g., Paroxetine and Fluoxetine). Given the inhibitory effects of these SSRIs on the 2D6 system, any TCAs which are given concomitantly with these SSRIs will be poorly metabolized and could cause toxic effects if the dosage is not reduced. Similarly, SSRIs such as Fluoxetine, and Sertraline are also inhibitors of the CYP 450 3A4 systems. When certain other drugs that use the same system such as Cisapride, a benzodiazepine (sedative-hypnotic), are administered, then the dosage of this latter drug will similarly need to be reduced to avoid toxic effects.

In contrast to inhibitors of the CYP450 system, there are also inducers. The *inducers* speed up or increase the efficiency of drug metabolism. Because the drug is metabolized much faster, the therapeutic efficacy of the drug is reduced and the dosage will therefore need to be increased. For example, chronic use of Carbamazepine (an anticonvulsant and mood stabilizer) causes this drug to become an inducer of the 3A4 system; therefore, dosages will need to be increased to prevent mood problems or seizures from developing. If Carbamazepine or other inducers are no longer administered, then the dosage of drugs that use the 3A4 system (e.g., Fluoxetine, Sertraline) will need to be reduced to prevent toxic effects. Another example of an inducer is smoking which uses the

KEY LEARNING POINTS:
Pharmacokinetics

- **Pharmacokinetics**—deals with how the body absorbs, distributes, metabolizes, and excretes a drug.
- **CYP450 Inhibitor**—reduces the efficiency of drug metabolism such that a lower dose is required to prevent toxic side effects.
- **CYP450 Inducer**—speeds up the efficiency of drug metabolism such that a higher dose is required to maintain a therapeutic level.
- Dosages will need to be adjusted according to race and non-prescription drug use to prevent toxic effects from developing.

1A2 system. Likewise, dosages for drugs that use this system will need to be increased for smokers and readjusted if they stop smoking. While this is a quick look at the CYP450 enzyme system, several points are worth noting. Firstly, depending on one's racial group, there may be differences in how drugs are metabolized and knowing this can provide for more accurate discussion of drug prescription levels and efficacy. Secondly, the importance of ensuring that patients are forthcoming with an accurate history of non-prescription drug or tobacco use is essential to ensure an accurate dosage.

In summary, it is no simple task to understand the complexities of the mechanisms associated with drug action. If one class of drug such as an SSRI does not produce meaningful results, it should not disqualify other drugs in the same category since they vary in their potency of serotonin reuptake and/or reuptake of norepinephrine and dopamine. Add to this the other mechanisms such as the SNRI, alpha 2 antagonists, NaSSA, and SARI, and the therapeutic efficacy increases. Moreover, the monotherapy approach seems to have given way to polypharmacy. It is the incremental synergistic properties that allow polypharmacy to be tweaked in relieving unwanted side effects while delivering the most potent therapeutic benefits. Having said that, the consumer is always cautioned against the stated unwanted side effects or the side effects that are not reported or will not become apparent until further research is conducted. Perhaps a greater risk may well be the relative lack of efficacy of psychotropic drugs when compared to placebo and/or therapy, especially since you may still get stuck with the monetary cost, expectations, and the side effects of drugs. For a more thorough review of psychopharmacology, the reader is referred to Stahl (2008).

The remaining section of this chapter will explore the characteristics and causes of depression from a psychopharmacological perspective. To this end, problems associated with psychotropic drug use and suicide will be explored along with alternate approaches to treating depression, such as cognitive/behavioral and electric convulsive therapy (ECT).

Depression

Approximately 2/3 of patients respond to any given antidepressant medication while 1/3 do not (Stahl, 2008). However, about 1/3 of patients will clinically respond to placebo while 2/3 will not. To that end, drug therapy may not be efficacious to all individuals with depression. Uncontrolled symptoms of depression may be a sign of an underlying neuropathological etiology. Although the role of monoamine neurotransmitters and depression has already been presented, the information below discusses some of the behavioral characteristics of depression, the effects of drugs and suicide, and alternative approaches to remit depression.

Mood Disorders

The reader can refer to the Diagnostic and Statistical Manual of Mental Disorders IV-Text Revision (DSM-IV-TR, American Psychological Association, 2000) for a complete description of the diagnostic features, associated features, prevalence, course, and differential diagnosis. For the most part, depression manifests in the following manner: loss of interest or pleasure in daily activities, significant problems with weight gain or loss, too little or too much sleep, psychomotor agitation, loss of energy, fatigue, reduced thinking and concentration, low self-esteem, recurrent thought of death, suicidal ideation, and related symptoms. Based on the data from the DSM-IV-TR (American Psychological Association, 2000), less than 1% of preschoolers, 2-3% of school age children, and 7-13% of adolescents present with mood disorders. These disorders consist of major depressive disorders, dysthymic disorders (milder form of depression), and depressive disorders, not otherwise specified (NOS). Based on information collected from a nationally representative sample of children by the U.S. Agency for Healthcare Research and Quality, antidepressant medication use increased from 0.9 million in 1997 to 1.4 million in 2002 (Vitiello, Zuvekas & Norquist, 2006). This study also found that adolescent use increased from 2.1% in 1997 to 3.9% in 2002 with higher use among whites than blacks and Hispanics. Additionally, data from 1998 to 2002 suggests that an overall increase in depression was greater in girls with a 68% increase than for boys with a 34% increase (Delate, Gelenberg, Simmons, & Motheral, 2004). Although Prozac was the first FDA drug approved for children, Zoloft appears to be the most prescribed for children for depression, obsessive compulsive disorders (OCD), and anxiety (Dopheide, 2006)

Theory of Depression

According to Stahl (2000, 2008), theories of depression have focused on three areas: 1) depletion of the monoamine neurotransmitters (5HT, NE, DA), 2) too few or too many receptors, and 3) signal transduction problem relating to a target gene for the brain-derived neurotrophic factor (BNDF). The monoamine hypothesis has focused on the depletion or scarcity of neurotransmitters available to bind with the receptors. The problem here has been the fact that antidepressants boost the neurotransmitters almost immediately; however, there is a delay of days or weeks before any therapeutic effect occurs. Research evidence for the monoamine hypothesis has been inconsistent and sketchy and is no longer a viable explanation for depression. When the receptor hypothesis was examined, it was found that receptors tend to up-regulate or increase when there is a deficiency of neurotransmitters. This up-regulation is an attempt to capture any of the neurotransmitters available for binding with the receptors. Some direct evidence for the neurotransmitter hypothesis has been found via postmortem positron emission tomography (PET) studies showing a large number of serotonin receptors in the frontal cortex for individuals who committed suicide. While there is some direct evidence for this hypothesis, this data is inconsistent with studies that have shown no immediate reduction of depression, despite adequate amounts of monoamine neurotransmitters available in the synapse (Stahl, 2000). It is the third area, the signal transduction to gene expression, which appears to be the target of current research. The role of the BNDF is to sustain the integrity or viability of the neurons. Under stress, the gene expression for BNDF is suppressed, and the end result is atrophy and apoptosis with an accompanying decrease in brain volume. With antidepressant treatment, it is believed that the gene expression for BNDF is reactivated.

Suicide and Drugs

Data from research indicates that 35-50% of depressed patients have made or will make a suicide attempt, and that over a 10 year span, 2-8% of these individuals will commit suicide (Virani, 2004). Perhaps the best executed study in this area is the Treatment for Adolescent Depression Study (TADS) (Emslie, Kratochvil, Vitiello, et al., 2006; March, 2004). The study consisted of 439 participants aged 12-17 years. In addition to looking at the effects of SSRIs on suicide, the study also examined the efficacy of using cognitive behavior therapy (CBT) as a conjunct therapy with antidepressants. The TADS was the largest random controlled trial where the clinicians and patients were "blind" to those individuals receiving either Prozac or placebo. After a 12 week treatment period, the Children's Depression Rating Scale—Revised was used to evaluate changes in symptoms. The results clearly suggest that Prozac combined with CBT was the most efficacious treatment with 71% ($p < .001$) improvement over placebo. Prozac alone improved symptoms by 61% ($p < .02$) in contrast to the placebo, while CBT improved symptoms 43% ($p < .01$) compared to a placebo. Prozac alone was found to be better than CBT alone ($p < .01$), however, placebo alone had no significant impact on reducing symptoms. Interestingly, all four groups improved suicidal ideation by 10% from a baseline of 29%. When the suicide and harm or self-injurious related events (e.g., cutting or violence) were examined more closely, 24 (5.5%) adolescents had either worsening suicidal ideation or made a suicide attempt. Of the seven who attempted suicide, six were in the Prozac group. When harm related events were examined, there were 33 (7.5%) adolescents involved. Of these, the largest group was in the Prozac group (11.9%), 8.4% for the Prozac and CBT combined group, 5.4% in the placebo group, and 4.5% in the CBT only group. Based on the data, patients in the Prozac group had the largest potential for self-harm, although Prozac also served to significantly reduce depressive symptoms. Suicidality may also be a temporal sequence of when and how long the antidepressant was taken. For example, Jick et al. (2004) used a large United Kingdom general practice research database and found that suicide risk decreased in adolescents who were on antidepressants for more than six months but increased for those who were treated with antidepressants for less than eight weeks. In addition, completed suicide risk is 38 times greater in the first nine days of starting on antidepressants than 90 after the treatment regimen. To that end, monitoring within the first two weeks seems critical to reduce self-harm.

Alternate Treatment Modalities

A regimen of drug action along with cognitive behavioral interventions has also proven efficacious with depression as discussed above. However, older techniques that may be looked upon as arcane, outdated, and perhaps prehistoric in today's venue, are emerging with some interesting data. Despite its stigma, electroconvulsive therapy is reviewed as a treatment modality, since it may prove to be a valuable last resort option.

Electroconvulsive Therapy (ECT)

When one thinks of ECT, the movie "One Flew Over the Cuckoo's Nest" or the ghoulish images of Frankenstein electrically stimulating a dead monster's brain to bring it back to life comes to mind. Although the face validity of ECT may look like something out of the Middle Ages, research paints a more optimistic picture. Guidelines provided by the American Academy of Child and Adolescent Psychiatry (AACAP, 2004) clearly state the parameters for using ECT with individuals who present with severe and persistent depression or mania with or without psychotic features, suicidality, schizoaffective disorders, schizophrenia, mania, and catatonia. For example, the individual's symptoms must be severe, persistent, and significantly disabling; they may include life-threatening symptoms such as refusal to eat or drink, or severe suicidality. Before considering ECT, there must be a failure to respond to at least two adequate trials of appropriate psychopharmacological agents (e.g., 5HT, NE, DA, polypharmacy) lasting 8-10 weeks and accompanied by other treatment modalities such as therapy, behavior modification and the like. Exceptions to the above are made for individuals who cannot tolerate drugs, are grossly incapacitated and unable to take drugs, or are a danger to themselves (Ghaziuddin, 2004). With adult patients, there appears to be no contraindications for the use of ECT, even with cases with cerebral tumor, chest infection, or myocardial infarction, although the American Psychological Association cautions against the use of ECT with individuals with intracranial tumors (Ghaziuddin). However, there is insufficient data with adolescents to make such categorical claims about the contraindications. The exact mechanisms underlying the therapeutic effects of ECT are unclear. It is speculated that ECT acts to release greater amounts of monoamines (5HT, NE, DA) or neuropeptides to produce the antidepressant effects. Other proposed mechanisms suggest that ECT trains the brain to resist seizures, and as such, helps to stabilize the individual's mood.

ECT Procedure

The preparation for ECT starts with a physical and cognitive exam, the latter of which evaluates short term memory and knowledge acquisition. The intent of these exams is to provide a baseline to assess the post ECT efficacy and any lingering side effects. In addition to consent from the individuals and/or parents/guardians, a second opinion is required to proceed. However, in some states, requirements are much more stringent. For example, Alabama requires consent and confirmation from four psychiatrists and one neurologist, in addition to monitoring by an attorney (Baldwin, Cowan, & Jones, 1998). The procedure itself involves fasting for at least 12 hours. An electrode is placed above the temple of the non-dominant side of the brain, and a second electrode is placed in the middle of the forehead (unilateral ECT) or above each temple (bilateral ECT). The individual is provided with anesthesia and a muscle relaxant in addition to being given pure oxygen. An electric current is presented for .02 to 8 seconds causing a seizure that lasts from 30 to 60 seconds. Throughout the process, an electroencephalogram monitors the seizure while an electrocardiogram monitors the heart rhythm. The individual usually wakes up 10 to 15 minutes after the procedure and is usually monitored for one to two hours afterwards. Side effects can consist of: short-term cognitive deficits (e.g., concentration, attention, verbal fluency), tardive seizures (those seizures that occur shortly after the treatment), along with very short term side effects such as headaches, nausea, vomiting, muscle aches, confusion, and agitation that typically last no more than one day. The usual course of ECT administration is three times weekly and consists of 10-12 treatments with initial improvement noted after 5-6 treatments.

ECT Efficacy

For the most part, the efficacy of ECT has been very positive ranging from 50-100% with higher response rates for those with mood disorders. For example, in 1990, Paillere-Martinot (see AACAP, 2004) found an 88% response rate or beneficial effects for eight adolescents who presented with schizophrenia, depression, mania, and head injury. Similarly, Ghaziuddin et al. (1996) found a 64% response rate in a heterogeneous group (depression, bipolar, and mood disorders) of adolescents who were unresponsive to three or more trials of antidepressants. Kutcher and Robinson (1995) studied 16 bipolars with either manic or depressive features and found that the ECT group had significantly shorter hospital stays (73 vs. 176 days). In an extensive review of 60 studies using 396 patients, Rey and Walter (1997) found that there was a 63% remission for depression, 80% for mania, and 42% for schizophrenia. When assessing the long term effects, Ghaziuddin (2000) did find significant impairments on cognitive tests one week post ECT in areas of concentration, attention, verbal and visual-delayed recall, and verbal fluency. However, when the same individuals were tested eight months later, the cognitive impairments were absent. To compare the side effects of ECT with psychotropic medication, Walter, Koster, and Ray (1999a) interviewed 26 patients and found that 85% had adverse side effects with ECT while 96% reported side effects with psychotropic medication. When the side effects of ECT were examined in more detail, the biggest complaints in rank order consisted of: memory impairment, confusion, and headaches, while for the medication group, the complaints focused on nausea or vomiting, confusion, and memory impairment. When the parents or guardians were interviewed, 82% reported the presence of side effects for ECT and 100% for medication (Walter, Koster, & Rey, 1999b). The rank order complaints for ECT according to the parents or guardians consisted of: headaches, memory impairment, and confusion while the complaints for the medication group focused on muscle aches, confusion, and a tie for third place for nausea/memory and memory impairment.

As a cautionary note, some of the studies referenced above used clinical impressions versus standardized tests, while others did not discuss treatment frequency. The above cautionary note notwithstanding, the overall data does suggest benefits of ECT for patients who are a threat to themselves and have not responded to previous psychopharmacological or behavioral treatments.

SUMMARY

The challenge of writing a chapter on psychopharmacology is like trying to hit a moving target. With the prolific release of new psychotropic drugs in recent years, the mechanism underlying their purported efficacy is not always understood (e.g., depression - neurotransmitter hypothesis). This is even more pronounced when it comes to the side effects. When SSRI's were first introduced, they were presented as safe with very few side effects. However, with the passage of time, one saw the full nature of the side effects (see appendix) along with data to warrant a black box warning of potential suicide. Besides the side effects, newer technology is casting doubt on our previously held notion of neurotransmitter depletion as a primary explanation of depression (see Stahl, 2008). Moreover, as technology advances, the explanations of drug action noted in this chapter may well be out of date. Although psychotropic drugs have provided some relief to patients with depression and related psychopathology, alternate approaches to augment a drug regimen are clearly warranted as noted by the TADS study. Likewise, while ECT has also shown efficacy in difficult to treat patients, the stigma may present a road block for this treatment modality. As a psychologist, educator, or parent, the reader is always encouraged to do his/her due diligence in weighing the relative efficacy of various therapeutic approaches with existing or perceived costs.

REFERENCES

American Academy of Child and Adolescent Psychiatry (2004). Practice parameter for use of electroconvulsive therapy with adolescents. *Journal of American Academy for Child and Adolescent Psychiatry, 43*(12), 1521-1539.

American Psychological Association. (1994). *Diagnostic and statistical manual of mental disorders* (4th ed.). Washington, DC: Author.

Baldwin, S., Cowan, E., & Jones, Y. (1998). Is Electroconvulsive Therapy Unsuitable for Children And Adolescents? *Adolescence, 33,* 645-655

Delate, T., Gelenberg, A. J., Simmons, V. A., & Motheral B. R. (2004). Trends in the use of antidepressant medication in a nationwide sample of commercially insured pediatric patients, 1998-2002. *Psychiatric Services, 55*(4), 387-391.

Dopheide, A. (2006). Recognizing and treating depression in children and adolescents. *American Journal of Health-System Pharmacy, 63*(3), 233-243

DuPaul, G. J., & Carlson, J. S. (2005). Child psychopharmacology: How school psychologists can contribute to effective outcomes. *School Psychology Quarterly, 20*(2), 206-221.

Emslie, G., Kratochvil, C, Vitiello, B., Silva, S., Mayes, T., McNutly, S., et al. (2006). Treatment for adolescents with depression study (TADS): Safety results. *Journal of American Academy for Child and Adolescent Psychiatry, 45*(12), 1440-1455.

Ghaziuddin, N. (2004). Practice parameter for use of electroconvulsive therapy with adolescents. *Journal of American Academy for Child and Adolescent Psychiatry, 43*(12), 1521-1539.

Ghaziuddin, N., King, C. A., Naylor, M. W., Ghaziuddin, B., Dequardo, J. R., Tandon, R., & Greden, J. (1996). Electroconvulsive treatment in adolescents with pharmacology-refractory depression. *Journal of Child and Adolescent Psychopharmacology, 6*(4), 259-271.

Handen, B. L., Breaux, A. M., Janosky, J., McAuliffe, S., Feldman, H., & Gosling, A (1992). Effects and non-effects of methylphenidate in children with mental retardation and ADHD. *Journal of the American Academy of Child and Adolescent Psychiatry, 31*(3), 455-461.

Herranz, J. L., Armijo, J. A., & Arteaga, R. (1988). Clinical side effects of phenobarbital, primidone, phenytoin, carbamazepine, and valproate during monotherapy in children. *Epilepsia, 29*(6), 794-804.

Jensen, P. S., Bhartara, V. S., Vitiello, B., Hoagwood, K., Feil, M., & Burke, L. (1999). Psychoactive medications practices for US children: gaps between research and clinical practice. *Journal of American Academy for Child and Adolescent Psychiatry, 38*, 557-565.

Jick, H., Kaye, J. A., & Jick, S. S. (2004). Antidepressants and the risk of suicidal behaviors. *Journal of the American Medical Association, 292*(3), 338-43.

Julien, R.M. (2001). *A primer of drug action.* New York, New York: Henry Holt and Company.

Kubiszyn, T. (2005). Introduction to the special issue: The division 16 task force on psychopharmacology, learning and behavior. *School Psychology Quarterly, 20*, 115-117.

Kubiszyn, T., & Carlson, C. I. (1995). School psychologists' attitudes toward an expanded health care role: Psychopharmacology and prescription privileges. *School Psychology Quarterly, 3*, 247-270.

Kutcher, S., & Robinson, H. A. (1995). Electroconvulsive therapy in treatment resistant bipolar youth. *Journal of Child and Adolescent Psychopharmacology, 5*(3), 167-175.

March, J. (2004). Fluoxetine, cognitive-behavioral therapy, and their combination for adolescents with depression: Treatment for Adolescents With Depression Study (TADS) randomized controlled trial. *Journal of the American Medical Association, 292*, 807-820.

Northwestern Memorial Hospital (October 2007). *Low tyramine diet.* Retrieved September 29, 2008 from http://www.nmh.org/nmh/pdf/pated/lowtyramine-diet07.pdf

Phelps, L., Brown, R. T., & Power, T. (2002). *Pediatric psychopharmacology: Combining medical and psychological interventions.* Washington, DC: American Psychological Association.

Rey, J. M., & Walter, G. (1997). Half a century of ECT use in young people. *American Journal of Psychiatry, 154*(5), 595-602.

Singh, N. N., Epstein, M. H., Luebke, J., & Singh, Y. N. (1990). Psychopharmacological intervention: I. Teacher perceptions of psychotropic medication for students with serious emotional disturbance. *Journal of Special Education, 24*(3), 283-295.

Stahl, S. M. (2000). Essential psychopharmacology: *Neuroscientific basis and practical applications* (2nd ed.). New York: Cambridge University Press.

Stahl, S. M. (2008). *Stahl's essential psychopharmacology: Neuroscientific basis and practical applications* (3rd ed.). New York: Cambridge University Press.

Vitiello, B., Zuvekas, S., & Norquist, G. (2006). National estimates of antidepressant medication use among U.S. children, 1997-2002. *Journal of the American Academy of Child & Adolescent Psychiatry, 45*(3), 271-279.

Virani, A. (2004) Antidepressants and the risk of suicide in children and adolescents: What's the link? *Child and Adolescent Psychopharmacology News, 9*(4), 1-6.

Walter, G., Koster, K., & Rey, J. M., (1999a). Views about treatment among parents of adolescents who received electroconvulsive therapy. *Psychiatric Services, 50*(5), 701-702.

Walter, G., Koster, K., & Rey, J. M. (1999b). Electroconvulsive therapy in adolescents: Experience, knowledge, and attitudes of recipients. *Journal of the American Academy of Child and Adolescent Psychiatry, 38*(5), 594-600.

Wilens, T., Biedderman, J., Kwon, A., Chase, R., Greenberg, L., Mick, E., et al. (2003). A systematic chart review of the nature of psychiatric adverse effects in children and adolescents treated with selective serotonin reuptake inhibitors. *Journal of Child and Adolescent Psychopharmacology, 13*(2), 143-152.

APPENDIX
Commonly Used Psychotropic Medication to Treat Emotional Disorders

The following drug chart provides information for some of the commonly used psychotropic medications for children with emotional disorders. This list is not exhaustive, and in the interest of space, this chart only provides abbreviated information regarding their side effects, signs of overdose, and contraindications. To that end, the reader is encouraged to check additional sources of information to ensure a more thorough understanding of how these drugs behave.

Brand Name	Generic Name	Function	Use for/Label	Dosage Range	Side Effects	Signs of Overdose	Contraindications
Abilify (ah–bil–li–fahy)	Aripiprazole (ay–ree–pip–ray–zole)	Dopamine partial agonist Atypical Antipsychotic	- Schizophrenia - Bipolar - Major Depressive Disorder	10-30 mg/day	The most common side effects include: Children and adolescents: - rausea - uncontrolled movements - sleepiness - headache - extrapyramidal disorder Adults: - dizziness - nausea - anxiety - constipation - insomnia - headache - vomiting - restlessness www.rxlist.com www.abilify.com www.accessdata.fda.gov	The most prevalent symptoms include: - tachycardia - phosphokinase increased - tremor - hypotension - bradycardia - aggression - aspartate - confusional state - vomiting - pneumonia aspiration - convulsion - hypertension - coma - hypokalemia - blood creatine lethargy - loss of consciousness www.abilify.com www.rxlist.com	Not recommended with: - breastfeeding - pregnancy - alcohol - patients with dementia-related psychosis - known hypersensitivity to the ingredients in the drug www.rxlist.com www.abilify.com www.accessdata.fda.gov

Brand Name	Generic Name	Function	Use for/Label	Dosage Range	Side Effects	Signs of Overdose	Contraindications
Adderall (ad-der-awl) XR	Amphetamine (am-fet-uh-meen)	DRI Stimulant	- Attention deficit hyperactivity disorder (ADHD)	Children 5–40 mg/day	The most common side effects include: - hypertension - headache - decreased appetite - stomach ache - loss of appetite - abdominal pain - insomnia - trouble sleeping - weight loss - dry mouth - nervousness - fast heart beat - mood swings - dizziness www.rxlist.com www.adderallxr.com www.healthsquare.com	The most prevalent symptoms include: - tremor - restlessness - confusion - convulsions - hallucinations - panic states - diarrhea - abdominal cramps - fatigue - depression - coma - circulatory collapse - nausea - vomiting - irregular heartbeat www.rxlist.com www.healthsquare.com www.adderallxr.com	Not recommended with: - cardiovascular disease - adrenergic blockers - phenobarbital - MAOIs - lithium carbonate - antihistamines - norepinephrine - acidifying agents - chlorpromazine - methenamine therapy - glaucoma - hyperthyroidism - history of drug abuse - tics - known hypersensitivity to the ingredients in the drug www.rxlist.com www.adderallxr.com www.healthsquare.com
Anafranil (an-ah-fray-nil)	Clomipramine (klo-mip-ruh-meen) Hydrochloride (hahy-druh-klawr-ahyd)	TCA	- Obsessive Compulsive Disorder (OCD)	25–250 mg/day	The most common side effects include: - dyspepsia - anorexia - nervousness - changed libido - ejaculatory failure - impotence - micturition disorder - increased appetite - weight gain	The most prevalent symptoms include: - seizures - flushing - loss of consciousness - dry mouth - drowsiness - confusion - fast or irregular heartbeat - agitation - enlarged pupils	Not recommended with: - MAOIs - pregnancy - Breast feeding - recovery period after a myocardial infarction - known hypersensitivity to the ingredients in the drug www.accessdata.fda.gov

Brand Name	Generic Name	Function	Use for/Label	Dosage Range	Side Effects	Signs of Overdose	Contraindications
					- somnolence - tremor - dizziness - headache - insomnia - increased - tremor - myoclonus - dry mouth - constipation - fatigue - abnormal vision - nausea www.accessdata.fda.gov www.rxlist.com www.medicinenet.com	www.accessdata.fda.gov www.medicinenet.com	www.rxlist.com www.medicinenet.com
Ativan (ay-ti-van)	Lorazepam (law-raz-uh-pam)	Benzodiazepine; modulates GABA receptor	- Anxiety	2-4 mg/day	The most common side effects include: - sedation - hostility - change in appetite - dizziness - unsteadiness - fatigue - euphoria - extrapyramidal symptoms - apnea - weakness - diarrhea www.biovail.com www.rxlist.com www.accessdata.fda.gov	The most prevalent symptoms include: - drowsiness - mental confusion - paradoxical reactions - dysarthria - lethargy - ataxia - hypotonia - hypotension - cardiovascular depression - respiratory depression - hypnotic state www.rxlist.com www.accessdata.fda.gov	Not recommended with: - acute narrow-angle glaucoma - pregnancy - breastfeeding - known hypersensitivity to the ingredients in the drug www.rxlist.com www.accessdata.fda.gov

Brand Name	Generic Name	Function	Use for/Label	Dosage Range	Side Effects	Signs of Overdose	Contraindications
Aurorix (aw-roh-iks)	Moclobemide (moe-kloe-be-mide)	MAOI	- Depression	300-600 mg/day	The most common side effects include: - dizziness - nausea - insomnia - restlessness - anxiety - confusion - diarrhea - upset stomach - constipation - blurred vision - headaches - skin rash www.depression-guide.com www.drugs.com www.virtualmedicalcentre.com	The most prevalent symptoms include: - dryness of mouth - trembling or shaking of arms or legs www.drugs.com	Not recommended with: - MAOIs - pregnancy - breast feeding - liver disease - high blood pressure - thyrotoxicosis - phaeochromocytoma - alcohol - known hypersensitivity to the ingredients in the drug www.depression-guide.com www.virtualmedicalcentre.com www.drugs.com
Aventyl (av-uh n-til) (Solution)	Nortriptyline (nawr-trip-tuh-leen)	TCA	- Major Depressive Disorder	25-100 mg/day	The most common side effects include: - fatigue - nausea - fast heart rate - blurred vision - dizziness - urinary retention - vomiting - dry mouth - constipation - change in weight - low blood pressure on standing - weakness	The most prevalent symptoms include: - agitation - drowsiness - confusion - fever - agitation - hallucinations - hypothermia - hyperpyrexia - blurred vision - vomiting - muscle stiffness - stupor - feeling hot or cold	Not recommended with: - pregnancy - breastfeeding - myocardial infarction recovery period - MAOIs - recent heart attack - known hypersensitivity to the ingredients in the drug www.accessdata.fda.gov www.rxlist.com www.nlm.nih.gov

Brand Name	Generic Name	Function	Use for/Label	Dosage Range	Side Effects	Signs of Overdose	Contraindications
					- disorientation - extrapyramidal symptoms - dry mouth www.accessdata.fda.gov www.rxlist.com	- fainting - seizure - dilated pupils - hyperactive reflexes www.accessdata.fda.gov www.rxlist.com www.nlm.nih.gov	
BuSpar (byou-spahr)	Buspirone (byou-spy-rown) Hydrochloride (hahy-druh-klawr-ahyd)	Partial Agonist for Serotonin 1A receptor	- General Anxiety Disorder (GAD)	15–60 mg/day	The most common side effects include: - nausea - headache - excitement - nervousness - dizziness - lightheadedness www.buspar.com www.bms.com www.accessdata.fda.gov www.healthcentral.com	The most prevalent symptoms include: - dizziness - vomiting - miosis - drowsiness - gastric distress www.bms.com www.accessdata.fda.gov www.healthcentral.com	Not recommended with: - MAOIs - grapefruit - haloperidol - impaired hepatic or renal function - known hypersensitivity to the ingredients in the drug www.buspar.com www.bms.com www.accessdata.fda.gov www.healthcentral.com
Carbatrol (kahr-bah-trol)	Carbamazepine (kahr-buh-maz-uh-peen)	Anticonvulsant and Mood Stabilizer	- Epilepsy - Seizures (not just from epilepsy)	400–1600 mg/day	The most common side effects include: - dizziness - vomiting - unsteadiness - nausea - drowsiness www.carbatrol.com www.accessdata.fda.gov	The most prevalent symptoms include: - tachycardia - hypotension - hypertension - ataxia - shock - dilated pupils - impairment consciousness - urinary retention	Not recommended with: - patients of Asian ancestry who have the HLA-B*1502 gene - pregnancy - breastfeeding - bone marrow problems - sensitivity to tricyclic antidepressants - MAOIs

Brand Name	Generic Name	Function	Use for/Label	Dosage Range	Side Effects	Signs of Overdose	Contraindications
					www.rxlist.com	- restlessness - psychomotor disturbances - loss of concentration - transient visual - irregular breathing - hallucinations - agitation - stupor - muscular twitching - drowsiness www.carbatrol.com www.accessdata.fda.gov www.rxlist.com	- alcohol - known hypersensitivity to the ingredients in the drug www.carbatrol.com www.accessdata.fda.gov www.rxlist.com
Celexa (she-lex-uh)	Citalopram (sahy-tal-uh-pram) Hydrobromide (hahy-droh-broh-mahyd)	SSRI	- Depression	20-60 mg/day	The most common side effects include: - coughing - tachycardia - hypotension - postural hypotension - paresthesia - migraine - increased saliva - confusion - change in weight - concentration - amnesia - polyuria - suicide attempt - flatulence - aggravated depression - amenorrhea - rash - taste perversion	The most prevalent symptoms include: - vomiting - dizziness - tremor - sweating - somnolence - nausea - sinus tachycardia www.rxlist.com www.frx.com/pi/celexa_pi.pdf	Not recommended with: - MAOIs - triptans - pregnancy - CNS drugs - Alcohol - breastfeeding - known hypersensitivity to the ingredients in the drug www.rxlist.com www.frx.com/pi/celexa_pi.pdf

Brand Name	Generic Name	Function	Use for/Label	Dosage Range	Side Effects	Signs of Overdose	Contraindications
Concerta (kon ser-ta)	Methylphenidate (meth-uh l-fen-i-deyt) HCl extended-release tablets CII	DRI (+NRI) Stimulant	- Attention deficit hyperactivity disorder (ADHD)	18-60 mg/day	The most common side effects include: - headache - dry mouth - dizziness - upper respiratory tract irritability - infection - abdominal pain - tachycardia - nausea - accidental injury - insomnia - decreased appetite www.rxlist.com www.concerta.net www.accessdata.fda.gov	The most prevalent symptoms include: - agitation - tremors - muscle twitching - cardiac arrhythmias - pyrexia - confusion - dry mouth - flushing - palpitations - hypertension - coma - vomiting - hallucinations www.rxlist.com www.concerta.net	Not recommended with: - cardiac abnormalities - patients with marked anxiety - clonidine - tension - agitation - family history of Tourette's - tics - MAOIs - vasopressor agents - glaucoma - esophagus narrowing - stomach narrowing - intestinal narrowing - known hypersensitivity to the ingredients in the drug www.rxlist.com www.concerta.net www.accessdata.fda.gov
Cymbalta (sim-buhl-tuh)	Duloxetine (dull-ox-eh-teen) Hydrochloride (hahy-druh-klawr-ahyd)	SNRI	- Major Depressive Disorder - Diabetic Peripheral Neuropathic Pain - Generalized Anxiety	40-120 mg/day	The most common side effects include: - nausea - dry mouth - sleepiness - constipation - decreased appetite - fatigue	The most prevalent symptoms include: - somnolence - tachycardia - serotonin syndrome - seizures - hypertension - hypotension vomiting	Not recommended with: - MAOIs - thioridazine - narrow glaucoma - inhibitors of CYP1A2 - inhibitors of CYP2D6 - NSAID pain relievers - known hypersensitivity to

Additional reference links (under Function/Side Effects for Concerta): www.rxlist.com, www.frx.com/pi/celexa_pi.pdf

SNRI (under Function, Concerta row)

182

Brand Name	Generic Name	Function	Use for/Label	Dosage Range	Side Effects	Signs of Overdose	Contraindications
			Disorder		- increased sweating insomnia - somnolence - dizziness www.rxlist.com www.cymbalta.com www.lilly.com	- coma www.rxlist.com www.cymbalta.com www.lilly.com	the ingredients in the drug www.lilly.com www.rxlist.com www.cymbalta.com
Desyrel (dez–er–al)	Trazodone (traz–oh–done)	SARI	- Depression	150-600 mg/day	The most common side effects include: - dry mouth - constipation - dizziness - blurred vision drowsiness - low blood pressure - fatigue - nausea - insomnia - agitation - headache - confusion www.rxlist.com mentalhealth.emedtv.com www.medicinenet.com	The most prevalent symptoms include: - vomiting - respiratory arrest - seizures - priapism - irregular heart rate - drowsiness - seizures mental-ealth.emedtv.com www.rxlist.com www.medicinenet.com	Not recommended with: - pregnancy - breast feeding - MAOIs - heart disease - liver disease - kidney disease - known hypersensitivity to the ingredients in the drug mental-health.emedtv.com www.rxlist.com www.medicinenet.com
Edronax (ed-rohn– aks)	Reboxetine (re- boks–eh– tahyn)	NRI	- Depression	2-10 mg/day	The most common side effects include: - dry mouth - insomnia - constipation - impotence - tachycardia	The most prevalent symptoms include: - hypotension - anxiety - hypertension www.healthyplace.com	Not recommended with: - MAOIs - Epilepsy - hypotension - urinary retention - glaucoma - kidney problems

Brand Name	Generic Name	Function	Use for/Label	Dosage Range	Side Effects	Signs of Overdose	Contraindications
						- vertigo - increased sweating - urinary retention www.healthyplace.com www.mentalhealth.com www.smart-drugs.com	www.mentalhealth.com www.smart-drugs.com	- liver problems - pregnancy - breast feeding - convulsive disorders - known hypersensitivity to the ingredients in the drug www.healthyplace.com www.mentalhealth.com www.smart-drugs.com
Effexor (eh-fek-sawr) XR	Venlafaxine (ven-luh-fak-seen) Hydrochloride (hahy-druh-klawr-ahyd)	SNRI	- Major Depressive Disorder - Generalized Anxiety Disorder (GAD) - Panic Disorder - Social Anxiety Disorder	75-225 mg/day	The most common side effects include: - nausea - dizziness - somnolence - dry mouth - nervousness - insomnia - abnormal ejaculation - sweating - headache - constipation - weakness - muscle pain - sore throat - loss of appetite www.rxlist.com www.effexorxr.com www.wyeth.com	The most prevalent symptoms include: - seizure - hallucinations, - vomiting - loss of consciousness - tachycardia - coma - hypotension www.rxlist.com www.wyeth.com	Not recommended with: - MAOIs - alcohol - warfarin - aspirin - pregnancy - breastfeeding - migraine medication - known hypersensitivity to the ingredients in the drug www.rxlist.com www.effexorxr.com www.wyeth.com

Brand Name	Generic Name	Function	Use for/Label	Dosage Range	Side Effects	Signs of Overdose	Contraindications
Eskalith (es-kah-lith)	Lithium (lith-ee-uh m) Carbonate (kahr-buh-neyt, -nit)	Mood Stabilizer	– Manic Depression	600–1800 mg/day	The most common side effects include: – discomfort – frequent urination – hand tremor – mild thirst – nausea – tremor – diarrhea – drowsiness – lack of coordination – muscle weakness – vomiting – dizziness – slurred speech – blurred vision – dry mouth www.rxlist.com www.accessdata.fda.gov www.pdrhealth.com	The most prevalent symptoms include: – diarrhea – giddiness – drowsiness – muscular weakness – lack of coordination – vomiting – weakness – ataxia – blurred vision – lithium poisoning www.accessdata.fda.gov www.pdrhealth.com	Not recommended with: – pregnancy – breastfeeding – alcohol – known hypersensitivity to the ingredients in the drug www.accessdata.fda.gov www.pdrhealth.com
Focalin XR (foh-kah-lin)	Dexmethylphenidate (dex-meth-ill-fen-eh-date) Hydrochloride (hahy-druh-klawr-ahyd) tablets	DRI Stimulant	– Attention deficit hyperactivity disorder (ADHD)	4–20 mg/day	The most common side effects include: – dizziness – weight loss – upset stomach – loss of appetite – nausea – headache – abdominal pain – dry mouth – tachycardia – dyspepsia	The most prevalent symptoms include: – euphoria – vomiting – mydriasis – agitation – convulsions – confusion – palpitations – hallucinations – delirium – sweating	Not recommended with: – heightened anxiety, agitation, or tension – pregnancy – glaucoma – MAIOs – motor tics – known hypersensitivity to the ingredients in the drug www.rxlist.com

Brand Name	Generic Name	Function	Use for/Label	Dosage Range	Side Effects	Signs of Overdose	Contraindications
					- insomnia - anxiety - feeling jittery - throat pain www.rxlist.com www.focalinxr.com www.fda.gov	- muscle twitching - hyperpyrexia - tachycardia - cardiac arrhythmias - hypertension - coma www.rxlist.com www.focalinxr.com www.fda.gov	www.focalinxr.com www.fda.gov
Geodon (jee-oh-duhn)	Ziprasidone (zih praise a don) HCl capsules	SDA Atypical antipsychotic	- Schizophrenia - Bipolar Mania - Acute Agitation in Schizophrenic Patients	40–160 mg/day	The most common side effects include: - extrapyramidal syndrome - dizziness - tremor - hypertonia - runny nose - dystonia - rash - dyskinesia - nausea - respiratory tract infection - dry mouth - somnolence - abnormal vision www.rxlist.com www.geodon.com http://media.pfizer.com	The most prevalent symptoms include: - slurring of speech - anxiety - pyramidal symptoms - transitory hypertension - somnolence - tremor - sedation www.rxlist.com http://media.pfizer.com	Not recommended with: - pregnancy - drugs that prolong the QT interval - alcohol - recent acute myocardial infarction - heart failure - known hypersensitivity to the ingredients in the drug www.geodon.com http://media.pfizer.com
Lamictal (lam-ik-tal)	Lamotrigine (la-moe-tri-jeen)	Anticonvulsant	- Bipolar - Epilepsy	2 mg every other day – 500 mg/day	The most common side effects include: - nausea	The most prevalent symptoms include: - ataxia	Not recommended with: - pregnancy - breast feeding

Brand Name	Generic Name	Function	Use for/Label	Dosage Range	Side Effects	Signs of Overdose	Contraindications
					- dizziness - blurred or double vision - rash - lack of coordination - sleepiness - vomiting - insomnia - headache - tremor www.lamictal.com http://us.gsk.com www.rxlist.com	- nystagmus - increased seizures - decreased level of consciousness - coma - intraventricular conduction delay http://us.gsk.com www.rxlist.com	- starting or stopping oral contraceptives - known hypersensitivity to the ingredients in the drug www.lamictal.com http://us.gsk.com http://us.gsk.com
Lexapro (leks-a-proh)	Escitalopram (es-sye-tal-oh-pram) Oxalate (ok-suh-leyt)	SSRI	- Major Depressive Disorder - Generalized Anxiety Disorder	10-20 mg/day	The most common side effects include: - nausea - insomnia - sexual problems - somnolence - drowsiness - sweating - fatigue - decreased libido - anorgasmia www.lexapro.com www.frx.com www.rxlist.com	The most prevalent symptoms include: - nausea - dizziness - insomnia - convulsions - coma - somnolence www.frx.com www.rxlist.com	Not recommended with: - MAOIs - pimozide - alcohol - pregnancy - breastfeeding - known hypersensitivity to the ingredients in the drug www.rxlist.com www.lexapro.com www.frx.com
Luvox (loo-voks) CR Extended-Release Tablets	Fluvoxamine (floo-voks-ah-meen) Maleate (mal-ee-eyt)	SSRI	- Obsessive compulsive Disorder (OCD) - Social Anxiety	25-300 mg/day	The most common side effects include: - nausea - tremor	The most prevalent symptoms include: - vomiting - blurred vision tachycardia	Not recommended with: - tizanidine - warfarin - thioridazine

Brand Name	Generic Name	Function	Use for/Label	Dosage Range	Side Effects	Signs of Overdose	Contraindications
			Disorder (SAD)		The most common side effects include: - asthenia - sweating - diarrhea - somnolence - anorexia www.luvoxcr.com www.accessdata.fda.gov www.revolutionhealth.com	- hypokalemia - coma - lack of coordination, - hypotension - diarrhea - nausea - fainting - respiratory difficulties - somnolence www.luvoxcr.com www.accessdata.fda.gov www.revolutionhealth.com	- ramelteon - alosetron - pimozide - serotonin syndrome - benzodiazepines - MAOIs - neuroleptic malignant syndrome - theophylline - triptans - TCAs - alcohol - pregnancy - breastfeeding - known hypersensitivity to the ingredients in the drug www.luvoxcr.com www.accessdata.fda.gov www.revolutionhealth.com
Nardil (narh–dil)	Phenelzine (fen–el–zeen)	MAOI	- Depressed (atypical, non–endogenous, or neurotic)	15–90 mg/day	The most common side effects include: - dizziness - headache - drowsiness - disturbances - myoclonic - fatigue - impotence - weakness - tremors - movements - hyperreflexia	The most prevalent symptoms include: - faintness - irritability - hyperactivity - agitation - headache - hallucinations - trismus - rigidity - convulsions - coma - rapid and irregular pulse	Not recommended with: - pregnancy - breast feeding - pheochromocytoma - dextromethorphan - guanethidine - congestive heart failure - renal impairment - history of liver disease - abnormal liver function - known hypersensitivity to the ingredients in the drug

Brand Name	Generic Name	Function	Use for/Label	Dosage Range	Side Effects	Signs of Overdose	Contraindications
					- constipation - weight gain - sleep - postural - dry mouth - hypotension - edema - anorgasmia www.healthyplace.com www.rxlist.com www.accessdata.fda.gov www.pfizer.com	- hypertension - hypotension - vascular collapse - respiratory depression - failure hyperpyrexia - clammy skin www.rxlist.com www.healthyplace.com www.accessdata.fda.gov www.pfizer.com	- Specific foods: tryptophan, pickled herring, liver, dry sausage, cheese, yogurt, beer and wine, yeast extract, meat extract, caffeine, foods aged, pickled, fermented, or smoked - OTC Medications cold and cough, nasal decongestants, hay-fever, sinus, asthma inhalant www.rxlist.com www.healthyplace.com www.accessdata.fda.gov www.pfizer.com
Paxil (pak-sil)	Paroxetine (pa-roks-e-teen)	SSRI	- Major Depressive Disorder - Obsessive Compulsive Disorder (OCD) - Panic Disorder - Social Anxiety Disorder (SAD) - Generalized Anxiety Disorder (GAD) - Posttraumatic Stress Disorder (PTSD)	20-50 mg/day	The most common side effects include: - asthenia - sweating - dizziness - impotence - abnormal vision - genital disorders - dry mouth - tremor - decreased appetite - yawning - nausea - injury - somnolence - constipation - insomnia	The most prevalent symptoms include: - manic reactions - urinary retention - tachycardia - confusion - vomiting - mydriasis - acute renal failure - convulsions - hypertension - aggressive reactions - syncope - hypotension - stupor - dystonia - rhabdomyolysis	Not recommended with: - thioridazine - pimozide - MAOIs - triptans - alcohol - pregnancy - breastfeeding - known hypersensitivity to the ingredients in the drug www.rxlist.com www.paxil.com http://us.gsk.com/ www.accessdata.fda.gov

Brand Name	Generic Name	Function	Use for/Label	Dosage Range	Side Effects	Signs of Overdose	Contraindications
					- weakness - nervousness - infection - sleepiness - diarrhea www.rxlist.com www.paxil.com http://us.gsk.com/ www.accessdata.fda.gov	- serotonin syndrome - tremor - myoclonus www.rxlist.com http://us.gsk.com/ www.accessdata.fda.gov	
Prozac (proh-zak)	Fluoxetine (flew-ox-eh-teen)	SSRI	- Major Depressive Disorder - Obsessive Compulsive Disorder	20-80 mg/day	The most common side effects include: - nervousness - drowsiness - tremors - yawning - weakness - loss of appetite - dry mouth - difficulty sleeping - sweating - decreased sex drive www.rxlist.com www.prozac.com www.lilly.com	The most prevalent symptoms include: - vertigo - abnormal accommodation - elevated blood pressure - confusion - seizures - unresponsiveness - nervousness - pulmonary dysfunction - abnormal gait - tremor - movement disorder - hypomania - somnolence - tachycardia www.rxlist.com www.lilly.com	Not recommended with: - thioridazide - pimozide - MAOIs - pregnancy - breastfeeding - known hypersensitivity to the ingredients in the drug www.lilly.com www.rxlist.com www.prozac.com

Brand Name	Generic Name	Function	Use for/Label	Dosage Range	Side Effects	Signs of Overdose	Contraindications
Remeron (rem-er-on)	Mirtazapine (mer-taze-uh-peen)	NaSSA Alpha 2 Antagonist	- Major Depressive Disorder	15-45 mg/day	The most common side effects include: - somnolence - increased appetite - weight gain - dry mouth - constipation www.rxlist.com www.pfizer.comwww.access data.fda.gov	The most prevalent symptoms include: - tachycardia - drowsiness - impaired memory - disorientation www.rxlist.com www.pfizer.com www.accessdata.fda.gov	Not recommended with: - disorientation - pregnancy - breastfeeding - alcohol - impaired memory - tachycardia - drowsiness - known hypersensitivity to the ingredients in the drug www.rxlist.com www.pfizer.com www.accessdata.fda.gov
Risperdal (ris-per-duhl)	Risperidone (ris-per-i-done)	SDA Atypical antipsychotic	- Bipolar mania - Schizophrenia - Irritability associated with Autism - Other Psychotic Disorders	Schizophrenia 1-6 mg/day Bipolar Mania .05-6 mg/day Autism .05-3 mg/day	The most common side effects include: - dystonia - agitation - dry mouth - upper respiratory tract infection - fatigue - increased appetite - insomnia - dizziness - headache - akathisia - urinary incontinence - saliva increase - somnolence www.rxlist.com	The most prevalent symptoms include: - exaggeration of listed side effects - extrapyramidal symptom - drowsiness - tachycardia hypotension - sedation - increased heart rate www.rxlist.com www.risperdal.com www.nami.org	Not recommended with: - seizure disorder - alcohol - cigarettes - pregnancy - breastfeeding - known hypersensitivity to the ingredients in the drug www.rxlist.com www.risperdal.com www.nami.org

Brand Name	Generic Name	Function	Use for/Label	Dosage Range	Side Effects	Signs of Overdose	Contraindications
					www.risperdal.com www.nami.org		
Seroquel (ser-oh-kw-il)	Quetiapine (kwe-tí´ah-pen) Fumarate (fyoo-muh-reyt)	SDA Atypical Antipsychotic	- Schizophrenia - Bipolar - Acute Mania	Schizophrenia 150–750 mg/day Mania 400–800 mg/day Depression 50–300 mg/day	The most common side effects include: - headache - agitation - dry mouth - drowsiness - sedation - dizziness - high blood sugar - weakness - abdominal pain - sudden drop in blood pressure upon standing - sore throat - upset stomach www.rxlist.com www.seroquel.com www.astrazeneca-us.com	The most prevalent symptoms include: - exaggeration of listed side effects www.rxlist.com www.astrazeneca-us.com	Not recommended with: - alcohol - known hypersensitivity to the ingredients in the drug www.rxlist.com www.seroquel.com www.astrazeneca-us.com
Sinequan (sin-uh-kwan)	Doxepin (dok-suh-pin)	TCA	- Depression - Anxiety	25–300 mg/day	The most common side effects include: - light sensitivity - rapid heart rate - nausea - constipation - water retention - urinary retention - rash - dizziness - dry mouth	The most prevalent symptoms include: - agitation - confusion - disturbed concentration - irregular heartbeat - hallucinations - dilated pupils - high or low body temperature - hyperactive reflexes	Not recommended with: - other dibenzoxepines - glaucoma - urinary retention - breastfeeding - known hypersensitivity to the ingredients in the drug www.pfizer.com www.sinequan.net

Brand Name	Generic Name	Function	Use for/Label	Dosage Range	Side Effects	Signs of Overdose	Contraindications
					- itchy or scaly skin weight gain or loss - drowsiness - blurred vision www.sinequan.net www.accessdata.fda.gov www.rxlist.com www.pfizer.com	- muscle rigidity - vomiting - convulsions - hypothermia - hyperpyrexia - severely low blood pressure www.pfizer.com www.sinequan.net www.accessdata.fda.gov www.rxlist.com	www.accessdata.fda.gov www.rxlist.com
Strattera (stra-tair-a)	Atomoxetine (at-oh-mox-eh-teen) HCl	NRI	- Attention deficit hyperactivity disorder (ADHD)	.05-100 mg/day	The most common side effects include: Children and adolescents: - decreased appetite - nausea - mood swings - upset stomach - vomiting - somnolence - abdominal pain - fatigue Adults: - nausea - constipation - hot flush - fatigue - urinary problems - dry mouth - insomnia - decreased appetite - trouble passing urine	The most prevalent symptoms include: - abnormal behavior - agitation - gastrointestinal symptoms - hyperactivity - mydriasis - somnolence www.rxlist.com	Not recommended with: - MAOIs - narrow angle glaucoma - pregnant - breastfeeding - known hypersensitivity to the ingredients in the drug www.rxlist.com www.strattera.com

Brand Name	Generic Name	Function	Use for/Label	Dosage Range	Side Effects	Signs of Overdose	Contraindications
					- dizziness - dysmenorrhea www.rxlist.com www.strattera.com www.accessdata.fda.gov		
Tofranil (toh-frey-nil)	Imipramine (i-mip-ruh-meen) HCL	TCA	- Depression	50-300 mg/day	The most common side effects include: Adults: - hallucinations - confusion - diarrhea - breast development - dry mouth - nausea - breast milk production - high blood pressure - low blood pressure upon standing - numbness - tremors - vomiting Children and Adolescents: - bedwetting - stomach and intestinal problems - nervousness - sleep disorders - tiredness www.tofranil-pm.com www.accessdata.fda.gov www.rxlist.com	The most prevalent symptoms include: - drowsiness - stupor - vomiting agitation - ataxia - restlessness - hyperactive reflexes - tachycardia - muscle rigidity - athetoid - convulsions - arrhythmia - cyanosis - hypotension - shock - coma - respiratory depression - mydriasis www.tofranil-pm.com www.accessdata.fda.gov www.rxlist.com	Not recommended with: - myocardial infarction recovery period - MAOIs - pregnancy - breastfeeding - known hypersensitivity to the ingredients in the drug www.tofranil-pm.com www.accessdata.fda.gov www.rxlist.com

Brand Name	Generic Name	Function	Use for/Label	Dosage Range	Side Effects	Signs of Overdose	Contraindications
Valium (val-ee-uh m)	Diazepam (dahy-az-uh-pam)	Benzodiazepine	- Anxiety - Convulsive Disorders - Acute Agitation	4-40 mg/day	The most common side effects include: - fatigue - muscle weakness - ataxia - drowsiness www.rxlist.com www.accessdata.fda.gov www.rocheusa.com	The most prevalent symptoms include: - drowsiness - confusion - lethargy www.rxlist.com www.accessdata.fda.gov www.rocheusa.com	Not recommended with: - myasthenia gravis - pregnancy - breastfeeding - respiratory insufficiency - sleep apnea - MAOIs - alcohol - acute narrow-angle glaucoma - known hypersensitivity to the ingredients in the drug www.rxlist.com www.accessdata.fda.gov www.rocheusa.com
Wellbutrin (well byu-trin) XL	Bupropion (byoh-proh-pee-uh n) Hydrochloride (hahy-druh-klawr-ahyd)	NDRI	- Major Depressive Disorder - Seasonal Affective Disorder	225-450 mg/day	The most common side effects include: - nausea - dizziness - insomnia - dry mouth - constipation - abnormal vision - sweating - anorexia - weight loss - dry mouth - headache - rash - agitation - fast heart rate	The most prevalent symptoms include: - seizures - hallucinations - loss of consciousness - fever - coma - hypotension - muscle rigidity www.rxlist.com www.us.gsk.com www.accessdata.fda.gov	Not recommended with: - MAOIs - liver problems - kidney problems - seizure disorder - anorexia - bulimia - nicotine - pregnancy - breastfeeding - known hypersensitivity to the ingredients in the drug www.us.gsk.com www.rxlist.com

Brand Name	Generic Name	Function	Use for/Label	Dosage Range	Side Effects	Signs of Overdose	Contraindications
							www.wellbutrin-xl.com www.accessdata.fda.gov
Xanax (zan-aks)	Alprazolam (al-prey-zuh-lam)	Benzodiazepine; modulates GABA receptor	- Anxiety - Generalized Anxiety Disorder - Panic Disorder	.75–10 mg/day	The most common side effects include: - hypotension - impaired coordination - depression - confusion - fatigue - palpitations - menstrual disorders - constipation - blurred vision - memory impairment - tremor - nasal congestion - irritability - changes in weight - sleepiness www.rxlist.com www.pfizer.com www.drugs.com	The most prevalent symptoms include: - diminished reflexes - coma - somnolence - impaired coordination - confusion - death www.rxlist.com www.pfizer.com www.drugs.com	Not recommended with: - open angle glaucoma - pregnancy - breast-feeding - alcohol - itraconazole - ketoconazole - narrow-angle glaucoma - known hypersensitivity to the ingredients in the drug www.xanax.com www.pfizer.com www.drugs.com
Zoloft (zoh-lawft)	Sertraline (ser-tra-leen) Hydrochloride (hahy-druh-klawr-ahyd)	SSRI	- Major Depressive Disorder - Obsessive Compulsive Disorder (OCD) - Panic Disorder	50–200 mg/day	The most common side effects include: - dry mouth - somnolence - fatigue - nausea - diarrhea/loose stools	The most prevalent symptoms include: - vomiting - tremor - nausea - dizziness - agitation	Not recommended with: - MAOIs - NSAIDs - aspirin - pimozide - pregnancy - breastfeeding

Brand Name	Generic Name	Function	Use for/Label	Dosage Range	Side Effects	Signs of Overdose	Contraindications
			- Posttraumatic Stress Disorder (PTSD) - Social Anxiety Disorder		- insomnia www.zoloft.com www.rxlist.com http://media.pfizer.com	- coma - hypertension www.zoloft.com www.rxlist.com http://media.pfizer.com	- antabuse - alcohol - known hypersensitivity to the ingredients in the drug www.rxlist.com www.zoloft.com http://media.pfizer.com

Note:

DRI = Dopamine Reuptake Inhibitor
MAOI = Monoamine Oxidase Inhibitor
NaSSA = Noradrenergic and Selective Serotonergic Antidepressant
NDRI = Norepinephrine and Dopamine Reuptake Inhibitor

NRI = Norepinephrine Reuptake Inhibitor
SARI = Serotonin 2A Antagonist/Reuptake Inhibitor
SDA = Serotonin–Dopamine Antagonist

SNRI = Serotonin-Norepinephrine Reuptake Inhibitor
SSRI = Selective Serotonin Reuptake Inhibitor
TCA = Tricyclic Antidepressant

CHAPTER 8

THE COMORBIDITY OF PSYCHOPATHOLOGY IN COGNITIVE AND ACADEMIC SLD SUBTYPES

Lisa A. Hain, Psy.D.
James B. Hale, Ph.D.
Jessica Glass Kendorski, Ph.D.

"With its hundred billion nerve cells, with their hundred trillion interconnections, the human brain is the most complex phenomenon in the known universe—always, of course, excepting the interaction of some six billion such brains and their owners within the socio-technological culture of our planetary ecosystem!"

—Steven Rose

Definition, Prevalence, and Identification of Specific Learning Disabilities

Children with specific learning disabilities (SLD) represent the largest disability category in school settings (National Research Center on Learning Disabilities, 2005). According to the President's Commission on Excellence in Special Education, between the years of 1990 to 2000 a 36 percent increase occurred in the SLD diagnosis (PCESE, 2002), representing over one-half of all classified students in the United States (Truscott, Catanese, & Abrams, 2005). Although exact SLD prevalence rates are difficult to discern, estimates suggest that 6 percent of students (2.72 million) nationwide are affected with SLD and need individual special education services (Fuchs, Deshler, & Reschly, 2004).

Given these national statistics, it is no surprise that the SLD population has been given such robust attention in recent times, leading us to a pivotal point in SLD practice. Do children with SLD experience developmental delays requiring greater intensity of intervention for success (e.g., Barnett,

Daly, Jones, & Lentz, 2004), or do they experience developmental *deficits* and require *individualized* intervention (e.g., Hale et al., 2008)? A review of legal, empirical, and clinical evidence suggests the latter position is more accurate (Hale, 2006). Understanding SLD within the context of cognitive, academic, and psychosocial assets and deficits provides us with a more solid foundation for understanding the SLD construct, so that targeted interventions can be developed to ameliorate the difficulties these children experience in their daily lives.

The IDEA 2004 legal definition defines a SLD in Title 20 United States Code Section 1401(30) [cited as 20 USC 1401(30)] as follows:

> (30) Specific Learning Disability.
> (A) In General. The term 'specific learning disability' means a disorder in one or more of the basic psychological processes involved in understanding or in using language, spoken or written, which disorder may manifest itself in the imperfect ability to listen, think, speak, read, write, spell, or to do mathematical calculations.
> (B) Disorders Included. Such term includes conditions such as perceptual disabilities, brain injury, minimal brain dysfunction, dyslexia, and developmental aphasia (34 C.F.R. 300.8).

Although the definition of SLD remains unchanged from previous IDEA legislation, SLD eligibility procedures underwent noteworthy modifications and additions. According to Title 20 of Section 1414, subsection b(6), [cited as 20 USC 1414(b)(6)], in determining whether a child has SLD, IDEA 2004 does not require a severe discrepancy between intellectual ability and achievement, and allows a process that determines if a child responds to scientific, research-based intervention. The ability-achievement discrepancy approach (AAD) has been heavily criticized on empirical grounds (see Berninger, 2001; Fuchs, Mock, Morgan, & Young, 2003; Hale, 2008; Kavale, Kaufman, Naglieri, & Hale, 2005; Lyon, 1995; Mather & Gregg, 2006; Vellutino, 2001), suggesting it is a weak methodology for identifying SLD (Fuchs, Mock, Morgan, & Young, 2003). More importantly, this approach has yielded inconsistent results with over-identification of children with high intelligence test scores and average achievement, but under-identification of children with low intelligence test scores and below-average achievement (Kavale, Holdnack, & Mostert, 2005; Semrud-Clikeman, 2005). In fact, an examination of national patterns suggests there is little consistency in identification practices across districts, states, and regions (Reschly & Hosp, 2005), leading to considerable SLD group heterogeneity and nebulous identification practices.

The response to intervention (RtI) approach was seen as an alternative to the discrepancy model (Gresham, 2002) and presented an opportunity to provide research validated instruction, early identification and treatment of SLD, and progress monitoring in general education (Deno, 2002; Fuchs, Deshler, & Reschly, 2004; Shinn, 2002). RtI approaches allow educators to intervene utilizing scientific, research-based instructional practices, thereby providing immediate assistance to the struggling student (Fletcher, Coulter, Reschly, & Vaughn, 2004) and not postponing intervention until placement in special education (Fuchs et al., 2003). RtI has the potential to reduce inappropriate referrals and the number of comprehensive SLD evaluations, and allow time for comprehensive assessment of learning strengths and weaknesses linked directly to classroom intervention (Hale, 2006). However, the RtI approach has received similar criticisms to the AAD approach, with both techniques ignoring the underlying psychological processing deficits that lead to the SLD, thereby disregarding statutory and regulatory SLD requirements under IDEA (Fiorello, Hale, & Snyder, 2006; Flanagan, Alfonso, Primavera, & Dynda, 2006; Hale, 2006; Hale, Kaufman, Naglieri, & Kavale, 2006; Ofiesh, 2006; Schrank, Miller, Catering, & Desrochers, 2006; Willis & Dumont, 2006; Wodrich, Spencer, & Daley, 2006). Multiple reasons could lead to poor responsiveness, such as inadequate teacher training, curricular or measurement issues, treatment integrity, and determining whether student progress actually reflects response or non-response (Hale et al., 2008).

The final Federal regulations (34 C.F.R. Parts 300 and 301; 2006) also permitted the use of alternative research-based procedures which have been termed the "Third Method" for SLD identification (§ 300.8(c)(10) (Hale, Flanagan, & Naglieri, 2008). Third methods can be considered hybrid approaches that include RtI and comprehensive evaluation, thereby addressing the statutory and regulatory IDEA requirements (Fiorello et al., 2006; Hale et al., 2006; Hale et al., 2008). Hale and colleagues proposed that RtI is highly warranted for widespread adoption in the schools at Tier 1 and Tier 2, but at Tier 3, comprehensive evaluation of the deficient basic psychological processes should be conducted for determination of special education eligibility and subsequent interventions (Fiorello et al., 2006; 2007; Hale et al., 2006; 2008). Using the standard error of the difference (Anastasi & Urbina, 1997), the concordance-discordance model (C-DM; Hale & Fiorello, 2004; Hale et al., 2008) was developed as an empirically-valid method for identifying a basic psychological processing deficit(s) that result in the academic deficit(s), and these cognitive and academic deficits must be different from the cognitive asset(s). This model notes that there can be multiple cognitive and/or neuropsychological causes for academic deficits, so pinpointing these cognitive-achievement relationships can lead to more targeted interventions (Hale & Fiorello, 2004). This methodology helps to reduce heterogeneity in the SLD population and was used successfully in a recent study (Hain, 2008) described later in this chapter.

Comorbidity Issues in SLD Identification and Intervention

This discussion of discrepancy and RtI limitations leads us to a critical point, namely that prior research using these identification methods have left us with empirical results for a heterogeneous, enigmatic SLD population. It is no wonder that some academics have questioned the validity of the SLD concept (Gresham et al., 2005; Ysseldyke & Marston, 1999). Despite this critical limitation of prior research, it is worth exploring this SLD heterogeneity and the comorbidity between SLD and other disorders. Prevalence rates of reading SLD vary between 5 percent and 17 percent (Semrud-Clikeman, Fine, & Harder, 2005) and approximately 6 percent of children are affected by math SLD (Geary, Hamson, & Hoard, 2000). Comorbidity estimates between math and reading disabilities approach 40 percent and likely co-occur (Geary, 1993). Rates for written language disorders are estimated to be as high as 17 percent in the population and typically co-occur with other language-based SLD (Hooper at al., 1994). Children with language disability may likely have difficulty with understanding receptive (language by ear) and/or expressive language (language by mouth or hand) which may impede learning across academic areas (Berninger & Richards, 2002).

SLD heterogeneity and comorbidity estimates are clarified when emerging evidence of reading, math, and written language SLD subtypes are explored. In the area of reading, phonological, orthographic, fluency, and global reading SLD subtypes have been identified, with the specific deficient psychological processes leading to the reading deficits identified in several studies (Bakker, Van Strien, Licht, Smit-Glaude, & Sietsia, 2007; Fiorello et al., 2006; King, Giess, & Lombardino,

2007; Zadina, Corey, & Casbergue, 2006). Five math SLD subtypes have been reported, including fluid/quantitative, mild executive/working memory, right hemisphere/NVLD, numeric/quantitative, and dyscalculia-Gerstmann Syndrome based upon performances across math achievement areas and neurocognitive functioning (Hale et al., 2008). These results suggest that multiple math deficits in numeric concepts, computational knowledge, working memory, long-term memory storage and/or retrieval, problem solving, and visual–spatial processes can likely lead to math SLD (Geary et al., 2000; Hale & Fiorello, 2004; Hale, Fiorello, Bertin, & Sherman, 2003; Mazzocco, 2005). Subtypes have been posited for written language disability as well. One written language subtype is characterized by fine motor and linguistic deficits; a second subtype with visual spatial deficits and poor handwriting, but good spelling and idea development; a third subtype with problems in spelling and organization; and a fourth subtype with poor letter production and sequencing deficits (see Sandler et al., 1992). Clearly, this SLD population heterogeneity obfuscates accurate identification and intervention, and differential assessment-intervention relationships could be strengthened through subtype examination (Hale et al., 2008, Zadina et al., 2006).

In addition to the comorbid academic disabilities, which is often the primary focus of educators, prevalence estimates of comorbid emotional/ behavioral disorders and SLD are 40% or higher (Taggart, Cousins, & Milner, 2007). According to the U.S. Surgeon General (U.S. Public Health Service, 2000), 1 in 5 children exhibits DSM-IV disorder symptoms and 5% suffer an emotional disorder that causes severe impairment. Comorbid SLD has been identified in children with bipolar disorder, attention deficit/hyperactivity disorder (ADHD) combined and inattentive types, and autism spectrum disorders (Mayes & Calhoun, 2006). Outcome studies of children with SLD suggest serious academic deficits which result in school failures (National Longitudinal Transition Study, 2005), and higher drop out rates when compared to typical peers (Bender & Wall, 1994). Youth with SLD are often overrepresented in the juvenile justice system (Quinn, Rutherford, Leone, Osher, & Poirer, 2005) with 55 percent of adjudicated youth being identified with learning difficulties (Ottnow, 1988). The comorbidity also extends into adulthood with SLD and mental illness affecting approximately 15 percent to 80 percent of adults (Bouras & Drummond, 1992). Obviously, the impact of SLD heterogeneity and comorbidity is significant, especially if the system is not designed to provide the intensive, individualized education these children need to address their significant learning and socioemotional problems.

Exploring SLD Psychosocial Subtypes

Despite direct advocacy from the Learning Disability Association of America (LDAA) for recognition of SLD psychosocial deficits, the emotional/behavioral needs of children with SLD are often overlooked (Elksnin & Elksnin, 2004). The comorbidity between cognitive, academic and psychosocial functioning is often discounted despite extensive research demonstrating that SLD affects more than learning, but leads to deficits in psychosocial functioning as well (Bryan et al., 2004; Forrest, 2004; Fuerst, Fisk, & Rourke, 1989, 1990; Hale, Rosenberg, Hoeppner, & Gaither, 1997; Hendriksen et al., 2007; Mattison, Hooper, & Carlson, 2006; Mayes & Calhoun, 2008; Nussbaum & Bigler, 1986; Nussbaum, Bigler, & Koch, 1986; Rock, Fessler, & Church, 1997; Rourke, 2008; Speece, McKinney, & Appelbaum, 1985, 1986; Wei-dong 2004; Ring, Zia, Lindeman, & Himlok, 2007). These studies substantiate the complex relationships between neuroarchitecture, academic, and psychosocial functioning, a fact now well recognized in the neuropsychological literature (Hale & Fiorello, 2004; Lichter & Cummings, 2001; Miller & Hale, 2008; Rourke, 2000).

Neuropsychological assets and deficits that underlie SLD are hypothesized to be the same deficits that lead to psychosocial dysfunction (Rourke, 2000) suggesting that more homogeneous subtypes of SLD can be discerned from neurocognitive, academic, and behavioral data. Speece and colleagues (1985) postulated the existence of seven subtypes of children with SLD that could be differentiated by emotional/behavioral variables (i.e., task orientation, independence, attention, distractibility, hostility, social skills, introversion-extroversion and considerateness), with a three-year longitudinal examination revealing SLD behavioral subtype stability over time (McKinney & Speece, 1986). Other studies have demonstrated SLD subtype differences on measures of depression, social withdrawal, hyperactivity, adjustment, and anxiety (Nussbaum & Bigler, 1986; Nussbaum, Bigler, & Koch, 1986).

Rourke and colleagues (see Rourke, 2000 for review) have identified SLD subtypes based on intellectual, neuropsychological, academic, and behavior ratings of psychosocial functioning. Studies have generally found normal psychosocial adjustment, internalized psychopathology, and externalized psychosocial subtypes (e.g., Fuerst et al., 1989). In a subsequent study, Fuerst and colleagues delineated six subtypes of psychopathology in children linked with specific patterns of neurocognitive processing. These patterns included normal, mild anxious, mild hyperactive, somatic, and internalizing and externalizing subtypes (Fuerst et al., 1990). Rourke suggests that children with stronger psycholingistic and language skills and weaker visual/spatial skills tend to demonstrate the most significant psychopathology (Rourke & Fuerst, 1991), postulating the existence of a white matter/nonverbal learning disability (NVLD) subtype (Fuerst et al., 1989; Fuerst et al., 1990; Rourke, 2000). The NVLD syndrome has been reviewed extensively by Rourke and colleagues who substantiate a single NVLD construct (Rourke, 1989; Rourke & Fuerst, 1991; Rourke, 1994; Rourke, 2008). Rourke postulates right hemisphere dysfunction in NVLD resulting in nonverbal, visual/spatial deficits due to deficits in white matter hindering intermodal integration (Rourke, 1995). These findings have been challenged because the NVLD construct suffers from heterogeneity, with some constellations of cognitive strengths and weaknesses not always eventuating in visual/perceptual, mathematics, and social perception difficulties (Forrest, 2004).

It is clear the comorbidity between SLD and psychosocial functioning can have deleterious effects on the learning, behavior, and socioemotional development of affected children. Collapsing children with cognitive, learning, and psychosocial problems into a single heterogeneous "SLD" group confounds differential diagnosis and service delivery for this enigmatic population, which can also lead to ambiguous research and clinical results (Fiorello et al., 2006; Hale & Fiorello, 2004; Miller & Hale, 2008; Rourke, 1994). To overcome these inadequacies, neurocognitive and psychosocial subtype studies are needed if relevant conclusions and implications are to be implemented in practice (Rourke, 2008).

SLD Subtypes Across Neurocognitive, Academic, and Psychosocial Factors
Our recent study (Hain, 2008) using data from school-based psychoeducational evaluations of children classified by multidisciplinary teams as having SLD is an initial attempt to explore homogeneous subtypes of children with SLD, and differentiate these subtypes based on neurocognitive, academic, and psychosocial variables. Standard scores from the Wechsler Intelligence Scale for Children-Fourth Edition (WISC-IV; Wechsler, 2003), the Woodcock Johnson Tests of Achievement-Third Edition (WJ-III; Woodcock, McGrew, & Mather, 2001), the Wechsler Individual Achievement Test-Second Edition (WIAT-II; Wechsler, 2001), or the Kaufman Tests of Educational

Achievement-Second Edition (KTEA; Kaufman & Kaufman, 2004) were used to establish Concordance-Discordance Model (Hale & Fiorello, 2004) psychometric SLD criteria, as this is a more stringent "Third Method" classification scheme than is offered by discrepancy or RtI methods. Psychosocial data included teacher ratings from the Behavioral Assessment System for Children-Teacher Rating Scale – Second Edition (BASC-2 TRS; Reynolds & Kamphaus, 2004). Cluster analysis of WISC-IV variables was performed, using the Average Linkage Within Groups variant of the Unweighted Pair-Group Method Arithmetic Average (UPGMA) as the amalgamation or linkage rule. This method combines clusters so that the average distance between all possible pairs of cases in the resulting cluster is as small as possible, minimizing within group variability and increasing subtype homogeneity. The cluster analysis yielded six cognitive SLD subtypes. The SLD subtypes were identified as Visual/Spatial (V/S)), Fluid Reasoning (FR), Crystallized/Language (C/L), Processing Speed (PS), Executive/Working Memory (E/WM), and High Functioning/Inattentive (HF/I), with subsequent MANOVA's and Bonferroni post-hoc analyses used to elucidate subtype differences.

Visual/Spatial Subtype

The Visual/Spatial learning disability subtype demonstrated deficiencies in visual and spatial processing, visual analysis and synthesis, understanding of part-whole relationships, and global processing (Groth-Marnat & Teal, 2000; Hale & Fiorello, 2004; Miller & Hale, 2008). Receiving the lowest Block Design (BD) subtest mean out of the six SLD subtypes, and difficulty with Symbol Search, this subtype appears to have visual processing or Gv deficits (e.g., Keith et al., 2006). However, deficits crossed over the outdated verbal-nonverbal dichotomy (e.g., Bryan & Hale, 2001), with poor Digit Span (DS) but not Letter-Number Sequencing (LNS) performance noted, suggesting difficulty with auditory attention and rote memory rather than working memory deficits (Hale, Hoeppner, & Fiorello, 2002). The Symbol Search (SS) mean score was lower than the Coding (CD) mean score indicating more difficulty with spatial processing (Gs), especially when considered in the context of BD (see Keith et al., 2006, confirmatory factor analysis of the WISC-IV). Difficulties with visual/spatial processing can lead to difficulties with awareness and integration of information, and attention to self and the environment, characteristics often found in children with right hemisphere parietal-dorsal stream processing problems, not frontal executive ones (Hale & Fiorello, 2004; Hale et al., 2006). This inattention secondary to poor self- and environmental awareness and visual/spatial deficits together suggest a right posterior NVLD subtype (Hale & Fiorello, 2004), which has been reported in the literature (Forrest, 2004).

This pattern of neurocognitive deficits likely results in poor math computation and reasoning skills, which was indeed the case in the Hain (2008) study. These results were consistent with right hemisphere deficits leading to poor column alignment, difficulty with place value, and inattention to operands (Mazzocco, 2004), which is highly similar to Rourke's (1995) NVLD/visual-spatial/math disability subtype. This subtype was primarily characterized by heightened Attention Problems and Learning Problems subscale scores on the BASC-2 TRS. Although prior studies have suggested internalizing disorders and heightened psychosocial disturbance in children with NVLD (Rourke & Fuerst, 1991; Hendriksen et al., 2007), this particular subtype had lower levels of depression and anxiety than the other subtypes. In addition, externalizing disorders were not evident, suggesting overall low levels of psychopathology, consistent with recent research demonstrating lower rates of psychopathology in children with NVLD when compared to controls and children with verbally-based SLD (Forrest, 2004).

TABLE 8-1
Visual/Spatial Subtype Profile

HIGHER PERFORMANCE	LOWER PERFORMANCE
COGNITIVE	
Concordant/Convergent Thought	Visual/Spatial Processing
Crystallized Ability	Sensory Integration
Rote Processing and Memory	Sensory/Motor Coordination
	Attention Allocation
ACADEMIC	
Word Reading	Math Calculation
Decoding	Math Reasoning
Spelling	

PSYCHOSOCIAL CONCERNS
Attention Problems
Learning Problems
School Problems
Attention to Self and Environment

Fluid Reasoning Subtype

The Fluid Reasoning subtype also appears to be a subtype of a right hemisphere learning disability, but might suggest more anterior involvement affecting attention and executive function (Hale & Fiorello, 2004; Miller & Hale, 2008). Fluid novel problem solving and categorical inductive reasoning was impaired in the Hain (2008) study, which would be suggestive of fluid reasoning or Gf deficits (e.g., Keith et al., 2006), which would be differentiated from the Visual/Spatial Subtype in that they appeared to have relatively intact visual-spatial or Gv skills. This group additionally scored lower on the socially-relevant Comprehension subtest, perhaps indicating difficulties with pragmatic language, novel problem solving, and inferential reasoning processes required to perform this socially relevant task (Hale et al., 2008; Miller & Hale, 2008). This subtype is congruent with certain aspects of Rourke's (1989) NVLD type, but it does not appear to have the visual-spatial deficits consistent with more posterior right hemisphere dysfunction. This subtype demonstrated reading comprehension, math reasoning, and math calculation deficits (Hain, 2008), suggesting that inferential divergent reasoning skills required in comprehension of reading passages and math problem solving may be hindered by poor fluid reasoning abilities (e.g., Bryan & Hale, 2001; Hale et al., 2008; Keith et al., 2006).

More comfortable with explicit, rote learning and comprehension, this subtype likely excels in early elementary school, but as the complexity of curricula and course demands increase in middle and high school, this subtype is particularly likely to struggle with fluid reasoning, novel problem solving, and right hemisphere language processes (Berninger & Richards, 2002; Bryan & Hale, 2001; Hale & Fiorello, 2004; Lindell, 2006; Rourke, 1994). These hypotheses fit nicely with the math reasoning and reading comprehension deficits found in Hain (2008), as both academic tasks require problem-solving skills and discordant-divergent thought processes to examine and identify patterns among both verbal and nonverbal information provided (Bryan & Hale, 2001; Hale & Fiorello, 2004).

In line with the Rourke and Fuerst (1991) NVLD subtype, this group had heightened scores on the BASC-2 across both internalizing and externalizing areas, suggesting increased risk for psychopathology. The right frontal lobe is critical for sustained attention and self-control (Hale et al., 2005), due to reciprocal interactions with the frontal-subcortical circuits (e.g., Hale & Fiorello, 2004), 2001), so it is not surprising this subtype would be more likely to experience behavioral problems and more overall psychopathology (e.g., Lichter & Cummings, 2001). This may be especially evident in older children, as the novelty and complexity of social exchanges interferes with adaptive, prosocial responding, resulting in overall psychosocial maladjustment (Hale et al., 1997).

TABLE 8-2
Fluid Reasoning Subtype Profile

HIGHER PERFORMANCE	LOWER PERFORMANCE
COGNITIVE	
Lexical/Semantic knowledge	Fluid reasoning
Crystallized ability	Discordant/Divergent thought
Auditory Encoding/Memory	Novel Problem Solving
Receptive/Expressive Language	Mental Flexibility
ACADEMIC	
Spelling	Math Reasoning
Decoding	Reading Comprehension
Word Reading	

PSYCHOSOCIAL CONCERNS
Externalizing Problems
Depression/Somatic Complaints/Withdrawal
Attention, Learning, School Problems
Atypicality

Crystallized/Language Subtype

The Crystallized/Language subtype evidently experiences acquired knowledge, concordant/convergent thought, and receptive and expressive language difficulties, which are all subsumed under crystallized ability or Gc (Berninger & Richards, 2002; Fiorello et al., 2006; Keith et al., 2006; Miller & Hale, 2008). It is very likely that this subtype is comparable to the verbal learning disability subtype (VLD) reported in other studies (Forrest, 2004; Hendriksen et al., 2007). Difficulty with language most likely hinders these children in understanding and processing language by either ear, mouth, or hand (Berninger & Richards, 2002).

Children with left hemisphere deficits will likely demonstrate poor crystallized and language skills, lacking concordant/convergent skills necessary for long-term memory and automaticity and routinization of academic skills (Hale & Fiorello, 2004), which leads to academic deficits in all subject areas. This subtype is likely a result of global left hemisphere/gray matter dysfunction and is a common cause of SLD (Berninger & Richards, 2002; Hale & Fiorello, 2004; Miller & Hale, 2008). These children are more likely to be identified in elementary school, since the curriculum at this age tends to be highly structured, routinized, and language based, all of which are areas of difficulty for the Crystallized/Language subtype. Goldberg's (2001) gradiential theory posits that there is a gradual shift from right to left hemisphere processes as tasks become learned and automatic, but these children always have to relearn content presented in the classroom, as they do not consolidate knowledge and skills into long-term memory, suggesting global left hemisphere grey matter impairment (Hale & Fiorello, 2004). This may account for fMRI findings that show increased right hemisphere activity in poor readers, and this declines with remediation of left hemisphere language processes (e.g. Shaywitz et al., 2003; Simos et al., 2007).

This subtype had evidence of aggression, conduct problems, and hyperactivity on the BASC-2. The Aggression subscale mean score was the highest mean for all subtypes. Children with crystallized and language deficits have been found to display withdrawn, anxious, and depressed symptoms (Boetsch, Green, & Pennington, 1996). This subtype may likely be emergent conduct-disordered children, possibly due to neuropsychological deficits or to continual school and social failures, characteristics that are likely found in the juvenile delinquency center population (Hale et al., 1997; Hale & Fiorello, 2004). Congruent with these findings, studies have suggested that children with VLD had higher rates of psychopathology, than did children with NVLD (Forrest, 2004). Perhaps the presence of intact right hemisphere emotion processing leads to higher rates of socialized delinquency in this subtype because these children may be socially aware, yet alienated by their continued academic failure (Hale et al., 1997; Hale & Fiorello, 2004). In combination with the executive deficits and working memory problems experienced by this group, it was not surprising that this subtype had the lowest levels of achievement and increased psychopathology in the Hain (2008) study, similar to the Forrest (2004) findings.

TABLE 8-3
Crystalized Language Subtype Profile

HIGHER PERFORMANCE	LOWER PERFORMANCE
COGNITIVE	
Meaningful Object Recognition	Crystallized Ability
	Receptive/Expressive Language
	Auditory Working Memory
	Long-Term Memory
	Symbolic relationships
ACADEMIC	
	Word Reading
	Reading Comprehension
	Math Calculation
	Math Reasoning
	Spelling
	Written Expression
PSYCHOSOCIAL CONCERNS	
Aggression	
Conduct Problems	

Depression
Inattention/Hyperactivity
Learning and School Problems
Atypicality

Processing Speed Subtype

The Processing Speed subtype was characterized by fairly adequate Verbal Comprehension, Perceptual Reasoning, and Working Memory Index scores, and a markedly lower Processing Speed Index score. Lowered mean SS and CD subtest scores suggested difficulties with visual-symbolic stimuli, simple cognitive processing on clerical tasks, working under time constraints, graphomotor skills, and/or psychomotor speed. These abilities are most aligned with the Processing Speed factor or Gs (Keith et al., 2006; Miller & Hale, 2008). Although there are multiple possible causes of this type of problem, this subtype could be the result of anterior cingulate/cingulate frontal-subcortical circuit dysfunction, which is primarily involved in motivation to perform well, persistence on tasks, and online monitoring of performance (Hale & Fiorello, 2004; Lichter & Cummings, 2001). This subtype is likely to have difficulty with sustained effort, balancing speed and accuracy, and efficient communication between the anterior and posterior brain regions (Hale & Fiorello, 2004). In addition to motor functions, the cerebellum has also been implicated in timing and implicit learning (Ivry, 1993), so this combination of frontal-subcortical circuit and cerebellar systems could result in impaired processing speed. The oculomotor circuit, with its relationship to motor control and visual attention and scanning, could also explain poor Coding and Symbol Search performance, as well as reading fluency, math fluency, and written language difficulties (Hale & Fiorello, 2004). As a result, a cognitive hypothesis testing (e.g., CHT) approach of these possibilities could further elucidate the nature of the processing speed problem, and therefore lead to more specific interventions.

In Hain (2008), the lowest mean subtest scores were found for Reading Comprehension and Written Expression subtests, suggesting only mild deficiencies in academics when compared to the other subtypes. They appeared to have problems with attention, learning, and atypical behaviors according to BASC-2 reports. Depression and withdrawal appeared to be borderline clinically significant, which would be consistent with the psychomotor and internalizing symptoms reported in individuals with cingulate dysfunction and depression (Mayberg, 2001). A psychomotor speed difficulty may affect new learning and automaticity of learned skills, and in the classroom, these children may appear "slow" or "unmotivated", similar to individuals who experience apathy and depressive symptoms due to abulia (Mayberg, 2001).

TABLE 8-4
Processing Speed Subtype Profile

HIGHER PERFORMANCE	LOWER PERFORMANCE
COGNITIVE	
Receptive/Expressive Language	Visual Sensory Memory
Crystallized Ability	Visual-Symbolic Learning
Auditory Working Memory	Rote Clerical Tasks
Visual Spatial Analysis/Synthesis	Processing Speed

Concordant/Convergent Thought
Discordant/Divergent Thought

Psychomotor Skill
Decision Making
Quick, Efficient Performance

ACADEMIC

Math Reasoning
Decoding
Word Reading

Reading Comprehension
Written Expression

PSYCHOSOCIAL CONCERNS
Depression
Withdrawal
Attention, Learning, and School Problems
Atypicality

Executive/Working Memory Subtype

The Executive/Working Memory subtype was most characterized by deficits in auditory-verbal working memory and visual-motor psychomotor speed. This type appears to be related to the SCAD profile described by Kaufman (1994). This profile, characterized by lower performance on the Symbol Search, Coding, Arithmetic and Digit Span subtests (and Letter-Number Sequencing), has been found in children with SLD and other disorders (Mayes & Calhoun, 1999; 2004; Fiorello et al., 2006; Hale et al., 2008). These more process-oriented indices/subtests are often impaired in children with executive dysfunction due to frontal-subcortical circuit dysfunction (Hale & Fiorello, 2004; Miller & Hale, 2008). As the frontal circuits serve as a check and balance between the left and right hemispheres, and the posterior to anterior axis, this subtype might not only display executive dysfunction, but this is also likely to affect higher level cognition and psychosocial adjustment (Hale & Fiorello, 2004).

Difficulty on these tasks could suggest difficulties with visual attention and scanning, speed of information processing, online monitoring of performance, or general apathy (Hale & Fiorello, 2004; Lichter & Cummings, 2001; Mayberg, 2001). The anterior cingulate is responsible for "executive-attention" functions which help the communication from posterior to anterior areas (Posner & Raichle, 1994). It is important for attention activation, decision-making, and online monitoring of performance, and attention (Hale & Fiorello, 2004; Hale, Fiorello, & Brown, 2005). Motor planning, organization, flexibility, and sustained attention are needed for Coding and Symbol Search, which could reflect dorsolateral prefrontal circuit dysfunction (Hale & Fiorello, 2004). Furthermore, the deficits noticeable on Digit Span and Letter-Number Sequencing suggest encoding, working memory, and retrieval difficulties necessary for higher level cognition (Hale & Fiorello, 2004). Given these findings, this Executive/Working Memory subtype is likely to experience multiple learning and psychosocial problems, especially given how the frontal-subcortical circuits are implicated in most psychopathologies (see Lichter & Cummings, 2001).

Not surprisingly, this subtype had severe emotional and behavioral deficits, with the highest BASC-2 clinical scale means of all SLD subtypes on the Hyperactivity, Conduct Problems, Anxiety, Depression, Attention Problems, Learning Problems, Atypicality, Withdrawal, Internalizing and Externalizing Problems, and Behavioral Symptoms Index scales. The seat of psychopathology is thought to lie in the prefrontal-subcortical circuits (Lichter & Cummings, 2001; Miller & Hale, 2008; Powell & Voeller, 2004), so this subtype pattern appears to lead to both global executive dysfunction and the most disabling emotional and behavioral deficits. In combination with the dorsal and ventral cingulate, the dorsolateral and orbital prefrontal circuit impairments likely lead to poor emotional response, disinhibition, and poor self-regulation (Hale & Fiorello, 2004; Hale et al., 2005). This subtype is most likely displaying what can be characterized as a dysexecutive syndrome that impairs cognitive, academic, and psychosocial functioning (Hanna-Pladdy, 2007).

TABLE 8-5
Executive Working Memory Subtype Profile

HIGHER PERFORMANCE	LOWER PERFORMANCE
COGNITIVE	
Receptive and Expressive Language	Working Memory
Crystallized Ability	Processing Speed
	Mental Flexibility and Manipulation
	Hypothesis Testing
	Memory Encoding and Retrieval
	Self-Monitoring and Evaluation
ACADEMIC	
Decoding	Math Calculation
Word Reading	Written Expression

PSYCHOSOCIAL CONCERNS
Attention/Hyperactivity
Aggression
Conduct Problems
Depression
Withdrawal
Atypicality
Somatic Complaints
Learning and School Problems

High Functioning/Inattentive Subtype

The High Functioning/Inattentive subtype was the highest functioning SLD subtype, with mild difficulty with basic encoding of auditory information into short-term memory, which could suggest attention/sensory memory, auditory processing problems, or sequential processing problems (Berninger & Richards, 2002; Hale & Fiorello, 2004; Miller & Hale, 2008). However, an examination of this subtype's profile, with high Letter-Number Sequencing and low Digit Span, with other subtests adequate, suggests there was an executive component for attention, sequencing, or encoding/retrieval, which would be more indicative of a more anterior (executive) as opposed to posterior (auditory processing) focus. For this subtype, the combined process requirements of auditory and sequential processing may be the problem, with both indicating left hemisphere regions for encoding sensory information into working memory for further manipulation (Berninger &

Richards, 2002; Hale & Fiorello, 2004; Hale et al., 2002; 2005).

Academic scores were generally adequate, suggesting only mild weaknesses in language-based tasks (e.g. word reading and written expression); however, this subtype did not display word decoding problems, which would have been more consistent with a phonological processing disorder and left superior temporal lobe dysfunction (Hale & Fiorello, 2004). Perhaps, if the frontal-subcortical circuits are implicated, the problems may lie in Broca's area for articulation, the basal ganglia for sequencing, or the oculomotor circuit for visual tracking (Hale & Fiorello, 2004); however, one would expect lower Coding performance if the latter was true. Inattention can be due to prefrontal dysfunction, but can also result from striatal dysfunction, part of the frontal-subcortical circuits. This could lead to sequencing problems, and processing of stimuli due to thalamic dysfunction, which registers auditory stimuli (Hale & Fiorello, 2004), rather than a left temporal lobe deficit in phonological processing. This subtype was characterized by attention and hyperactivity problems and appears to have characteristics of mild Attention-Deficit/Hyperactivity Disorder (ADHD), a disorder characterized by striatal underactivity that secondarily affects dorsolateral and orbital prefrontal functioning (see Hale et al., 2005 for discussion).

TABLE 8-6
High Functioning Inattentive Profile

HIGHER PERFORMANCE	LOWER PERFORMANCE
COGNITIVE	
Crystallized Ability	Auditory Attention
Processing Speed	Working Memory
Visual spatial processing	Sequencing
Concordant/Convergent Thought	
Discordant/Divergent Thought	
ACADEMIC	
Word Reading	Written Expression
Reading Comprehension	
Calculation	
Math Reasoning	
Spelling	

PSYCHOSOCIAL CONCERNS
Hyperactivity
Attention
Impulse Control

Contrasting Neurocognitive, Academic and Psychosocial Characteristics of SLD Subtypes: Clinical Implications

Several meaningful subtype differences emerged in the Hain (2008) study. Two of the subtypes, Fluid Reasoning and Visual/Spatial, appear to be aligned with deficits in Gf and Gv respectively (Keith et al., 2005; Miller & Hale, 2008). This may suggest manifestations of the NVLD syndrome

(Rourke, 2000) or a right hemisphere learning disability (RHLD) affecting both verbal and nonverbal information processing and expression (e.g., Bryan & Hale, 2001). The differentiation of these subtypes suggests further delineation of RHLD processing deficits may be worth exploring in clinical practice, but is generally consistent with current research (Forrest, 2004; Hendriksen et al., 2007; Mammarella et al., 2006). Two subtypes, the Processing Speed and Executive/Working Memory groups, appeared to have difficulties with executive processes mediated by the frontal-subcortical circuits, reflecting previous research demonstrating either SCAD or ACID profiles in children with SLD (Fiorello et al., 2006; Hanna-Pladdy, 2007; Kaufman, 1994; Mayes & Calhoun, 2004; Prifitera & Dersh, 1993). Two other subtypes emerged with opposite patterns, a High Functioning/Inattentive subtype, characterized by higher mean scores across most cognitive areas, but difficulty with auditory attention, sensory memory, and/or sequential processing, and a Crystallized/Language subtype with global cognitive deficits, particularly in the areas of prior knowledge, receptive and expressive language, and executive function, with somewhat spared visual object recognition and categorization skills.

Academically, significant group differences occurred across all achievement measures, with the Crystallized/Language and the Executive/Working Memory subtypes demonstrating significantly lower performance across the achievement variables. Reading difficulties were pronounced for the Crystallized/Language subtype as well as for the Executive/Working Memory subtype, suggesting phoneme-grapheme correspondence, lexical/semantic information, receptive/expressive language, rapid naming/processing speed, and working memory are important for successful reading (Fiorello et al., 2006; 2007; Hale & Fiorello, 2004; Miller & Hale, 2008; Shaywitz et al., 2002; Simos et al., 2007). The Crystallized/Language subtype had deficits across all areas of reading, perhaps suggesting that these children are experiencing double or triple deficit reading disabilities and are at greatest risk for reading failure (Lovett, Steinbach, & Frijters, 2000; Wolf & Bowers, 1999), consistent with the Global reading disability subtype found in the Fiorello et al. (2006) study. The Executive/Working Memory subtype demonstrated more difficulty in word reading and reading comprehension suggesting possible deficient sequential processing and rapid naming ability, possibly leading to reading fluency and hence comprehension deficits (Bowers, 2001), which is also aligned with the Fluency-Comprehension subtype reported by Fiorello et al. (2006). Reading comprehension concerns were evident for the Fluid Reasoning subtype, possibly due to difficulties with higher order divergent/discordant reasoning, which would be consistent with right hemisphere language-based disabilities (Bryan & Hale, 2001; Miller & Hale, 2008).

The Executive/Working Memory subtype also experienced difficulties with math reasoning and calculation, consistent with frontal-executive subtype of math disability reported in the literature (Hale et al., 2003; 2008; Mazzocco, 2001). Contrary to previous conceptualizations of math SLD being due to right hemisphere dysfunction (Rourke, 2000), this subtype is similar to the executive or procedural math SLD subtypes that have impaired executive functions that limit strategy use, algorithm computation, and working memory (Geary, Hoard, & Hamson, 1999; Hale et al., 2008). This is consistent with the position that a math disability can result from many causes, not only right hemisphere dysfunction (Forrest, 2004; Hale & Fiorello, 2004). Both RHLD groups experienced difficulty with math calculation and math reasoning, however, likely due to different causes. These two subtypes were differentiated by visual-spatial and fluid reasoning/novel problem solving processes, both of which are related to math achievement (Hale & Fiorello, 2004; Hale et al., 2003; 2008; Langdon & Warrington, 1997). The Fluid Reasoning subtype appears aligned with the Fluid/Quantitative subtype in the Hale et al., (2008) study; whereas, the Visual/Spatial subtype appears to be aligned with their Right Hemisphere/NVLD math disability subtype. The Crystallized/Language subtype evidenced difficulty with the math areas as well, indicating that math disabilities appear to be the result of both left and right hemisphere bilateral processes (Benbow & Lubinski, 1997; Hale et al., 2003; 2008a; 2008b; Hale & Fiorello, 2004). The Crystallized/Language subtype may represent a semantic type of math disability with difficulties noted in number association and math fact automaticity (Geary, 1993) or they may represent the Dyscalculia-Gerstmann Syndrome math disability subtype documented by Hale et al. (2008).

Written expression difficulties were apparent for the Crystallized/Language, the Executive/Working Memory, and the two RHLD subtypes. These results suggest that linguistic processes, executive impairments, visual-spatial deficits, and difficulties with divergent thought processes may all be related to written expression disabilities (Hale & Fiorello, 2004; Hooper et al., 2006; Sandler et al., 1992). The difficulties with written language in the Crystallized/Language subtype may very well relate to language by hand difficulties (see Berninger & Richards, 2002). The Executive/Working Memory subtype is likely having written language difficulties due to the constraint placed upon the executive system, and the increase in working memory involvement in creating and revising a written product (Wilson & Proctor, 2000). The difficulties noted in the RHLD groups could likely be due to visual/spatial deficits, fine motor deficits, or possible right hemisphere linguistic deficits (see Bryan & Hale, 2001; Berninger & Richards, 2002; Sandler et al., 1992). Therefore, interventions aimed at remediating written expression disabilities will need to be geared to the specific underlying cognitive assets and deficits (Berninger & Abbott, 1992), consistent with findings of cognitive patterns interacting with written language interventions to produce successful outcomes (Hooper et al., 2006).

As Rourke (2008) suggests, there is no single psychosocial profile for children with SLD. Nevertheless, research suggests there are many different subtypes of psychosocial functioning in children with SLD, ranging from the typical behavior to severe psychopathology (Rourke, 2008). Furthermore, variability among heterogeneous groups and ineffective identification practices has undermined our research and clinical efforts (Hale et al., 2008) in establishing clear cognitive, academic, and behavioral profiles for SLD subtypes. Overall, each subtype in the Hain (2008) study had a different profile of neurocognitive, academic, and psychosocial functioning, suggesting both clear and subtle differences that warrant careful clinical examination and differentiated instructional programs (Hale et al., 2008).

The Crystallized/Language and Executive/Working Memory subtypes had the highest levels of psychopathology, consistent with the comorbidity of SLD and externalizing and internalizing disorders (Hale et al., 1997; Willcutt & Pennington, 2000). Despite Rourke's (2000) suggestion that children with left hemisphere dysfunction are less likely to experience significant psychosocial problems, this was not consistent with the Hain (2008) findings. Certainly, poor crystallized/language skills most notably lead to a host of academic and social difficulties in the school setting (Bryan et al., 2002). Because of their learning problems, and difficulty with oral communication, these children may become aggressive or noncompliant, and display more "socialized" delinquency (Hale & Fiorello, 2004). This subtype is also aligned with previous cluster analytic studies in which verbal deficits led to a moderate degree of behavioral impairment (Forrest, 2004; Nussbaum & Bigler, 1986; Nussbaum et al., 1986).

Whenever executive functions, such as working memory and processing speed, appeared to be impaired in the SLD subtypes reported in Hain (2008), they often had considerable overall levels of psychopathology. This is aligned with research stipulating that neurocognitive executive deficits due to frontal-subcortical circuit dysfunction (e.g., Lichter & Cummings, 2001) lead to dysexecutive syndromes in some children with SLD, which affects cognitive, academic, and emotional/behavioral functioning (Hanna-Pladdy, 2007). Similar subtypes have been frequently reported in other cluster analytic studies (see McKinney & Speece, 1986; Nussbaum & Bigler, 1986; Speece et al., 1985). Remarkably, the Visual/Spatial, Processing Speed, and High Functioning/Inattentive subtypes demonstrated low levels of psychopathology, displaying mainly attention and learning problems with reduced adaptive skills. However, the High Functioning/Inattentive subtype demonstrated characteristics of mild ADHD; whereas, the inattention observed in the Visual/Spatial subtype could be due to posterior attentional processes and neglect (Posner & Raichle, 1994; Reddy & Hale, 2007; Voeller, 2001), suggesting that attention problems are not all due to ADHD, which is considered a frontal-subcortical circuit disorder due to striatal hypoactivity (Hale et al., 2005). In addition, neurocognitive, academic, and behavioral differences among High Functioning/Intattentive, Executive/Working Memory, and Processing Speed subtypes could reflect comorbidities of ADHD-Inattentive, ADHD-Combined, and Depression psychosocial patterns respectively.

The Fluid Reasoning subtype demonstrated similar characteristics as Rourke's (2006) NVLD syndrome, displaying difficulty with nonverbal problem solving and mathematics, as well as psychosocial disturbance and psychopathology in the areas of depression, withdrawal, somatic complaints, atypicality, attention, hyperactivity, aggression, and conduct problems; however, the Visual/Spatial subtype experienced few significant psychosocial concerns. Perhaps the heterogeneous group of NVLD children may account for the differences found among studies (Forrest, 2004), with only the anterior Fluid subtype experiencing the most psychosocial concern. As Mammarella et al. (2006) suggested, specific subtypes such as the visuospatial subtype of NVLD should be further explored especially since the right hemisphere is not seen as purely "nonverbal" and can be better differentiated by concordant/convergent (left hemisphere) and discordant/divergent (right hemisphere) functions (Bryan & Hale, 2001; Lindell, 2006).

TABLE 8-7
Summary of Learning Constructs

(Hain, 2008)

Learning Constructs	Behavior Manifestations
Crystallized/Language	Moderate impairment with psychopathology, aggression, conduct problems, and delinquency.
Working Memory	Psychopathology and dysexecutive syndrome hindering cognitive, academic, and emotional functioning.
Visual/Spatial & Processing Speed	Attention and learning problems and reduced adaptive skills.
Fluid Reasoning	Depression, withdrawal, somatic complaints, atypical attention, hyperactivity, aggression, conduct problems.

Cognitive Hypothesis Testing Model and Balance Theory

Studies like this one help to shed light into the enigmatic picture of children with SLD, especially when one considers the comorbidity between SLD neurocognitive profiles, academic deficits, and psychosocial functioning. Clearly, given the considerable variability found among SLD subtypes, a "one size fits all" approach to assessment and intervention will not work. However, the final IDEA regulations did allow for a model that could meet both the statutory and regulatory requirements and the balanced practice approach advocated by Hale's empirical method of SLD determination (Hale & Fiorello, 2004). A Cognitive Hypothesis Testing model (CHT; Hale & Fiorello, 2002, 2004; Hale et al., 2003; 2006; 2007; 2008, Reddy & Hale, 2007) provides a framework for integrating cognitive, academic, and emotional/behavioral assessment into a problem-solving RtI model for children with SLD and comorbid disorders who do not respond to standard interventions.

FIGURE 8-1
Cognitive Hypothesis Testing Model

Theory
1. Presenting Problem
5. Cognitive Strengths/Weaknesses
9. Intervention Consultation
13. Continue/Terminate/Modify

Interpretation
4. Interpret IQ or Demands Analysis
8. Interpret Constructs/Compare
12. Determine Intervention Efficacy

Hypothesis
2. Intellectual/Cognitive Problem
6. Choose Related Construct Test
10. Choose Plausible Intervention

Data Collection
1. Presenting Problem
5. Cognitive Strengths/Weaknesses
9. Intervention Consultation
13. Continue/Terminate/Modify

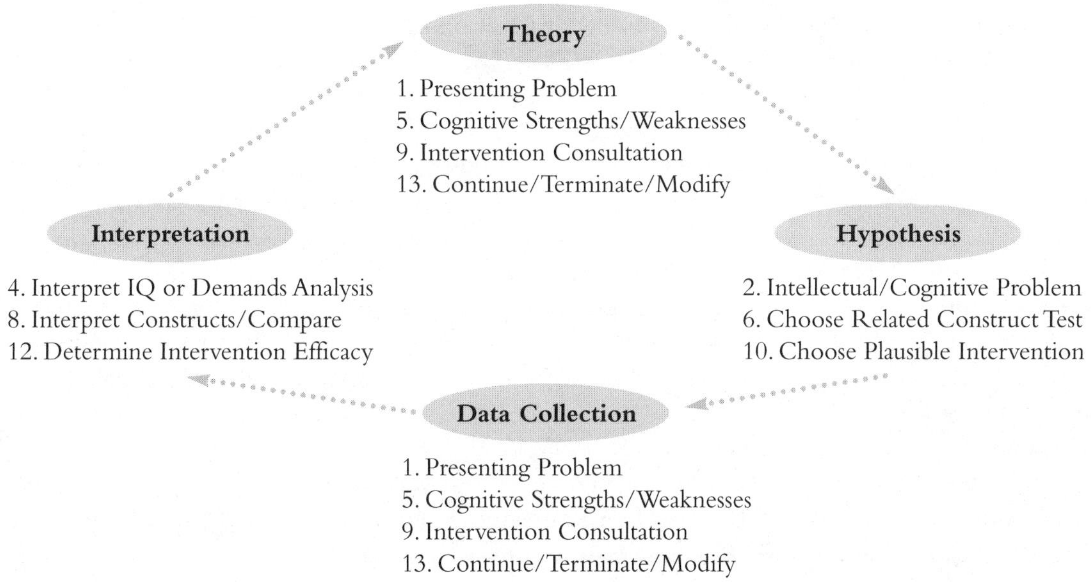

This balanced practice model combines the best of RtI and comprehensive evaluation in the determination of SLD. It also provides a methodology for linking assessment practices to successful interventions. In their balanced practice model (Hale et al., 2006), children receive standard protocol RtI and progress monitoring during Tier 1, and more individualized problem-solving RtI approach at Tier 2, both of which can be accomplished in the general education setting (Fiorello et al., 2006; Hale, 2006; Hale et al., 2006). However, prior to SLD determination and Tier 3 instruction, children then receive a CHT evaluation using multiple data sources that helps to address the underlying causes of the learning and/or psychosocial deficits. This method ensures accurate diagnosis (i.e., reducing false positives or negatives), and links assessment data to empirically supported interventions (Hale et al., 2008). We conclude this chapter with a case study in which the CHT approach was applied to a young child with comorbid learning and emotional/behavioral deficits. This child was served in the second author's externally funded SNAP-FIT (Student Neuropsychological Assessment Profiles for Innovative Teaching) project. This project is evaluating the efficacy of the Hale et al. (2006) model by combining the best of RTI and CHT in a balanced practice approach to meeting children's needs.

Case Study: Kai's "Here and Now" Cognitive Behavior Therapy Intervention
Relevant Background Information

Kai's gestation, delivery, and early development were unremarkable except for stuttering until age 4 and occasional nocturnal enuresis. Although she was always "shy" and "quiet," her mother and teacher noted increased academic and work completion problems in the 4th grade, and Kai appeared more and more inattentive, withdrawn, and, at times, depressed. A physician evaluation led to an ADHD-Inattentive Type diagnosis, and Kai was treated with Concerta, which only seemed to make her worse, as she frequently "zoned out" on medication.

At the time of evaluation, Kai lived with her employed mother and an older sister, who was described as "very bright" and "controlling". The father, who was reportedly illiterate, was not involved in the family. The mother reported that Kai "likes to be to herself and draw," seldom interacting with her sister unless there was a conflict. The family history was positive for emotional and learning problems, but no other information was provided.

Kai was a 5th grade student in a general education classroom in a diverse, urban school setting. Her mother described Kai as "slow," and that her school motivation and effort had deteriorated. Although her teacher reported Kai was a "strong reader," she reportedly had comprehension problems and difficulty with written language. Following her poor response to fluency instruction, and having continued difficulty with attention, work completion, depressed mood, and "strange" behavior, Kai was referred for a SNAP-FIT (Student Neuropsychological Assessment Profiles for Innovative Teaching) evaluation.

Classroom and Testing Observations

Kai was observed to be compliant but frequently inattentive and disengaged during whole group instruction in the classroom. She often looked down or toward the wall, and occasionally stared blankly ahead. When off-task, Kai occasionally displayed subvocal lip movements. After being inattentive, Kai occasionally shook her head slightly, as if to say "no" to herself, and then looked at her work or wrote on her paper. Kai occasionally glanced at her teacher and peers, but was quiet during the entire observation period, and had no meaningful interactions with others.

During testing, Kai presented as a quiet, pleasant 10 year, 7 month old child who seemed preoccupied or disengaged at times. Her verbal output was adequate, but she had some difficulty with word choice and occasionally responded with off-task or tangential comments. Kai showed a pattern of cautious but accurate responding, reluctance to respond when uncertain, and difficulty with unstructured or ambiguous tasks, often leading to slow and inefficient responding. Problems with decision-making, mental flexibility, and self-monitoring were evident. The results appeared to be a reliable and valid indicator of her current pattern of cognitive, academic, psychosocial functioning.

Assessment Results and Clinical Impressions
Intellectual/Cognitive Screening

On the WISC-IV, Kai obtained a WISC-IV Full Scale SS of 106 (M = 100, SD = 15), which was at the 66% compared to her same age peers. However, her Perceptual Reasoning (SS = 112), Verbal Comprehension (SS = 108), and Working Memory (SS = 102) scores were somewhat higher than her Processing Speed Index (SS = 88) score. Due to both between and within factor variability, Kai's Full Scale score was not considered to be a reliable and valid measure of her level of cognitive and intellectual functioning (see Hale et al., 2007).

An examination of Kai's subtest scores suggested that she fit the Processing Speed SLD subtype described earlier, but there were differences among other subtests that warranted further investigation. As can be seen in Table 8-8, Kai performed quite well on Perceptual Reasoning tasks, indicating good fluid reasoning, novel problem solving, understanding of part-whole relationships, and perceptual analysis and synthesis. Although the Verbal Comprehension score was in the average range, Kai's crystallized factual and vocabulary knowledge appeared to be better than her common sense problem solving skills. It is interesting to note that in an earlier study of SLD and behavior problems on the Child Behavior Checklist, Comprehension was a strong indicator of psychopathology (Hale et al., 1997), and this was Kai's lowest VC score. Although receptive and expressive language was deemed adequate, she appeared to have some qualitative difficulty with language formulation and/or word retrieval, and there were several tangential comments made during verbal tasks. Kai did fairly well on Working Memory tasks, but "lost" several sequences. For instance, her Digits Forward (ss = 9) and Digits Backward (ss = 6) scores were fairly comparable, though she performed better when asked to repeat letters and digits presented in mixed up sequence (ss=12). Qualitatively, Kai appeared to have better skill at rote recall or orally presented information than mental manipulation of information. Nevertheless, Processing Speed was a relative weakness for Kai. She struggled with quick, efficient responding when asked to match symbols to numbers according to a template and decide whether target stimuli were contained within a group of distracters (ss=7). This could suggest spatial or motor difficulties, but her symbols were carefully formed and she only made two errors on the Symbol Search subtest.

TABLE 8-8
Kai's WISC-IV Subtest Performance

Verbal Comprehension	Scaled Score	Perceptual Reasoning	Scaled Score
Similarities	12	Block Design	12
Vocabulary	14	Picture Concepts	11
Comprehension	9	Matrix Reasoning	13
Working Memory	Scaled Score	**Processing Speed**	Scaled Score
Digit Span	9	Coding	7
Letter Number Sequencing	12	Symbol Search	9

Cognitive Hypothesis Testing (CHT)

On the basis of history, prior data collection, and intellectual/cognitive screening, several hypotheses were developed and subsequently evaluated. First, despite adequate verbal and crystallized abilities, it was apparent that Kai had subtle language formulation issues and possible difficulty with social problem solving, especially given her reportedly poor peer relationships. Since visual, spatial, and fluid reasoning skills appeared to be adequate, no further evaluation was undertaken in this domain.

However, some evidence of inflexibility and perseveration suggested executive difficulties might be present, and this could account for variable performance on working memory and considerably impaired processing speed. Although likely to be related to executive deficits, an evaluation of visual-spatial, motor, and visual-motor integration skills would be necessary to rule out this possible cause for low processing speed.

To examine language and language retrieval issues in relation to crystallized abilities, first the WISC-IV Information subtest (ss = 7), and WISC-IV Integrated Information (ss = 11) and Comprehension (ss = 7) subtests were administered. Next, the Delis-Kaplan Executive Function System (D-KEFS) Verbal Fluency Letter (ss = 5), Category (ss = 12), and Category Switching = (ss = 8) and NEPSY-II Speeded Naming (ss = 6) were administered. These findings suggest Kai has difficulty with quick, efficient verbal retrieval from long-term memory, but good lexical-semantic and categorical thinking, unless she is required to shift cognitive set, all of which point to expressive difficulties being related to executive deficits for verbal information.

Processing speed was further evaluated to determine if it was indeed related to problems with speed of performance, or whether it was due to visual, motor, or integration problems. First, Kai had no difficulty on the Arrows subtest (ss = 11), and the NEPSY-II Design Copy (ss = 9) subtest, with Global and Local scores both adequate (ss = 10), and Motor qualitatively lower (ss = 7). Her Visuomotor Precision was accurate (51–75th percentile), but slow (ss = 5). Finger tapping was adequate for both hands (26 – 50th percentile), yet she had some difficulty with sequencing (6–10th percentile right hand, 11–25th percentile left hand). Although visual-spatial explanations for Kai's processing speed issues could be ruled out on the basis of hypothesis testing results, the findings suggested some difficulty with motor coordination and control (praxis), which could secondarily affect visual-motor coordination and processing speed.

However, a majority of the CHT findings pointed to executive problems, particularly in the areas of quick efficient performance, decision speed, resolving conflict and ambiguity, and online monitoring of performance, all executive functions related to frontal-subcortical circuits, particularly the cingulate circuit. Kai's performance on the WJ-III Decision Speed subtest was in the low average range (SS = 77), suggesting difficulty with quick, efficient decision making. Although she struggled with the D-KEFS Trail Making Test Letter-Number Switching (ss = 5), Kai performed adequately on the Visual Search (ss = 10), Motor Speed (ss = 8), Number Sequencing (ss = 10), or Letter Sequencing (ss = 9) subtests, which also require quick performance. She had considerable difficulty with Color-Word Interference Test Inhibition and Inhibition/Switching subtests, but not the Color Naming (ss = 11) or Word Reading (ss = 9) ones. As noted earlier, she had difficulty with letter fluency and switching on the D-KEFS Verbal Fluency Test. Her performance on both measures on the NEPSY-II Auditory Attention and Response Set (ss = 5 and SS = 7) were below average, and she struggled with Animal Sorting (ss = 4), as she repeatedly tried variations of the same initial sort. Given that this NEPSY-II task also requires novel problem solving, one might wonder why her WISC-IV Matrix Reasoning score was so high. Perhaps the multiple choice format for the latter subtest could account for her adequate performance. Given her lack of improvement on the WISC-IV Integrated Comprehension subtest, and Kai's reported social problems, the NEPSY-II Affect Recognition (ss = 5) and Theory of Mind (6–10th percentile) were administered, both indicating that social information processing deficits extended beyond the language domain.

Academic Achievement Functioning

Kai did fairly well on the WJ-III Tests of Achievement. She had no difficulty on the Calculation (SS = 116) or Applied Problems (SS = 115) subtests, but her Math Fluency performance was accurate and slow (SS = 82). Spelling (SS = 106) and Writing Samples (SS = 111) scores were quite good, despite the teacher's report of writing difficulties. Perhaps the structured format and that the task requires only brief sentences fostered her performance. Kai wrote creative sentences that were quite advanced for the most part, but she occasionally added irrelevant information. Despite having good single word reading (Letter-Word Identification SS = 102), Kai struggled with Reading Fluency (SS = 73), which likely affects her reading comprehension (Passage Comprehension SS = 88), however, the latter score could have been affected by the word retrieval difficulties noted earlier, as this is not a timed test and items are relatively short. Although speeded performance appears to be an issue in all academic areas, it is interesting to note that Kai had four uncommon errors to false statements on the Reading Fluency subtest, suggesting speed is further reduced when decision-making is involved.

Behavioral Functioning

According to the teacher report, Kai was in the average range for the BASC-II Externalizing Problems subscales. Although she reportedly had few somatic complaints (*Somatization T = 53*), Kai had significant elevations on the Internalizing Anxiety (*T = 67*), Depression (*T = 73*) subscales. Her Withdrawal (*T = 67*), Atypicality (*T = 74*), Attention Problems (*T = 64*), and Learning Problems (T = 64) subscales also reflected the difficulties reported by informants and observed during testing. Adaptive behavior was reportedly low in Social Skills (*T = 32*) and Adaptability (*T = 36*) areas. Significant items endorsed included "seems out of touch with reality," "does strange things," "acts confused," "seems unaware of others," "avoids other children," "refuses to join group activities," "prefers spending time alone," "is sad or lacks enjoyment," "is negative about things," and "is lonely."

During the clinical interview, Kai complained the teacher was "into magic" and that it bothered her, that she couldn't listen to talk about things that weren't "real" because they made her feel "weird." She also indicated she had no friends, and peers were often mean to her and always picking on her. She reported a good relationship with her mother, and enjoyed drawing and playing in her room during free time. Although she indicated a desire to read, she said it was getting harder, and the content did not always "make sense."

Intervention Development and Evaluation

After consultation with the teacher and parent, two areas were targeted for intervention. The first area addressed was processing speed. Two interventions were developed, one designed to improve automaticity of word reading and math computation skills, and the second required Kai to self-monitor timely performance of daily academic tasks. The second intervention consisted of weekly individual cognitive-behavior therapy (CBT) sessions with the school psychologist, which is the focus of this discussion. The therapist worked with Kai to understand how her "different" thoughts and behaviors could undermine her chances for success in the classroom and with her peers. The school psychologist helped Kai focus on the *"Here and Now"* times for thinking and behaving. During these periods, Kai was taught to focus her attention, remain on-task, complete her work, and have prosocial peer and adult interactions, but during "Kai Time" she could think and behave how she wanted. As a result, CBT strategies including self-monitoring attention, confronting irrational thoughts, and engaging in prosocial replacement behaviors. Social skills instruction and role playing were also used within CBT sessions. Using items endorsed by the parent and teacher on the BASC-

II subscales as an outcome measure, weekly teacher and school psychologist ratings were completed, and averaged across raters to determine response to intervention.

Although these findings do not reflect normative changes in behavior, a consensus emerged between the teacher, school psychologist, and parent that Kai's affect appeared brighter and she was more engaged. Irrelevant comments and social impairments seemed to improve. However, she continued to demonstrate atypical comments and behaviors, particularly during conversations. This often followed periods of withdrawal, so the therapeutic goals changed to focus on maintaining social contact with others. Despite continuing to have difficulty with idiosyncratic behaviors that competed with her on-task performance, Kai appeared to show improvement in CBT, and most importantly, in the classroom as well.

REFERENCES

Anastasi, A. & Urbina, S. (1997). *Psychological testing* (7th ed.). Upper Saddle River, NJ: Prentice-Hall.

Bakker, D. J., Van Strien, J. W., Licht, R., & Smit-Glaude, & Sietsia, S. W. D. (2007). Cognitive brain potentials in kindergarten children with subtyped risks of reading retardation. *Annals of Dyslexia, 57*, 99-111.

Barnett, D. W., Daly, E. J., Jones, K. M., & Lentz, F. E. (2004). Response to intervention: Empirically based special service decisions from single-case designs of increasing and decreasing intensity. *The Journal of Special Education, 38*, 66-79.

Benbow, C. P., & Lubinski, D. (1997). Psychological profiles of the mathematically talented: Some sex differences and evidence supporting their biological basis. In M. R. Walsh (Ed.), *Women, men, and gender* (pp. 271-287). New Haven, CT: Yale University Press.

Bender, W. N., & Wall, M. E. (1994). Social-emotional development of students with learning disabilities. *Learning Disability Quarterly, 17*, 323-341.

Berninger, V. W. (2001). Understanding the "lexia" in dyslexia: A multidisciplinary team approach to learning disabilities. *Annals of Dyslexia, 51*, 23-48.

Berninger, V. W. & Richards, T. L. (2002). *Brain literacy for educators and psychologists*. New York: Academic Press.

Berninger, V. W. & Abbott, R. D. (1992). The unit of analysis and the constructive processes of the learner: Key concepts for educational neuropsychology. *Educational Psychologist, 27*, 223-242.

Boetsch, E. A., Green, P. A., & Pennington, B. F. (1996). Psychosocial correlates of dyslexia across the lifespan. *Development and Psychopathology, 8*, 539-562.

Bouras, N. & Drummond, C. (1992). Behavior and psychiatric diagnosis of people with mental handicaps living in the community. *Journal of Intellectual Disability Research, 36*, 349-357.

Bowers, P. (2001). Exploration of basis for rapid naming's relationship to reading. In M. Wolf (Ed.), *Dyslexia, fluency, and the brain* (pp. 41-63). Timonium, MD: York Press

Bryan, K. L. & Hale, J. B. (2001). Differential effects of left and right hemisphere accidents on language competency. *Journal of the International Neuropsychology Society, 7*, 655-664.

Bryan, T., Burstein, K., & Ergul, C. (2004). The social-emotional side of learning disabilities: A science based presentation of the state of the art. *Learning Disability Quarterly, 27*, 45-51.

Deno, S. L. (2002). Problem solving as "best practice". In A. Thomas, & J. Grimes (Eds.), *Best practices in school psychology IV* (pp. 37-56). Bethesda, MD: National Association of School Psychologists.

Elksnin, L. K. & Elksnin, N. (2004). The social-emotional side of learning disabilities. *Learning Disability Quarterly, 27*, 3-9.

Fiorello, C. A., Hale, J. B., & Snyder, L. E. (2006). Cognitive hypothesis testing and response to intervention for children with reading problems. *Psychology in the Schools, 43*, 835-853.

Fiorello, C. A., Hale, J. B., Holdnack, J. A., Kavanagh, J. A., Terrell, J. & Long, L. (2007). Interpreting intelligence test results for children with disabilities: Is global intelligence relevant? *Applied Neuropsychology, 14*, 2-12.

Flanagan, D. P., Ortiz, S. O., Alfonso, V. C., & Dynda, A. M. (2006). Integration of response to intervention and norm-referenced tests in learning disability identification: Learning from the Tower of Babel. *Psychology in the Schools, 43*, 807–825.

Fletcher, J. M., Coulter, W. A., Reschly, D. J., & Vaughn, S. (2004). Alternative approaches to the definition and identification of learning disabilities: Some questions and answers. *Annals of Dyslexia, 54*, 304-331.

Forrest, B. J. (2004). The utility of math difficulties, internalized psychopathology, and visual-spatial deficits to identify children with the nonverbal learning disability syndrome: Evidence for a visuospatial disability. *Child Neuropsychology, 10(2)*, 129-146.

Fuchs, D., Mock, D., Morgan, P., & Young, C. (2003). Responsiveness-to-intervention: Definitions, evidence, and implications for the learning disabilities construct. *Learning Disabilities Research and Practice, 18*, 157-171.

Fuchs, D., Deshler, D. D., & Reschly, D. J. (2004). National Research Center on Learning Disabilities: Multimethod studies of identification and classification issues. *Learning Disability Quarterly, 27*, 189-196.

Fuerst, D. R., Fisk, J. L., & Rourke, B. P. (1989). Psychosocial functioning of learning-disabled children: Replicability of statistically derived subtypes. *Journal of Consulting and Clinical Psychology, 57*, 275-280.

Fuerst, D. R., Fisk, J. L., & Rourke, B. P. (1990). Psychosocial functioning of learning-disabled children: Relations between WISC Verbal IQ-Performance-IQ discrepancies and personality subtypes. *Journal of Consulting and Clinical Psychology, 58*, 657-660.

Geary, D. C. (1993). Mathematical disabilities: Cognitive, neuropsychological, and genetic components. *Psychological Bulletin, 114*, 345-352.

Geary, D. C., Hoard, M. K., & Hamson, C. O. (1999). Numerical and arithmetical cognition: Patterns of functions and deficits in children with learning disability. *Journal of Experimental Child Psychology, 74*, 213-239.

Geary, D. C., Hamson, C. O., & Hoard, M. K. (2000). Numerical and arithmetical cognition: A longitudinal study of process deficits in children with learning disabilities. *Journal of Experimental Child Psychology, 77*, 236-263.

Goldberg, E. (2001). *The executive brain: Frontal lobes and the civilized mind*. New York: Oxford University Press.

Gresham, F. M. (2002). Best practices in social skills training. In A. Thomas & J. Grimes (Eds.), *Best practices in school psychology IV* (pp. 1029-1040). Bethesda, MD: National Association of School Psychologists.

Gresham, F. M., Reschly, D. J., Tilly, D. W., Fletcher, J., Burns, M., Crist, T., et al. (2005). Comprehensive evaluation of learning disabilities: A response to intervention perspective. *The School Psychologist, 59* (1), 26-29.

Groth-Marnat, G., & Teal, M. (2000). Block design as a measure of everyday spatial ability: A study of ecological validity. *Perceptual and Motor Skills, 90*, 522-526.

Hain, L. A. (2008). *Exploration of specific learning disability subtypes differentiated across cognitive, achievement, and emotional/behavioral variables*. Unpublished doctoral dissertation, Philadelphia College of Osteopathic Medicine, Philadelphia.

Hale, J. B. & Fiorello, C. A. (2002). Cross-battery cognitive assessment approaches to test interpretation: Are you a clumper or a splitter? *Communiqué, 31*(1), 37-40.

Hale, J. B. (2006). Implementing IDEA with a three-tier model that includes response to intervention and cognitive assessment methods. *School Psychology Forum: Research and Practice, 1*, 16 – 27.

Hale, J. B., Fiorello, C. A., Miller, J. A., Wenrich, K., Teodori, A. M., & Henzel, J. (2008a). WISC-IV assessment and intervention strategies for children with specific learning disabilities. In A. Prifitera, D. H. Saklofske, & L. G. Weiss (Eds.), *WISC-IV clinical use and interpretation: Scientist-practitioner perspectives*. New York, NY: Elsevier Science.

Hale, J. B. (2008). *Response to intervention: Guidelines for parents and practitioners*. Retrieved July 1, 2008, from http://www.wrightslaw.com/idea/art/rti.hale.pdf

Hale, J. B., Flanagan, D. P., & Naglieri, J. A. (2008b). Alternative research-based methods for IDEA 2004 identification of children with specific learning disabilities, *Communiqué, 36* (8), 14-17.

Hale, J. B., Hoeppner, J. B., & Fiorello, C. A. (2002). Analyzing digit span components for assessment of attention processes. *Journal of Psychoeducational Assessment, 20*, 128-143.

Hale, J. B., Fiorello, C. A., & Brown, L. L. (2005). Determining medication treatment effects using teacher ratings and classroom observations of children with ADHD: Does neuropsychological impairment matter? *Educational and Child Psychology, 22*(2), 39-61.

Hale, J. B., Fiorello, C. A., Bertin, M., & Sherman, R. (2003). Predicting math achievement through neuropsychological interpretation of WISC-III variance components. *Journal of Psychoeducational Assessment, 21,* 358-378.

Hale, J. B. & Fiorello, C. A. (2004). *School neuropsychology: A practitioner's handbook.* New York: The Guilford Press.

Hale, J. B., Kaufman, A., Naglieri, J. A., & Kavale, K. A. (2006). Implementation of IDEA: Integrating response to intervention and cognitive assessment methods. *Psychology in the Schools, 43,* 753-770.

Hale, J. B., Rosenberg, D., Hoeppner, J. B., & Gaither, R. (1997, April). *Cognitive predictors of behavior disorders in children with learning disabilities.* Paper presented at the annual convention of the National Association of School Psychologists, Anaheim, CA.

Hale, J. B., Fiorello, C. A., Kavanagh, J. A., Holdnack, J. A., & Aloe, A. M. (2007). Is the demise of IQ interpretation justified? A response to special issue authors. *Applied Neuropsychology, 14,* 37-51.

Hanna-Pladdy, B. (2007). Dysexecutive syndromes in neurologic disease. *Journal of Neurologic Physical Therapy, 31*(3), 119-127.

Hendriksen, J. G. M., Keulers, E. H. H., Feron, F. J. M., Wassenberg, R. W., Jolles, J. & Vles, J. S. H. (2007). Subtypes of learning disabilities: Neuropsychological and behavioural functioning of 495 children referred for multidisciplinary assessment. *European Child and Adolescent Psychiatry, 16,* 517-524.

Hooper, S. R., Montgomery, J., Swartz, C., Reed, M. S., Sandler, A. D., Levine, M. D. et al. (1994). Measurement of written language expression. In G. R. Lyon (Ed.), *Frames of reference for the assessment of learning disabilities* (pp. 375-415). Baltimore: Brookes.

Individuals With Disabilities Education Improvement Act of 2004 (IDEA), Pub. L. No. 108–446, 118 Stat. 2647 (2004). [Amending 20 U.S.C. §§ 1400 et seq.].

Ivry, R. B. (1993). Cerebellar involvement in the explicit representation of temporal information. *Annals of the New York Academy of Sciences, 682,* 214-230.

Kaufman, A. S. (1994). *Intelligent testing with the WISC-III.* New York: Wiley.

Kaufman, A. S., & Kaufman, N. L. (2004). *Kaufman Test of Educational Achievement, Second Edition Manual.* Circle Pines, MN: AGS.

Kavale, K. A., Holdnack, J. A., & Mostert, M. P. (2005). Responsiveness to intervention and the identification of specific learning disability: A critique and alternative proposal. *Learning Disability Quarterly, 28,* 2-16.

Kavale, K. A., Kaufman, A. S., Naglieri, J. A., & Hale, J. (2005). Changing procedures for identifying learning disabilities: The danger of poorly supported ideas. *School Psychologist, 59,* 16-25.

Keith, T. Z., Goldenring-Fine, J., Taub, G. E., Reynolds, M. R., & Kranzler, J. H. (2006). Higher order, multisample, confirmatory factor analysis of the Wechsler Intelligence Scale for Children-Fourth Edition: What does it measure? *School Psychology Review, 35,* 108-127.

King, W. M., Giess, S. A., & Lombardino, L. J. (2007). Subtyping of children with developmental dyslexia via bootstrap aggregated clustering and the gap statistic: Comparison with the double deficit hypothesis. *International Journal of Language & Communication Disorders, 42,* 77-95.

Langdon, D. W., & Warrington, E. K. (1997). The abstraction of numerical relations: A role for the right hemisphere in arithmetic? *Journal of the International Neuropsychological Society, 3,* 260-268.

Lichter, D. G., & Cummings, J. L. (Eds.) (2001). *Frontal–Subcortical Circuits in Psychiatric and Neurological disorders.* New York, NY: Guilford Press.

Lindell, A. K. (2006). In your right mind: Right hemisphere contributions to language processing and production. *Neuropsychology Review, 16,* 131-148.

Lovett, M. W., Steinbach, K. A., & Frijters, J. C. (2000). Remediating the core deficit of developmental reading disability: A double-deficit perspective. *Journal of Learning Disabilities, 33,* 334-358.

Lyon, G. R. (1995). Toward a definition of dyslexia. *Annals of Dyslexia, 45,* 3-27.

Mammarella, I. C, Cornoldi, C., Pazzaglia, F., Toso, C., Grimoldi, M., Vio, C. (2006). Evidence for a double dissociation between spatial-simultaneous and spatial-sequential working memory in visuospatial (nonverbal) learning. *Brain and Cognition, 62*(1), 58-67.

Mather, N., & Gregg, N. (2006). Specific learning disabilities: Clarifying, not eliminating a construct. *Professional Psychology: Research & Practice, 37,* 99-106.

Mattison, R. E., Hooper, S. R., & Carlson, G. A. (2006). Neuropsychological characteristics of special education students with serious emotional/behavioral disorders. *Behavioral Disorders, 31*(2), 176-188.

Mayberg, H. (2001). Depression and frontal-subcortical circuits: Focus on prefrontal-limbic interactions. In D. G. Lichter & J. L. Cummings (Eds.), *Frontal-subcortical circuits in psychiatric and neurological disorders* (pp. 177-206). New York: Guilford Press.

Mayes, S. & Calhoun, S. (2006). WISC-IV and WISC-III profiles in children with ADHD. *Journal of Attention Disorders, 9*, 486-493.

Mayes, S. & Calhoun, S. (2008). WISC-IV and WIAT-II profiles in children with high-functioning autism. *Journal of Autism and Developmental Disorders, 38*, 428-439.

Mazzocco, M. M. M. (2001). Math learning disability and math SLD subtypes: Evidence from studies of Turner syndrome, fragile X syndrome, and neurofibromatosis type 1. *Journal of Learning Disabilities, 34*, 520-533.

Mazzocco, M. M. M. (2005). Challenges in identifying target skills for math disability screening and intervention. *Journal of Learning Disabilities, 38*, 318-323.

McKinney, J. D. & Speece, D. L. (1986). Academic consequences and longitudinal stability of behavioral subtypes of learning disabled children. *Journal of Educational Psychology, 78*, 365-372.

Miller, D. C., & Hale, J. B. (2008). Neuropsychological applications of the WISC-IV and WISC-IV Integrated. In A. Prifitera, D. H. Saklofske, & L. G. Weiss (Eds.), *WISC-IV clinical assessment and intervention* (2nd ed.) (pp. 445-495). New York, NY: Elsevier Science.

National Research Center on Learning Disabilities. (2005). *Specific learning disability: Building consensus for identification and classification.* Washington, DC: U.S. Department of Education.

National Longitudinal Transition Study (2005). *The academic and functional performance of youth with disabilities.* Washington, DC: U.S. Department of Education.

Nussbaum, N. L. & Bigler, E. D. (1986). Neuropsychological and behavioral profiles of empirically derived subtypes of learning disabled children. *The International Journal of Clinical Neuropsychology, 18*, 82-89.

Nussbaum, N. L., Bigler, E. D., & Koch, W. R. (1986). Neuropsychologically derived subgroups of learning disabled children. *Journal of Research and Development in Education, 19*, 57-67.

Ofiesh, N. (2006). Response to intervention and the identification of specific learning disabilities: Why we need comprehensive evaluations as part of the process. *Psychology in the Schools, 43*, 883-888.

Ottnow, L. (1988). Neuropsychiatric, psychoeducational, and family characteristics of 14 juveniles condemned to death in the United States. *American Journal of Psychiatry, 145*, 584-589.

Posner, M. I. & Raichle, M. (1994). *Images of mind.* New York: Scientific American Library.

Powell, K. B., & Voeller, K. K. S. (2004). Prefrontal executive function syndromes in children. *Journal of Child Neurology, 19*, 785-797.

President's Commission on Excellence in Special Education (2002). *A new era: Revitalizing special education for children and their families.* Jessup, MD: U.S. Department of Education.

Prifitera, A., & Dersh, J. (1993). Base rates of WISC-III diagnostic subtest patterns among normal, learning-disabled, and ADHD samples. In B. A. Bracken, & R. McCallum (Eds.), *Wechsler Intelligence Scale for Children: Third edition* (pp. 43-55). Brandon, VT, US: Clinical Psychology Publishing Co.

Quinn, M., Rutherford, R., Leone, P., Osher, D., & Poirer, J. (2005). Youth with disabilities in juvenile corrections: A national survey. *Exceptional Children, 71*(3), 339-345.

Reddy, L. A., & Hale, J. B. (2007). Inattentiveness. In A. R. Eisen (Ed.), *Clinical Handbook of Childhood Behavior Problems: Case Formulation and Step-by-Step Treatment Programs* (pp.156-211). New York, NY: Guilford Press.

Reschly, D. J., & Hosp, J. L. (2004). State SLD policies and practices. *Learning Disability Quarterly, 27*, 197-213.

Reynolds, C. R., & Kamphaus, R. W. (2004). *Behavior Assessment System for Children, Second Edition.* Circle Pines, MN: American Guidance Service.

Ring, H., Zia, A., Lindeman, S., & Himlok, K. (2007). Interactions between seizure frequency, psychopathology, and severity of intellectual disability in a population with epilepsy and a learning disability. *Epilepsy & Behaviors, 11*, 92-97.

Rock, E. E., Fessler, M. A., & Church, R. P. (1997). The concomitance of learning disabilities and emotional/behavior disorders: A conceptual model. *Journal of Learning Disabilities, 30* (3), 245-263.

Rourke, B. P. (1989). *Nonverbal learning disabilities: The syndrome and the model.* New York: Guilford Press.

Rourke, B. P., & Fuerst, D. R. (1991). *Learning disabilities and psychosocial functioning: A neuropsychological perspective.* New York: Guilford Press.

Rourke, B. P. (1994). Neuropsychological assessment of children with learning disabilities. In G. R. Lyon (Ed.), *Frames of reference for the assessment of learning disabilities* (pp. 475–509). Baltimore, MD: Brooks.

Rourke, B. P. (1995). *Syndrome of nonverbal learning disabilities: Neurodevelopmental manifestations*. New York: Guilford Press.

Rourke, B. P. (2000). Neuropsychological and psychosocial subtyping: A review of investigations within the University of Windsor Laboratory. *Canadian Psychology, 41*, 34–51.

Rourke, B. P. (2008). Neuropsychology as a (psycho) social science: Implications for research and clinical practice. *Canadian Psychology/Psychologie Canadienne, 49*, 35–41.

Sandler, A. D., Watson, T. E., Footo, M., Levine, M. D., Coleman, W. L., & Hooper, S. R. (1992). Neurodevelopmental study of writing disorders in middle childhood. *Journal of Developmental and Behavioral Pediatrics, 13*, 17–23.

Schrank, F. A., Miller, J. A., Catering, L., & Desrochers, J. (2006). American Academy of School Psychology survey on the independent educational evaluation for a specific learning disability: Results and discussion. *Psychology in the Schools, 43*, 771–780.

Semrud-Clikeman, M. , Fine , J. , & Harder , L. (2005). The school neuropsychology of learning disabilities. In R. K. D'Amato, E. Fletcher-Janzen , & C. R. Reynolds (Eds.), *Handbook of school neuropsychology*. New York, NY: John Wiley & Sons.

Semrund-Clikeman, M. (2005). Neuropsychological aspects for evaluating learning disabilities. *Journal of Learning Disabilities, 38*, 563–569.

Shaywitz, B. A., Shaywitz, S. E., Pugh, K. R., Mencl, W. E., Fulbright, R. K., Skuldlarski, P. et al. (2002). Disruption of posterior brain systems for reading in children with developmental dyslexia. *Biological Psychiatry, 53*, 101–110.

Shaywitz, S. E., Shaywitz, B. A., Fulbright, R., Skudlarski, P., Mencl, W. E., Constable, R. T., et al. (2003). Neural systems for compensation and persistence: Young adult outcome of childhood reading disability. *Biological Psychiatry, 54*, 25–33.

Shinn, M. R. (2002). Best practices in using curriculum-based measurement in a problem-solving model. In A. Thomas, & J. Grimes (Eds.), *Best practices in school psychology IV* (pp. 671–697). Bethesda, MD: National Association of School Psychologists.

Simos, P. G., Fletcher, J. M., Sarkari, S., Billingsley, R. L., Denton, C., & Papanicolaou, A. C. (2007). Altering the brain circuits for reading through intervention: A magnetic source imaging study. *Neuropsychology, 2*, 485–496.

Speece, D., McKinney, J. D., & Appelbaum, M. (1985). Classification and validation of behavioral subtypes of learning-disabled children. *Journal of Educational Psychology*, 77, 67–77.

Taggart, L., Cousins, W. , & Milner , S. (2007). Young people with learning disabilities living in state care: Their emotional, behavioural and mental health status. *Child Care in Practice, 13*, 401–416.

Truscott, S. D., Catanese, A. M., & Abrams, L. M. (2005). The evolving context of special education classification in the United States. *School Psychology International, 26*, 162–177.

U.S. Public Health Service, *Report of the Surgeon General's Conference on children's mental health: A National action agenda*. Washington, DC: Department of Health and Human Services, 2000.

Vellutino, F. R. (2001). Further analysis of the relationship between reading achievement and intelligence: A response to Naglieri. *Journal of Learning Disabilities, 34*, 306–310.

Voeller, K. K. S. (2001). Attention-deficit/hyperactivity disorder as a frontal-subortical disorder. In D. G. Lichter & J. L. Cummings (Eds.), *Frontal-subcortical circuits in psychiatric and neurological disorders* (pp. 334–371). New York: Guilford Press.

Wechsler, D. (2001). *Wechsler Individual Achievement Test-Second Edition*. San Antonio, TX: Psychological Corporation.

Wechsler, D. (2003). *Wechsler Intelligence Test for Children-Fourth Edition*. San Antonio, TX: Psychological Corporation.

Wei - dong, J. (2004). A comparative study on cognitive function and self-concept in children with learning disability. *Chinese Journal of Clinical Psychology, 12*(4), 375–376.

Willcutt, E. G., & Pennington, B. F. (2000). Psychiatric comorbidity in children and adolescents with reading disability. *Journal of Child Psychology and Psychiatry, 41*, 1039–1048.

Willis , J. O. , & Dumont , R. (2006). And never the twain shall meet: Can response to intervention and cognitive assessment be reconciled? *Psychology in the Schools, 43*, 901–908.

Wilson, B. M., & Proctor, A. (2000). Oral and written discourse in adolescents with closed head injury. *Brain and Cognition, 43*, 425-429.

Wodrich, D. L., Spencer, M. L., & Daley, K. B. (2006). Combining RTI and psychoeducational assessment: What we must assume to do otherwise. *Psychology in the Schools, 43*, 797-806.

Wolf, M., & Bowers, P. G. (1999). The double-deficit hypothesis for the developmental dyslexias. *Journal of Educational Psychology, 91*, 415-438.

Woodcock, R. W., McGrew, K. S., & Mather, N. (2001). *Woodcock-Johnson III*. Itasca, IL: Riverside.

Ysseldyke, J., & Marston, D. (1999). Origins of categorical special education services in schools and a rationale for changing them. In D. Reschly, W. D. Tilly III, & J. Grimes (Eds.), *Special education in transition: Functional assessment and noncategorical programming* (pp. 1–18). Longmont, CO: Sopris West.

Zadina, J. N., Corey, D. M., & Casbergue, R. M. (2006). Lobar asymmetries in subtypes of dyslexic and control subjects. *Journal of Child Neurology, 2*, 922-931.

CHAPTER 9

SCHOOL ACHIEVEMENT, NEUROPSYCHOLOGICAL CONSTRUCTS, AND EMOTIONAL DISORDERS

John M. Garruto, M.S., NCSP
Gurmal Rattan, Ph.D.

"The problem with most emotional words is that each has multiple and thus ambiguous meanings. Language tends to throw away information in order to construct a tidy package for the consumer."

—Jerome Kagan

Introduction

The passage of No Child Left Behind (2002) has increased accountability for ensuring that students are meeting with success in school. Similarly, the passage of the reauthorization of the Individuals with Disabilities Education Act (IDEA) of 2004 has placed an increased onus on identifying researched based interventions. Clearly, there is a wealth of research on the importance of accurate identification of the problem before an appropriate intervention can be selected (Deno, 2002; Hale & Fiorello, 2004; Reschly & Ysseldyke, 2002). In recent years, there has also been increasing momentum related to the "Response to Intervention" (RTI) movement as a paradigm for problem solving. Many school districts have begun to implement RTI through the presence of problem solving teams. These are not new concepts; they have been host to a variety of names such as Child Study Teams, Instructional Support Teams, or School-Based Intervention Teams. Research has demonstrated that these teams, when implemented with fidelity, can lead to better outcomes for students and fewer referrals to special education (Kovaleski, Gickling, & Morrow, 1999).

Establishing taxonomies for children with problems is not new to the field of education, given

IDEA and the various state regulations. It is of little surprise, then, that problem solving teams are often restricted to the same taxonomies as the list of existing services. To that end, academic and behavior problems tend to be viewed as singular entities, as opposed to a constellation of emotional, neuropsychological, cognitive, academic, motivational, familial, and other factors. Consequently, this framework lends problem solvers to just choose interventions related solely to the suspected problem identified. This conceptualization is identified in Figure 9-1.

FIGURE 9-1

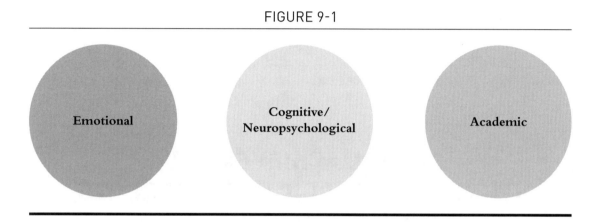

However, what if the problems were to overlap? Can a neuropsychological or cognitive problem also relate to emotional problems and can those problems relate to academic problems? For instance, consider a child who has an impulsive style of answering questions. It is conceivable that this child may also be prone to becoming quickly frustrated in class since problems with impulsivity often lead to poor test performance. Consider a child with planning difficulties. Perhaps this child might consider writing a message on the bathroom stalls at the urging of a friend, and may not bother to think through the act to consider the consequences. This same child may also become completely overwhelmed with the nature of a complex academic problem solving task, and because of poor planning, have no idea where to start. Figure 9-2 shows an alternative example of how clinicians might view neuropsychological problems as they relate to both emotional and academic outcomes.

FIGURE 9-2

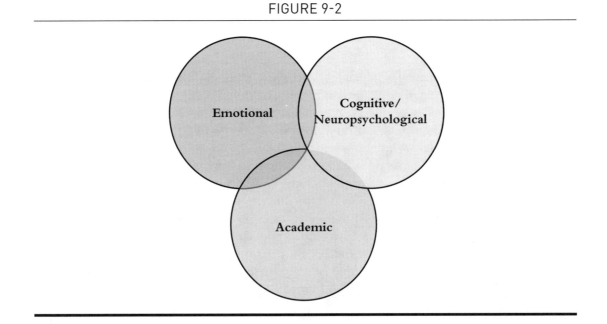

The purpose of this chapter is to review the existing research and highlight the concurrence of various neuropsychological problems hindering both emotional functioning and achievement. Specifically, this will encompass executive dysfunctions, right hemisphere dysfunction (specifically as they result nonverbal learning disabilities), and clinically internalizing emotional concerns that have a basis in neuropsychology (such as anxiety and depression). Although some of these issues are discussed more in depth elsewhere in this volume, this chapter will focus on the concurrence of achievement and emotional consequences with similar neuropsychological origins. Research relating to the three components presented in Figure 9-2 will be discussed in terms of their influence on both academic achievement and social-emotional adjustment. Furthermore, interventions related to all three dimensions will also be explored.

RESEARCH RELATED TO NEUROPSYCHOLOGICAL PROCESSES AND ACHIEVEMENT/SOCIAL-EMOTIONAL OUTCOMES

Executive Function Disorders

Jimmy is an eleven-year-old male who is struggling significantly in school. He receives below average to failing grades in school. When he was assessed by the school psychologist, he presented with average intellectual development and low average-to-average skills in reading, writing, and math. Rating scales have shown clinically significant concerns related to hyperactivity, attention problems, apathy toward school, and aggression. However, since he was learning general information appropriately, Jimmy

KEY LEARNING POINTS: Overview

- Remember: when attempting to define a child's problem in school, the nature of the problem may not solely be cognitive, emotional, or academic. In fact, most problems often hinder each of these areas, and thus require multi-modal methods of intervention as well.

was not identified with an educational disability. Instead, he was identified with an Attention Deficit Hyperactivity Disorder (ADHD), and placed on Ritalin (Methylphenidate). Nevertheless, Jimmy is still failing in school.

Jimmy is not unique as there are many students just like him in most schools. Teachers, parents, and even school psychologists often prematurely stop their evaluations at the special education eligibility process, and thus overlook an important component to the learning dynamic, namely, executive functioning. Executive functioning is a very broad term, and discussed more substantially in this volume, though a brief summary will be offered here. Executive functioning is the ability to regulate one's thoughts and actions. Skills related to executive functioning include planning, inhibition, concept formation, working memory, and set shifting. An often cited analogy (e.g., Goldberg, 2002) to help conceptualize executive function is to picture the band conductor of an orchestra. The conductor is directing specific parts of the orchestra to play and times them appropriately. By listening skillfully to the sounds of the band, the conductor not only flags which parts of the orchestra to play, but at which intensity and at what tempo. A poor conductor may have orchestra members who might chime in at the wrong time or play somewhat sluggishly. On the other hand, certain members knowingly or unknowingly may play too quickly.

Children with executive functioning problems often manifest a variety of different behaviors. For instance, one child may have problems keeping behavior under control (emotional dysregulation), while another may be blurting out the answer without thinking of the ramifications (inhibition problems). Some children may be unable to complete a test because they allocated too much time to a specific item (planning problems), while another child confuses computational signs when confronted with a mixed array of math problems (set shifting problems). When the "conductor" is not keeping the orchestra in line, problems inevitably result. The players still know how to play (hence they are able to demonstrate specific skills when individually assessed), but they are not terribly efficient.

Can problems with executive functioning also interfere with behavior? Certainly, a diagnosis of ADHD could be rendered when the problem is actually an executive functioning problem. In reality, however, ADHD is an executive functioning problem. The child who has problems set shifting may not have sensed that the topic in the class has changed. The child with problems related to inhibition control may deliver a hurtful comment without first silently rehearsing the comment to anticipate the likely consequence. Perhaps psychopharmacological treatment can lead to effective results (see the chapter on psychopharmacology in this volume). However, a greater understanding of problems associated with executive functioning can help the teacher, parent, or school psychologist better understand not only what is going on with a child, but also how to best intervene.

Children who have problems with ADHD also tend to meet criteria for conduct disorders, which may later evolve into antisocial personality disorders. As has been discussed, these types of problems often transcend the behavioral and social-emotional realms. Academically, students with ADHD are much more likely in school to be retained, suspended, or expelled (Barkley, 1998). Furthermore, students with executive functioning deficits often experience problems in many core academic subjects. For example, research has substantiated that problems with executive functioning relates to problems in both reading (Hale & Fiorello, 2004) and emotional disorders (Feifer & Rattan, 2007). To assess the latter relationship between emotional disorders and executive functions, Feifer and

Rattan administered the BRIEF (Gioia et al., 2000), a behavior rating scale of executive functioning, to three groups of students with varying degrees of emotional disorders. The results indicated that the BRIEF Shift variable was significantly different between groups 1 (students educated in a self-contained facility) and 3 (contrast group). These results suggested that students with more severe emotional problems had difficulty shifting their attention from one task to another. Likewise, the BRIEF Emotional Control and Self-Monitor variables were found to be significantly different between groups 1 and 3 as well. This suggested that students with more severe emotional problems had greater difficulty regulating their emotional impulses and self-monitoring their behavior, respectively. These findings are consistent with other research students noting a significant relationship between executive functioning and behavioral disorders (Giancola et al., 1998; Morgan & Lilienfeld, 2000).

There is a general consensus that executive functions generally take place in the prefrontal region of the brain (Barkley, 1998; Hale & Fiorello, 2004; Miller, 2007). The prefrontal lobe is responsible for maintaining inhibition control, filtering out sensory distractions, engaging in metacognitive processes, in addition to numerous functions relating to the organization and planning of activities. Specific areas of the brain that have been implicated for ADHD are the cingulate and orbital prefrontal cortex, although there is also evidence of parietal-occipital involvement (Hale & Fiorello, 2004). Lezak (1982) also indicated that children with damage to the right hemisphere, as well as damage to subcortical structures in the limbic regions, display problems with executive functioning as well.

Executive functions overlap with both emotional development and academic achievement, and deficits can adversely impact student performance. In fact, Gordon, Cantor, Ashman, and Brown (2006) have identified what they call the "executive plus" model. In this model, these researchers identify how executive dysfunction relates to difficulties with a variety of problem-solving mechanisms. For instance, emotional dysregulation can impact the problem solving process due to "attentional" neglect, which results in an inadequate exploration of all possible alternatives to find a solution. Once again, it bears restating that executive functioning is a broad term and comprises a series of narrow abilities. These include (but are not limited to) planning, inhibition, set shifting, concept formation, and working memory. For the purposes of this chapter, the skills of planning and inhibition will be discussed in greater detail, since they relate to achievement as well as social-emotional development.

Planning

Planning is a skill that is often required for success in school. Students who do not have adequate planning ability often have problems with social-emotional adjustment as well. Planning is not necessarily related to fulfilling goal attainment, but is more related to reaching a specific goal in the most efficient manner. The logical consequences of good versus poor planning abilities are readily apparent both in the academic arena as well as social-emotional areas. For instance, when engaged in a timed test that requires reading, the good planner will look ahead to the questions and think them through while reading the passage. The implications for planning in writing are readily apparent when it comes to organizing one's thoughts and ideas into meaningful sentences. Furthermore, when a child is engaged in a conflict resolution task, the student with good planning abilities will analyze different solutions and think about their consequences before rendering a decision. Although the ramifications of planning can disrupt both cognitive and emotional domains, the neuropsychological functioning of students with planning problems tends to be more of a cognitive factor (Miller, 2007). In fact, Miller (2007) noted that problems with planning are often related to problems with the dorsolateral prefrontal circuit. Consequently, deficits in this area can lead to difficulties with learning, organization, focusing, and a shifting cognitive set, as well as time management skills. Nevertheless, the student with poor planning abilities can also present with social-emotional difficulties. According to Lezak (1982), "Defective planning can be identified in patients who have no difficulty formulating goals but lose track of their intentions or activities, do not generate plans, or come up with plans that are unrealistic if not simply silly" (p. 288). Therefore, difficulties with planning, even in the absence of poor impulse control, can still lead to profound social-emotional consequences. For instance, consider a child who is playing a game of checkers with a classmate, then abruptly and whimsically decides to play cards with another classmate before the game of checkers has been completed. Most children with good planning ability would recognize that simply walking away from a game prematurely to pursue another activity with a different friend would be rather rude, inconsiderate, and hurtful.

Most problems with planning become readily apparent in academic achievement areas, particularly with writing and study skills. According to Feifer and DeFina (2002), multiple executive functioning domains including planning can readily disrupt the writing process leading to deficits with verbal fluency, incorrect spacing of words, a lack of cohesive ties between sentences and paragraphs, and poor use of lines when writing. Consider two students who wrote the following simple paragraphs on birds.

Student 1:
> *Birds are very different from other animals. Unlike most animals who are stuck on the ground, birds can fly and take to the sky. Also, even though most animals grow inside their mothers until they are born, baby birds grow in eggs until they are born. Birds are amazing creatures!*

Student 2:
> *Birds can fly. I love birds. I have a bird named Polly at home. They eat worms even though most animals don't like them. Birds are pretty and they are a lot of fun. Birds also lay eggs.*

Based upon these writing samples, the child with the planning difficulties is rather easy to spot. However, this child is probably not going to be identified as having a learning disability. Most standard tests of achievement, such as the Wechsler Individual Achievement Test-2nd Edition (Wechsler, 2001), or the Test of Written Language-3rd Edition (Hammill & Larson, 1996) only ascribe a small portion of the student's "writing ability" to planning and organization. Let's look at the second child. As can be seen, the child uses appropriate vocabulary, has complete sentence structure and adequate spelling, capitalization, and punctuation. However, there is no logical flow to this student's writing, and there is little planning or organization. Therefore, this student may not be eligible as a student with a learning disability since the deficit is not so much a language based deficit, but rather a deficit in performance. Still, the need for intervention is just as important given the multiple academic tasks that poor planning skills may impact. Indeed, having an understanding of both the academic and social-emotional consequences of planning deficits will allow the informed educator, school psychologist, or parent to advocate for these children when standardized assessments and traditional diagnostic protocols may simply "miss" them.

Inhibition

One area that is frequently mentioned by teachers as disrupting the learning process is impulsivity. Problems with impulsivity and response inhibition often accompany referrals that are suspect for ADHD. Although students who present as having problems of attention (daydreaming or "wandering off") are probably not seen as having significant inhibition problems, students who are impulsive or hyperactive may likely have more trouble in this area. From a neuropsychological perspective, planning is more related to the dorsolateral prefrontal circuit, whereas problems with inhibition often implicate the orbitofrontal circuit. Therefore, the dorsolateral prefrontal circuit is often associated with more academic concerns, and the orbitofrontal circuit tends to be associated with more behavioral concerns (Miller, 2007).

From a behavioral standpoint, the majority of problems associated with response inhibition are strikingly obvious. A child with inhibition problems may say inappropriate comments, commit social blunders, and be oblivious to their own inquisitive nature. For instance, telling the teacher she is overweight, blurting out that an assignment is "stupid," or cursing loudly at oneself in class for making a mistake are examples of students who have problems related to inhibition control. In addition, there are also difficulties noted with emotional inhibition as well. For instance, if a student is acting out in class (perhaps because the student has a goal to amuse classmates and has not considered the consequences of waiting for a more appropriate occasion) the teacher will quite naturally redirect the student. This may cause the student to feel "judged" by the teacher or perhaps even belittled. Next, the student becomes angry and offended, and then launches into a verbal tirade toward the teacher by yelling and screaming. Clearly, a student with better response inhibition may also feel "judged" or upset by being singled out and reprimanded in front of peers. However, a student with better emotional control chooses to refrain from a similar reaction in order to avoid the consequences of being sent to the office; therefore, the student inhibits their response and remains quiet. Although "repeat offenders" may be viewed as having "behavior problems" or being "incorrigible," it is possible that their difficulties may be related to problems with inhibition.

KEY LEARNING POINTS: Executive Function

- Executive functions are directive processes related to our brain's ability to engage in purposeful thinking. They include planning, inhibiting, sustaining and dividing attention, and engaging in higher level reasoning. Most executive functioning takes place in the frontal area of the brain.
- Attention Deficit Hyperactivity Disorder (ADHD) is an executive function problem.
- Students with executive dysfunction often exhibit problems with both behavior and academic achievement. Often times, traditional psychological evaluations do not detect the nuances associated with executive dysfunction, though neuropsychological evaluations almost always examine this key learning construct.
- An important brain region related to executive functioning is the dorsolateral prefrontal cortex, which is involved with the regulation of planning, focusing, and set shifting.
- A second important brain region related to executive functioning is the orbitofrontal cortex, which is involved with inhibition control and behavioral regulation.

Not only are there emotional and behavioral concerns associated with poor inhibition skills, there are also academic implications. For example, when a student with inhibition problems is taking a test, they may choose an answer that looks right without carefully reading the question or evaluating other possibilities. When solving a math problem, a student with inhibition difficulties may quickly subtract the smaller number from the larger one regardless of orientation to the problem, failing to "inhibit the prepotent response." In other words, the student immediately does the first thing that comes to mind, rather than taking the time to evaluate the problem. Furthermore, a study by Savage, Cornish, Manly, and Hollis (2006) found a variety of executive functioning skills were related to reading achievement, including inhibition control. Students' performances on a measure of response inhibition such as "continuous performance tasks" were related to success in reading accuracy and reading comprehension, even when IQ was statistically removed. In addition, response inhibition was also associated with reading disabilities, even for students not diagnosed with ADHD (Wilcutt, Pennington, Olson, Chhabildas, & Hulslander, 2005). Lastly, problems with response inhibition can also affect written language skills. For instance, a study by Altmeirer et al. (2006) revealed that while measures of inhibition were not the strongest academic predictor, they still meaningfully predicted how effectively both third and fifth grade students took notes while reading.

One academic area where the research is inconsistent regarding problems with response inhibition is mathematics. Some research has shown that disinhibition may adversely impact early math skills (Mazzocco & Kover, 2007); however, inhibition is not necessarily viewed as a long-term predictor of success in math (Censabella & Noel, 2008; Mazzocco & Kover, 2007). One aspect of math that requires further exploration is those students who have trouble with operational signs, and therefore confuse simple addition and subtraction markers. According to Bull and Scerif (2001), this type of mistake could be related either to response inhibition (orbitofrontal cortex) or cognitive set-shifting (dorsolateral prefrontal cortex), just like with planning (Miller, 2007). With respect to inhibition, the student may be unable to inhibit a prepotent response (for example-always adding or subtracting the smaller number from the larger). With respect to set-shifting, the student may have problems related to "shifting gears" (for example-always adding even when one should be subtracting.)   It is always helpful to cross reference academic pitfalls with other behavioral observations to determine the precise nature of the problem, which can hopefully lead to developing more appropriate interventions.

The ADHD Conundrum

There is a wealth of research relating response inhibition to ADHD (Hale & Fiorello, 2004; Miller, 2007; Riccio, Homack, Jarratt, & Wolfe, 2006; Wodka et al., 2007). Although ADHD wears many different "faces," problems with inhibition control, most likely stemming from orbitofrontal dysfunction, has been shown to be highly predictive of the "externalizing" or acting out/impulsive signs of ADHD (Riccio et al., 2006; Wodka et al., 2007). Nevertheless, it would be premature to assume that only the orbitofrontal cortex is associated with deficits in behavioral inhibition, and various facets of attention. According to Hale and Fiorello (2004), the inattentive subtype of ADHD may be more related to the dorsolateral cortex, and the hyperactive/impulsive subtype may be more related to the orbitofrontal cortex. Furthermore, the inattentive subtype of ADHD that is found in children with nonverbal learning disabilities may be associated more with parietal lobe dysfunction than with frontal lobe problems. To that end, use of stimulant medications with this latter group of children does not seem to be as effective as it would be with frontal lobe types of attention disorders. Therefore, simply identifying ADHD on its own does little to guide intervention. It is imperative that the informed school psychologist, teacher, or parent look beyond this diagnosis. With respect to

Jimmy, the case study presented earlier, the relationship of aggression and hyperactivity as well as the emotional implications of apathy toward school probably stem more from dysfunctions in the orbitofrontal area. However, what matters most is not necessarily pinpointing the precise brain region impaired, but rather using this information to determine an appropriate intervention plan for students who may not qualify for special education services, but rather need a formalized treatment plan in order to derive academic and behavioral success in school.

Nonverbal Learning Disabilities

Holly is an eight-year-old third grade girl who is experiencing numerous academic and behavioral challenges in school. To the casual observer, Holly presents as a well functioning child with few outward signs or concern. She is very articulate and verbose, has an encyclopedic knowledge base, and always filled with factual information. Nevertheless, Holly is struggling in school. In particular, she has difficulty in the area of math. For instance, she often becomes confused aligning numbers when problem solving, and when she is given a word problem, she has difficulty understanding what she is required to do. Holly is also socially awkward, and completely misses innuendo and nonverbal body language. Her teacher has complained that when Holly is talking to her neighbor, she will often look at Holly in such a way that anyone should know to be quiet, but Holly keeps on talking until explicitly told to stop. Lastly, she has a trouble fitting in with the other classmates in school. In summary, Holly has a nonverbal learning disability that impacts both academics and social-emotional development.

The field of learning disabilities continues to perplex school psychologists, teachers, parents, administrators, and other professionals alike. School psychologists spend much of their time assessing children for a variety of disabilities. In fact, the recent reauthorization of IDEA (2004) has sought to address changes in how learning disabilities are identified, given concerns with the use of the discrepancy analysis and the "wait-to-fail" problem solving paradigm (Reschly, 2005; Reschly & Ysseldyke, 2002). These concerns have done much to change the face of how reading disabilities are addressed, first through good teaching and then through a specific identification process. Consequently, there has been a trend toward the assessment of disabilities in a more proactive fashion, through the use of a Response-To-Intervention (RTI) model. However, there is little research generalizing the effectiveness of RTI to math, writing, or even certain subtypes of emotional disorders.

It is perhaps ironic that recent education law is coined as "No Child Left Behind" because this framework has the potential to leave some children behind, specifically those with math, writing, and social-emotional deficits. For instance, nonverbal learning disabilities are not acknowledged in federal legislation when identifying learning disabilities, though there is extensive research relating how nonverbal learning disabilities adversely impact education (Hale & Fiorello, 2004; Rourke, 2005; Rourke, 2000; Petti, Voelker, Shore, & Hayman-Abello, 2003). Given the substantial amount of research in this area and the significant educational implications for children who present with nonverbal learning disabilities, it is important for the informed practitioner (teacher, parent, administrator) to be aware of this needy, albeit often overlooked child.

Rourke (2000) identified two specific subtypes of learning disabilities. The first subtype is consistent with a basic phonological processing deficit (BPPD), and the second subtype falls under the category of a nonverbal learning disability (NLD). According to Rourke (2000), the BPPD subtype tends to have stronger visual and tactile perceptual skills, better problem solving skills, and better social-

KEY LEARNING POINTS:
Nonverbal Learning
Disabilities (NLD)

- Students with NLDs often have strong rote problem solving skills, but difficulty with higher level thinking skills. Specific academic difficulties include higher level mathematics and inferential reading comprehension skills.
- Students with NLDs may have difficulty with interpersonal relationships, often missing the meaning behind nonverbal body language, struggle to read emotional cues and markers, and have difficulty interacting with others.
- Students with NLDs tend to present with significant visual-spatial deficits.

emotional skills. The problems for these children reside with hearing and sequencing sounds in words, as well as with auditory memory skills. Conversely, NLD students have relative success with auditory memory and hearing sounds. Their deficits are more with social-emotional skills, visual-spatial skills, nonverbal communication, and problem solving. In school, the BPPD student tends to have more problems with word reading and spelling, whereas the NLD student will have more problems encountering new experiences, struggle with mathematics, and also reading comprehension as the content becomes more inferential. Furthermore, students with nonverbal learning disabilities clearly have problems understanding emotional cues and interpreting facial expressions and nonverbal cues (Petti et al., 2003).

Rourke (2000) added there are differing types of neuropsychological and medical disorders that often lead to NLD profiles. The most common of these include Asperger Syndrome (a type of high functioning autism), Williams Syndrome, Hydrocephalus (excess fluid in the brain), Turner Syndrome, and damage or dysfunction of the right cerebral hemisphere. In fact, sometimes the term nonverbal learning disability and right hemispheric dysfunction are interchangeable terms, that is to say, both profiles appear to be related to deficits in the right hemisphere (Hale & Fiorello, 2004). For further research on nonverbal learning disabilities, please refer to the chapter by Yalof in this volume.

Upon closer inspection, the psychopathology noted by Rourke (2000) suggests that NLD students seem more prone to internalizing disorders, such as depression and anxiety. However, these students frequently show attentional problems as well. According to Hale and Fiorello (2004), dysfunction in the anterior right hemisphere may lead to more "externalizing" types of attention problems, such as hyperactivity and aggression, whereas dysfunction in the posterior part of the right hemisphere may lead to more inattentive but non externalizing problems, such as NLD. Hale and Fiorello (2004) indicated that this particular subtype of attention may not be as influenced by stimulant medication. Therefore, practitioners should not automatically assume that deficits in attention reflect ADHD, but instead may be manifestations from symptomalogy associated with a nonverbal learning disability, a depressed child, or an anxious child. Still, diagnosing NLD in children can be extremely difficult, and the prudent examiner should proceed with caution. For instance, Forrest (2004) conducted a study that revealed there are some students with NLDs who actually demonstrated good math abilities. In this study, Forrest (2004) noted that students identified with NLD did better on certain subtests of the Keymath-Revised Test (Connolly, 1988) than their verbally learning disabled counterparts. Furthermore, in contrast to other studies (e.g. Casey, Rourke, & Picard, 1991) some students who showed nonverbal learning disabilities actually had lower rates of psychopathology than their verbal learning disabled (BPPD) peers (Forrest, 2004). Therefore, the problem resides not with the manifestation of the syndrome, but more likely in the search for exclusive symptoms based on preset criteria of NLD leading to nomenclature that can be misleading. Forrest (2004) indicated that practitioners should be cautious with either loosely applying the NLD criteria, or simply ignoring alternate symptoms for those already identified with NLD. In fact, Forrest (2004) illustrates a very important absolute when it comes to assessing any type of disability; namely, do not overlook presenting symptoms that simply do not fit the pre-existing nomenclature for the condition. Similarly, Watkins, Glutting, and Youngstrom (2005) reiterated that certain profiles, such as the Wechsler ACID (Arithmetic, Coding, Information, and Digit Span) and SCAD (Symbol Search, Coding, Arithmetic, and Digit Span) profiles only identify a small portion of children with learning disabilities.

Notwithstanding, all practitioners should attempt to seek specific cognitive and emotional behavioral patterns in order to determine which interventions to select, and also to guide further assessments that can either confirm or refute a hypothesis (Hale & Fiorello, 2004). Perhaps the case study shown in Hale, Kaufman, Naglieri, and Kavale (2006) best demonstrates this point. In their case study, Hale et al. discussed a student who presented as ADHD-primarily inattentive type; however, the stimulant medication prescribed did not work. Further assessment suggested right–hemisphere dysfunction consistent with a nonverbal learning disability, and interventions were subsequently targeted toward that end. Soon, measurable success was quickly observed. This example highlights the importance of not adhering to a "fixed profile" but rather to allow a thorough and comprehensive assessment to be the catalyst for appropriate interventions to follow.

Biological Basis of Internalizing Disorders

Barbara and Joseph are once again in the same sixth grade class. Their school experiences have been fairly unremarkable until the past year, as school work started to become very challenging for them both. Barbara has recently become very anxious in class, and worries about all sorts of things. For instance, she worries that she will fail her tests, she worries that others may not accept her, and she even worries that her mother may die. Barbara often thinks the children around her think negatively about her, so she approaches them cautiously. As a result, Barbara has not been finishing her homework or tests in a timely manner, and has been reluctant to come to school each morning.

Joseph, on the other hand, has lost almost all interest in school as well as most other endeavors. In addition, Joseph has a hard time getting out of bed in the morning, has little to look forward to, and participates in no extracurricular activities such as football or video games. He appreciates the help his friends and family try to give, but he simply feels that life is no longer fun anymore. Consequently, Joseph is not motivated to complete much work and seems indifferent about the possible consequences.

Some educators, parents, and even practitioners may attribute Joseph and Barbara's school related difficulties to sheer laziness. However, most can probably make the intuitive connection on how emotional disorders such as anxiety or depression may be falsely masked as problems with motivation or behavior. To illustrate the complexities of diagnosing internalizing types of emotional disorders, Baxter and Rattan (2004) assessed a sample of 86 males between the ages of 9-11 years that were previously diagnosed as having ADHD. To assess the presence of internalizing disorders, the Behavior Assessment System for Children (BASC) Parent Scale, Teacher Rating Scale, and Self-Report of Personality (Reynolds & Kamphaus, 1992) in addition to the Revised Children's Manifest

KEY LEARNING POINTS:
Internalizing Disorders

- Depression may be associated with under-activity in the prefrontal cortex of both hemispheres, though the right hemisphere shows the greatest under-activity.
- Anxiety may be related to an *over-activity* of processes in numerous brain regions. These regions include the basal ganglia, striatum, caudate nucleus, putamen, orbitofrontal circuit, and anterior cingulate circuit.
- Similar to executive functioning deficits and problems with NLDs, internalizing disorders are associated with poor academic performance, as well as with social-emotional dysfunction.
- The anterior cingulate circuit is often associated with task motivation, reward anticipation, and the development of empathy and rational decision making.

Anxiety Scale (Reynolds & Richmond, 1985) were compared to the normative sample for each respective measure. The results found that ADHD children presented with significantly higher levels of both anxiety and depression on the BASC, as well as higher anxiety scores on the RCMAS, when ratings were completed by parents, teachers, and self-report measures. This suggested that differential assessment may be required to detect the presence of internalizing disorders despite the fact that externalizing behaviors such as ADHD were the primary reason for referral.

With respect to brain functioning, there are three neurotransmitters that are often implicated with emotional problems. These include serotonin, norepinephrine, and dopamine. Specific agents that affect the activity of neurotransmitters are known as enzymes. According to Stahl (2008), two important neurotransmitters related to depression are norepinephrine and serotonin. For instance, having less serotonin or norepinephrine available impacts the frequency of signals between neurons, and the net result could lead to depression. See the chapter by Rattan in this volume for a more detailed account of the psychopharmacology associated with depression.

With respect to actual brain structures, there have been numerous areas implicated with depression as well. According to Levin, Heller, Mohanty, Herrington, and Miller (2007), depression may be associated with under-activity in the prefrontal cortex of both hemispheres; however, the right hemisphere shows the greatest under-activity. In addition, a decrease of activity in the dorsal anterior cingulate cortex, as well as an increase in the activity of the limbic system has been noted. According to Levin et al. (2007), cognitive skills are also impacted in children with depression, including memory, attention, and visual-spatial deficits. Such deficits certainly hold ramifications for both learning as well as social-emotional functioning.

While depression has often been related to an under-activity of neurological processes in the prefrontal cortex, anxiety may be related to an over-activity of processes in numerous brain regions. For instance, Stahl (2008) indicated that too much norepinephrine can result in symptoms of anxiety including heart racing, tremors, and sweating. Stahl (2000, 2008) also noted that obsessive compulsive disorder may stem from the basal ganglia being unable to put the breaks or inhibit behavior as well. In addition, the striatum, the caudate nucleus, and the putamen have also been implicated in obsessive-compulsive disorders, in addition to the orbitofrontal circuit and anterior cingulate circuit (Schwartz & Begley, 2002; Miller, 2007). The anterior cingulate circuit is often associated with motivation, reward anticipation, and empathic behavior as well. See the chapter by Feifer in this volume for a more detailed account of the neurobiology of mood and anxiety disorders.

The implications of relating depression and anxiety to learning as well as to the obvious social-emotional ramifications are somewhat intuitive. For example, the depressed child may not be motivated to engage in daily academic tasks. Conversely, the anxious child may be overly vigilant to virtually everything in the classroom, and therefore struggle to derive meaningful information from the daily class lesson. One group that seems regularly highlighted as having internalizing difficulties are those children with nonverbal learning disabilities. Greenham (1999) reviewed research supporting this conclusion, citing that students with nonverbal learning disabilities, "experience a variety of psychosocial difficulties, including poor peer relationships, immature and socially irresponsible behavior, misinterpretation and poor enactment of nonverbal emotions, increased risk for internalizing symptoms, and high rates of self-referral for psychotherapy" (p. 188). Other researchers have found an overlap of anxiety with neuropsychological problems and learning problems (Kusche, Cook, & Greenberg, 1993; Mayfield-Arnold et al., 2005), as well as depression with various neuropsychological, learning, and attentional problems (Arnett et al., 1999; Baxter & Rattan, 2004; Mayfield-Arnold et al., 2005).

In summary, the precise relationship between internalizing emotional disorders, neuropsychological deficits (particularly nonverbal learning disabilities) and academic achievement is still unclear (Forrest, 2004). However, what remains clear is that internalizing disorders such as anxiety and depression have multiple impacts on the students they affect. There are clearly neuropsychological consequences and implicated areas of the brain that impact both academics as well as social-emotional adjustment for students of all ages.

Interventions

It is important to note that there is a great deal of behavioral overlap in the three areas discussed, namely, executive functioning, nonverbal learning disabilities, and internalizing disorders. For example, students with nonverbal learning disabilities also exhibit executive function disorders in addition to possible internalizing disorders. Likewise, children with executive function disorders often exhibit internalizing disorders as well. The complexity of overlapping disorders cannot be stressed enough. Psychological and educational researchers have often sought to categorize a variety of behaviors that are readily observed, although overlapping conditions and similar behavioral manifestations makes this very challenging. The astute school psychologist, teacher, administrator, or parent is not as concerned with identification and labels, but with finding appropriate solutions to address the problem. The next section also highlights this tenet.

Given that similar behaviors can arise from different etiologies, it is important to first determine the underlying or core condition within the child, and then choose an appropriate intervention. Affective neuroscience allows psychologists the opportunity to determine the root causes for underlying core conditions based upon a brain-behavioral paradigm, as opposed to simply labeling various symptomalogies based upon observable behavior only. Clearly, an incorrect diagnosis may lead to interventions that probably will not be helpful for children (Hale et al., 2006). The following subsections will overview various interventions for children with executive function problems, nonverbal learning disabilities, and internalizing disorders.

PSYCHOPHARMACOLOGY

Executive Functioning

As previously stated, ADHD is a disorder related to executive dysfunction. As most educators are aware, stimulant medication has largely been used as a first-line treatment for ADHD. Although there is a substantial amount of research related to the success of medication for treatment of ADHD, there are some who may question this approach (e.g., Breggin, 1991). Still, it is incumbent upon school psychologists to discuss with parents what "scientifically-based" interventions are available for any disorder, though caution should be given toward school personnel who forcefully request parents to place children on any medication. As noted by Jacob and Hartshorne (2007), "To receive IDEA 2004 funds, states must prohibit school personnel from requiring parents to obtain a prescription for a controlled substance as a condition of attending school" (p. 226).

Stimulant medication is often used for the treatment of ADHD. Popular psycho-stimulants include Methylphenidate (Ritalin, Concerta, Metadate), and mixed amphetamine salts (Adderall). The side effects most often seen include loss of appetite and sleeplessness. However, more significant side effects can be present including blood pressure changes and cardiac arrhythmia (Jacob & Hartshorne, 2007). Research has indicated the success of Methylphenidate in helping to control attention, but overall enhancement of cognitive abilities has not been shown to occur (Rees, Marshall, Hartridge, Mackie & Weiser, 2007). It is important to understand that the success of psycho-stimulants on attention is not necessarily a "smoking gun" for ADHD. Rather it is the effect that stimulant medication has on neurotransmission that ultimately helps children sustain their attention (Stahl, 2000, 2008).

Psychopharmacological interventions for other brain areas implicated in executive functioning are currently limited and often relate to the comorbidity of executive functions to other disorders (such as schizophrenia). Although one study (Bush et al., 2008) indicated that Methylphenidate has resulted in increased activity in the dorsolateral prefrontal cortex and parietal cortex, others (Hale & Fiorello, 2004) have indicated that stimulants seem to have a negligible response on those who exhibit ADHD symptoms when problems are located in the parietal area. Until further research is conducted, it seems clear that other interventions are likely preferable when ADHD or other executive function problems are only mildly disrupting the learning process.

Nonverbal Learning Disabilities

There is very little research data indicating the effectiveness of psychopharmacological intervention related to nonverbal learning disabilities. According to Hale and Fiorello (2004):

> *"However, as noted earlier, others suggest that the inattentive type is related to parietal dysfunction and nonverbal LDs, and indeed this may be the case for many children diagnosed with ADHD. However, we would argue that children with this type of attention problem will be unlikely to respond to medication because their symptoms are actually secondary to parietal lobe dysfunction" (p. 270).*

Given this statement and the dearth of references related to the treatment of nonverbal learning disabilities by medication, it is clear that other interventions including counseling services, using social scripts, behavioral incentive charts rewarding prosocial behaviors, participating in after school activities with other children, direct academic tutoring, and/or special education services are more appropriate for this type of difficulty.

Internalizing Disorders

Anxiety and depression are often treated using psychopharmacological interventions. As Stahl (2008) indicates, most anxiety disorders are treated with similar types of medications, such as selective serotonin or norepinephrine reuptake inhibitors. Monoamine oxidase inhibitors (MAOIs) are also sometimes used in the treatment of depression. The overall function of both of these medications is to increase the number of neurotransmitters available for binding with their respective receptor sites. Again, one must be careful with selective serotonin reuptake inhibitors (SSRIs) given the recent concern that for some children, SSRIs have been linked to suicidal ideation as well as other side effects (Jacob & Hartshorne, 2007). Nevertheless, given the significant consequences related to untreated depression (such as suicidal ideation or disinterest in attending to school) or anxiety (such as fear of school, fear of what others are thinking, obsessions/compulsions, and/or panic attacks), it might be important for parents to consult with a highly trained pediatric psychiatrist about these options if other treatments fail.

DIRECT INTERVENTIONS

Executive Functions

Oftentimes, prescribing medication is a frequently used treatment choice for those who present with executive functioning disorders consistent with ADHD. However, it is critical that additional interventions be considered in conjunction with, or in lieu of, psychopharmacological interventions for children with these types of deficits. One such technique is direct skills instruction and repeated practice for specific skills that are impaired. Ylvisaker and Feeney (2002) highlight four skills needed to be proficient with executive dysfunction including: 1) autonomy (making one's own choices without outside influences), 2) self-regulation (formulating and carrying out plans of action), 3) psychological empowerment (acting on the belief that one can change one's future), and 4) self-realization (having an accurate perception of one's own strengths and limitations) (p. 52). Ylvisaker and Feeney describe a technique where organizing a 12-step self-questioning method under three phases (setting a goal, taking action, and then adjusting the goal or plan) has shown success. Some questions include, *"What do I want to learn?"*, *"What can I do to learn what I don't know?"*, and *"What has changed about what I don't know?"* (p. 60-61).

Ylvisaker and Feeney (2002) further describe the importance of teaching actual metacognitive (or thinking about thinking) strategies. These researchers indicate the importance of pretesting and goal setting with the student, as well as describing the strategy, modeling the use of the strategy, practicing the strategy verbally, practicing the strategy in a controlled setting with feedback, practicing the strategy in a different (advanced) context with feedback, having the student commit to applying these strategies in all settings, and helping them with generalization (see p. 61). Explicitly teaching techniques such as self questioning, and engaging in a step-by-step process can also help the student with poor planning and self-monitoring skills develop additional techniques on their own.

The use of group training has also been successful in remediating executive functioning deficits as well. Rees et al. (2007) analyzed the effects of a 16-week program to improve self-awareness and self-regulation. The results of this study indicated that positive effects were found, although these results were not maintained at a six-month follow-up. Perhaps one reason the results were not maintained lies in the importance of context relative to the problem. Context is very important and the students likely required generalization of their newly acquired skills into new settings as well.

A very effective strategy, especially for students with poor response inhibition, is cueing. Students who have problems with inhibition control may not be cognizant they are blurting out responses in class or responding reflexively and impulsively to most environmental situations. Having teachers developing nonverbal cueing systems, such as holding up a color-coded card, making a subtle gesture, or simply a light tap on the shoulder may be extremely helpful for students to draw attention to their current behavior. Again, the importance of providing feedback cannot be overstated. Certainly, using a behavior modification system or some sort of token economy can be helpful to reinforce and promote on-task behaviors and assist with basic self-regulation skills as well. Of course, the reinforcer has to be of substantive value to the student.

Another helpful intervention is Positive Behavioral Interventions and Supports (PBIS or PBS). PBIS is a fast growing initiative that explicitly teaches positive behavior and seeks to suppress negative behavior. There is ample evidence that has shown the utility of PBIS (OSEP, 2008). Feeney and Ylvisaker (2006) highlight the utility of PBIS and use of functional behavioral assessment, as well as the importance of context in order to make interventions work. To learn more about PBIS, visit http://www.pbis.org. Also, see the chapter by Sudano in this volume for a more detailed account of PBIS.

KEY LEARNING POINTS: Interventions

- Psychopharmacology is often a first line treatment for executive function problems and internalizing disorders. However, a combination of medication plus cognitive/behavioral therapy seems to be the most efficacious.
- Many students presenting with nonverbal learning disabilities may not be eligible for special education services. Nevertheless, early interventions including explicit teaching of social skills, using social stories, providing classroom accommodations to assist with organizational skills, and using specific social programs can be helpful.
- Direct intervention including counseling and universal mental health initiatives (such as positive behavioral interventions and supports) can provide much needed assistance to students who have both internalizing and externalizing emotional conditions.

Lastly, there are packaged programs for educators and psychologists that can be very effective in providing successful intervention for children with executive functioning difficulties. One such program is the Promoting Alternative Thinking Strategies (PATHS) program (Greenberg, 2006). According to Greenberg, this program focuses on exerting "verbal control" over limbic impulses (having thoughts override the emotional impulses). It is a universal program that has been shown to have positive effects on student performance, as measured by ratings of inhibition control as well as externalizing (acting out) emotional ratings. In fact, Greenberg indicated that two subcortical structures (the dorsolateral prefrontal cortex and the anterior cingulate) are often positively affected after participation in this curriculum. Table 9-1 provides a listing of the aforementioned executive functioning interventions.

TABLE 9-1
Executive Functioning Interventions

- Stimulant medication
- Teaching metacognitive strategies
- Group training
- Context generalization
- Classroom cueing systems
- Behavior modification plans
- Positive Behavior Instructional Supports
- Packaged programs (PATHS)

Nonverbal Learning Disabilities

As previously mentioned, there is some overlap with NLD and autism spectrum disorders, particularly Asperger's Syndrome. From a neuropsychological perspective, there is agreement that both disorders impact the right hemisphere. With respect to nonverbal learning disabilities, auditory memory and rote verbal skills including decoding skills are relative strengths for NLD students, while motor skills, math reasoning skills, and social interaction skills tend to be areas of greater weakness. If the child is found eligible for special education services, occupational therapy services are often recommended to assist with fine motor concerns. Furthermore, the school psychologist, school counselor, or school social worker can assist in enhancing social skills through counseling intervention services. Lastly, a speech-language pathologist may focus therapy on social pragmatic language goals, while a special education teacher may be needed to help with the higher level reasoning needed for mathematics or inferential comprehension.

However, many students presenting with a nonverbal learning disability may not be found eligible for special education services. In many respects, these students are often overlooked by the system, particularly in early elementary school. For instance, the "early years" often require memorization of rote math facts, and the use of basic psychological skills that are often not lacking for students with NLD. Nevertheless, early intervention continues to be important regardless of whether a child is eligible for direct special education services. Telzrow and Bonar (2002) offer helpful interventions for the NLD student including the importance of teaching social skills (such as making eye contact and greeting one another), teaching explicit strategies for making friends, and assisting students in generalizing discrete skills to other social environments. Motor problems can be compensated for by providing extended time on paper and pencil tasks, using word processors, and using specialty lined-paper to accommodate for perceptual concerns. Telzrow and Bonar (2002) further endorse the use of memory aides, as well as graph paper to help with organizational problems surrounding arithmetic difficulties. Finally, specific social skills programs such as the PATHS program (Greenberg, 2006) as well as the *"I Can Problem Solve"* curriculum (Shure, 1992) can be extremely beneficial, along with social stories such as those promoted by Carol Gray (Gray, 2000). The use of social stories can help explain everyday social practices, as well as model correct behavior for social situations in school. Table 9-2 highlights the interventions for students with nonverbal learning disabilities.

243

TABLE 9-2
Nonverbal Learning Disabilities Interventions

- Research regarding psychopharmacological intervention is currently mixed
- Direct social skills instruction
- Pragmatic language skill instruction provided by a speech language pathologist
- Fine motor remediation provided by an occupational therapist
- Packaged Programs:
  - PATHS
  - I Can Problem Solve
- Social Stories

Internalizing Disorders

Similar to ADHD, medication is often used as a first line treatment for anxiety and depression; however, psychotherapeutic techniques can be extremely beneficial as well. One technique that has shown good success with internalizing disorders is cognitive behavioral therapy (CBT), and has been related to changes in the brain due to *neuroplasticity* (Schwartz & Begley, 2002). In other words, teaching children to reinterpret traumatic or stressful experiences in a more positive and adaptive fashion can actually alter brain chemistry. For instance, Felmingham et al. (2007) discovered that changes to the amygdala and the anterior cingulate occurred after providing CBT in patients who suffered from Post-Traumatic Stress Disorder (PTSD). For further review of the merits of CBT, see the works of Aaron Beck, Albert Ellis, and Donald Meichenbaum.

Additionally, it is important for school personnel to be cognizant of students with anxiety disorders, and to create a learning environment sensitive to the needs of these students. For instance, creating "safety zones" in class or throughout the school environment can help students reduce their stress, as well as providing a mentor or coach who can periodically check in with the student. Clearly, providing counseling services and having the student work in a stress management group with the school counselor is important as well. Consideration of modifying homework demands, such as shortening the number of problems, refraining from calling on these students unexpectedly to read aloud or perform a problem on the board, and constantly reinforcing independent work completion can be beneficial as well. Keeping these considerations in mind will allow the school psychologist, teacher, counselor, administrator, and parent to best advocate for the child with internalizing disorders. Table 9-3 summarizes the interventions for students with internalizing disorders.

TABLE 9-3
Internalizing Disorders Interventions

- Use of medication for depression or anxiety (SSRI, NRI, SNRI, SARI, NaSSA – see chp 7 for more details)
- Cognitive Behavior Techniques
- Other counseling techniques including stress management, relaxation, systematic desensitization, etc.
- Modify demands of homework and classroom setup to accommodate for the student with internalizing disorders.

SUMMARY

The worlds of education and special education have sought to categorize students into discrete categories with an assumption that each has its own exclusive venue for assessment and intervention and that etiologies (or causes) do not overlap. As can be seen, neuropsychological dysfunctions can impact both social-emotional as well as academic success. Hopefully, by becoming more cognizant of how various brain functions can impact social-emotional development and achievement, specific interventions can be tailored to meet the needs of each student.

REFERENCES

Arnett, P., Higginson, C., Voss, W., Bender, W., Wurst, J., & Tippin, J. (1999). Depression in multiple sclerosis: Relationship to working memory capacity. *Neuropsychology, 13*(4), 546-556.

Barkley, R. A. (1998). *Attention Deficit Hyperactivity Disorder: A handbook for diagnosis and treatment-second edition.* New York: Guilford Press.

Baxter, J., & Rattan, G. (2004). Attention deficit disorder and the internalizing dimension in males, ages 9-0 through 11-11. *International Journal of Neuroscience, 114*, 817-832.

Breggin, P. (1991). T*oxic psychiatry: Why therapy, empathy and love must replace the drugs, electroshock, and biochemical theories of the "new psychiatry".* New York: Author.

Bull, R., & Scerif, G. (2001). Executive functioning as a predictor of children's mathematics ability: Inhibition, switching, and working memory. *Developmental Neuropsychology, 19*(3), 273-293.

Bush, G., Spencer, T., Holmes, J., Shin, L., Valera, E., Seidman, L., et al. (2008). Functional magnetic resonance imaging of methylphenidate and placebo in attention-deficit/hyperactivity disorder during the multi-source interference task. *Archives of General Psychiatry, 65*(1), 102-114.

Casey, J., Rourke, B., & Picard, E. (1991). Syndrome of nonverbal learning disabilities: Age differences in neuropsychological, academic, and socioemotional functioning. *Development and Psychopathology, 3*(3), 329-345.

Censabella, S., & Noël, M. (2008). The inhibition capacities of children with mathematical disabilities. *Child Neuropsychology, 14*(1), 1-20.

Connolly. A.J. (1988). *KeyMath - revised.* Circle Pines, MN: American Guidance Service.

Deno, S. L. (2002). Problem solving as "best practice." In A. Thomas & J. Grimes (Eds.), *Best practices in school psychology IV* (pp. 37-56). Bethesda, MD: National Association of School Psychologists.

Feeney, T., & Ylvisaker, M. (2006). Context-sensitive cognitive-behavioural supports for young children with TBI: A replication study. *Brain Injury, 20*(6), 629-645.

Feifer, S. G., & DeFina, P. D. (2002). *The neuropsychology of written language disorders: Diagnosis and intervention.* School Neuropsych Press: Middletown, MD.

Feifer, S.G., & Rattan, G. (2007). Executive functioning skills in male students with social-emotional disorders. *International Journal of Neuroscience, 117*, 1565-1577.

Felmingham, K., Kemp, A., Williams, L., Das, P., Hughes, G., Peduto, A., et al. (2007). Changes in anterior cingulate and amygdala after cognitive behavior therapy of Posttraumatic Stress Disorder. *Psychological Science, 18*(2), 127-129.

Forrest, B. (2004). The utility of math difficulties, internalized psychopathology, and visual-spatial deficits to identify children with the Nonverbal Learning Disability Syndrome: Evidence for a visualspatial disability. *Child Neuropsychology, 10*(2), 129-146.

Giancola, P. R., Mezzich, A. C., & Tarter, R. E. (1998). Executive cognitive functioning, temperament, and antisocial behavior in conduct disordered females. *Journal of Abnormal Psychology, 107*(4), 629-641.

Gioia, G. A., Isquith, P. K., Guy, S. C., & Kenworthy, L. (2000). *Behavior rating inventory of executive functioning: Professional manual.* Odessa, Florida: Psychological Assessment Resources.

Goldberg, E. (2002). *Executive brain: Frontal lobes and the civilized mind.* New York: Oxford University Press.

Gordon, W., Cantor, J., Ashman, T., & Brown, M. (2006). Treatment of post-TBI executive dysfunction: Application of theory to clinical practice. *Journal of Head Trauma Rehabilitation, 21*(2), 156-167.

Gray, C. (2000). The new social story book: Illustrated edition. Arlington, TX: Future Horizons.

Greenberg, M. (2006). Promoting resilience in children and youth. *Annals of the New York Academy of Sciences, 1094*(1), 139-150.

Greenham, S. (1999). Learning disabilities and psychosocial adjustment: A critical review. *Child Neuropsychology, 5*(3), 171-196.

Hale, J.B. & Fiorello, C.A. (2004). *School neuropsychology: A practitioner's handbook.* New York: Guilford.

Hale, J., Kaufman, A., Naglieri, J., & Kavale, K. (2006). Implementation of IDEA: Integrating response to intervention and cognitive assessment methods. *Psychology in the Schools, 43*(7), 753-770.

Hammill, D.D., & Larsen, S.C. (1996). *The test of written language* (3rd Ed.). Austin, TX: Pro-Ed.

Individuals with Disabilities Education Improvement Act of 2004. (PL No. 108-446, 20 USC 1400).

Jacob, S. & Hartshorne, T.S. (2007). *Ethics and law for school psychologists* (5th Ed.). New York: John Wiley & Sons.

Kovaleski, J., Gickling, E., Morrow, H., & Swank, P. (1999). High versus low implementation of instructional support teams: A case for maintaining program fidelity. *Remedial and Special Education, 20*(3), 170-183.

Kusche, C., Cook, E., & Greenberg, M. (1993). Neuropsychological and cognitive functioning in children with anxiety, externalizing, and comorbid psychopathology. *Journal of Clinical Child Psychology, 22*(2), 172.

Levin, R., Heller, W., Mohanty, A., Herrington, J., & Miller, G. (2007). Cognitive deficits in depression and functional specificity of regional brain activity. *Cognitive Therapy & Research, 31*(2), 211-233.

Lezak, M. (1982). The problem of assessing executive functions. *International Journal of Psychology, 17*(2/3), 281.

Mayfield-Arnold, E., Goldston, D., Walsh, A., Reboussin, B., Sergent Daniel, S., Hickman, E., et al. (2005). Severity of Emotional and Behavioral Problems Among Poor and Typical Readers. *Journal of Abnormal Child Psychology, 33*(2), 205-217.

Mazzocco, M., & Kover, S. (2007). A longitudinal assessment of executive function skills and their association with math performance. *Child Neuropsychology, 13*(1), 18-45.

Miller, D.C. (2007). *Essentials of school neuropsychological assessment.* New York: Wiley.

Morgan, A. B., & Lilienfeld, S. O. (2000). A meta-analytic review of the relation between antisocial behavior and neuropsychological measures of executive functions. *Clinical Psychology Review, 20*(1), 113-136.

Office of Special Programs (2008). *OSEP Technical Assistance Center on Positive Behavioral Interventions and Supports.* Retrieved May 27, 2008 from http://www.pbis.org.

Petti, V., Voelker, S., Shore, D., & Hayman-Abello, S. (2003). Perception of nonverbal emotion cues by children with nonverbal learning disabilities. *Journal of Developmental & Physical Disabilities, 15*(1), 23-36.

Rees, L., Marshall, S., Hartridge, C., Mackie, D., & Weiser, M. (2007). *Cognitive interventions post acquired brain injury. Brain Injury, 21*(2), 161-200.

Reschly, D. J. (2005). Learning disabilities identification: Primary intervention, secondary intervention, and then what? *Journal of Learning Disabilities, 38*(6), 510-515.

Reschly, D. J., & Ysseldyke, J. E. (2002). Paradigm shift: The past is not the future. In A. Thomas & J. Grimes (Eds.), *Best practices in school psychology IV* (pp. 3-20). Bethesda, MD: National Association of School Psychologists.

Reynolds, C. R., & Kamphaus, R. W. (1992). *Behavior assessment system for children.* MN: American Guidance Services, Inc.

Reynolds, C. R., & Richmond, B. O. (1985). *Revised children's manifest anxiety scale.* DA: Western Psychological Services.

Riccio, C., Homack, S., Jarratt, K., & Wolfe, M. (2006). Differences in academic and executive function domains among children with ADHD Predominantly Inattentive and Combined Types. *Archives of Clinical Neuropsychology, 21*(7), 657-667.

Rourke, B. (2005). Neuropsychology of learning disabilities: Past and future. *Learning Disability Quarterly, 28*(2), 111-114.

Rourke, B. (2000). Neuropsychological and psychosocial subtyping: A review of investigations within the University of Windsor laboratory. *Canadian Psychology/Psychologie Canadienne, 41*(1), 34-51.

Savage, R., Cornish, K., Manly, T., & Hollis, C. (2006). Cognitive processes in children's reading and attention: The role of working memory, divided attention, and response inhibition. *British Journal of Psychology, 97*(3), 365-385.

Schwartz, J.M. & Begley, S. (2002). *The mind & the brain: Neuroplasticity and the power of mental force*. New York: HarperCollins.

Shure, M.B. (1992). *I can problem solve*. Champaign, IL: Research Press.

Stahl, S. M. (2000). *Essential psychopharmacology: Neuroscientific basis and practical applications* (2nd ed.). New York: Cambridge University Press.

Stahl, S. M. (2008). *Stahl's essential psychopharmacology: Neuroscientific basis and practical applications* (3rd ed.). New York: Cambridge University Press.

Wechsler, D. (2001). *The Wechsler Individual Achievement Test-2nd Edition*. San Antonio, TX: The Psychological Corporation.

Watkins, M.W., Glutting, J.J., & Youngstrom, E.A. (2005). Issues in subtest profile analysis. In D. Flanagan & P. Harrison (Eds.), *Contemporary intellectual assessment: Theories, tests, and issues* (2nd Ed, pp. 251-268). New York: Guilford.

Willcutt, E., Pennington, B., Olson, R., Chhabildas, N., & Hulslander, J. (2005). Neuropsychological analyses of comorbidity between reading disability and Attention Deficit Hyperactivity Disorder: In search of the common deficit. *Developmental Neuropsychology, 27*(1), 35-78.

Wodka, E., Mahone, E., Blankner, J., Larson, J., Fotedar, S., Denckla, M., et al. (2007). Evidence that response inhibition is a primary deficit in ADHD. *Journal of Clinical and Experimental Neuropsychology, 29*(4), 345-356.

Ylvisaker, M., & Feeney, T. (2002). Executive functions, self-regulation, and learned optimism in pediatric rehabilitation: a review and implications for intervention. *Pediatric Rehabilitation, 5*(2), 51-70.

CHAPTER 10

BEST PRACTICES IN THE ASSESSMENT OF EMOTIONAL DISORDERS

Amy Gabel, Ph.D.

"The human brain is generally regarded as a complex web of adaptations built into the nervous system, even though no one knows how."

—Michael S. Gazzaniga

The purpose of this chapter will be to outline a specific protocol to assist educators and clinicians in developing an assessment plan for students with emotional disorders. Without proper diagnosis or description of needs, key elements may be ignored in the development of behavioral intervention plans used to assist students with emotional difficulties function more adequately in a classroom setting. Consequently, a well-conceived assessment plan is imperative so that proper areas of emotional functioning are properly evaluated, with interventions targeted toward specific needs. The following vignette portrays a referral not uncommon in the school setting:

Vignette #1: Sam continues to exhibit: a) problems paying attention; b) difficulty focusing on salient material in class; c) difficulty following directions; d) problems with recall and following through on tasks; and e) completion of homework in a sloppy manner. In addition, Sam also: a) seems lost or confused; b) makes the same mistakes over and over again; c) distracts the class; d) has emotional outbursts; e) appears bored and disinterested in classroom activities; f) wants to be in control; and g) reacts impulsively.

Based upon this vignette, many hypotheses could be developed regarding why Sam may be experiencing such an array of difficulties in the classroom. Clearly, if educators or school psychologists attempted to write a behavior intervention plan for each of the areas or symptoms described above, it would make for a rather complex and convoluted intervention. Furthermore, if each symptom were addressed in a behavior plan, no understanding would be gained regarding the underlying cause of the behavior dysfunction. Consequently, without the underlying cause being identified, only temporary relief may be achieved from treating each symptom, and it is likely that the behaviors will either return or be replaced by another maladaptive response in time.

In previous chapters, readers were familiarized with the foundations of the neurological systems underscoring emotional disorders. These neurological foundations should always be considered when an assessment plan is developed. As noted in the groundbreaking work of Luria (1973), the human brain is the seat of all learning and behavior, and is made up of a series highly integrated, complex systems. Therefore, when one system is compromised, the functioning and development of most other systems are compromised as well. For instance, if a student has a dysfunction related to frontal lobe functioning (i.e., difficulties with regulation, poor inhibitory capabilities, etc.), then other systems, may also be affected. While our initial impression may be that the impact will be a negative, we also know that because of the plasticity of the human brain, particularly for younger students, major problems in daily functioning may not necessarily occur. Rather, because neurons are still in the process of being committed for specific functions in younger children, there is greater opportunity for some functions to be adopted by, or compensated for, in other systems before those uncommitted neurons become more specialized or circuit redundancies are created (Kandel, Schwartz, & Jessell, 2001; Neville & Bavelier, 2000).

Because of the inter-relatedness among various neurological systems, assessment should involve multiple measures of behavioral and emotional functioning, answering specific questions relevant to the current situational demands under which the child must function. Therefore, the specific tools or methods selected by the examiner must take into account critical factors such as: a) who made the referral; b) the type of school setting in which the student is placed; c) precipitating factors upon which the referral was made; d) past assessment data; and e) the current challenges/situations which the student will face. Therefore, it is imperative that multiple sources of information be collected to evaluate all facets of an apparent emotional disorder. As will be described, a comprehensive evaluation using the best practices of assessment involves much more than a simple evaluation of emotion and behavior via the completion of a single behavior rating scale.

KEY LEARNING POINTS: Assessment

1. Proper assessment helps to identify interventions that are tailored to meet the needs of the individual.
2. Any assessment should take into account best practices, which always entails gathering multiple pieces of data through multiple means and sources.

The fundamental aim of this chapter is to present relevant information related to planning and conducting assessments for students with emotional disorders. Consequently, there will be a decreased emphasis on the linkage of tests or test results to specific areas or systems of the brain. Rather, a series of questions or areas of functioning will be explored to assist psychologists in planning their evaluations. Specific constructs to investigate include social and emotional skills, executive functioning (i.e., elements of attention, self-regulation, self-monitoring, etc.), language skills, and other processing capabilities highlighted later in the text. Examples of evaluation tools will also be presented in the areas described. It is important to note that tables highlighting sample instruments are not meant to be exhaustive; rather, they are provided as a starting point for practitioners seeking measures in these areas. Not only is the diagnosis of emotional disorders complex, there is also tremendous co-morbidity between emotional disorders and other learning conditions (Martinez & Semrud-Clikeman, 2004). Consequently, it is important that other conditions be ruled out via proper assessment tools when a student is evaluated for social and emotional concerns.

Response to Intervention (RTI): Tier I Measures

Response to Intervention or Instruction (RTI) has been primarily applied to early reading skills, and to some extent early math difficulties, though several important concepts are relevant to emotional disorders. First, the underlying components of RTI processes; namely, universal screening and data collection for all students should be applied to cases involving suspected social and emotional disorders (Gresham, 1991). A critical component of RTI is determining which screening measures to use to appropriately measure behavioral and emotional constructs so that early intervention may be provided. Studies have shown that students with mild disabilities often exhibit difficulties with basic social and affective skills (Gresham & MacMillan, 1997). Clearly, research has demonstrated that behavioral interventions provided sooner, rather than later, are ultimately more successful (Lyon, Fletcher, Shaywitz, Shaywitz, Torgesen, & Wood, 2001; Torgesen, Alexander, Wagner, Rashotte, Voeller, & Conroy, 2001; Chrisophersen & Mortweet, 2001; Kratochwill, Elliott, & Busse, 1995). Furthermore, early interventions are ultimately a cost effective way to provide treatment since it is easier to ameliorate a mild behavioral problem before maladaptive emotional patterns become ingrained and evolve into major issues. This is particularly important for students with emotional and behavioral issues, as their interactions with peers and adults will necessarily impact how others in the environment respond to them. Most clinicians and educators who have worked with students with behavioral challenges realize a vicious circle can develop when the student continues to have negative behaviors reinforced as a result of maladaptive social interaction systems.

However, it is not only important to conduct early screenings to detect behavioral difficulties, but it is equally vital to screen for the presence of adaptive capabilities related to social competence (Stoiber, 2004; Guralnick, 1990). These skills include behaviors such as exhibiting self-control, in addition to social cooperation. In previous chapters, the complexity of many neurological systems comprising the emotional brain centers were discussed, including a relatively new area of research related to mirror neurons. If we are to link research to practice and consider the ramifications of these mirror neurons, then early intervention and exposure to age-appropriate peers modeling prosocial behaviors will be critical toward developing long-term success for students with emotional and behavioral challenges.

One of the important keys to a successful universal screening program is the effective use of school-based resources to address the needs of small groups of students that may be identified as having social and emotional needs. The importance of early detection enables one to capitalize on the strengths that may exist within a student's overall behavioral profile. Although an exhaustive list of behavioral measures will not be provided, a few are listed below that can be used to screen or benchmark larger numbers of students (see Table 10-1).

TABLE 10-1
Universal Screening Tools

TOOL	AGE RANGE	AUTHOR(S)
Reynolds Bully and Victimization Scales	Grades 3-12	William Reynolds
BASC-2 Behavioral and Emotional Screening System (BESS)	Preschool – Grade 12	Randy Kamphaus, Cecil Reynolds
Social Skills Improvement System (SSIS) Performance Screening Guide/SSIS Family	Preschool through Secondary	Stephen Elliott, Frank Gresham
Functional Assessment and Intervention System (Social Competence Performance Checklist)	Children and Adolescents	Karen Stoiber

Another important component of RTI paradigms is monitoring the effectiveness of interventions (i.e., student progress). Progress monitoring is especially important for students with emotional disorders in order to adequately assess the course of treatment and interventions. Examples of brief assessment instruments that may be used for progress monitoring of social and emotional conditions are shared in Table 10-2.

TABLE 10-2
Progress Monitoring Tools

MEASURE	AGE RANGE	PROGRESS MONITOR AREA(S)	AUTHOR(S)
Beck Youth Inventory, Second Edition (BYI-II)	7-18	Discrete behavioral or emotional skills (anger, depression, etc.)	Judith S. Beck, Aaron T. Beck, John B. Jolly
Functional Assessment and Intervention System (FAIS)	Children and Adolescents	Decrease of challenging behaviors; increase of prosocial behavior	Karen Stoiber
BASC Progress Monitor (in press)	Children and Adolescents	Decrease of challenging behaviors; increase of prosocial behavior	Cecil Reynolds, Randy Kamphaus
Social Skills Improvement System – SSIS (family of products)	3-19	Social Skills Improvement	Stephen Elliott & Frank Gresham

Utilizing an RTI method of tiered interventions often requires additional data collection besides simple screening measures. If it is necessary to conduct further diagnostic assessments to pinpoint appropriate interventions, the assessment areas and instruments described later in this chapter may also prove helpful. As our assessment practices change with RTI, it will be important for examiners to think differently about the purpose of their assessments, and what questions they are attempting to answer. If a student's behavioral and/or emotional functioning is such that more specialized interventions need to be pursued, data collected as part of an RTI process should naturally be incorporated into the comprehensive assessment. Hopefully, the additional data will provide important insights into how a student has already responded to attempted interventions, and assist in developing new interventions as well.

There is little doubt that when concerns are presented regarding a student's social and emotional functioning, the consequences of *"doing nothing"* can be dire. Therefore, regardless of whether eligibility for special education services is one of the assessment goals, there are many questions to be addressed by an evaluation that may prove highly relevant for social success in both the school and home environment. For instance, the results of more targeted diagnostic measures can yield important intervention information within an RTI environment. This is particularly true when there is an emphasis placed on understanding *why* a symptom is occurring, and not just providing a standard response to the behavior without really understanding its foundation. Consequently, it is suggested that practitioners think broadly about the purposes behind their assessments, and choose assessment tools accordingly.

Tier 2: The Importance of Interview and Observation

When developing an assessment protocol to engage in a more "individual" or problem solving approach, it is extremely helpful to receive referrals that contain specific examples related to the referring source's concerns. Then, detailed questions may be formed by the clinician through the development of an appropriate assessment protocol. This stage is usually referred to Tier 2 within an RTI model of service delivery. The first step for clinicians is to observe the student in multiple environments and interview key teachers and caregivers as part of the evaluation process. Observation and interview data provide crucial information to assist in the refinement of referral questions, thus narrowing the scope of the testing process, and leading to better intervention suggestions. Furthermore, observations of students in their natural environment also assist clinicians in understanding behavioral manifestations within certain contextual settings, rather than over-relying on the opinion of others through rating scale information. Although an observation or interview may be considered an extra step, it ultimately may save time by helping the clinician narrow or refine the scope of the questions to be answered by the assessment, thus decreasing the number of instruments that must be used and the time required for testing. Consider the following vignette:

Vignette #2: Michael has been previously evaluated, and receives special education services for students with emotional disabilities. Although Michael has cognitive abilities in the Superior range, he continues to experience behavioral difficulties in the classroom. Recently, his aggressive behaviors have escalated, particularly toward some of the less capable students in the classroom. When Michael participates in the general education classroom, fewer behavioral difficulties are noted, though he produces little to no work and often lacks the organization and planning skills for meaningful learning to occur.

A number of referral questions could be generated from the aforementioned vignette, all of which may lead to the development of an appropriate assessment protocol. Clearly, there are a number of reasons why Michael's aggressive behavior could be intensifying, and include: a) Michael has been diagnosed with bipolar disorder and is cycling through a difficult phase; b) the class has been preparing for high stakes testing to occur shortly after the holiday break; c) Michael is avoiding a particular task that he dislikes; and/or d) another student in the classroom is provoking Michael, prompting him to react in an aggressive manner.

In order to pinpoint the nature of Michael's behavioral difficulties, the school psychologist observed Michael in two different educational settings and noticed that his aggressive behaviors appeared to increase when asked to complete writing assignments. For instance, he was observed listening attentively to lectures, but took no notes, rarely participated in verbal discussions, and interacted little with peers. Furthermore, Michael often came unprepared to class, appeared bored and disinterested, and often needed to borrow materials from his classmates. He rarely participated in tasks and activities that involved writing without extensive prompting. In fact, the process of writing appeared somewhat slow and laborious for him, with limited output noted. Michael was quick to *show off* how much he knew about a particular topic when directly queried by his teacher, and spoke in a rather loud manner as if attempting to impress his peers as well.

Based upon these observations, the clinician developed a battery of assessment measures that tapped cognitive skills, language skills, executive functioning skills, visual perceptual and fine motor skills, and emotional functioning as well. The assessment battery was primarily focused on the hypotheses generated based upon the referral question, classroom observations, and practical considerations all clinicians should adhere to when conducting school based evaluations. In other words, targeted assessments should focus on the skill areas in question, and not overburden children nor remove them from their academic learning environment for an undo period of time. Based on the overall assessment, the clinician arrived at the following conclusions:

1. Michael's overall cognitive skills were very strong.
2. Michael's fine motor skills were interfering with written language output.
3. Michael has noted executive functioning difficulty with task initiation, organization and planning skills which may be hindering writing as well.
4. Michael had difficulty with auditory working memory tasks.

Further assessment suggested that Michael's frustration in class often became intensified due to a constellation of cognitive factors hindering written language output. Michael had difficulty organizing and planning his thoughts long enough for the execution of an output response requiring fine motor coordination. His low frustration tolerance and emotional impulsivity usually led to frequent behavioral outbursts in class. Since the clinician was able to focus the assessment protocol on addressing key cognitive areas and obtaining targeted information relevant to Michael's situation in the classroom and at home, several specific interventions were implemented in the classroom. Many of the targeted interventions addressed Michael's fine motor weaknesses, as well as the use of graphic organizers, story maps, and computer technology to circumvent his fine motor deficits. Both occupational therapy and counseling services were recommended as well.

Due to the complexity in understanding behavior and emotion, the above vignette underscores the importance of assessing the underlying reasons contributing to the behaviors observed in class.

Simply attempting to deal with behaviors without investigating the underlying causes would likely not have led to long-term success. Clearly, one of the important lessons from neuropsychology is how the disruptions in one system can affect the operation of other systems. Although Michael's case is complex, at a very basic level, not only was he trying to protect a fairly fragile sense of self, he was also reacting to the frustration associated with the difficulties he experienced when forming letters and numbers in an accurate and efficient manner. Although fine motor output is a relatively low-level skill, it still must be developed to automaticity in order to facilitate the production of more complex sentences and paragraphs. Michael knew he was bright, and could not comprehend why he was unable to put his thoughts on paper. Furthermore, he was mad at himself for not being able to write as accurately and efficiently as peers, and livid at his classmates because they did not present with similar difficulties. Had Michael not experienced other emotional challenges, he may have been able to compensate more effectively with either accommodations in writing on his own, or experience a less intense, more appropriate reaction to his difficulties.

Tier 3: Assessment of Executive Functions

The case of Michael provides a suitable introduction to executive functioning as one of the major areas that should be considered in a comprehensive evaluation for students who have or are suspected to have social and emotional disorders. One of the primary reasons why executive function skills should be assessed is that difficulties in self-regulation (a component of executive functioning) can cause major problems for students in both classroom and community settings. Self-regulatory disorders often affect a student's capability to deal effectively with noise, emotion, thoughts, moods, actions, pain, feelings, and sensation. Greene's (1998) work on the "explosive child" provides outstanding examples of the chaos and turmoil that can occur when emotional and behavioral self-regulation is lacking in children. Since regulatory difficulties so clearly impact the expression of social and emotional disorders, they, and other related executive functioning constructs are critically important to assess with students experiencing these concerns.

It is important to note that executive functioning skills are not a unitary construct, but rather are a constellation of several overarching behaviors used to manage cognitive and emotional functioning (Stuss & Benson, 1997). These include planning and sequencing of complex behaviors; the ability to pay attention to several components at once; the capacity for grasping the gist of a complex situation; resistance to distraction and interference; inhibition of inappropriate response tendencies; and the ability to sustain behavioral output for relatively prolonged periods of time. Welsh and Pennington (1988) define executive functioning as the ability to maintain an appropriate problem-solving set for attainment of future goals involving one or more of the following: a) intention to inhibit/defer response; b) strategic plan of action sequences; c) mental representation of the task including relevant stimulus information and desired future goal state. When observed in the classroom, most educators see executive dysfunction manifested as difficulties with initiating and executing (getting things started and paced appropriately from start to finish), goal setting, planning (educational tasks as well as behaviors), and prioritizing, inhibiting, organizing, and shifting flexibly from one course of action or thought to another.

Clearly, there are serious behavioral consequences for students who have relatively poor executive functioning skills; therefore, all assessment protocols should include a screening of executive function capabilities. Regardless of whether emotions and actions are directed inward or outward, the consequences of making an impulsive decision, or being unable to inhibit an impulse can be

KEY LEARNING POINTS: Executive Functioning and Emotional Disorders

- Executive functioning skills are not a unitary construct, but rather are a constellation of several overarching behaviors used to manage cognitive and emotional functioning (Stuss & Benson, 1997).
- According to Moffit and Lynam (1994), students with poor executive functioning skills often have significant behavioral concerns for three primary reasons.
  1. They have difficulty learning from environmental consequences, and may not comprehend the negative impact of their behavior on others.
  2. These students may demonstrate relative poor working memory skills, rendering them vulnerable to sustaining abstract ideas about ethical values and future rewards when confronted with a compromising situation.
  3. Lastly, students low in *executive functioning* skills may have difficulty adapting their behavior to changing social circumstances.

disastrous. In many situations, either the referral source or the precipitating event will provide insight to the psychologist regarding the severity of concerns. Should screening measures reveal that executive dysfunction is present, additional evaluations will most likely be warranted.

Vignette #3: Larry is sitting in his 6th grade social studies class. Instead of going through the last minute preparations for an upcoming geography presentation with his classmates, he becomes distracted by his teacher setting up a computer to prepare for the next lesson. While staring at his teacher, he inadvertently knocks his notebook off of his desk just as his nemesis, Jerry, walks by. Quite naturally, Jerry believes that Larry has intentionally thrown a book at him, and immediately retorts using inappropriate language. Upon hearing the inappropriate remark, his teacher glances upward and immediately chastises Jerry for his vulgar language and warns him that his next classroom infraction will cost him recess for the day. Jerry becomes enraged at the unfairness of his teacher's accusation, and immediately begins to scream at his teacher in an uncontrolled manner. Needless to say, recess is lost for the day.

There are many false assumptions and incorrect accusations in the aforementioned vignette causing Jerry to make a snap judgment and formulate a maladaptive response, and the situation escalates from there. This example magnifies the importance of executive functioning skills being such a critical component in the evaluation of social and emotional disorders. Simply put, regardless of what may have caused Jerry to assume that the book was deliberately thrown at him (i.e., low self-esteem, oppositional-defiant- disorder, depression, etc.), it is Jerry's inability to evaluate the accuracy of his perceptions, response, and subsequent overreaction that lead to a relatively innocuous classroom situation escalating to an explosive meltdown.

Previous research (Moffit & Lynam, 1994; Barkley, 2001) has suggested that *executive functioning* skills are of critical importance for establishing and maintaining socially appropriate interactions within a classroom setting, by allowing students to self-monitor emotional impulses and regulate motoric processes in order for successful adaptation to their learning environment. Furthermore, measurable deficits in executive functioning skills may be extremely important in determining specific modes of treatment for children with behavioral difficulties. Therefore, executive functioning is important not only for understanding Jerry's emotional reactions within the classroom setting, but also for understanding the types of interventions that may produce the greatest benefit. For instance, if counseling/therapeutic interventions were provided to Jerry, it would not be terribly effective simply to work with him on identifying alternative interpretations, or choose from among more adaptive responses. Rather, he would need to take a more behavioral approach by first working on stopping and thinking in less emotionally charged situations, and then receive guided practice in using these skills in the day-to-day classroom environment via coaching and signaling. According to Barkley (2001), effective school performance requires, in part, successful social and emotional management through a milieu of interpersonal encounters and challenges.

TABLE 10-3
Key Questions to Answer by Measuring Executive Functioning

Key questions that may be answered via assessment of executive functioning.
1. Are there difficulties in thinking flexibly about options for problem solving?
2. What kinds of structure seem to benefit the student's problem-solving?
3. Is the student able to resist impulses?
4. Does the student perseverate on problem-solving activities?
5. Can the student regulate (manage) their responses to difficult situations?
6. Does the student use clues or feedback when problem-solving?
7. Can the student sustain attention during boring tasks?
8. Is the student able to establish plans to achieve short- or long-term goals?

There are a number of tools, procedures, and methods for evaluating executive functioning in children, though best practices usually involve a combination of instruments used in a multimodal format. Although rating scales and checklists offer a quick and easy method of evaluation, there are limitations associated with their use. Obviously, one of the greatest limitations of behavior rating scales such as the BRIEF is that ratings are always provided through the filter of the observer. Suppose Jerry continued to exhibit behavioral outbursts in class, then perhaps a *"reverse halo effect"* might occur causing the teacher (rater) to have an overall negative perception of him. Unfortunately, there are times where students who are chronically disruptive in the classroom present such a challenge to the instructional process that teachers become frustrated and quite naturally lose their objectivity. Therefore, a chronically disruptive student with many behavioral challenges is often rated more negatively than students who are more reserved and less disruptive. In order to minimize rater biasness, it is essential that clinicians collect rating scales from more than one teacher in more than one setting, in addition to input from parents as well. Collecting data from more than one source is beneficial so that the expectations associated with environments in which the child performs well can be compared to those environments in which difficulties are encountered. Students may perform better in some environments because a greater degree of structure is offered or there are fewer demands for certain types of *"difficult to perform"* behaviors. Additionally, collecting data from multiple raters helps to counterbalance different levels of tolerance and expectations that influence our perceptions of children.

It is good practice to not only directly measure executive functioning through assessment instruments, but also use observational based rating scales in conjunction with these performance-based measures. Barkley (2001) defined executive functioning skills as a set of mind tools that greatly facilitated adaptive behavior functioning during real world encounters. Therefore, behavior ratings of executive functioning, such as the BRIEF checklist, may be particularly useful when examining executive functioning skills within a classroom context. Given the numerous elements of executive functioning, there are many choices among instruments in this area to further evaluate organization and planning capabilities, flexibility in thinking, working memory, emotional self-control, behavioral inhibition, attentional capacity, and the like. Table 10-4 provides a list of some of the most commonly used assessments to evaluate elements of executive functioning and attention.

TABLE 10-4
Measures of Executive Functioning

TOOL	AGE RANGE	AUTHORS(S)	ASSESSMENT TYPE
Delis-Kaplan Executive Function Scale (DKEFS)	8-89	Dean C. Delis, Edith Kaplan, Joel H. Kramer	Performance-based measure
Wisconsin Card Sort Test	6.5-89	David A. Grant & Esta Berg	Performance-based measure
WCST Computer Version 4 Research Edition	6.5-89	Robert K. Heaton	Performance-based measure
NEPSY-II	3-16	Marit Korkman, Ursula Kirk, Sally Kemp	Performance-based measure
Behavior Rating Inventory of Executive Function (BRIEF, BRIEF-P, BRIEF SP)	2.5-adult	Gerald Gioia, Peter Isquith, Steven Guy, Lauren Kenworthy	Rating Scale
Brown ADD Scales	3-adult	Thomas E. Brown	Rating Scale
TEACh	6-16	Tom Manly, Ian H. Robertson, Vicki Anderson, Ian Nimmo-Smith	Performance-based measure
Luria-Nebraska Neuropsychological Battery (LNNB), LNNB Children's Revision	15 and up (LNNB), 8-12 (LNNB-C)	Charles J. Golden, Arnold D. Purisch, Thomas Hammeke	Performance-based
Stroop Color and Word Test (Adult and Child Forms)	5-14 and 15 and up	Charles J. Golden, Shawna M. Freshwater	Performance-based
Conners Continuous Performance Test II Version 5 (Kiddie Version also available)	6 and up, Kiddie version 4-5	C. Keith Conners	Performance-based
Test of Variables of Attention (TOVA)	4-80	Lawrence Greenberg, Robert A. Leark, Tammy R. Dupuy, Clifford L. Corman, Carol L. Kindschi, Michael Cenedela	Performance-based
Tower of London DX 2nd Edition	7 and up	William C. Culbertson, Eric Zillmer	Performance-based
Halstead-Reitan Category Test (computerized version preferred)	9-14	Ralph Reitan	Performance-based

Assessment of Language Functions

Based on the evolution of the brain, we know that higher cortical functions have developed to mediate the understanding and expression of emotion. One of these higher functions is the application of language to emotion. Specifically, both internal and external language may mediate both the perception and expression of emotion. Furthermore, numerous studies have documented the relationship between language deficits and social and emotional difficulties (Marton, Abramoff, & Rosenzweig, 2005; Fujiki, Brinton, Morgan, & Hart, 1999; Craig, 1993). According to Stuss and Levine (2002), verbal retrieval skills allow students to both rehearse and develop alternative strategies for uncompromising situations. In essence, verbal abilities are essential toward developing behavioral self-control.

Language difficulties are not only observed in receptive and expressive capabilities, but also in an important area of social language called pragmatics. Pragmatics involves the understanding of the subtle aspects of communication such as understanding language in: context, irony, sarcasm, and how attributes such as tone, facial expression and gesture influence meaning. Social language is one form of pragmatic capabilities, and relates directly to a student's capability to interact with others. Table 10-5 details important social components of pragmatic language.

TABLE 10-5
Social Components of Pragmatic Language

Social language includes important skills such as:

- turn-taking during conversations;
- attention to and understanding of non-verbal cues such as gestures and facial expressions;
- the ability to initiate conversation on a topic;
- the ability to maintain conversation and provide elaboration on a topic;
- the ability to change topics in conversations appropriately; and
- the ability to appropriately end conversations.

Clearly, students who have deficits in the above areas will be at a disadvantage in most social encounters at school. It is important to assess these skills so an appropriate intervention plan can be tailored toward specific needs. If a student continues to experience deficits in key social and pragmatic language skills, then despite all of the behavioral programming that is implemented, the student will continue to manifest a core language deficit hindering social success.

In addition to social pragmatic language, there is another subcategory of language-related skills that can have a dramatic impact on social and emotional functioning, namely, *"theory of mind."* Theory of mind refers to an individual's ability to understand and reflect on other people's mental states, emotions, and intentions. It involves understanding that another person can exhibit thoughts and beliefs that are different from one's own. Theory of mind involves, above all else, perspective taking. In the second vignette involving Michael, he may have lacked some of the core characteristics associated with this construct, since his affective/social recognition capabilities were somewhat compromised. During treatment for emotional disorders, it is important that affect recognition and the ability to take the perspective of another be considered for evaluation. When deficits in this area are uncovered during assessment, critical information relevant to the length and content of treatment is gained. Specifically, treatment will need to begin at a much more basic level, and be comprised of more direct instruction if affect recognition and perspective-taking remain problematic. Just as in academics, many students acquire these skills during incidental learning experiences at home and in the classroom. However, those students who have compromised skills in these areas will most likely need explicit training and instruction. Table 10-6 illustrates some of the common instruments used to assess language-related capabilities of affect recognition and social perception skills.

TABLE 10-6
Language Measures

MEASURE	AGE RANGE	AREAS ASSESSED	AUTHOR(S)
Clinical Evaluation of Language Fundamentals – Fourth Edition (CELF-4), CELF Preschool 2	5-21	Overall Language, including pragmatics	Elisabeth H. Wiig, Wayne A. Secord, Eleanor Semel
CASL	3-0 to 21-11	Overall Language	Elizabeth Carrow-Woolfolk
Children's Communication Checklist-2 (CCC-2)	4-0 to 16-11	Social Language	Dorothy Bishop
OWLS: Oral and Written Language Scales, Listening Comprehension (LC) Scaleand Oral Expression (OE) Scale	3-21	Overall Language	Elizabeth Carrow-Woolfolk,
TELD-3: Test of Early Language Development-Third Edition	2-0 to 7-11	Overall Language	Wayne P. Hiresko, Kim Reid, Donald D. Hammill
Test of Language Development, Fourth Edition	4-0 though 17-11	Overall Language	Phyllis L. Newcomer, Donald D. Hammill
Test of Pragmatic Language, Second Edition	6-0 to 18-11	Pragmatics	Diana Phelps-Terasaki, Trisha Phelps-Gunn
NEPSY-II (Selected Subtests)	3-16	Theory of Mind, Social Perception, Affect Recognition	Marit Korkman, Ursula Kirk, Sally Kemp

Assessment of Social and Emotional Functioning

When a student is referred for a comprehensive psychological or school-based neuropsychological evaluation due to social-emotional concerns, it is imperative to incorporate tools that properly address the emotional symptomalogy in question. Therefore, the battery of social and emotional assessment measures each clinician utilizes will often vary greatly. For instance, if there is a need to capture information on a wide array of acting-out types of behaviors, then it may be beneficial to use a broad-band behavioral checklist. On the other hand, if there are already specific areas of distress that have been identified, or if there is a need to assess concerns at a finer level of detail, then a narrow-band checklist or structured interview related to a specific area might suffice. Since most observable behaviors in the home or school setting often represent a set of symptoms manifesting from neurological dysfunction, it is important to evaluate social and emotional functioning via multiple methods to ensure valid interpretations and the development of more precise interventions. Table 10-7 provides clinicians with a set of basic questions to address in the initial stages of an evaluation for social-emotional disorders, while Table 10-8 provides examples of commonly used assessment measures for students with social emotional dysfunction.

TABLE 10-7
Specific Questions to Address in the Assessment of Social-Emotional Functioning

1. Does the student manifest a pattern of behaviors that are primarily internally nor externally-focused?
2. If internally-focused, are there feelings associated with depression or anxiety that impact perception and behavior?
3. Have there been traumatic events that have influenced the student's emotional reactivity?
4. Does the student manifest obsessions or ritualistic behaviors interfering with the ability to function in the school setting?
5. Are there indications of distortions in thinking or reality perceptions hindering social skill development and emotional behavior?
6. How does the student cope with emotionally challenging situations as well as modulate typical feelings of frustration, annoyance, or disappointment?

TABLE 10-8
Measures of Pro-Social Skills and Strengths

MEASURE	AGE RANGE	TYPE OF SCALE	AUTHOR(S)
BASC-II	2-21	Broad-band	Randy Kamphaus, Cecil Reynolds
Conners Comprehensive Behavior Rating Scales	6-18	Broad-band	C. Keith Conners
Achenbach System of Empirically Based Assessment (ASEBA)	6-18	Broad-band	Thomas M. Achenbach, Leslie Rescorla
Devereux Behavior Rating Scale – School Form	5-18	Broad-band	Jack A. Naglieri, Paul A. LeBuffe, and Steven I. Pfeiffer
Beck Youth Inventory-II	7-18	Broad or Narrow	Judith S. Beck, Aaron T. Beck, John B. Jolly
Children's Depression Inventory	7-17	Narrow-band	Maria Kovacs
Revised Children's Manifest Anxiety Scale -2	6-19	Narrow-band	Cecil R. Reynolds, Bert O. Richmond
MMPI-A			Robert P. Archer
Clinical Assessment of Behavior (CAB)	2-18	Broad-band	Bruce A. Bracken, Lori K. Keith
Reynolds Child Depression Scale (RCDS)/Reynolds Adolescent Depression Scale, 2nd Edition	Grades 3-6/ 11 to 20 yrs	Narrow-band	William Reynolds
Emotional Quotient Inventory: Youth Version	7 -18	Broad-band	Reuven Bar-On, James D.A. Parker
Social Skills Rating System (SSRS)	3-18	Broad-band	Frank M. Gresham, Stephen N. Elliott
Personality Inventory for Children, Second Edition	5-19	Broad-band	Robert D. Wirt, David Lachar, James E. Klinedinst, Philip D. Seat, William E. Broen
Piers-Harris Children's Self Concept Scale, 2nd Edition	7-18	Narrow-band	Ellen V. Piers, Dale B. Harris, David S. Herzberg
Children's PTSD Inventory	6-18	Narrow-band	Philip A. Saigh

In addition to checklists and structured interviews, there are other methods for clinicians to consider when collecting data pertaining to social and emotional functioning. These methods include projective assessment. Projective assessments should not be used in isolation, but at times can assist psychologists in delving into social emotional attributes not readily shared by some children. These techniques involve showing pictures or other vague stimuli that students must describe, elaborate upon, or tell a story. Projective techniques are somewhat controversial, and not as psychometrically sound as many rating scales, though they can provide a degree of insight, especially when teasing out depression, anxiety, or reality awareness. Some of the more common tools are noted in Table 10-9.

TABLE 10-9
Projective Measures

MEASURE	AGE RANGE	AUTHOR(S)
Robert's Apperception Test for Children:2	6-18	Glen E. Roberts, Chris Gruber
Rorschach Psycho-Diagnostic Technique	Primarily for Adolescents and up	Hermann Rorschach
House-Tree-Person Projective Drawing Technique		
Children's Apperception Test	3 and up	John N. Buck
Thematic Apperception Test	3-10	Leopold Bellak, Sonia Bellak
	10 and up	H.A. Murray

Cross–Battery Assessment: The Link to Interpretation

Cross-battery approaches to assessment encourage an analysis of the process or conditions in which a student performs well, and those in which a student experiences difficulty. This *"compare and contrast"* process places the emphasis on how a child performs a given task, rather than just an analysis of the overall result, and allows school based teams to develop more effective intervention plans. In the case of emotional disorders, this process can also assist in further understanding why a student may be struggling with the emotional rigors of an academic setting. Therefore, it is recommended that educators and clinicians consider a flexible battery approach to assessment where the selection of tests and measures vary, tapping various psychological constructs based upon a hypothesis testing model (see Hale & Fiorello, 2004).

Clearly, an analysis of both cognitive and emotional areas will need to be evaluated with students suspected of having an emotional disorder. A school-based neuropsychological model emphasizing a cross-battery assessment approach emphasizes multiple assessment measures measuring constructs such as sensory-motor functioning, attention, visual-spatial functioning, language processing, memory and learning, executive functioning skills, general intellectual functioning, and academic achievement (Miller, 2007). All of these cognitive and emotional constructs are manifestations of a single brain attempting to manage the emotional challenges of a dynamic and vibrant academic setting. Some constructs such as sensory-motor functioning or attention may seem like relatively lower level skills, but these constructs are vital in determining the integrity of more "higher" level cognitive functioning skills. As Blair (2002) noted, children characterized by negative emotionality stemming from an inability to inhibit emotional impulses are more likely to experience difficulty in the application of higher order cognitive processes due to their inability to practice planning and reflective problem solving when in socially compromising situations. Table 10-10 provides an example of ten core cognitive and/or emotional constructs to assess in the evaluation of students with social and emotional disorders.

TABLE 10-10
School Neuropsychological Assessment of Emotional Disorders

(Miller, 2007)

Sensory-Motor Functioning
Attentional Skills
Visual-Spatial Functioning
Language Skills
Memory and Learning Skills
Executive Functioning
General Intellectual Functioning
Executive Functions
Academic Achievement
Social Emotional Functioning

A challenge that many examiners face is how to interpret conflicting or unclear results. Through a process-oriented, hypothesis testing approach, a pattern of results is investigated in order to confirm, disconfirm, or explain a specific result or hypothesis. The tests themselves are merely tools, sections of a comprehensive analysis of how students respond to various types of tasks. It is important to note that tests do not diagnose, but rather skilled clinicians trained in interpreting data from multiple sources, including data from tests, ultimately arrive at a diagnostic conclusion. Therefore, evaluators should not fall into the cerebral trap of being a slave to a test score, but should seek to explain the rationale behind conflicting data, such as differences between parent and teacher rating scales, to assist with decision-making.

Lastly, context remains an important element of the overall assessment process. Although an appropriate assessment battery may be constructed by the examiner, if the results are not interpreted within the context of the student's overall functioning, then errors in judgment or inappropriate conclusions may arise. For example, the role of ability measures has not yet been presented within this chapter. However, it remains important to interpret a student's social and emotional skills within the framework of a child's age, cognitive ability, and environmental supports. For instance, we would not expect a preschool-aged child to be able to appropriately cope with frustration in the same manner as a 16-year-old. Furthermore, children with rather limited cognitive capabilities may cope with social and emotional challenges more like a younger student, as opposed to a similar age peer with adequate cognitive capabilities. As clinicians develop their assessment batteries, there may be a need to administer a comprehensive cognitive assessment, while in other cases, a screener (surveillance) or brief measure is more appropriate. A list of some of the comprehensive and screening cognitive ability measures is found below in Table 10-11

TABLE 10-11
Cognitive Ability Screening Measures

MEASURE	AGE RANGE	AUTHOR(S)
Wechsler Abbreviated Scale of Intelligence (WASI)	6 – 89	Brief
Kaufman Brief Intelligence Test – Second Edition (KBIT-II)	4-90	Brief
RIAS	3-94	Described as Comprehensive
Wechsler Intelligence Scale for Children – Fourth Edition (WISC-IV)	6 – 16	Comprehensive
Kaufman Assessment Battery for Children – Second Edition (KABC-II)	3-18	Comprehensive
Stanford Binet Intelligence Scale – Fifth Edition	2-85+	Comprehensive
Differential Ability Scales- Second Edition (DAS-II)	2-6 to 17-11	Comprehensive
Wechsler Nonverbal Test of Ability (WNV)	4 through 21-11	Brief or Comprehensive
Universal Nonverbal Intelligence Test (UNIT)	5 to 17-11	Brief or Comprehensive
Woodcock-Johnson Test of Cognitive Abilities – NU	2-90+	Brief or Comprehensive

The Importance of Assessing Strengths

Thus far, many of the assessment tools and areas discussed have been within the framework of uncovering weaknesses or reasons as to why a student experienced social and behavioral concerns. In addition to this focus, however, a well-rounded assessment should also provide information regarding student strengths, especially when attempting to link results with specific interventions offering the greatest chance for success. Examples of assessment instruments that have been developed to assist practitioners in describing student strengths are summarized in Table 10-12.

TABLE 10-12
Measures of Pro-Social Skills and Student Strengths

MEASURE	AGE RANGE	AUTHOR(S)
Resiliency Scales for Children and Adolescents	9-18	Sandra Prince-Embury
School Motivation and Learning Strategies Inventory (SMALSI)	8 to 18	Kathy Stroud, Cecil Reynolds
Academic Competence Evaluation Scales (ACES) and Academic Intervention Monitoring System (AIMS)	Kindergarten through College	James C. DiPerna, Stephen N. Elliott
Emotional Quotient Inventory: Youth Version	7 -18	Reuven Bar-On, James D.A. Parker
Social Skills Rating System (SSRS)	3-18	Frank M. Gresham, Stephen N. Elliott

SUMMARY AND CONCLUSIONS

Throughout this chapter, a multi-source, multi-method approach to the assessment of social and emotional disorders has been described. In defining the appropriate assessment battery for any student, the clinician must apply a broad understanding of the complexity of social and emotional functioning. It is not enough to simply ask whether or not a student qualifies for special education services. Rather, a framework of differential diagnosis, and asking a variety of *"how"* and *"why"* questions is essential to building an appropriate assessment plan that is linked to intervention. Depending upon the stage or level of investigation, different choices in assessment tools may be selected. It is important to think flexibly, however, and not reserve diagnostic tools only for eligibility considerations. In contrast, these tools should be used to understand why students are behaving in a particular manner, and generate specific interventions to assist them in reaching their learning potential. Perhaps through early identification procedures of specific core processing deficits, such as faulty language skills, poor inhibitory control and self-regulation skills, sensory-motor awareness and sensitivity, and executive functioning skills, proper treatment may then be directed toward students in hopes of diminishing the rising tide of emotional dysfunction in our schools.

REFERENCES

Beck, J.S., Beck, A.T., Jolly, J.B. (2005). *Beck Youth Inventories – Second Edition*. San Antonio, TX: Harcourt Assessment, Inc.

Bishop, D.V.M. (2003). *CCC-2 Children's communication checklist-2*. San Antonio, TX: Harcourt Assessment, Inc.

Barkley, R. (2001). The executive functions and self regulation: an evolutionary neuropsychological perspective. *Neuropsychology Review, 11*(1), 1-29.

Blair, C. (2002). School readiness. Integrating cognition and emotion in a neurobiological conceptualization of children's functioning at school entry. *American Psychologist, 57*, 111-127.

Bracken, B.A. & McCallum, R.S. (1998). *Universal Nonverbal Intelligence Test (UNIT)*. United States: Riverside Publishing.

Christophersen, E.R. & Mortweet, S.L. (2001). *Treatments that work with children: Empirically supported strategies for managing childhood problems*. Washington, DC: American Psychological Association.

Craig, H.K. (1993). Social skills of children with specific language impairment: Peer relationships. *Language, Speech, and Hearing Services in Schools, 24*(4), 206-215.

Delis, D.C., Kaplan, E., Kramer, J.H. (2001). *Delis-Kaplan executive function system (DKEFS)*. San Antonio, TX: The Psychological Corporation.

Elliott, S.N. & Gresham, F.M. *Social skills improvement system*. Minneapolis, MN: Pearson.

Fujiki, M., Brinton, B., Morgan, M. Hart, C.H. (1999). Withdrawn and sociable behavior of children with language impairment. *Language, Speech, and Hearing Services in the Schools, 30*(2), 183-195.

Gioia, G.A., Isquith, P.K., Guy, S.C., Kenworthy, L. (2000). *Behavior rating inventory of executive function (BRIEF)*. Florida: Psychological Assessment Resources.

Grant, D.A. & Berg, E.A. (1993). *Wisconsin card sorting test*. Florida: Psychological Assessment Resources.

Greene, R. (1998). *The explosive child*. New York: Harper Collins Publishers.

Gresham, F.M. (1991). Conceptualizing behavior disorders in terms of resistance to intervention. *School Psychology Review, 20*, 23-36.

Guralnick, M.J. (1990). Social Competence and early intervention. *Journal of Early Intervention, 14*, 3-14.

Hale, J. B. & Fiorello, C. A. (2004). *School neuropsychology: A practitioners handbook*. New York: Guilford Press.

Heaton, R.K. (2003). *WCST: Computer version 4 research edition*. Florida: Psychological Assessment Resources.

Kamphaus, R.W. & Reynolds, C.R. *Behavioral and Emotional Screening System for Children (BESS)*. Minneapolis, MN: Pearson.

Kandel, E.R., Schwartz, J.H., and Jessell, T.M. (2001). *Principles of Neural Science*. (4th ed.), New York: McGraw-Hill.

Kratochwill, T.R., Elliott, S.N., & Busse, R.T. (1995). Behavior consultation: A five-year evaluation of consultant and client outcomes. *School Psychology Quarterly, 10*, 87-117.

Korkman, M., Kirk, U., Kemp, S. (2007). *NEPSY – Second Edition*. San Antonio, TX: Harcourt Assessment, Inc.

Marton, K., Abramoff, B., & Rosenzweig, S. (2005). Social cognition and language in children with specific language impairment (SLI). *Journal of Communication Disorders, 38*, 143-162.

Miller, D. C. (2007). *Essentials of school neuropsychological assessment*. New Jersey: Wiley & Sons.

Moffitt, T. E., & Lynam, D. Jr. (1994). The neuropsychology of conduct disorder and delinquency: implications for understanding antisocial behavior. *Progress in Experimental Personality and Psychopathology Research*, 233-262.

Neville, H.J. and Bavelier, D. (2000). Specificity and plasticity in neurocognitive development in humans. In Gazzaniga, M.S. (Ed). *The New Cognitive Neurosciences*. (2nd ed.), Cambridge, MA: The MIT Press, pp. 83-99.

Lyon, G. R., Fletcher, J. M., Shaywitz, S. E., Shaywitz, B. A., Torgesen, J. K., Wood, F., et al. (2001). Rethinking learning disabilities. In C. E. Finn Jr., A. J. Rotherham, & C. R. Hokanson Jr. (Eds.), *Rethinking special education for a new century* (pp. 259–287). Washington, DC: Thomas B. Fordham Foundation. Retrieved from http://www.excellence.net/library/special ed/index.html

Luria, A.R. (1973). *The Working Brain: An Introduction to Neuropsychology*. Translated by Basil Haigh. Penguin Books, Ltd.

Martinez, R., & Semrud-Clikeman, M. (2004). Emotional adjustment of young adolescents with different learning disability subtypes. *Journal of Learning Disabilities, 37*, 411–420.

Prince-Embury, S. (2007). *Resiliency scales for children and adolescents: A profile of personal strengths*. San Antonio, TX: Harcourt Assessment, Inc.

Reynolds, C.R., & Kamphaus, R.W. *BASC-2 (Behavior Assessment System for Children, Second Edition)*.

Reynolds, W. (2003). *Reynolds bully victimization scales for schools*. San Antonio, TX: Harcourt Assessment, Inc.

Roley, S.S., Blanche, E.I., Schaaf, R.C. (2001). *Understanding the nature of sensory integration with diverse populations*. United States: Therapy Skill Builders, a Harcourt Health Sciences Company.

Saigh, P.A. (2004). *Children's PTSD Inventory*. San Antonio, TX: Harcourt Assessment, Inc.

Semel, E., Wiig, E.H., Secord, W.H. (2003). *Clinical evaluation of language fundamentals*. San Antonio, TX: The Psychological Corporation.

Stoiber, K. (2004). *Functional Assessment and Intervention System*. San Antonio, TX: Harcourt Assessment, Inc.

Stuss, D.T., Alexander, M.P., Benson, D.F. (1997). Frontal lobe functions. In J.L.C.E. Michael & R. Trimble (Eds.), *Contemporary behavioral neurology. Blue books for practical neurology*, (Vol. 16, pp. 169-187). Boston: Butterworth-Heinemann.

Stuss, D. T., & Levine, B. (2002). Adult clinical neuropsychology: lesson from studies of the frontal lobes. *Annual Review of Psychology, 53*, 401-433.

Torgesen, J. K., Alexander, A. W., Wagner, R. K., Rashotte, C. A., Voeller, K. S., & Conroy, T. (2001). Intensive remedial instruction for children with reading disabilities: Immediate and long-term outcomes from two instructional approaches. *Journal of Learning Disabilities, 34*, 33–58, 78.

Wechsler, D., Kaplan, E., Fein, D., Kramer, J., Morris, R., Delis, D. (2004). *Wechsler intelligence scale for children-fourth edition integrated.* San Antonio, TX: Harcourt Assessment, Inc.

Wechsler, D. & Naglieri, J.N. (2006). *Wechsler nonverbal scale of ability.* San Antonio, TX: Harcourt Assessment, Inc.

Welsh, M.C. & Pennington, B.F. (1988). Assessing frontal lobe functioning in children: Views from developmental psychology. *Developmental Neuropsychology, 4*, 199-230.

Woodcock, R.W., McGrew, K.S., Mather, N. (2006). *Woodcock-Johnson-III NU.* United States: Riverside Publising.

CHAPTER 11

MINDFUL DISCIPLINE FOR DISTRESSED LEARNERS

Mary Fowler, B.A.

"Teachers not only must coerce and cajole students to learn; they must also be mature enough to deal with the emotional messiness implicit in working so closely with young people."
—David Labaree, Professor of Education, Stanford University

Steven, a ninth grader pushes into the classroom and slams his books on the desktop where the previous occupant has left a pen. Suddenly, the pen explodes and goopy ink spreads everywhere. Steven immediately reacts with a verbal arsenal of expletives as his peers and classmates begin to laugh. Feeling embarrassed and socially threatened, Steven's *flight or fight* response takes over and he instinctively lashes out at his closest classmate in a physical manner. Acting swiftly and decisively, his teacher orders Steven to leave the room, and then spends the next few minutes feverishly writing a referral.

Sally, a third grader, dashes off the school bus and makes a run to be first in line. She's in full speed, intently concentrating with her eye trained on her desired goal. Suddenly, another child bursts to the head of the line at the moment Sally arrives. Sally responds by shoving the girl out of her way. The line monitor orders Sally to the office, where the principal decides to suspend her for the rest of the day. Once the weight of the consequences looms over Sally, she reflects upon her actions and realizes she should never put her hands on another student. However, in the heat of the moment, Sally has such difficulty controlling her emotions when her desired goal is so close to fruition.

Tommy, a middle-school student, has adopted a new persona to carve out his rightful place among his peers. He is determined to become a malcontent, disobey rules, and essentially become bad to the bone, only Tommy is unable to play this role fully. His half-hearted attempts to become unruly and wield a false sense of bravado are easily exposed by his peers, who see through his phony demeanor and simply laugh at him. However, to his teachers, Tommy's disruptive behavior is becoming more and more problematic in the classroom. Beneath the surface, Tommy presents as an angry, confused, and somewhat emotionally challenged student whose edginess has impacted both his academic and social skill development.

What Do These 3 Students Have in Common?

Most school psychologists have frequently encountered a Steven, Sally, or Tommy as these types of behaviors are often quickly referred to school support teams for further assessment. Each student may be diagnosed with a host of neurological issues such as disruptive, behavioral or mood disorders like ADHD, ODD, OCD, Bipolar Disorder, Anxiety, Depression, or PTSD. Regardless of the label, these students share an underlying issue. They are distressed learners. As such, they are naturally prone to being emotionally distraught, difficult to manage in a class setting, and quickly driven to reaction. These students misbehave, miss social cues, and draw wrong conclusions. Fearful, anxious and defensive, they often react with emotional volatility, anger, and unusual displays of aggression. In the face of such behavior, it may be hard to read their emotional sub-story. Clearly, each of these students requires a teacher or building administrator who can respond to their behavioral outburst with "grace under pressure". Unfortunately, emotionally messy students have a way of pushing the inner switches and emotional boundaries of the very persons who want to assist them most. Therefore, when the situation calls for a cool, calm, collected, response, teachers may find that they, too, have been driven to an emotional reaction that subsequently fuels the situation even more.

Many classroom management interventions often focus on the by-products of the emotional messiness—the obvious behavior disruptions that occur in the school or home setting. This chapter is about *managing* distress—the precursor to emotional messiness or disturbance. It focuses on prevention and intervention techniques that calm and quiet distress—theirs, yours, and that of other learners. Simply put, parents and educators need to understand why certain techniques are needed to diffuse certain types of behavioral situations for distressed learner. These techniques are essential, and once there is an understanding of how they work, hopefully most educators will use them to complement solid classroom management and practice. Hence, this chapter will focus upon a 3-step holistic approach known as *"Mindful Discipline."* This approach draws upon research in the fields of social psychology, neuroscience, behavior, and mindfulness to foster stress reduction.

Mindfulness Defined as a Classroom Management Practice

Mindfulness is the practice of becoming intentionally aware of our own internal thoughts and actions, and not necessarily the thoughts and actions of others. Only by developing and enhancing our own self-awareness can human beings illuminate what beliefs or experiences might be shaping our thoughts, feelings, and ultimately our behavioral responses. This intentional awareness relies upon the power of observation. The purpose of observation is bidirectional, as it allows us to look for causes of our own internal responses, as well as the external behaviors from others that trigger these self-same responses. Therefore, rather than focusing on the behavior and its emotional ramifications, the focus takes a more objective and rational turn toward analysis and understanding. Soon, our understanding replaces judgment with evaluation. Evaluation leads to seeing more facets of a problem and generating thoughtful, responsive possibility. (Langer, 1989)

Through mindfulness, teachers are able to disengage from the emotional messiness being played out before their eyes. This cognitive disengagement allows teachers to observe the behavior from a different perspective, and thus attend to the student's messiness using a reasoned, problem-solving approach. In other words, there is an opportunity that presents itself each time a student misbehaves. This opportunity allows teachers a window of insight to "see" behavior in an objective fashion, without pre-judging or superimposing stereotypical names such as *"bad kid, trouble maker, wise guy, etc."* Table 11-1 is a simple three-part technique that should assist teachers in curbing self serving judgments about students. After all, the goal of all educators is not to label students, but rather educate them academically as well as socially on their emotional journey through school.

TABLE 11-1
Three-Step Technique to Curb Emotional Judgments

1. *Observe:* What about the situation or the context is contributing to the maladaptive behavior?
2. *Empathize:* How would you or others act in similar situation given the emotional sub-story.
3. *Search:* Look for *"hidden"* clues or unseen factors that explain what's driving the behavior. Always seek to answer this question: **"What is the student working for?"**

Learned Reactive Patterns and Self-Defeating Behaviors

The techniques of *"observe, empathize, and search"* have the added benefit of not fueling an emotional fire, and therefore allow to teachers to sidestep the drama of learned reactive patterns such as those demonstrated by distressed students such as Tommy. Most disruptive students often mask their true feelings with many behavioral disguises, which often erupt from the stress and strains of previous interpersonal experiences. These students develop a repertoire of behaviors that psychiatrist Robert Brooks (2007) categorizes as *self-defeating*. According to Brooks (2007), common self-defeating behaviors include quitting, avoiding, clowning, controlling, bullying, and denying. Brooks (2007) labeled these behaviors as self-defeating because they represent feeble attempts on the part of the student to protect and defend against a perceived threat, real or imagined, in the hopes of achieving a goal such as gaining attention, power, or control (Center for Collaborative Practice, 2001). For some educators, volitional behavior aimed at disrupting the learning environment simply represents a lack of moral character. Consequently, the notion of self defeating behavior being nothing more than an attempt to mask more painful emotions may be hard to accept. Nevertheless, the class clown may be laughing on the outside yet crying on the inside because their antics are not producing the desired goal, namely, approval and a sense of belonging. When teachers begin to understand the emotional sub-story driving inappropriate behavior, they are more likely to act mindfully instead of mindlessly. Table 11-2 depicts the differences between mindful and mindless behavior.

TABLE 11-2
Mindful Versus Mindless Behavior Patterns

Mindful—to be aware and attentive	Mindless—to sense and react
Mindful—to observe and respond	Mindless— to judge and condemn
Mindful—to act with intention	Mindless—to act out of desperation
Mindful—to solve problems	Mindless—to stir or create problems

The Biology of Stress, Threat, and Distress

Our brains are a system of networks, systems, and subsystems. Though we sometimes refer to our *"emotional"* selves and our *"thinking"* selves, in actuality the neural systems that govern emotion and thought are highly interactive. Still, at the present time in human evolution, connections from the emotional system to the cognitive system are much stronger for children than those connections traveling from the cognitive centers in our brain back toward the emotional centers. Despite our advanced cognitions, human behaviors remain first and foremost a survival species. For instance, part of human consciousness is always on alert, and always appraising incoming stimuli for any harmful potential. Often times, there is a natural tendency to react with lightning speed in a flight or fight manner when our survival appears threatened (Sapolsky, 1998). In addition, human beings also react to psychosocial, emotional, and mental stressors in the same neurobiological manner as physical threats, by making a quick appraisal of the stimuli with respect to its detrimental effects on our emotional psyche (LeDoux, 1996)

According to the preeminent neuroscientist Joseph LeDoux (1996), an emotional stimulus presents itself through one or more sensory pathways; visual, auditory, olfactory, or somatic as the incoming stimuli travels toward the thalamus. The thalamus receives all incoming stimuli from the outside world, with the exception of smell, and then relays the information for further processing to the prefrontal cortex. Housed in the anterior regions of the brain, the prefrontal cortex is associated with both cognitive and emotional executive functioning skills including thinking, planning, problem solving, reflecting, and evaluating. The prefrontal cortex allows us to *"think"* about what we are sensing, and ascribe some emotional value to the stimuli. The thalamus also serves to relay information from the prefrontal cortex to the amygdala, which is the brain's early warning threat detector, via an emotional pathway referred to as the *"high road"* (LeDoux, 1996). The *high road* allows us to respond in a more rational and cerebral fashion by intellectualizing a perceived threat, as opposed to allowing unbridled passion and aggression to subvert our behavioral responses in a reflexive fashion.

The signal the thalamus sends to the amygdala that is independent of the prefrontal cortex, travels along what LeDoux (1996) referred to as a quick and dirty processing pathway or *"the low road."* The amygdala, which lies deep within the limbic structures of our brain in the temporal lobes, is our brain's rapid fire, emotional appraisal threat detector. It signals the body to order up an array of neurochemical ingredients in case it senses a perceived threat or danger requiring us to fight, flee, or freeze. This "low road" pathway allows us to react instantaneously if need be, and is not dependent upon the prefrontal cortex to take action. The key word here is react. Reaction is driven by the brain's limbic system and has important evolutionary significance, especially when hesitation might result in a disaster (LeDoux,1996)

Whether to respond in a cerebral manner or react in a reflexive manner has much to do with how the brain perceives the stimuli. For example, a 10-year-old boy is swimming in a Florida river, and there is something floating nearby. Immediately, there is an elevation in respiration and breathing patterns, and the boy's body activates adrenaline in response to a perceived threat. There is no more enjoyment, but rather just intense focus and concentration to determine the closest exit from the water. This bodily response and change in psychological thought patterns occurs because of the confusion surrounding a particular visual stimulus within a contextual situation; namely, is this a log or an alligator floating in the water? If circumstances allow some time to pause, then chances are the executive network in the prefrontal cortex will make a reasoned assessment of the situation. If the object in question is determined to be just a log floating nearby, the boy becomes engaged in an internal and private monologue: *"Hold up. That's not an alligator, silly! No need to scream for help! Go ahead. Enjoy yourself. Finish your exercise. Keep swimming."*

The overarching design of the brain is indeed very useful. Of course, there are times when it can become extremely difficult to recognize the difference between a log and an alligator. Similarly, in a classroom learning environment, it can also be extremely difficult to interpret a perceived threat when there is none. That's where the emotional messiness comes in. The more emotionally taxed a child becomes, the more likely the child will react emotionally, instead of responding in a rational manner. If a child is over-stressed, tired, not feeling well, or has an underlying neurological condition, the chances of a reaction tend to increase (LeDoux, 2008). Clearly, our day to day experiences also color our judgment. For instance, suppose the 10-year-old boy had previously come dangerously close to an alligator while swimming. It stands to reason that each time the child swims in a river, the emotional memories of the previous danger will no doubt flood into the child's psyche to cloud further judgments and perceptions.

For emotionally distressed learners, certain school environments, tasks, or social encounters can cast shadows from earlier traumatic experiences to the present day. Most teachers will be unaware of these earlier experiences that trigger the behavioral reactions for each learner. To further compound the process, the limbic system is geared to identify patterns of stimuli, and does not necessarily distinguish between past or present tense. (VanDerKolk, 2006) Consequently, many students often find themselves in reaction, as opposed to reflection, with little clue as to what led them there.

The Neural Short Circuit—the Angry, the Aggressive, the Anxious

As previously stated, reaction has an evolutionary advantage to immediately ward off an impending threat. These behaviors are highly adaptive and appropriate depending upon the context. Nevertheless, unless there is clear and present danger, it is crucial for children to activate cortical regions that override emotionally driven reactions in order to facilitate emotional control and order emotionally appropriate behavioral responses. It other words, children need to think before they act.

Herein lies the problem for distressed or emotionally messy students. The behavioral trend is for these students to be *low road* processors, and subsequently become vulnerable to emotional triggers. Unfortunately, these students often react in a maladaptive manner during situations that call for a more tempered response. Thus, their behavior is often inappropriate for the context, and their reactions tend to be volatile. In the face of a frothing student, it may be especially hard for teachers to read the fear and anxiety that is fueling an aggressive or anger-driven reaction. Clearly, such reactions can generate fear in others and stimulate an emotional reaction from teachers, when a thoughtful response would be better. Thus, not only are certain students low road processors, but there are also many educators who respond to these behaviors in a similar (low road) fashion as well. Many ineffective classroom management practices such as yelling, threatening, or even ridiculing tend to occur when teachers are operating from a position of reacting, and not reflecting. Reactive behaviors can happen to all educators, in part, because they *"discharge"* behaviors, meaning these behaviors help release unpleasant physical and emotional sensations (Scaer, 2007)

In the vignette with Steven, the ninth grader described at the beginning of this chapter, anger had carried over from a previous situation. Consequently, Steven had slammed his books causing his pen to explode, which resulted in a discharge behavior of inappropriate language. The ideal response would have required his teacher to ignore the behavior until Steven was calm, and then discuss the situation in a rational manner to encourage Steven to make better choices. However, before his teacher could speak, another student had reacted with laughter, also a *discharge behavior*, to relieve tension. After all, loud noises startle and elevate the fight, flight, or freeze chemical cascade in the brains of others as well. In response to the laughter, Steven then reacted by verbally threatening the other student, yet another discharge behavior. Consequently, his teacher reacted in a rather emotional manner, thereby prompting Steven to storm out of the room.

To some, Steven's behavior pattern is typical of an emotionally disturbed student, and he may certainly have a history of ADHD, ODD, or another emotional condition. Being a ninth grader, he may be headed toward an alternative educational placement setting, and also have an increased risk of dropping out of school. It is important to understand that *emotional disturbance* is nothing more than a diagnostic category reflecting the lack of success a child has in modulating the neurobiology of distress and reactivity. The teacher who understands that anger and aggression are basically fear-driven reactions will be less likely to respond in a reactive manner, and in turn, more apt to respond in a rational and effective manner. Clearly, Steven's behavior merited a disciplinary response. In the case of a highly distressed learner, timing and a sense of calmness means everything. Unfortunately, all too often schools require an emotionally distressed student to exhibit the use of self-control skills before actually being taught the specific interventions or strategies needed to modulate behavior.

The Felt Sense of Distress—Reaction Junkies

Throughout the course of a school day, all children experience a rise and fall in the levels of stress chemicals in their bodies. Stress chemicals, such as adrenalin, cortisol, and norepinephrine are in a constant state of flux in response to specific environmental demands. Children or adults who are constantly under stress, or who suffer a traumatic brain injury, often develop an elevated level of baseline stress chemicals in their bodies. Consequently, their bodies become accustomed to these heightened levels of stress chemicals. When the cascade of fight, flight, or freeze chemicals subside in their bodies, there is a tendency to feel as if something is terribly wrong (Sapolsky, 1998). In essence, there is a natural human tendency to adapt to feeling "high" on stress chemicals, and the body habituates to this stress response. Therefore, when there is a rise and fall in the levels of stress chemicals in their bodies, the baseline has been sufficiently raised to not return to pre-trauma norms, at least not without deliberate use of stress reduction techniques (McEwen, 2000).

Similarly, children with behavioral or emotional disorders are predisposed to limbic-driven, stress reactive behavior. This reactive behavior makes it more likely these children will have an elevated stress chemical baseline. Consequently, children with emotional disorders often find themselves in more frequent negative social exchanges, thus under more stress and trauma, and locked in a self-defeating cycle (Goleman, 1995).

Among the harmful effects of chronic elevated stress chemicals are coronary heart disease, immunosuppression, and also cognitive inefficiency. For instance, McEwen's (2000) research revealed that excess stress chemicals destroy neurons in the hippocampus, the brain structure associated with memory functions. Elevated levels of stress chemicals can also impair the optimal functioning of the brain's executive network in the prefrontal cortex. Thus, the ability to think, plan, problem solve, make reasoned decisions, and follow through with goals and objectives is affected as well (LeDoux, 1996).

This reactive cycle sheds a new light on the plight of Sally, the third grade student described in the second vignette. Sally has ADHD and though she's not necessarily oppositional defiant or emotionally disturbed in the way these labels are currently used, she is highly reactive. Sally's ADHD makes it difficult for her to modulate her behavior and exercise self-control when flooded with stress. Her anger was impulsive and reactive, almost like a lightening strike, without any reason or forethought. Nevertheless, her reaction may have also served to discharge elevated levels of stress chemicals pending from a desired goal (being first in line) being so suddenly thwarted (Sapolsky, 1998). In a different context, Sally's behavior could have been highly appropriate if her behavioral response was to shove her classmate away from an oncoming bus. Still, once this neural circuit becomes activated, the brain does not differentiate between situation and context; it simply summons a reaction (LeDoux, 2008).

Effective classroom management must help students deal with the source of their distress, as well as help them interpret the physical sensation of stress through a specialized technique called *Mindful Discipline*. Mindfulness, the act of being aware, of witnessing without judgment, of letting go of belief systems that trigger reactive behavior patterns, or of recognizing unquieted body sensation is an effective way to help students with emotional disorders better manage their emotional worlds (VanDerKolk, 2008). Simply put, *Mindful Discipline* is the electrical tape wrapped around a frayed, emotionally disturbed cord to keep it from short circuiting.

Mindful Discipline in Practice

> *"The more mindful we are, the more choices we have and the less reactive we become."*
> —Ellen Langer from *The Art of Mindful Creativity*

There are three types of general strategies that help students who have difficulty with reactive behavior patterns. The goal of these strategies is to rewire the internal behavioral tendencies in the brain by forging newer and more powerful circuits leading to a more adaptive emotional response to stress.

Step 1. Training Response-ability

Clearly, if an emotionally distressed learner were capable of stopping and thinking in the heat of an emotional moment, there would be no need to simply react. Cognitive therapeutic approaches encourage children to stop and think—to use the same mind that created the problem to solve the problem. Since the brain is already emotionally reactive and unlikely to think clearly in the heat of the moment, the first strategy that needs to be explicitly taught, trained, and habituated is to **STOP**

AND BREATHE. When an emotionally reactive student is asked to stop and think, the child is actually being asked to shift cognitive gears rapidly by first shifting their own physiological state. Often times, distressed learners such as Steven and Sally are incapable of exhibiting self-control until there has been an actual physical discharge. The goal is to train *"Stop and Breathe"* so that it becomes the student's first discharge reaction. There is evidence-based research emerging regarding the effectiveness of utilizing stress management techniques such as breathing, mindfulness, and similar practices in schools to dispel reactive behavior patterns (Bradley et.al., 2007, Zylowska, 2008).

How "Stop and Breathe" Works

Stop and Breathe engages the mind and discharges uncomfortable physical sensations. *"Stop"* diverts a child's attention, while *"breathe"* refocuses the attention on a conscious deliberate action to physically discharge stress in a more appropriate manner. The act of breathing brings more oxygen into the system and thereby reduces the cascade of stress chemicals that have been flooding the body. According to Sapolsky (2004), cortisol is the primary stress hormone that leads to increased heart rates, higher blood pressure, and immune system dysfunction. Conversely, lower levels of cortisol are associated with positive moods and a more relaxed bodily state. From a neuropsychological perspective, there are three core executive functioning deficits that arise from a stressful brain: namely, deficits with behavioral inhibition, diminished working memory skills, and limited cognitive flexibility (Lupien et al., 2005). All three executive functioning skills allow children to respond to an emotional crisis in a more reflective and contemplative manner, as opposed to reacting in a reflexive and impulsive fashion. Once cortisol is released in the blood stream, it takes approximately 45 minutes for the body to return to baseline rates; however, controlled breathing can enhance this process. For most students, there are four types of learning experiences that often elevate stress levels (Lupien et al., 2005):

TABLE 11-3
Four Types of Stressful Learning Experiences

1. ***Novelty situations***—teachers can reduce stress in their students by developing a daily schedule and reviewing it periodically throughout the day
2. ***Unpredictable situations***—developing a structure and routine to the day is critical to reducing the chances of unpredictable events. However, assemblies, fire-drills, change of schedules, and substitute teachers are part of any school experience. Preparing children in advance for inevitable changes as well as discussing back-up contingencies for these events can be helpful.
3. ***Perceived threats to the ego***—teachers can control their verbal and nonverbal (body language) behavior so it is less threatening. Kneeling down to talk to a student, becoming cognizant of personal space, using a quiet voice, discussing misbehavior in private rather than in front of peers, avoiding empty threats, empathizing with emotions, using reflective listening techniques, diffusing anger with humor, and simply knowing each student well enough to avoid putting them in an uncomfortable situation (*i.e. calling on a learning disabled student to read out loud in front of the class*) can help defuse emotional outbursts.
4. ***Sense of control is lost***—allowing students choices rather than dictating a particular behavioral response or providing an in class time-out area to relax can help students feel more in control to make better decisions.

In most classrooms, children have been conditioned to repress physical discharges, much to our biology's detriment. For instance, students who elicit a yawn, or perhaps an exasperated sigh or even a grunt, usually receive negative feedback from their teacher. As previously discussed, negative feedback actually elevates the stress reaction, especially for students with emotional disturbances. Once the biology is quieted, the student has a chance to demonstrate a more rational response, as opposed to an emotional reaction. Once again, a reactive biology has to calm before it can become response-enabled.

How Do You Teach Students to "Stop and Breathe"?

This technique is very easy to train and even easier when appropriately demonstrated. One of the keys is to observe whether or not students breathe from the top of their chest or their diaphragm. Often times, shallow-chested breathers tend to exhibit more stress and therefore need explicit training in this technique. Table 11-4 provides a framework for teaching the stop and breathe technique for distressed students. In addition, for teachers who are prone to reactive behaviors and engage in combative practices with students such as yelling, making empty threats, or other ineffective discipline practices, this technique provides an extra cushion of self-control.

A daily practice of stress management techniques such as breathing has proven effective in reducing anxiety and behavior problems, improving emotional regulation, and increasing academic performance and attendance (Bradley, 2007; Zylowska, 2006). Table 11-5 provides a training regimen for students to practice daily, and is an important component of social-emotional academic learning. Following this protocol will allow students to better manage their emotions and ultimately guide the development of social integration through trust, empathy, and attachment, while simultaneously learning to temper emotional aggression and reactivity.

TABLE 11-4
Teaching the Stop and Breathe Technique

1. At this very moment take a deep breath and just observe the feel of the air going in and out of your lungs. Breathe in and out. Got it? Okay.
2. Now, place your hand on your lower abdomen. When you breathe in, imagine your lower abdomen is a balloon filling with air. Breathe in and try to fill the balloon slowly. Breathe out and let the balloon slowly collapse.
3. Do this deep belly breathing to the count of four for a full minute. Eventually, we will work our way up to five minutes.
4. Now breathe in 1-2-3-4. Hold for a full second. Now breathe out 4-3-2-1. Breathe in. Hold. Breathe out.
5. As you breathe, notice how you feel. Calm? Quiet? Perhaps even peaceful? Did you notice that you were not thinking about anything else, and focusing all your attention on breathing in and out? The simple act of breathing has not only calmed your nervous system; it has also disengaged you from any thoughts that might be spiraling through your head and leading to unpleasant feelings.

Once students have been taught the proper techniques of breathing, the next step is to utilize a nonverbal cue to signal them when they need to calm their biology. A nonverbal gesture or signal is highly recommended since words can have a disquieting effect. For instance, teachers can hold up their hand instead of verbalizing stop, and then motion to *breathe* in with an index finger drawing a line from your nose to your belly as you model the breath. Whatever gesture is decided upon, it is important to practice this technique with the entire class. Keep practicing so this technique eventually sets the physical state for each learner. Ideally, each student will be trained to stop and breathe, and also be in a position not only to self-monitor their own emotional levels, but also be in a better position to monitor their peers as well. Through practice, students are learning an effective and lifelong self-control technique.

TABLE 11-5
Breathing and Relaxation Protocol

1. Be relaxed and authentic. Discuss with students the nature of breathing and the control they can develop over their body and emotions by consciously altering the pace of drawing a breath.
2. Prepare students.
   a) Teach a brain lesson on the sympathetic nervous system, the parasympathetic nervous system and homeostasis.
   b) Acknowledge uncomfortable feelings and try to diffuse tension through games and activities. For instance, encourage students to tighten one arm as hard as they can, hold it, and then release. Ask them to notice what the release feels like. Have them repeat the exercise holding even longer, and then discuss the results.
   c) Next, ask students to pay attention to their breathing. Have them notice whether they are breathing from the chest or the belly. Explain that chest breathing is shallow and inefficient intake of oxygen, while belly breathing is calming and efficient intake.
   d) Practice breathing as a group exercise.
   e) Guide students in daily practice. Begin day 1 by practicing for 30 seconds, then add 30-60 seconds each day up to 3-5 minutes a day. The following techniques will also be helpful:

      • Use a calm, steady voice.

      • Provide an alternative for students who need to move (e.g. breathing and walking, or breathing and making figure 8's with their fingers on the desk.)

      • Provide an alternative, quiet activity for resistant students. These students usually need extra time to feel more comfortable.

      • Encourage home base breathing for 10-15 minutes. Consider making this a homework assignment and reward students for their commitment.

      • Consider creating a class-wide reinforcement contingency. For instance, if everyone completes their breathing homework for one week the class receives a special snack, or five minutes of down time, or even a no-homework night.

Step 2. Make "IT" Safe

The *"IT"* to make safe is referring to the identification of whatever is going on that provokes student reaction. It could be a particular type of task, an unpredictable environment, content that is perceived too difficult, another classmate, personal history, family drama, or a number of other possibilities. Resilience research findings show that children exposed to multiple risks and adversities can overcome them with the right complement of protective influences (Masten, 2001). Interestingly, it is the ordinariness of influences that surprised researchers the most. For instance, important adults in their lives and turning point experiences were essential when helping children with neurologically based difficulties overcome their childhood adversities (Katz, 2006).

What can a teacher do? The answer lies in tending to three basic human needs cited by researchers Ryan and Deci (2000) in their work on intrinsic human motivation and self-determination. These needs are centered around the emotional constructs of relatedness, autonomy, and competence. When a student does not feel secure, albeit physically or emotionally, one of these three basic needs is most likely not being met (Ryan & Deci, 2000). In fact, all issues of safety and security must be addressed or the student will be *"mis-engaged"* in behavior that takes them further away from meeting these essential needs. Table 11-6 highlights three ways to foster social emotional health and wellness in students.

Step 3. Act With Intention

The idea behind mindful discipline is to *"ACT"* and not *"REACT"*. Although no method is foolproof, one way to increase the probability of success is to develop an intention to guide your teaching practice. Intentions are simple, straightforward guidelines for behavior. They are one sentence descriptions of your ideal state of being.

For instance, suppose there is a student who tends to promote a reactive behavior through their persistence noncompliance and oppositional behavior in class. In this case, your guiding intention may be *"I am competent, kind, and concerned."* If still ready to react, you simply repeat your intention silently and as many times as necessary so that you do not say or do something that you will regret, that is ineffective, or that violates this fundamental postulate.

TABLE 11-6
Three Ways to Nurture Student Health and Well-Being

1. Foster relatedness through connection and belonging. Some characteristics of safe environments are:
   * Constant, predictable, and non-reactive. Students respond best to highly structured but not rigid environments, consistent routines, rules that are created collaboratively and are consistently reinforced with pre-set consequences. In other words, the students know what to expect and behavior is reinforced.
   * Spirit of community and collaboration. This includes team mentality, no put-downs, a sense of connection and belonging, differentiation in tasks and activities, and personal strengths celebrated. Social isolation is taboo.
   * Abundance of positive feedback. Develop a realistic appraisal of frequency by monitoring yourself for a week. Put a check mark down every time you give positive feedback. Is it abundant?
   * Have a sense of humor that is truly funny, though never at another's expense.
   * Challenges are opportunities. Teachers need to break down challenging tasks into stepping stones and provide encouragement and support along the way.

2. Cultivate autonomy and self-determination by allowing choices and decision making.
   - Provide choices of preferred activities and rewards whenever possible.
   - Allow alternate methods of response.
   - Treat behavior as a choice. Allow the student the opportunity to calm first and then decide wisely.
   - Train students to **SBTR**—stop, breathe, think, respond. During *"think"* the student makes a choice between appropriate or inappropriate behavior. During *"respond"*, the student follows through on the choice and evaluates the result. Use prompts to coach each step of this process. The *"think"* part works best once the student's biology has quieted a bit. If the shift to cognitive activity reactivates the stress, go back to quieting.
   - Provide a setting where student is most comfortable and relaxed.

3. Develop competence through authentic participation in meaningful activities and successful experiences.
   - Identify strengths and talents. Provide multiple opportunities to use them.
   - Provide differentiated or universal design for learning instruction.
   - Use portfolio assessments.
   - Provide positive feedback for increments of appropriate behavior and completed work.

It is important for teachers to have flexible intentions, and perhaps to have different guiding intentions for different patterns of behavior. An intention should be relatively brief, usually between 3-5 words, and simple enough that it can be recalled during stressful situations. Silently reciting a guiding intention replaces the need to put forth conscious energy to refrain from saying something regrettable or unprofessional that will only serve to entice even more inflammatory behavior. In addition, intentions can help teachers interact in a way that builds safety, trust, consistency, and predictability. For many traumatized children, the school often represents a beacon of hope by providing a learning environment that fosters resilience and reinforces pro-social behavior to allow children to develop an effective skill set to best manage their emotional worlds.

> *"I will act as though what I do makes a difference"*
>
> —William James

REFERENCES

Bradley et. al. (2007). *Reducing test anxiety and improving performance in America's schools: Summary of results from the test edge national demonstration study.* Boulder Creek, CA: Institute of Heart Math.

Brooks, R. (2007). *The power of mindsets: Nurturing resilience in our youth and ourselves.* Keynote address. Learning & The Brain Conference: Cambridge, MA.

Center for Collaborative Practice (2001). *Creating positive behavioral interventions and supports.* Available: www.cecp.air.org.

Fowler, M. (2001) *Maybe you know my teen.* New York: Random House.

Goleman, D. (1997). *Emotional intelligence.* New York: Bantam Books.

Katz, M. (1997). *On playing a poor hand well.* New York: Norton.

Langer, E. (1989). *Mindfulness. Reading,* MA: Addison-Wesley.

Langer, E. (2005) *On becoming an artist:* New York: Ballantine Books.

LeDoux, J. (1996). *The emotional brain.* New York: Simon and Schuster.

LeDoux, J. (2008). *The emotional brain.* Presentation at the 92nd Street YMCA: New York.

Lupien, S. J., Fiocco, A., Wan, N., Maheu, F., Lord, C., Schramek. T., & Tu M.T. (2005). Stress hormones and human memory function across the lifespan. *Psychoneuroendocrinology, 30*(3), 225-242.

Masten, A.S. (2001). Ordinary magic: Resilience processes in development. *American Psychologist, 56,* 227-238

McEwen, B. (2000). Allostasis and allostatic load: Implications for neuropsycho-pharmacology. *Neuropsychopharmacology, 22,* 108-124.

Ryan, R.M. & Deci, E.L. (2000) The "what" and "why" of goal pursuits: Human needsand the self-determination of behavior. *Psychological Inquiry, 11,* 227-268.

Sapolsky, R.M. (2004, 1998). *Why zebras don't get ulcers.* New York: W.H. Freeman and Company.

Scaer, R. (2007). *The body bears the burden: Second edition.* New York: Hayworth Press.

VanDerKolk:, (2006) Clinical implications of neuroscience research in PTSD. *Annals of New York Academy of Sciences.* Available: www.thetraumacenter.org

Zylowska, L. (2006). *Mindful awareness program (MAP) for AD/HD: A pilot study of mindfulness meditation training for AD/HD adults and teens.* Presentation at the eighteenth annual conference of CHADD (Children and Adults with Attention Deficit/Hyperactivity Disorders), Chicago.

Zylowska, L. et al. (2008). Mindfulness meditation training in adults and adolescents with ADHD. *Journal of Attention Disorders, 11,* 737-746.

CHAPTER 12

WELLNESS, MENTAL HEALTH, AND RESILIENCE IN SCHOOL

Beth Doll, Ph.D.

"If there is anything that we wish to change in the child, we should first examine it and see whether it is not something that could better be changed in ourselves."

—Carl Jung

Overview

In the decade following World War II, researchers in child development began a series of powerful longitudinal studies to identify which factors predicted children's social and emotional success or failure. For example, the Newcastle Thousand Family Study (Kolvin et al., 1988) began to track characteristics of the child, family, and community for all children born in May and June of 1947. They were hoping these records could be used to predict which children would commit criminal offenses as adolescents. Soon after, Werner (1989) and her colleagues (Werner & Smith, 1992) began to carefully document individual child characteristics along with the family and community lives of all children born in 1955 on the Hawaiian island of Kauai. These researchers were seeking to understand the factors that might predict developmental disabilities in children. Similarly, at least a dozen other longitudinal studies were also initiated to tease out childhood characteristics that preceded and predicted adolescent or adult development of mental illness, learning disabilities, economic dependence, or other social or psychological disturbances (Doll & Lyon, 1996; Werner, 2006).

The results of these studies were remarkably consistent and unexpected. For instance, the most powerful predictors of children's developmental failures were characteristics associated with their families and communities rather than of the children themselves (Doll & Lyon, 1998; Werner, 2006).

In fact, chronic adversities such as poverty, neglect or abuse, marital discord, or parental illness were more powerful predictors of poor outcomes than were acute adversities such as the death of a family member, or childhood illness. Moreover, it was the *number* of adversities rather than the *type* of adversity that significantly raised children's likelihood of social or emotional disturbance. For example, children appeared to be capable of weathering one or two chronic life adversities, but were much more likely to succumb to risk in the face of three or more.

These longitudinal studies of childhood risk shifted our understanding of children's development in several important ways. First, it became clear that children's developmental success or failure emerged out of the interface between children and their caretakers (Brehm & Doll, 2008; Masten, 2001). Notwithstanding, this phenomenon was articulated by Bronfenbrenner (1979) in his ecological model of childhood development. Second, any isolated risk factor might contribute to a variety of psychosocial disturbances, and similar developmental failures might emerge out of multiple alternative risk factors. Finally, and of particular importance for this chapter, these studies documented that a key to preventing developmental failures is strengthening the families and communities that care for, and raise, society's children.

Clearly, if this were an exhaustive list of the available literature, this chapter would focus upon preventing adversities in children's lives. However, Rutter (1985) noted that all of these longitudinal development studies included children who were supposed to be failing (since they were growing up with multiple chronic life adversities) but in fact were not. The capacity to overcome adversity was termed 'resilience.' Subsequently, many researchers reanalyzed their data to identify the early characteristics of vulnerable children, their families, and their communities that predicted their social and emotional success against the odds (Doll & Lyon, 1998). Nevertheless, the results were remarkably consistent. Some of the resilience factors that were identified were actually intrinsic characteristics of the children, such as satisfying friendships, a strong sense of efficacy, and a capacity for self-regulation. However, just as many were characteristics of the families and communities, such as access and support from at least one caring adult, connection to positive community organizations, and access to high quality schools. An essential contribution of these studies of resilience was in establishing the very important role that psychological wellness plays in moderating the impact of life adversity and promoting developmental success.

Schools are a primary site where communities can promote and enhance psychological wellness. As Rutter and Maughan (2002) pointed out, children spend over 15,000 hours in school from the time they enter kindergarten to graduation from high school. Moreover, schools were frequently identified in studies of developmental risk and resilience as the place where much of children's success was supported. Therefore, the purpose of this chapter is to describe children's mental health as both the absence of disturbance and the presence of wellness, and to explain how mental health can be nourished by the routines and practices of schools that promote wellness and moderate the effects of psychological disturbances.

A Practical Definition of Children's Mental Health

The earliest definitions of children's mental health focused on pediatric social and emotional disturbances. These were subsequently codified as psychiatric disorders in the American Psychiatric Association's (1952) Diagnostic and Statistical Manual of Mental Disorders (DSM), currently in its fourth revision (American Psychiatric Association, 2000). The diagnosis of these disorders has been the traditional first step in the provision of mental health services for children. Debates continue ranging from the number of disorders that exist, to the overall nomenclature, to how these disorders should be further subdivided into specific categories. Fortunately, there is essential agreement among mental health professionals on certain key points. For example, there is widespread agreement that most mental health disorders arise out of an interaction between children's biological predisposition to the disorder (nature) combined with less than optimal caretaking environments (nurture), and that the relative contribution of nature or nurture will differ for different disorders and children. Second, mental health professionals generally agree on the symptoms that characterize children's social, emotional, and psychological disorders. For simplicity's sake, these can be collapsed into six important indicators of mental disorders in children as noted in Table 12-1:

TABLE 12-1
Six Indicators of Mental Disorders in Children

1. *Emotional disturbances*, including excessive worry, fearfulness, sadness or pessimism. All of these emotions are typical for most children at some time. However, these are symptomatic of a disorder when the core emotions are significantly more intense than those of typical children, and when children are unable to regulate their actions in response to these emotions.
2. *Avoidance behaviors*, including instances in which children actively avoid certain places, people, or activities to the point where it is life-impairing. In some cases, children's insistence on avoidance behaviors becomes so marked that it is interpreted as stubbornness, non-compliance, or evidence that a child has *shut down*.
3. *Self injurious behaviors*, including instances in which children jeopardize their own physical well-being. These include suicidal behaviors (thinking about or planning suicide, making minor attempts, or making lethal attempts), but also include cutting behaviors and under-eating or over-exercising in order to restrict bodyweight.
4. *Peer relationships*, especially ones that are unusually intense or disturbing including social isolation, in which children have very few or no peer friendships; peer conflict, in which children have many or unusually severe arguments and fights; or peer bullying, in which children frequently victimize or are victimized by peers.
5. *Impulsive behaviors*, in which children are much more likely than their peers to carelessly act without thinking. In many instances, extremely impulsive children are also physically overactive, or they may be described as immature and acting like younger children.
6. *Rules and authority*, in which children frequently disobey adults' rules and are often defiant or even hostile towards them. In some cases, these children may be described as deliberately cruel or highly aggressive towards peers or adults.

These indicators of psychological, social, and emotional disorders are generalizations across the multiple syndromes and disorders that have been codified within the DSM IV_TR (APA, 2000). Subtle nuances characterize the many different ways in which children's competence might be disrupted, or the pathways that various children might follow into disruptive disorders or maladaptive behaviors. Within traditional conceptual frameworks, mental health has been tacitly defined as the absence of these indicators (that is, the absence of mental illness). However, the developmental risk and resilience studies, as well as studies in the field of developmental psychopathology, demonstrated that these emotional disturbances may be more or less destructive for children depending upon the presence of essential social protective factors. These positive factors have been organized into a working description of psychological wellness as noted in Table 12-2.

Clearly, the absence of an emotional disturbance and the presence of psychological wellness interact to comprise the mental health of children and adolescents (Masten, 2001). Defined in this manner, mental health emerges out of the adversities and psychological supports that exist within the individual children, their families, and their communities (see Figure 12-1). Embedded within this definition is the critical assumption that the absence of an emotional disturbance is not the same as the presence of wellness, and both must be addressed to promote children's life success. An important benefit of this definition for children's mental health is that it provides a clear and practical explanation of the purpose of school mental health services, namely, to maximize emotional wellness and minimize adversity for the developing child. A second assumption is that all natural caretakers of children are important providers of mental health services, including families as well as the many different educational professionals in the life of a child.

TABLE 12-2
Six Indicators of Psychological Wellness

1. Has strong and caring relationships with adults:
   - Is comfortable interacting with adults; has fun with adults.
   - Follows instructions and attends to rules.
   - Is appropriately independent but asks for help when needed.
   - Offers to help.
2. Has effective relationships with peers:
   - Enjoys interacting with peers; is fun to be with.
   - Can make new friends.
   - Has at least 3 good friends to play with or eat lunch with.
   - Helps friends and takes care of them.
   - Is able to 'fix' conflicts with peers when these arise.
   - Can compromise with peers.
   - Can solve social problems effectively.
   - Can stand up for themselves when necessary.
   - Deflects bullying and stands up for other kids.
3. Is highly bonded with family:
   - Makes caring comments about parents.
   - Wants to be like one or both parents.
   - Talks about what parents think or do.
   - Is reliable in carrying messages or notes back and forth from home.
4. Expects to be successful at most tasks (efficacious):
   - Expects to be successful.
   - Persists at tasks even when they are difficult.
   - Concentrates harder and attempts different strategies when work is difficult.
5. Makes thoughtful decisions and sets personal goals to achieve:
   - Keeps track of assignments and work to-be-completed.
   - Has future aspirations.
   - Recognizes choices and can explain why one choice was made over another.
   - Makes decisions comfortably and in a reasonable amount of time.
   - Shows good judgment in making choices and decisions.
6. Can regulate personal behavior to match rules or to meet personal goals:
   - Remembers the rules and follows them most of the time.
   - Does not rely upon adults for discipline.

FIGURE 12-1
Psychological Wellness

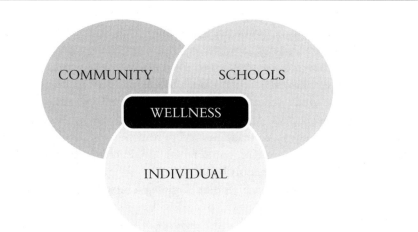

School Practices That Promote Children's Mental Health

School mental health interventions are generally divided into three groups: 1) *Universal strategies* that are used with all children enrolled in a school to promote their psychological well-being, 2) *preventive strategies* that are used with children who are at special risk for developing a disorder, and 3) *therapeutic strategies* that are used with children who already meet the diagnostic criteria for one or more disorders (Institute of Medicine, 1994). The provision of the third group of interventions, therapeutic mental health services to children with identified mental illnesses, is a highly specialized skill that is guided by comprehensive theoretical frameworks often requiring expert supervised experience. Consequently, it is easy to presume that therapeutic interventions are the most important of all mental health service, and also have the most impact on children's well being. This is not necessarily true. Instead, the universal strategies that are blended into the natural, daily practices of families and schools are much more effective in meeting children's mental health needs (Masten et al., 2005). This is most likely because these strategies are modeled by adults who are highly influential in children's lives; namely, their families and teachers. Furthermore, by being integrated in a seamless and natural fashion, children learn to use the strategies in context and immediately understand how to apply them in actual situations. Finally, the skills that are conveyed through each strategy can be reinforced more often and more appropriately in natural settings than skills taught by community or school mental health professionals in pull-aside settings. Therefore, some of the best work of school mental health professionals is done through active collaboration with children's caretakers.

Universal Strategies to Promote the Mental Health of All Children

The research literature of childhood risk and resilience provides a roadmap for the most important strategies used to promote universal mental health of all children. The following seven strategies are supported by research evidence that links them not only to children's mental health in the immediate present, but also to their life success in adulthood.

1. One of the most important ways that schools can promote mental health is by fostering strong, caring, and respectful relationships between adults and children in the building. Both in the developmental resilience research and in the effective teaching research, children tend to be significantly more successful academically, socially, and personally when they have supportive relationships with caring adults (Doll & Lyon, 1998; Pianta, 1999). In fact, the quality of teachers' relationships with children is even more important in socially disadvantaged communities, where schools may be the island of safety in children's otherwise unpredictable days (Hamre & Pianta, 2005). Schools foster critical interpersonal relationships by ensuring that teachers take the time to check in with children, share their successes and struggles, and show their interest and respect. These simple acts of kindness are not random, but rather are deliberate and systematic, to make sure every student feels welcomed by the adults in their school. Some schools appoint mentors for children who seem to be fading into the background, while other schools build *"talking time"* into daily schedules. For example, in one school, the principal made a point of giving a birthday card to every student, while in another school the counselor passed out HERO slips for students who tried their best. Taken together, these moments are not at the expense of lost instructional time, but instead help to seal a child's social commitment and sense of value toward school (Elias & Weissberg, 2000).

2. A second important way that schools promote mental health is by creating peer environments that predispose children to form healthy and satisfying friendships with one another (Wentzel & Caldwell, 1997). Friendships provide an essential source of social support for children in school, as well as a sense of company, guidance, and assistance for children (Wentzel, 2002). Schools can prompt friendships by ensuring that the recess playground has multiple, highly enjoyable games for children to play, and games that are appropriate for all ages and grades (Doll, 1996). In today's world of working parents and supervised daycare, children have few opportunities to learn the simple playground games that previously were passed down from older children to younger ones. Having fun together is certainly not limited to play. Learning together can be fun as well, and schools can promote mental health by ensuring that some instructional activities occur within tutoring pairs or smaller peer groups. Children who are naturally shy and tentative in making friends sometimes find large groups very difficult to navigate. However, when smaller and more intimate groups are created for learning or play activities, these children's opportunities for friendships can often flourish.

3. Third, mentally healthy schools coach children in resolving the inevitable conflicts they have with one another. In fact, most arguments and disagreements are verbal and not physical, and most of these conflicts occur with friends whom children spend time with on a daily basis (Gropeter & Crick, 1996). Children often agonize over these conflicts because underlying every painful disagreement is their nagging worry that they may have lost a friend. Perhaps an apt comparison is to consider these conflicts merely *"social accidents."* Simple problem solving strategies can be highly effective in helping children make repairs to these accidents (Pellegrini, 1995; Smith, Daunic, & Miller, 2002). For instance, having children pose questions such as,*"What is the problem?"* (What is the nature of the children's disagreement?) "What are the possible solutions?" (The longer the list of solutions, the more likely it is to include a good choice.) *"Which choice is most fair?"* Try it out. An essential key to success is for children to be coached in these problem solving skills during teachable moments when the conflicts have just occurred (i.e., on the playground, in the classroom, on the bus, in the cafeteria,

etc.). Coaching in problem solving is even more powerful when consistent problem solving steps are used across all settings and all adults in the school. When a classroom or school is struggling with high numbers of peer conflicts or conflicts that are unusually severe, class-wide problem solving strategies have been an effective way to identify and implement solutions (Murphy, 2002). In a classroom meeting, all children are engaged to describe the problem, propose possible solutions, vote on the best solution, and subsequently carry them out in an effective fashion.

Inevitably, children will differ in their social influence and status depending upon their social competence, physical attractiveness, athletic ability, or length of time they have been enrolled in school. Therefore, schools need to intervene only when these status differences evolve into an inflexible pecking order in which low social status makes them vulnerable to bullying and intimidation, and ultimately threatens their mental health. Schools can interrupt harmful pecking orders by encouraging socially influential children to adopt values of caring and courtesy. In addition, school-wide *"no bullying"* rules are also important and can be enforced by adults as well as other children.

The last three universal strategies for promoting children's mental health have the purpose of strengthening a child's developing capacity to act in an autonomous and responsible fashion (Masten & Coatsworth, 1998). This autonomy has also been called *self-determination* (meaning the child can take charge of their daily decisions and plan for their futures) or *self-agency* (meaning that the child can act as their own agent to shape and promote their own future). In summary, a child's capacity for autonomy together with the ability to maintain effective interpersonal relationships ultimately defines mental health.

4. A fourth strategy that strengthens a child's autonomy is the promotion of expectations they can achieve in order to be successful (Bandura, 1997). Children who expect to be successful in school are more likely to act in ways that support success, such as taking on more challenging tasks, persisting when the task becomes difficult, asking for help when necessary, and adopting a variety of problem solving strategies to help them succeed (Pajares & Schunk, 2002). Bandura (1997) has demonstrated that these expectations for success are not just a property of individual children but also are shared, collective expectations of an entire class or school. Adults can encourage children's success expectations by expressing confidence in them, and by not always rescuing children too quickly from challenging but achievable tasks. Instead, children are reassured when performing well, and encouraged to brainstorm on alternative strategies to see a tough task through to completion. Peers can also encourage success expectations, as successful children can model high expectations for the rest of the group. Class-wide success expectations are much more likely to occur when children are encouraged to master the task, rather than by competitive goals to perform better.

5. A fifth strategy for promoting children's autonomy is frequent and meaningful experience with goal-setting and decision-making. This raises a curious quandary for adults in schools. Most children's capacities for goal-setting and decision-making are obviously forged through practice, yet adults are understandably reluctant to permit children to make risky decisions or set inappropriate goals. Consequently, the first inclination for most adults is to make important and responsible decisions for children. Although this might lead to better decision

making in the short run, the capacity to make high quality decisions in the long run can be stymied. Table 12-3 describes appropriate steps that adults can take to support decision-making and goal setting while still permitting children to make the primary choice.

Even when children have high quality goals and have made responsible decisions, their ultimate success requires that they be able to act upon these. Mentally healthy schools also contribute to children' developing self-control: their capacity to govern moment-to-moment behaviors so that they act consistent with the goals and decisions that they have made (Bear, 2008).

TABLE 12-3
Supporting Children's Goal-Setting and Decision-Making

Goal-setting:
1. Help children set goals that are so specific they will know immediately whether or not they have met them.
2. Help elementary age children set manageable goals that they can reach within one or two weeks; help middle school age children set goals they can reach within a month.
3. Let children set goals that are a bit more challenging than you think they can reach.
4. Help children set goals that use problem solving strategies to accomplish a task.
5. Allow children to set goals for themselves at least monthly. When children cannot set their own goals, it is permissible to set one for them.

Decision-making:
6. When children are in the process of making decisions, they should start by listing their different choices.
7. If their list of choices is too short, feel free to add more choices to the list.
8. Do not let children make a choice until they have thought about other information they might need to know.
9. Prompt children to stop and think about the reliability of the information they are using to make their choices. Is the information accurate? Was the person who gave them the information trying to influence their decision?
10. Help children think about the risks and benefits of their choices.
11. Ask children to "think aloud" about their decisions, so you can assess their reasoning skills.
12. When children endorse decisions that are unnecessarily risky, explore the values they attach to the anticipated risks, being open to the possibility that their beliefs about risks may be inconsistent with your own adult needs.
13. Sometimes children's emotions interfere with their decision making. It is important to slow the decisions down so as not to make a hasty or biased decision.

Both goal-setting and decision-making
14. Ask children to commit in writing to the goals or decisions they have made.
15. Help children monitor the impact of their goals and decisions and allow them to make changes when they find that these are not effective.

The acid test of self-control is whether children can act in ways that are less attractive in the short term in order to meet the long-term goals that they have set for themselves. Self control can be divided into five discrete steps: (1) knowing the rules and standards for behavior; (2) noticing in the moment when it is time to follow a rule; (3) noticing whether or not you are following the rule; (4) stopping, thinking, and making a conscious decision to follow the rule (and doing it!); and (5) evaluating your rule-following behavior and taking steps to improve it if it is inadequate. Each of these steps can be deliberately prompted by adults. Children are most likely to know the rules if they are given direct instruction in a school's rules, actively participate in setting and promoting the rules, and if the rules are described in consistent and familiar terms by all adults in a school. Although children may not always notice when it is time to follow a rule, they can be taught signals or prompts that adults will use to remind them. Initially, the prompts can be very obvious or loud (a loud bell or command), but over time and as children become more familiar with the routines, the prompts can be made more subtle or eliminated altogether. To prompt children to notice whether or not they are following the rules, they can be taught to keep simple records of their own rule-following behaviors, and in some cases, they can even graph or tally their records across a day or week so that they can follow their progress over time. To remind them to stop and think about the rules before they act, children can be taught simple delaying routines ("First count to five." Or "Say to yourself, What is the rule here."). Finally, to prompt children to evaluate their behavior over time, brief classroom meetings can be convened when all children discuss their progress and brainstorm ways to improve it.

These kinds of universal strategies for promoting children's autonomy and effective relationships can be embedded into the routines and practices that are used on a daily basis in throughout a school. Done well, these can foster children's psychological wellness and diminish their vulnerability to emotional and social disturbances.

Preventive strategies for children at high risk of disorders. Despite our best efforts, some children will still demonstrate the early signs of social or emotional disorders. Sometimes this is because they are struggling hard to overcome multiple social or emotional risk factors. Alternatively, they may have a strong biological predisposition towards a psychosocial disorder. The universal school mental health strategies that are available to all children will be especially important for these children. In addition, effective school mental health programs will include programs to directly teach important social or emotional competencies to these children as a preventive strategy. In some cases, like the universal mental health strategies, preventive school mental health interventions might be provided through teachers or other educators; in other schools, this instruction will be provided by one of the school mental health professionals. Regardless, four key components must be part of this instruction if it is to truly impact children's daily adjustment in school. The skill must be taught together with examples of how to use the skill in everyday situations. Adults in the actual playground or classroom setting must remind the children to use the skill there, and in some cases coach the children through using the skill. Then, the children need immediate feedback on their performance. In some cases, children are also given homework assignments of keeping records of their skill practice, and report back on their experiences.

Social problem solving is a particularly useful skill to teach to children in this manner (Shure & Digeronimo, 1995). While problem solving strategies underlay some universal mental health strategies, the social problem solving instruction that occurs here is more intense and opportunities will be created for children to practice the skills with adult coaching on the playground and in the classroom. Children are taught to memorize a precise script to use when they encounter a problem, and then repeatedly rehearse the script with examples and then with actual problems that they encounter in the school. Social problem solving has been particularly helpful in guiding socially awkward children through the resolution of social conflicts or accidents (What should I do when my friend and I can't agree about which game to play?), helping very anxious children overcome their need to flee (How can I come to school when its feeling really scary?), or prompting very impulsive children to stop and think before they act (What am I supposed to do when I don't remember the directions for this worksheet?)

One aspect of many social or emotional disturbances is the unhelpful scripts that children play over and over in their minds. For example, children who are overanxious often have critical scripts playing in their minds ("Everyone's going to see how bad I am at soccer"), children who tend to be depressed often play pessimistic scripts in their minds ("None of my friends will ever like me the way that I am"), and overaggressive children often play blaming scripts in their minds ("He's deliberately bumping into me to make me drop my books"). This self-talk is not only disturbing and disruptive for children, but it seems to be entirely out of their control, even when their rational self knows that these self-statements are not really true. However, children can be taught new scripts that help them handle these situations more effectively, and they can be taught how to deliberately chant the adaptive talk in their minds whenever they are overcome with the negative self-talk (Mennuti, Freeman, & Christner, 2006). This is called a cognitive behavioral strategy because it treats 'cognitions' in the mind as if they were simple behaviors. Like other kinds of psychosocial instruction, interventions that teach children adaptive talk work best when the talk is prompted and coached by adults in the everyday settings where children will use it.

Some children are so overwhelmed by the adversities that they face in their own lives that they forget to notice the feelings, dilemmas, or discomfort of the other children that they interact with. With empathy training, they can be reminded to stop and notice the feelings of others, and that will make it possible for them to adjust their responses to the other children's mood. This skill of 'perspective-taking' requires that children recognize that what other people are seeing, hearing, thinking, feeling, and experiencing may be different from themselves. Recognizing what other people are seeing is the easiest of these; for example, perspective taking allows children to know that a child on one side of a wall will not be able to see objects or events on the other side. Similarly, it is relatively easy for children to recognize that children across the room will not be able to hear a whispered voice. These simple perspective-taking tasks are often used to convince children of the importance of anticipating another person's perspective. Recognizing what other people are thinking or feeling is much more difficult, and will require that children stop and reflect thoughtfully on the other children's situation: Are they struggling to complete a very difficult task? (They might be frustrated.) Are they caught in a frightening situation? (They might be scared.) As an aid to perspective taking, children can be directly taught to read the facial expressions of children around them, and think carefully about what the expression conveys. (Does their expression look happy or content? Is it distressed or unhappy?)

For some children, concentrated instruction in self regulation and goal setting/decision making is very useful. This instruction will be similar to that which is taught as a universal prevention strategy but, because it is taught in a smaller group, it will be more intense, can occur more often, and can be directly adapted to the challenging situations that these children face. Often small rewards are provided to fully engage the children in the skills instruction

Therapeutic strategies to promote the mental health of children with identified disorders. In some cases, the provision of comprehensive universal strategies and small group preventive strategies will still not be enough to assure the social and emotional success of children who already meet the criteria for mental disorders. These children may need intensive therapeutic mental health services, which may be provided by school mental health professionals (e.g., school counselors, school psychologists, or school social workers), community mental health professionals, or both. Current best practice is to create a 'wrap around' plan for the children—a coordinated plan for school and community services provided through public and private agencies that 'wraps the services' around the children and their families. These therapeutic services are most effective when provided in addition to (rather than instead of) the universal and preventive strategies because, in every case, the school milieu will continue to play a critical role in the children's mental health. Moreover, best practice is for these services to provide evidence-based interventions—therapeutic procedures that are comprehensively described in treatment manuals and that have been demonstrated by rigorous research to bring about meaningful improvements in the child's mental health (Brehm & Doll, 2008; Kratochwill & Stoiber, 2002).

SUMMARY

Within the model described in this chapter, school mental health services have the dual purpose of promoting all children's psychological well-being and minimizing the negative impact of adversities on children's life successes. These goals are addressed at three levels. All adults in the school provide universal mental health supports to promote children's autonomy and prompt their effective relationships with adults and peers. Many adults in the school also contribute to preventive interventions for children who are still at high risk for social or emotional disturbances. When interventions at these two levels are not sufficient, therapeutic mental health services are provided to strengthen the wellness and minimize the disturbance of children who are identified with disorders. Ultimately, high quality school mental health services will raise the life successes of most children enrolled in the school.

REFERENCES

American Psychiatric Association. (1952). *Diagnostic and statistical manual of mental disorders.* Washington, DC: Author.

American Psychiatric Association. (2000). *The diagnostic and statistical manual of mental disorders - Fourth edition, text revised.* Washington, DC.: Author.

Bandura, A. (1997). *Self-efficacy: The exercise of control.* New York: W. H. Freeman.

Bear, G. (2008). School-wide approaches to behavior problems. In B. Doll & J. A. Cummings (Eds.), *Transforming school mental health services: Population-based approaches to promoting the competency and wellness of children* (pp. 103–142). Thousand Oaks, CA: Corwin Press in cooperation with the National Association of School Psychologists.

Brehm, K., & Doll, B. (2008). Building resilience in schools: A focus on population-based prevention. In R. Christner and R. Mennuti (Editors), *School-based mental health: A practitioner's guide to comparative practices* (pp. 55-85). Oxford: Taylor and Francis Publishing.

Bronfenbrenner, U. (1979). *The ecology of human development: Experiments by nature and design.* Cambridge, MA: Harvard University Press.

Deci, E. L., Koestner, R., & Ryan, R. M. (2001) Extrinsic rewards and intrinsic motivation in education: Reconsidered once again. *Review of Educational Research, 71*, 1–27.

Doll, B. (1996). Children without friends: Implications for practice and policy. *School Psychology Review, 25*, 165–183.

Doll, B., & Lyon, M. (1998). Risk and resilience: Implications for the practice of school psychology. *School Psychology Review, 27*, 348-363.

Elias, M. J., & Weissberg, R. P. (2000). Primary prevention: Educational approaches to enhance social and emotional learning. *Journal of School Health, 70*, 186–190.

Grotpeter, J. K. & Crick, N. R. (1996). Relational aggression, overt aggression, and friendship. *Child Development, 67*, 2328–2338.

Hamre, B. & Pianta, R. (2005). Can instructional and emotional support in the first-grade classroom make a difference for children at-risk for school failure? *Child Development, 76*, 949–967.

Institute of Medicine. (1994). *Reducing risks for mental disorders: Frontiers for preventive intervention research.* Washington, DC: National Academy Press.

Kolvin, I., Miller, F. J. W., Fleeting, M., & Kolvin, P. A. (1988). Social and parenting factors affecting criminal offense rates: Findings from the Newcastle Thousand Family Study. *British Journal of Psychiatry, 152*, 80-90.

Kratochwill, T. R., & Stoiber, K. C. (2002). Evidence-based interventions in school psychology: The state of the art and future directions. *School Psychology Quarterly, 17*, 341–389.

Masten, A. S. (2001). Ordinary magic: Resilient processes in development. *American Psychologist, 56*, 227–238.

Masten, A. S., & Coatsworth, J. D. (1998). The development of competence in favorable and unfavorable environments. *American Psychologist, 53*, 205–220.

Masten, A., S., Roisman, G. I., Long, J. D., Burt, K. B., Obradovic, J., Riley, J. R., et al. (2005). Developmental cascades: Linking academic achievement and externalizing and internalizing symptoms over 20 years. *Developmental Psychology, 41*, 733–746.

Mennuti, R., Freeman, A., & Christner, R. (2006). *Cognitive behavioral interventions in educational settings: A handbook for practice.* New York: Brunner-Routledge.

Murphy, P. (2002). *The effect of classroom meetings on the reduction of recess problems: A single case design.* Unpublished doctoral dissertation, University of Denver, Denver, CO.

Pajares, F., & Schunk, D. H. (2002). Self and self-belief in psychology and education: A historical perspective. In J. Aronson (Ed.), *Improving academic achievement: Impact of psychological factors on education* (pp. 3–21). San Diego: Academic Press.

Pellegrini, A. D. (1995). *School recess and playground behavior.* Albany: State University of New York Press.

Pianta, R. C. (1999). *Enhancing relationships between children and teachers.* Washington, DC: American Psychological Association.

Rutter, M. (1985). Resilience in the face of adversity: Protective factors and resistance to psychiatric disorder. *British Journal of Psychiatry, 147*, 598-611.

Rutter, M., & Maughan, B. (2002). School effectiveness findings, 1979–2002. *Journal of School Psychology, 40*, 451–475.

Ryan, A. M., Gheen, M. H., & Midgley, C. (1998). Why do some children avoid asking for help? An examination of the interplay among children' academic efficacy, teachers' social-emotional role, and the classroom goal structure. *Journal of Educational Psychology, 90*, 528–535.

Shure, M. B., & Digeronimo, T. F. (1995). *Raising a thinking child workbook: Teaching young children how to resolve everyday conflicts and get along with others.* Champaign, IL: Research Press.

Smith, S. W., Daunic, A. P., & Miller, M. D. (2002). Conflict resolution and peer mediation in middle schools: Extending the process and outcome knowledge base. *Journal of Social Psychology, 142*, 567–586.

Wentzel, K. R. (2002). Are effective teachers like good parents? Teaching styles and student adjustment in early adolescence. *Child Development, 73*, 287–301.

Wentzel, K. R., & Caldwell, K. (1997). Friendships, peer acceptance, and group membership: Relations to academic achievement in middle school. *Child Development, 68*, 1198–1209.

Werner, E. E. (1989). High-risk children in young adulthood: A longitudinal study from birth to 32 years. *American Journal of Orthopsychiatry, 59*, 72-81.

Werner, E. E. (2006). What can we learn about resilience from large-scale longitudinal studies? n S. Goldstein & R. B. Brooks (Eds), *Handbook of resilience in children* (pp. 91-105). New York, NY: Springer.

Werner, E. E., & Smith, R. S. (1992). *Overcoming the odds: High risk children from birth to adulthood*. Ithaca, NY: Cornell University Press.

CHAPTER 13

POSITIVE BEHAVIOR SUPPORT AND EMOTIONAL DISORDERS: A FRAMEWORK FOR SUPPORTING SOCIAL, EMOTIONAL AND ACADEMIC WELLNESS

Ronald A. Sudano, Ed.S., NCSP

"While school systems are not responsible for meeting every need of their students, schools must meet the challenge when the need directly affects student learning."
—*The Carnegie Council Task Force on Education of Young Adolescents* (1989)

Almost two decades ago, well before the initiation of the federal legislation known as the *No Child Left Behind Act of 2000* (NCLB), the Carnegie Council Task Force recognized the inherent need for schools to address nonacademic barriers to learning for students. Since then, some schools have taken up the challenge, while others continue to resist. Many hold to the teaching of the "3-Rs" (reading, 'riting, and "'rithmetic) or, more generally, academics, as the sole mission of schools, while ignoring the intra-individual and external factors that may positively or negatively impact a student's learning.

In addition to requiring research-supported curricula and effective teaching for students to achieve at a high level, there needs to be the recognition that peak performance for students in school also results from the reciprocal interaction of social, emotional, and neuropsychological make-up of the learner. When these factors constitute a barrier to learning, it is incumbent on a school to remove or ameliorate them to the maximum extent possible.

The following vignettes, aptly titled *"A Tale of Two School Districts,"* describe the approaches of two school districts with differing approaches to nonacademic barriers (e.g., emotional disorders) affecting its students. The stories will illuminate the ideas that nonacademic barriers to learning must be addressed for many students to be successful, that current research-validated approaches can effectively address them, and that when they are addressed learner performance and by extension school achievement are improved.

Dexcel School District

Tavona is a second grade student who attends Rosserger Elementary School in Dexcel School District. Teachers have noticed that Tavona always appeared sad and had difficulty playing with the other children, seeming to choose to be aloof and alone. Peers tended to avoid her and reluctantly chose her last in activities when selecting teams. Teachers described Tavona as a somewhat timid child who was reserved and quiet during classroom discussions or activities. Tavona's second grade teacher once referred her to the elementary school guidance counselor. The counselor talked with Tavona and then advised the teacher to provide Tavona a little "TLC" and to try to boost her self-esteem with a little more attention.

The teacher spoke with Tavona's parents, who said, "Well, that's how she's always acted. We don't know what to do with her." Although Tavona's grades were below average, each of her teachers believed she had the ability to do better and she seemed to do well on the standardized tests administered at the end of each year. Tavona was rarely a behavior problem and the teachers dutifully passed Tavona, secretly hoping she would someday fulfill her potential. Fast forward to high school: Tavona gravitates to socializing with students who frequently find themselves in trouble, but who accept her. They regularly party with alcohol and dabble in drugs. Her school performance deteriorates to the point where she now fails her major subjects and she is at risk for not graduating and dropping-out of school. The administrators, teachers, and counselors chalk up her performance to a poor attitude and "running with the wrong crowd."

While recognizing Tavona had difficulties over the years, school administrators and staff espoused the philosophy that children should come to school ready to learn. They felt services for "marginal students" were available to students somewhere in the community. Furthermore, they maintained it was not the school's responsibility to attend to such student needs, but rather the parents' responsibility. Thus, having referred her to the building's Student Assistance Program, the school's principal deems the district's obligation "satisfied."

This district's students typically perform poorly on statewide proficiency tests. Staff and student morale is poor, leading to frequent use of absence due to illness and high staff turnover rate. Administrators spend excessive amounts of time embroiled in issues involving absenteeism, aggression, school violence, student discipline problems, and high referral rates to investigate students' needs for special education programs.

Excel School District

In a neighboring town is Excel School District where, Tessa, a student of the same age and with similar issues as Tavona, attends Progress Elementary School. Excel's administrators and staff recognize the interrelationship of social and emotional wellness and academic learning and its impact on academic performance. Given that knowledge, the district has instituted a three-tiered prevention model, Response to Intervention for both academics and behavior from elementary through high school.

Fortunately for Tessa and for students like her, Progress Elementary's first priority is to ensure that all students are meeting benchmark (i.e., grade level) expectations in academics as well as in social, emotional, and academic learning (SEAL). With respect to the latter, the school utilizes a School-Wide Positive Behavior Support (SWPBS) framework that clarifies school-wide rules and expectations and provides exciting and fun recognition activities to individuals and groups of students who follow school rules, routines, and procedures and who demonstrate standards-based competencies for social, emotional and academic skills. The Board of Education has embedded most of these skills, e.g., self-awareness, self-management, social awareness, relationship skills, and responsible decision-making, in the state's academic standards.

Schools using SWPBS adopt a set of school-wide expectations (or standards), e.g., "Respect, Responsibility, and Readiness," that communicate the values and culture of social relationships that should be demonstrated by ALL students and staff. Any student who has difficulty with the acquisition of these skills is selected through a screening process for more structured monitoring and prevention strategies at increasingly more intensive levels as necessary. In addition, the school has invested in a cognitive-behavioral program, Promoting Alternative Thinking Strategies (PATHS), for its students. The teaching staff uses PATHS, a K-6 program, to develop social and emotional competence, to develop awareness and management of feelings, to improve critical thinking skills, and to improve classroom climate.

Tessa followed rules quite well, but various staff observed her having difficulties with peer relationships and demonstrating problems with critical thinking skills. The teacher engaged the parent in home-based activities with the PATHS program. As part of the SWPBS process, Tessa received acknowledgment for appropriate interactions with her peers and school staff. Tessa received these recognition supports randomly and by different staff at least once every two weeks. Tessa's peer relationships began to improve and she began to make friends and socialize in class. Had she not done so, however, the school's Resource Team may have screened Tessa for social and emotional problems (e.g., Systematic Screening for Behavior Disorders/SSBD) and referred her to a school counselor or, perhaps, to one of the community provider agencies who has established a partnership with the school to provide school-based behavioral health supports.

If Tessa were found to have mental health problems such as depression or anxiety, research-validated interventions could be initiated among provider, school, and parent systems. Screening, triage, and referral processes are in place for students through high school, including the Teen Screen Program (9th grade) provided to all students enabling parents to have their teenager receive a voluntary mental health check up.

The students in the Excel District typically perform at high levels on state proficiency tests. Staff and student morale are high in part because all implement instruction and provide support to meet students' academic, social, and emotional needs in a safe and secure environment. Furthermore, administrators are able to spend the necessary time to provide instructional leadership to the staff and to interact positively with students. *(The preceding are fictional vignettes; the interventions are currently available and research-validated.)*

Why should schools adopt and integrate frameworks such as School-Wide Positive Behavior Support (SWPBS) and Response to Intervention (RtI) and integrate them as a primary structure for establishing school-based mental/behavioral health supports?

Policy, Regulatory, and Research Foundations

Some may dismiss Excel District's vignette as "Pollyannaish." Yet, many school districts across the country are implementing variations of this approach that are unique to their needs and resources. The catalyst for this movement is three-pronged:

1. Policy studies indicating the deplorable state of mental health among the nation's school children, (i.e., President's New Freedom Commission on Mental Health, 2003; U.S. Public Health Service, Report of the Surgeon General's Conference on Children's Mental Health: A National Action Agenda, 2000); therefore, schools have an ethical and moral responsibility to address situations that impair student learning;

2. Legal mandates (federal and/or state) that school systems must address. For example, the Federal No Child Left Behind Act (NCLB, 2001) requires that schools support all children, including those with serious emotional disturbances, in reaching their optimal potential and achievement by removing the emotional, behavioral, and academic barriers that interfere with student success. This legislation now aligns with the provisions under the Individuals with Disabilities Education Improvement Act (IDEIA, 2004) for special needs students that also requires *Child Find* (i.e., early identification of students who may need more support), *Early Interventions, and Least Restrictive Environment* (LRE); and,

3. Research that has increasingly corroborated the link between academic achievement and social-emotional-academic learning (e.g., Adelman & Taylor, 2005; CASEL, 2005; Weisberg & O'Brien, 2004; Weist et al., 2002). There is also emerging research to support the adoption of School-Wide Positive Behavior Support (Sugai & Horner, 2007) and other school-wide positive support systems that incorporate a 3-tier model of prevention/intervention (e.g., Knoff, 2007, Project Achieve; Sprick, 2007, Safe and Civil Schools).

Aligning Frameworks to Support Social-Emotional-Academic Learning

Knowing that we should address needs for all students (and that we are required to do so) begs the question, "How?" In addition, once the *how* is known then implementation is frequently hampered by resistance from staff who are overwhelmed with the myriad of requirements thrust on them to get students to required levels of academic performance. Educators understandably balk at "just one more thing" added to their plate. Nevertheless, the question remains as to how policies, legislation, and research may be addressed through an alignment of frameworks and processes that work synergistically to enhance the performance of students. For example, school staff, parents, and community agencies need to understand that SEAL constructs may be developed through appropriate implementation of School-Wide Positive Behavior Support (SWPBS) and that they are a Response to Intervention (RtI) process. When schools provide foundational instruction and opportunities for social, emotional, and academic learning skills and measure student response, they are implementing RtI. Thus, the school system is not deploying three separate programs to improve student achievement and social-emotional development but rather using elements of various frameworks in synchrony.

The dynamic interplay of these frameworks provides foundational supports for the development of *resiliency* in students. Benard (1991 p. 18, in 2004) describes the formation of resiliency in this way: "The development of human resiliency is none other than the process of healthy human development." Henderson (2007) defines a primary demonstration of resilience in children as the ability to bounce back from frustrations and to recover from setbacks. Resilient individuals adapt to change, stress, or problems and are able to take things in stride. The result of this bouncing back is a feeling of success and confidence. This capacity observed in resiliency research demonstrates itself in the data that despite adversities in early life, most individuals have satisfactory outcomes. Key elements that Henderson (2007) describes as "resiliency-building 'hidden' predictors of academic success" are: (1) school climate, (2) social and emotional learning, and (3) arts education curricula.

Henderson calls them "hidden" because, while research demonstrates they have strong linkages for improving academic achievement, they are often overlooked. A key outcome of SWPBS is a more positive school climate, more connectedness with staff and with the school system, and a safer and more secure learning environment. Through SWPBS, students have opportunities to learn, to practice and to receive positive acknowledgment for developing appropriate social skills. Additional programs may be offered to enhance social awareness, relationship building, and responsible decision-making. Therefore, SWPBS as an interactive system for building SEAL skills that can easily contribute to fostering resiliency in both students and staff.

FIGURE 13-1
Alignment of Frameworks Contributing to Improved Student Performance

• Social Competence
• Problem-Solving
• Autonomy
• Sense of Purpose
(Benard, 2004)

• Data-Supports
  Decision-making
• Practices Support
  Students
  - School-wide
    Expectations
  - Teaching
  - + Reinforcement
  - Reductive
    Consequences
  - Problem Solving
  - + School Climate
• Systems Support
  Teachers & Families
(Sugai & Horner, 2007)

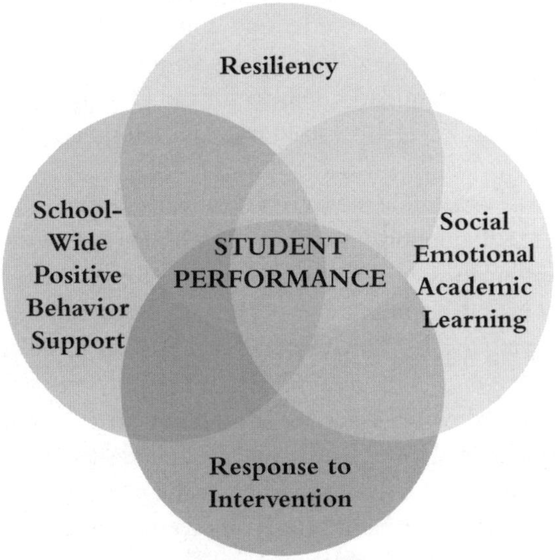

Resiliency

School-Wide Positive Behavior Support

STUDENT PERFORMANCE

Social Emotional Academic Learning

Response to Intervention

Standards-based
Instruction &
Opportunities to Practice
• Self-Awareness
• Self-Management
• Social Awareness
• Relationship Skills
• Responsible Decision-
  making
(CASEL, 2003)

• High Quality Academic and
  Behavioral Instruction
• Problem-Solving Model
• Multi-tiered Support
• Scientifically-validated
  Interventions/Standard Protocols
• Progress Monitoring
(IDEA Partnership, 2007)

Let's now explore each of these frameworks and how they naturally and dynamically provide a scaffold for processes that address the policies, legislation, and research that require schools to address nonacademic barriers to learning. More importantly, it is crucial to understand how this scaffolding provides needed supports for students like Tavona and Tessa.

SEAL (Social-Emotional-Academic Learning)
Moving Toward a Positive Reconceptualization of "BEHAVIOR"

Researchers have suggested the term Social, Emotional, and Academic Learning (SEAL) as appropriately describing the basic skills that provide the foundation for student achievement and performance (Weissberg & O'Brien, 2004). Historically, the term behavior narrowly and reactively referred to the disciplinary issues for students that have a negative impact on school performance. Often, these behaviors in the extreme tend to be attributed to "social, emotional, or behavioral disorders." To break the shackles of such constricted thought that narrows our focus of action, the term *"behavior"* should be viewed in the broader context of Social Emotional Academic Learning (SEAL). This complex system lends itself to explicit instruction or modeling strategies and positive reinforcement supported by designing standards-based curricula as well as school culture and classroom environments for student success. Using this conceptualization of the learner's behaviors provides a structure for positively and proactively preventing disorders. Moreover, it can guide intervention planning to prevent emerging disorders or reduce the negative effects of existing social, emotional, or behavior disorders.

The "Big Ideas" of SEAL

In disciplines such as reading and math, researchers have identified seminal ideas and key constructs that form the basis upon which all higher order and complex skills build. For example, reading researchers refer to big ideas such as *phonemic awareness, phonological processing, word recognition, vocabulary,* and *comprehension* as the foundation blocks for the mastery of skills essential for effective reading (National Institute of Child Health and Human Development, 2000).

Similarly, research in the area of social and emotional learning informs us of five building blocks for the development of appropriate social, emotional, and academic learning skills necessary for the development of effective social and emotional growth. The Collaborative for Academic, Social, and Emotional Learning (CASEL, 2003), a national center for research and practices in the area of social-emotional learning, promotes the following five research-validated components for SEAL [Figure 13-2]:

1. **Self-Awareness:** knowing what we are feeling in the moment; having a realistic assessment of our own abilities and a well-grounded sense of self-confidence.
2. **Social Awareness:** sensing what others are feeling; being able to take their perspective; appreciating and interacting positively with diverse groups.
3. **Self-Management:** handling our emotions so that they facilitate rather than interfere with the task at hand; being conscientious and delaying gratification to pursue goals; persevering in the face of setbacks and frustration (resiliency).
4. **Relationship Skills:** handling emotions in relationships effectively; establishing and maintaining healthy and rewarding relationships based on cooperation; resistance to inappropriate social pressure; negotiating solutions to conflict; and seeking help when needed.
5. **Responsible Decision Making:** accurately assessing risks, making decisions based on a consideration of all relevant factors and the likely consequences of alternative courses of actions; respecting others; and taking personal responsibility for one's actions and decisions.

FIGURE 13-2
What Does SEAL Address?

(Collaborative for Academic, Social, and Emotional Learning, 2006)

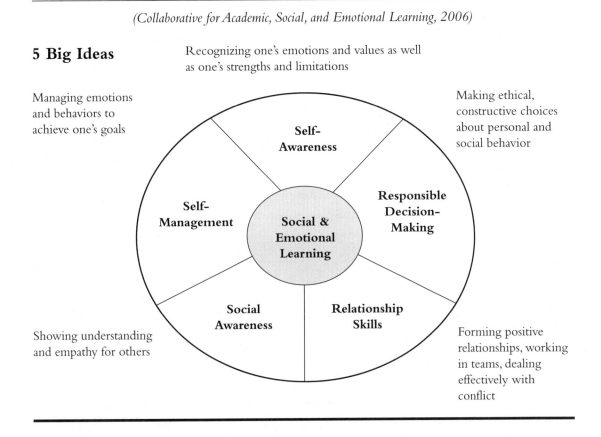

5 Big Ideas

Recognizing one's emotions and values as well as one's strengths and limitations

Managing emotions and behaviors to achieve one's goals

Making ethical, constructive choices about personal and social behavior

Showing understanding and empathy for others

Forming positive relationships, working in teams, dealing effectively with conflict

These are the 5 core groups of social and emotional competencies identified by the Collaborative for Academic, Social and Emotional Learning (CASEL) that provide the foundation for student wellness and success (academically, socially, emotionally, and behaviorally). Physical wellness in the health domain also supports student functioning in addition to addressing their needs. Students who develop these competencies will be better able to perform well within school, classroom, family, and community environments. The establishment of these competencies fosters resilience in students, enabling them to cope with daily stresses and challenges.

The prudent clinician may easily recognize these abilities or skills relate to underlying neuropsychological processes typically ascribed to executive functioning. Governing internal thoughts and self-regulation enables learners to manage stressful or challenging situations and emotions effectively, interact appropriately in social situations, and make choices regarding environmental, task, or social demands that support successful outcomes.

The logic-model [Figure 13-3] for the SEAL framework holds that through research-based SEAL programming schools can create safe, caring, and well-managed participatory learning environments embedding the 5 Big Ideas, each dynamically supporting the other. Creating safe and positive learning environments leads to the establishment of greater attachment, engagement, and commitment to school. It is vital for schools to explicitly teach social-emotional-academic learning skills in order to enhance positive development and reduce the risk for more negative behaviors. The outcomes for students include better academic performance and success in school and life.

FIGURE 13-3
SEAL Logic Mode

(Collaborative for Academic, Social, and Emotional Learning, 2006)

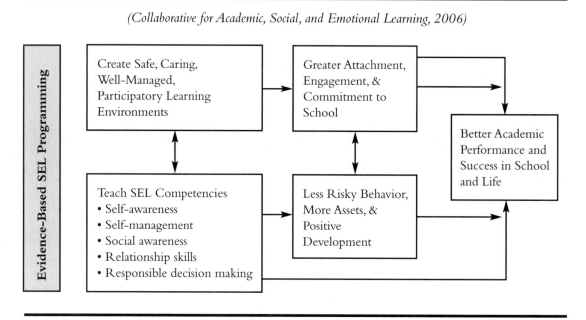

As with reading, math, and other academic subjects in school, these skills should be taught using a **standards-based** approach in order to measure the effectiveness of student outcomes along the way. Applying these constructs to the scenarios with Tavona and Tessa, both schools could have used this framework to offer therapeutic supports for each child; however, only one school did. Progress Elementary School screened, intervened early, monitored progress, and was poised to offer additional supports in the event that Tessa responded poorly to the initial strategies developed to address her nonacademic barriers to learning.

School-Wide Positive Behavior Support and Response to Intervention (RtI) Connection
With the knowledge that academic success is a consequence of physical, social, and mental wellness, schools and communities need to ensure that these *enabling* factors are supported. Students will then be optimally situated to benefit from effective instruction with research-validated curricula. School staff, parents, and community agencies can establish a scaffold for improving student achievement by aligning frameworks such as SEAL, the three-tiered frameworks known as Response to Intervention (RtI) and School-Wide Positive Behavior Support, as well as integrated school-based behavioral health supports as part of the process.

RtI is a multi-tier (i.e., 3 to 4 Tier), team problem-solving model that emphasizes "high quality instruction and interventions matched to student need." By monitoring student response to these interventions, student progress is evaluated at each Tier. The decisions based on student outcome data determine changes that need to be made in instruction or intervention for school-wide, small group, or individual student systems.

The following graphic organizer [Figure 13-4] depicts the types of supports a school might establish when applying the elements of RtI to academic and behavioral systems. For the purposes of this discussion, let us focus on the right side of the triangle, **Behavioral Systems**.

FIGURE 13-4
Behavioral Support Systems

(IDEA Partnership, 2007)

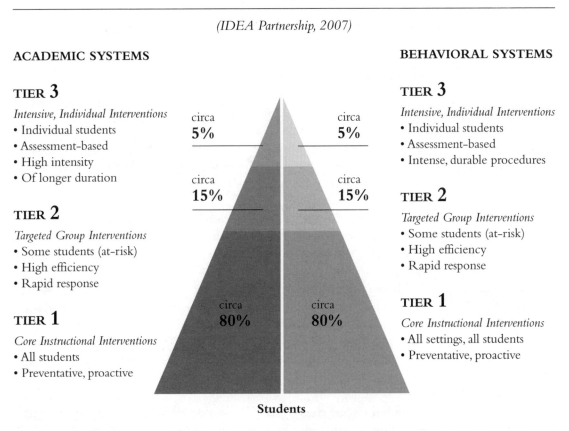

ACADEMIC SYSTEMS

TIER 3

Intensive, Individual Interventions
• Individual students
• Assessment-based
• High intensity
• Of longer duration

TIER 2

Targeted Group Interventions
• Some students (at-risk)
• High efficiency
• Rapid response

TIER 1

Core Instructional Interventions
• All students
• Preventative, proactive

circa **5%**

circa **15%**

circa **80%**

BEHAVIORAL SYSTEMS

TIER 3

Intensive, Individual Interventions
• Individual students
• Assessment-based
• Intense, durable procedures

circa **5%**

circa **15%**

TIER 2

Targeted Group Interventions
• Some students (at-risk)
• High efficiency
• Rapid response

circa **80%**

TIER 1

Core Instructional Interventions
• All settings, all students
• Preventative, proactive

Students

At Tier 1, RtI provides the process for schools to conduct universal benchmark screening; progress monitoring; and effective instruction in academics, social, and emotional learning. This should provide appropriate services for most students. While there is no definitive research on the number of students who are positive responders to prevention efforts, most estimate a range of eighty (80) to eighty-five (85) percent.

At Tier 2, students "at-risk" for developing mild to moderate social or emotional difficulties receive standard protocol interventions, usually in small groups within the regular education program. Approximately, fifteen (15) percent of students may benefit from these secondary prevention efforts.

Students with significant social or emotional difficulties, approximately one to five (1-5) percent, receive intensive interventions at Tier 3. Such interventions provide intensive individual social-emotional skill instruction or specialized strategies or treatment for social/emotional problems. These specialized interventions may be provided by school staff or through contracted services with external providers that partner with schools and deliver supports on-site. School-provider partnerships may also offer school-based behavioral health prevention and treatment services at any Tier. Students who do not demonstrate improvement based upon progress monitoring at Tier 3 may be referred for special education services and more intensive treatments or placements, if necessary.

An RtI framework provides a structure and learning environment within which to embed SEAL for all students, thereby enhancing each child's capacity to be a safe, secure, competent learner within the school environment. The proactive framework of RtI allows schools to shift toward a more positive conceptualization of student performance. The 3-tiered model may take the following format:

- **Tier 1**—All students receive instruction in social, emotional, and academic learning skills. The goal is to support most students in the development of the basic skills necessary to participate fully in regular education and to prevent the development of problem behaviors that become nonacademic barriers to learning.
- **Tier 2**—Students who may be "at-risk" or show signs of emerging problems that may negatively impact the development of social, emotional, or academic learning receive mildly to moderately intensive skill reinstruction, strategies, and/or interventions to build their skills and to prevent any existing problems from becoming worse.
- **Tier 3**—Students who have developed serious problems or emotional disorders that negatively impact social, emotional, and academic learning receive intensive interventions and supports to reduce the effects of these barriers to learning and to prevent the problem/disorder from getting worse.

School staff accomplish the above goals by following the basic tenets of RtI and consistently applying the same process for social-emotional-academic learning as they would for academics. One practical and efficient method to implement RtI in this context is through the aligned elements comprising the framework of **School-Wide Positive Behavior Support (SWPBS)**. There are a number of school-wide positive behavior support systems, among them Project Achieve (Knoff, 2007) and Safe and Civil Schools (Sprick et al., 2002) that schools can adopt to implement an RtI approach to proactively instill social and emotional skills, reduce problem behaviors, and intervene when social, emotional, or behavioral health disorders emerge. Each has similar elements in terms of adopting a multi-tier model and providing supports at each Tier, and is driven by data analysis to guide social/emotional skill instruction and intervention. The following section will explore an approach encouraged by the Office of Special Education Programs (OSEP) Center for Positive Behavioral Interventions and Supports, known as **School-Wide Positive Behavior Support**.

School-Wide Positive Behavior Support (SWPBS)

School administrators and staff have to deal with ever increasing levels of minor and major incidents of problem behavior and with large numbers of students who present with a myriad of emotional and social deficits. In the case scenario for Tavona, she depicted a fairly typical progression of an emerging emotional and social disorder all too common among students in schools. Unfortunately, typical responses to these problems have been for the most part reactive, or, just as devastating, nonreactive and punitive. This usually results in an inordinate reliance on office discipline referrals, suspensions, and expulsions in a vain attempt to gain compliance and reduce the problem behaviors. Other attempts to deal with these issues include referral and assignment of students to out-of-school placements. The fact that these problems are on the increase is one indicator that punitive approaches rarely work over time.

SWPBS provides educators with a much needed alternative (Sugai & Horner, 2007). SWPBS is a comprehensive and proactive response to students' antisocial and problematic behaviors. It provides a structure for preventing the emergence of significant emotional and social disorders. In addition, SWPBS is based on the principle that when faculty and staff actively teach expectations and positively acknowledge them, the number of students with serious behavior problems will be reduced and school climate in general will improve.

There are three primary components in which the SWPBS process is organized: prevention, multi-tiered support, and data-based decision-making. First, SWPBS establishes universal prevention foundation (Tier 1) by defining and teaching core behavioral expectations, by acknowledging and rewarding appropriate behavior (e.g., compliance to school rules, safe and respectful peer to peer interactions, academic effort/engagement), and by developing a consistent continuum of consequences for problem behavior. In addition, depending on school-based data, individual schools may elect to incorporate research-validated preventions programs (e.g., PATHS, Second Step Violence Prevention Program, etc.) to establish and promote social, emotional, and academic learning skills. Setting this foundation provides a school climate and culture where behavioral expectations are explicitly taught, consistently acknowledged, and actively monitored.

Multi-tiered support (Tiers 2 & 3) applies prevention for students at risk for developing social and emotional difficulties. Additionally, those students that have significant identified social, emotional, or neuropsychological disorders (e.g., severe depression, anxiety, autism, schizophrenia, etc.) may warrant increasing levels of intervention. At these tier levels, SWPBS emphasizes the principles of applied behavioral analysis as a foundation for defining challenging behavior and conducting functional behavioral assessments for individuals. The results of these assessments can then be used in the process of wraparound planning to develop interventions that address patterns of inappropriate behavior, and to enhance natural and logical support systems that enable student success.

Data-based decision-making is used throughout the process. Teams routinely use data to identify early patterns of inappropriate behavior by groups or individuals (universal screening) and to monitor and evaluate the effectiveness of school-wide and individualized interventions (progress monitoring). SWPBS includes the adoption of practical ways to collect, analyze, and report data on regularly scheduled cycles. For SWPBS, schools are encouraged to use a web-based software application for collecting and analyzing student discipline data known as the School-Wide Information System, or SWIS. The SWIS system collects information on many elements of student discipline but analysis begins with five basic data sets around problem behaviors : (1) who was involved (e.g. student, peers, teacher), (2) when it occurred (time of day), (3) what type of problem behavior took place (disrespect, fighting, skipping class), (4) location of the event (classroom, hallway, cafeteria, etc.), and (5) average number of discipline referrals per day per 100 students. The last statistic permits staff to analyze occurrences in a consistent and reliable manner without confounding variables such as months with fewer days or fluctuation in number of students. SWIS easily converts data to graphs (Figure 13-5) that may be reviewed by school staff to identify patterns of behavior so that both system-wide and individual behavior problems can be addressed. Eventually, school staff can move toward more advanced reporting including analysis of skewed or disproportional referrals or discipline actions among subgroups of students (e.g., ethnicity, IEP, low SES, etc.).

FIGURE 13-5
Example of School Wide Information System (SWIS)

Year	Month	Days Count	Referral Count	Avg Referrals
2007	Aug	0	0	0.00
2007	Sep	17	28	1.65
2007	Oct	20	17	0.85
2007	Nov	15	8	0.53
2007	Dec	9	11	1.22
2008	Jan	19	15	0.79
2008	Feb	18	11	0.61
2008	Mar	20	9	0.45
2008	Apr	19	13	0.68
2008	May	17	9	0.53
2008	Jun	6	3	0.50
2008	Jul	5	0	0.00
Totals		**165**	**124**	

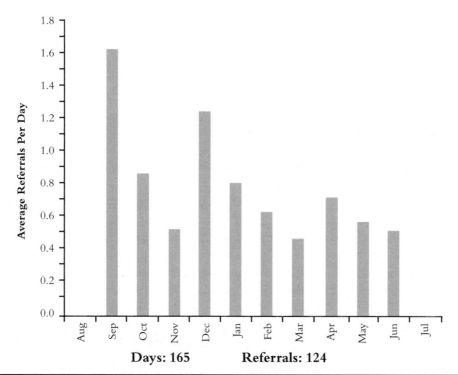

Note: Adapted from www.swis.org demo site: https://app.swis.org/swis.php?pid=3000

The Core Elements of SWPBS as an RtI Approach
- **Tier 1: Core Elements**
  - Establishment of school-wide expectations that may incorporate SEAL skills that are explicitly taught or modeled and a process for teaching or developing them.
  - Integration and coordination of commercially available, research-supported social-emotional skills programs (e.g., PATHS, Second Step, Olweus Bullying Prevention) as determined by analysis of school's data [Figure 13-6. – Examples].
  - Continuum of reinforcement for appropriate social, emotional, and academic learning skills.
  - Continuum of re-teaching strategies and mild reductive consequences for inappropriate behavior.
  - Use of data collection and management systems to identify patterns of problematic behavior issues in non-classroom, classroom, and individual student systems.
  - Data analysis teaming on a continuing basis to analyze discipline patterns and to recommend intervention strategies.
  - Universal screening 2 to 3 times per year to identify students who are at risk and who may need early intervening strategies in regular education settings.
    - Use of a multi-gated system for students who need more support.
      - Teacher nomination, Formal Screening, Observation & Record Review, Referral to Supports.
  - Involvement of parents, families, youth and community providers in these processes as appropriate.

FIGURE 13-6
Tier 1 Practices and Programs That Support Social Emotional and Academic Learning for all Students

Tier 1: Universal Prevention

1. School-wide Positive Behavior Support
2. Social and Emotional Academic Learning (SEAL)
3. Resilience Training
4. Effective Instruction
5. Classroom Group Contingencies
6. *I Can Problem Solve* (Shure)
7. *Promoting Alternative Thinking Strategies* (Greenberg)
8. *Bullying Prevention* (Olweus)
9. Single School Culture
10. Community Programs
11. Parent Involvement
(This is not an all inclusive list of examples)

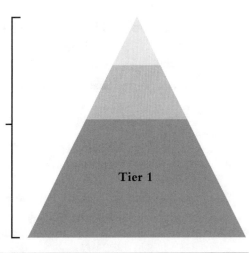

Tier 1

Note: Adapted from PaTTAN, 2005

309

- **Tier 2: Core Elements**
  - Consolidation and/or integration of teams (e.g., Student Assistance Program, behavior core team, building level team, etc.) to identify, recommend, and coordinate supports for students who are at-risk.
  - Analysis of data (e.g., Systematic Screening for Behavior Disorders (SSBD), School-Wide Information System (SWIS), attendance records, school/family surveys, etc.) for decision-making **at a minimum of once a month** for general population and **at a minimum of bi-weekly** for students who are at-risk.
  - Use of Standard Protocol Interventions for small groups of students and individual students who may have a moderate degree of need to support SEAL.
  - Targeted group interventions (Check-in/Check-out, Check and Connect, social or academic skills groups, tutor/homework clubs, etc.) [Figure 13-7].
  - Targeted group with a unique feature for an individual student.
  - Individualized function based assessment (FBA) for a student focused on one specific problem behavior.
  - Behavior Support Plan across all settings (i.e., home, school, community).
  - Hi-Fidelity Wraparound: More complex and comprehensive plan that address multiple life domain issues across home, school and community (i.e. basic needs, mental health treatment as well as behavior/academic interventions).
  - Involvement of parents, families, youth and providers in these activities as appropriate.

⋆While Tier 2 usually focuses on group intervention and some poorly responding students that demonstrate more severe problems. With this latter group, individualized strategies should be initiated as soon as possible in order to prevent a disorder from becoming established or to provide support, realizing the student will likely develop a more severe disorder and require Tier 3 level support.

FIGURE 13-7

Tier 2 Practices and Programs That Support Social Emotional and Academic Learning for Students "At-Risk"

Tier 2: Behavior/Emotional-Social Intervention

SWPBS: Behavior Education Plan (BEP)
    Check-in/Check-out
    Functional Behavior Assessment (FBA/BSP)
Peer/Adult Mentoring or Mediation
Strategic Behavioral Interventions
    (Group Contingencies, Cognitive-Behavioral
    Strategies, functional assessments, etc.)
Special situation groups
    (divorce, COA, D&A, anxiety, depression)
Conjoint Behavioral Consultation
(This is not an all inclusive list of examples)

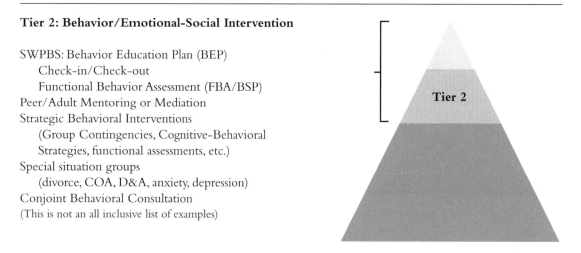

Note: Adapted from PaTTAN, 2005

- **Tier 3: Core Elements**
  - Consolidation and/or integration of teams (i.e., behavior core team, building level team, etc.) to identify, recommend, and coordinate supports for students who have serious emotional disorders.
  - Analysis of data for decision-making - **at a minimum weekly** or more frequently for students who have need of intensive supports.
  - Use of Standard Protocol Interventions for individual students who have a significant degree of need to support SEAL [Figure 13-8].
  - Individualized function-based analysis for a student focused on one or more specific problem behavior(s).
  - Positive Behavior Support Plan across all settings, (i.e., home, school, community).
  - Hi-Fidelity Wraparound: More complex and comprehensive plan that address multiple life domain issues across home, school and community (i.e. basic needs, MH treatment as well as behavior/academic interventions).
  - Involvement of parents, families, youth and providers in these activities as appropriate.

FIGURE 13-8
Tier 3 Practices and Programs That Support Social Emotional and Academic Learning for Students With Severe Problems or Identified Disorders

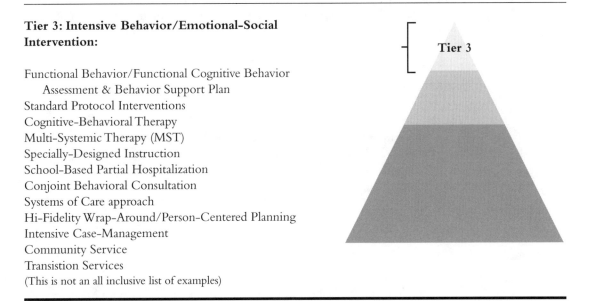

Tier 3: Intensive Behavior/Emotional-Social Intervention:

Functional Behavior/Functional Cognitive Behavior
    Assessment & Behavior Support Plan
Standard Protocol Interventions
Cognitive-Behavioral Therapy
Multi-Systemic Therapy (MST)
Specially-Designed Instruction
School-Based Partial Hospitalization
Conjoint Behavioral Consultation
Systems of Care approach
Hi-Fidelity Wrap-Around/Person-Centered Planning
Intensive Case-Management
Community Service
Transistion Services
(This is not an all inclusive list of examples)

Note: Adapted from PaTTAN, 2005

The difference between Tier 2 and Tier 3 supports relates more to difference in intensity and complexity rather than differences in types of supports.

SUMMARY
The programs and interventions previously described within each Tier are examples of the types of strategies that may be used at each level, but this is not an exhaustive list at any Tier. It is the responsibility of the school and school district to provide an array of supports at each Tier that can

provide the continuum of supports required for *all* students.

To ensure successful implementation of any systems approach, school districts must provide top-level administrative support, designate internal and external coaches to provide guidance, train staff and provide technical assistance on a regular basis, and commit to making SEAL improvement a top priority for the school district. Without such system support and resources, there would be an insufficient foundation to initiate it successfully, let alone sustain the effort.

This chapter also outlined why social-emotional-academic learning and resiliency are key factors in student academic achievement. In addition, there was a discussion on the legal, policy, and research foundation for supporting these factors as well. Using scientifically-based approaches, namely RtI and SWPBS to enhance these skills, emotional disorders can be reduced through prevention efforts. However, when emotional and behavioral problems are present, a proactive SWPBS/RtI systems approach can address emerging problems early and quickly. As a result, there may be fewer students with identified emotional disorders, and these individuals may then be treated with standard protocol interventions and Hi-Fidelity Wraparound planning and support.

Administrators armed with the knowledge of how SEAL contributes to emotional and behavioral wellness and its effect on academic achievement will have the ability to recommend an effective school-based behavioral support system with school boards, community providers, and parents. Identification of research-validated practices for academic and behavioral skill development and intervention is burgeoning. There is access to training and technical support through federal and state technical assistance agencies, along with a legal mandate to galvanize action. There only remains our resolve to take action to ensure the implementation of appropriate supports so that *all* students may experience successful academic and social-emotional performance, thereby improving academic achievement.

The hypothetical scenarios at the beginning of this chapter demonstrated how two schools took differing approaches to two students with emerging social-emotional problems. One scenario demonstrated how these frameworks supported students like "Tessa." Educators now have a professional, ethical, and, some may hold, a moral obligation to ensure such approaches are available to the "Tavonas" of the world as well.

REFERENCES

Adelman, H. & Taylor, L. (2002; Updated 2005). A center concept paper & accompanying resource aids: Rethinking Student Support to Enable Students to Learn and Schools to Teach. Center for Mental Health in Schools at UCLA. Los Angeles, CA. Copies available at: http://smhp.psych.ucla.edu.

Benard, B. (2004). *Resiliency: What we have learned.* San Francisco: WestEd.

Collaborative for Academic, Social, and Emotional Learning (2003). *Safe and sound: An educational leader's guide to evidence-based social and emotional learning (SEL) programs.* Chicago, IL: Author.

Henderson, N. (2007). Resiliency-building "hidden" predictors of academic success. In Henderson, N. (Ed.), with Benard, B. & Sharp-Light, N., *Resiliency in action: Practical ideas for overcoming risks and building strengths in youth, families, and communities* (pp. 39-43). Ojai, CA: Resiliency in Action, Inc.

IDEA Partnership (2007). Response to Intervention: Policy Considerations and Implementation--PowerPoint Presentation. Retrieved August 30, 2008, from the IDEA Partnership website, http://www.ideapartnership.org/page.cfm?pageid=18

Knoff, H. M. (2007). Positive Behavior Support System/Implementation Fact Sheet: *Building Strong Schools to Strengthen Student Outcomes*. Project Achieve website: Retrieved August 30, 2007, from the Project Achieve website, http://www.projectachieve.info/images/PBSS_Fact_Sheet_108.pdf

National Institute of Child Health and Human Development. (2000). *Report to the National reading panel, teaching children to read: An evidence-based assessment of the scientific research and its implications for reading instruction.* Washington, DC: Author.

New Freedom Commission on Mental Health: Achieving the Promise: Transforming Mental Health Care in America. Final Report. DHHS pub no SMA-03-3832. Rockville, MD: Department of Health and Human Services, 2003. Available at www.mentalhealthcommission.gov/reports/finalreport/fullreport-02.htm

Pennsylvania Training and Technical Assistance Network (PaTTAN). *Response to Intervention: A Schoolwide Framework for Student Success.* Power point presentation. Retrieved November 2, 2005 from http://www.pattan.k12.pa.us/teachlead/SpecialProjects1.aspx

School Wide Information System (SWIS). Retrieved August 30, 2008 from https://app.swis.org/swis.php?pid=3000.

Social and Emotional Learning (SEL): What it is and how does it contribute to students' academic success? Retrieved November 19, 2006 from http://www.casel.org.

Sprick, R. (n.d.). *Safe and Civil Schools Overview.* Retrieved August 30, 2008, from the Safe and Civil Schools website, http://www.safeandcivilschools.com/media/SCS_overview.pdf

Sprick, R. S., Garrison, M., & Howard, L. (2002). *Foundations: Establishing positive discipline policies.* Sopris West.

Sugai, G. & Horner, R. (2007). Is School-Wide Positive Behavior Support an evidence-based practice? *Journal of Evidence-Based Practices for Schools,* 8 (1) [Electronic version]. Retrieved August 30, 2008, from the OSEP Center on Positive Behavioral Interventions and Supports website, http://www.pbis.org/files/101007evidencebase4pbs.pdf

U.S. Department of Education, Office of Elementary and Secondary Education, *No Child Left Behind: A desktop reference,* Washington, D.C., 20202.

U.S. Public Health Service, Report of the Surgeon General's Conference on Children's Mental Health: A National Action Agenda. Washington, DC: Department of Health and Human Services, 2000. Stock No. 017-024-01659-4 ISBN No. 0-16-050637-9

Weissberg, R. P., & O'Brien, M. U. (2004). What works in school-based social and emotional learning programs for positive youth development. *Annals of the American Academy of Political and Social Sciences.* 591:86-97.

Weist, M. D., Evans, S. W., & Lever, N. A. (2002). Advancing mental health practice and research in schools. In Weist, M. D., Evans, S. W., & Lever, N. A. (Eds.) *Handbook of school mental health: Advancing practice and research.* (pp. 1-7). New York: Plenum.

APPENDIX

One possible approach to establishing an alignment of frameworks for student success:

Strategies, Activities, and Tasks:
In order to implement a district or statewide plan to encourage schools to apply the evidence-based practices that support the frameworks of SEAL, Resiliency, RtI, and SWPBS there needs to be an alignment of frameworks and a structure that supports communication from the state-level to the local school-building level.

The state/district structure supports system resources that supports the practices that teachers use to support students (e.g., development of SEAL, among others) and that also supports data collection and data-driven decision-making that informs those practices.

Strategy #1: Adopt a Systems approach that administrators and educators can clearly envision how the State's requirements may be embedded within it.

313

Strategy #2:   Resiliency is a framework that embraces a student's capacity to withstand and bounce-back from negative impacts on his/her life and environment. It is an overarching framework for children and youth development. Offer resiliency training to staff and parents. Provide opportunities for integrating resiliency building elements into the curricula and school-wide support system.

Strategy #3:   RtI and SWPBS are conceptual and operational frameworks that can support the implementation of practices for academics and behavior. Provide professional development for all staff so they may understand how they align with the mission, vision, and goals of the state, district, and school.

Strategy #4:   Consider that the SWPBS/RtI framework provides the structure, process, and strategies to assist students to achieve the necessary social, emotional, and academic learning skills (SEAL) as well as renew school climate and this may support the development of wellness and resiliency.

Strategy #5:   The conceptual schema of entwining Resiliency and SEAL may be linked to a state's academic standards. If these skill opportunities do not exist, then a state will need to adopt them. The required teaching of these skills will be less problematic if a state embeds resiliency and social-emotional-academic learning within its academic domains. SWPBS/RtI then becomes the operational framework to support the educational and school-based behavioral health practices that staff may use to accomplish this.

- Essential elements:
  - Establish a State Leadership Team to advise and to promote dissemination, fiscal, and legislative infrastructure
  - Identify a cadre of State Trainers to provide professional development and technical assistance to school districts
  - External (state/district) and Internal (school building) coach to support school-based core teams (e.g., SAP teams)
  - Core teams (e.g., SAP) that provide training to school staff
  - Data-driven decision making by administrators and staff

Assessment:

- System level process measurement: Fidelity checks, consumer surveys, and team functioning
- Formative and Summative Assessments using student discipline data base, student records, staff surveys, state academic proficiency data; school-wide screening for internalizing problems of students

Communication:

- Websites, Newsletters, state and regional publications, conferences and workshops
- Check-out the idea of Social Entrepreneurism to assist organization to take this to scale